Focus on Grammar

An **ADVANCED** Course for Reference and Practice

SECOND EDITION

Jay Maurer

Longman

Focus on Grammar: An **Advanced** Course for Reference and Practice

Pearson Education, 10 Bank Street, White Plains, NY 10606

Editorial director: Allen Ascher
Executive editor: Louisa Hellegers
Director of design and production: Rhea Banker
Development editor: Margaret Grant
Production manager: Alana Zdinak
Managing editor: Linda Moser
Production editor: Robert Ruvo
Senior manufacturing manager: Patrice Fraccio
Manufacturing manager: David Dickey
Photo research: Beaura Kathy Ringrose
Cover design: Rhea Banker
Cover image: *Frost, Penpont, Dumfriesshire,
    3 December 1989.* Copyright © Andy Goldsworthy
    from his book *A Collaboration with Nature,*
    Harry N. Abrams, 1990.
Text design: Charles Yuen
Text composition: Preface, Inc.
Illustrators: Moffitt Cecil: p. 246; Ronald Chironna: p. 15; Brian Hughes:
    p. 48; Jock MacRae: pp. 58, 102, 221, 311, 325, 326, 356, 375, 388, 440,
    471, 472, 483; Don Martinetti: pp. 41, 42, 334, 448, 449; Paul McCusker:
    pp. 49, 50, 74, 90, 93, 94, 150, 166, 170, 171, 207, 234, 242, 249, 250,
    277, 284, 288, 315, 339, 340, 372, 390, 464, 465, 479, 487; Andy Meyer:
    pp. 348, 349, 350, 386, 434; Dusan Petricic: pp. 2, 9, 29, 73, 77, 78, 87,
    88, 131, 148, 152, 182, 211, 230, 258, 267, 273, 292, 293, 300, 301, 302,
    318, 364, 376, 399, 400, 420.
Photo credits: See p. xv.

Library of Congress Cataloging-in-Publication Data

Maurer, Jay
    Focus on grammar; An advanced course for reference and grammar /
    Jay Maurer—2nd ed.
        p. cm.
    ISBN 0-201-38309-8 (alk. paper)
    1. English language textbooks for foreign speakers. 2. English language—
Grammar problems, exercises, etc. I. Title.

PE1128.F794 1999
428.2'4'076—dc21

                                                99-76095
                                                CIP

2 3 4 5 6 7 8 9 10—CRK—04 03 02 01 00

CONTENTS

APPENDICES

ABOUT THE AUTHOR

Jay **Maurer** has taught English in binational centers, colleges, and universities in Portugal, Spain, Mexico, the Somali Republic, and the United States. In addition, he taught intensive English at Columbia University's American Language Program. He was also a teacher of college composition and literature for sixteen years at Santa Fe Community College and Northern New Mexico Community College. He is the co-author of the three-level *Structure Practice in Context* series, co-author of the five-level *True Colors* series, and co-author of the *True Voices* video series. Currently he writes and teaches in Seattle, Washington. *Focus on Grammar: An Advanced Course for Reference and Practice*, Second Edition, has grown out of the author's experiences as a practicing teacher of both ESL and college writing.

INTRODUCTION

THE **FOCUS ON GRAMMAR** SERIES

Focus on Grammar: An Advanced Course for Reference and Practice, **Second Edition**, is part of the four-level **Focus on Grammar** series. Written by practicing ESL professionals, the series focuses on English grammar through lively listening, speaking, reading, and writing activities. Each of the four Student Books is accompanied by an Answer Key, a Workbook, an Audio Program (cassettes or CDs), a Teacher's Manual, and a CD-ROM. Each Student Book can stand alone as a complete text in itself, or it can be used as part of the series.

BOTH CONTROLLED AND COMMUNICATIVE PRACTICE

Research in applied linguistics suggests that students expect and need to learn the formal rules of a language. However, students need to practice new structures in a variety of contexts to help them internalize and master them. To this end, **Focus on Grammar** provides an abundance of both controlled and communicative exercises so that students can bridge the gap between knowing grammatical structures and using them. The many communicative activities in each unit enable students to personalize what they have learned in order to talk to each other with ease about hundreds of everyday issues.

A UNIQUE FOUR-STEP APPROACH

The series follows a unique four-step approach. In the first step, **grammar in context**, new structures are shown in the natural context of passages, articles, and dialogues. This is followed by a **grammar presentation** of structures in clear and accessible grammar charts, notes, and examples. The third step is **focused practice** of both form and meaning in numerous and varied controlled exercises. In the fourth step, **communication practice**, students use the new structures freely and creatively in motivating, open-ended activities.

A COMPLETE CLASSROOM TEXT AND REFERENCE GUIDE

A major goal in the development of **Focus on Grammar** has been to provide Student Books that serve not only as vehicles for classroom instruction but also as resources for reference and self-study. In each Student Book, the combination of grammar charts, grammar notes, and expansive appendices provides a complete and invaluable reference guide for the student.

THOROUGH RECYCLING

Underpinning the scope and sequence of the series as a whole is the belief that students need to use target structures many times in many contexts at increasing levels of difficulty. For this reason, new grammar is constantly recycled so that students will feel thoroughly comfortable with it.

COMPREHENSIVE TESTING PROGRAM

SelfTests at the end of each part of the Student Book allow for continual assessment of progress. In addition, diagnostic and final tests in the Teacher's Manual provide a ready-made, ongoing evaluation component for each student.

THE **ADVANCED** STUDENT BOOK

Focus on Grammar: An Advanced Course for Reference and Practice, Second Edition, is divided into ten parts comprising twenty-five units. Each part contains grammatically related units, with each unit focusing on a specific grammatical structure or related groups of structures.

In this advanced-level text, some structures are grouped together because of their related application to writing. The infinitive of purpose, for example, is taught together with participial phrases because both kinds of structures function adverbially. But, more importantly, they have similar applications to the acquisition of two important concepts: sentence combining and avoiding dangling modifiers.

Each unit has one or more major themes relating the exercises to one another and providing a context that serves as a vehicle for the structures. All units have the same clear, easy-to-follow format:

GRAMMAR IN CONTEXT

Grammar in Context presents the grammar focus of the unit in a natural context. The texts, all of which are recorded, present language in various formats. These include newspaper and magazine articles, stories, conversations, and other formats that students encounter in their day-to-day lives. In addition to presenting grammar in context, this introductory section raises student motivation and provides an opportunity for incidental learning and lively classroom discussions. Topics are varied, ranging from birth order, marriage, money, and humor to cloning, sports, and compassion. Each text is preceded by a pre-reading activity called **Questions to Consider**. These pre-reading questions are intended to create interest, elicit student knowledge about the topic, help point out features of the text, and lead students to make predictions about the reading.

GRAMMAR PRESENTATION

This section is made up of grammar charts, notes, and examples. The grammar **charts** focus on the form of the unit's target structure(s). The clear and easy-to-understand boxes present each grammatical form in all its combinations. These charts provide students with a clear visual reference for each new structure.

The grammar **notes** and **examples** that follow the charts focus on the meaning and use of the structure(s). Each note gives a clear explanation of the grammar point and is always accompanied by one or more examples. BE CAREFUL! notes alert students to common ESL / EFL errors. Usage Notes provide guidelines for using and understanding different levels of formality and correctness. Reference Notes provide cross-references to related units and the Appendices.

FOCUSED PRACTICE

The exercises in this section provide practice for all uses of the structure presented in the Grammar Presentation. Each Focused Practice section begins with a recognition exercise called **Discover the Grammar**. Here, the students are expected to recognize the form of the structure with its meaning and often to explain why alternate forms could or could not be substituted. This activity raises awareness of the structures as it builds confidence. Occasionally, creative activities such as writing endings to stories complete this section.

Following the Discover the Grammar activity are exercises that practice the grammar in a controlled, but still contextualized, environment. The exercises proceed from simpler to more complex. There is a large variety of exercise types including fill-in-the-blanks, matching, multiple choice, question and sentence formation, and editing (error analysis). Exercises are cross-referenced to the appropriate grammar notes so that students can review the notes if necessary. As with the Grammar in Context section, students are exposed to many different written formats, including letters, postcards, journal entries, news articles, stories, and conversations. Some exercises are art-based, providing a rich and interesting context for meaningful practice. All Focused Practice exercises are suitable for self-study or homework. A complete **Answer Key** is provided in a separate booklet.

COMMUNICATION PRACTICE

The exercises in this section are intended for in-class use. The first exercise is **Listening**. Having had exposure to and practice with the grammar in its written form, students now have the opportunity to check their aural comprehension. They hear a variety of listening formats, including conversations, radio announcements, interviews, and phone recordings. After listening to the tape (or hearing the teacher read the tapescript, which can be found in the Teacher's Manual), students complete a task that focuses on either the form or the meaning of the structure. It is suggested that students be allowed to hear the text as many times as they wish to complete the task successfully.

The listening exercise is followed by a variety of activities that provide students with the opportunity to use the grammar in open-ended, interactive ways. Students work in pairs, small groups, or as a whole class in surveys, information gaps, discussions, games, and other problem-solving activities. Every unit gives students an opportunity to write an essay especially formulated to elicit practice of the unit's structures using the unit's theme. Finally, a **Picture Discussion** in each unit enables students to apply their mastery of structure. The subjects of the Picture Discussion range from reproductions of famous paintings to cartoons to drawings.

REVIEW OR SELFTEST

After the last unit of each part, there is a review feature that can be used as a self-test. The exercises in this section test the form and use of the grammar content of the part. These tests include questions in the format of the Structure and Written Expression sections of the TOEFL®. An **Answer Key** is provided after each test.

FROM GRAMMAR TO WRITING

At the end of each part, there is a writing section called From Grammar to Writing. This feature is designed to help students bridge the gap between writing in the ESL / EFL classroom and the less controlled writing they may need to do outside of class, whether in everyday or academic settings. These optional units occur after the SelfTests and focus on such writing issues as the sentence; subject-verb and pronoun-antecedent agreement; topic sentences; parallelism; avoiding fragments, run-on sentences, and comma splices; punctuating adjective clauses; writing direct and indirect speech; and unity, support, and coherence. Although these writing issues are not solely ESL / EFL related, they are highly important to the ESL / EFL student who wants to write successfully.

In most of the From Grammar to Writing units, the topic presented is related to the grammar content of the part just concluded. For example, the second writing unit on parallelism naturally and logically accompanies the gerund and infinitive part, since mixing gerunds and infinitives in a series is a common parallelism error. Two units deal with important issues in the structuring of a composition: writing good topic sentences and ensuring that a piece of writing is unified and coherent and has enough supporting details to make the writer's point. A new feature of the From Grammar to Writing units in this edition is a final writing section called **Apply It to Your Writing.** In this activity, students apply the principles they have just learned in a short composition and then work with a partner to edit each other's work.

APPENDICES

The Appendices provide useful information, such as lists of common irregular verbs, phrasal verbs, spelling rules, and names of countries. The Appendices can help students do the unit exercises, act as a springboard for further classroom work, and serve as a reference source.

NEW IN THIS EDITION

In response to users' requests, this edition has:

- new and updated texts for Grammar in Context
- a new easy-to-read format for grammar notes and examples
- rewritten grammar notes
- cross-references that link exercises to corresponding grammar notes
- authentic reading selections in most units
- more photos and art
- information gaps and games
- a vocabulary development component called Understanding Meaning from Context

SUPPLEMENTARY **COMPONENTS**

All supplementary components of *Focus on Grammar, Second Edition* —the Audio Program (cassettes or CDs), the Workbook, and the Teacher's Manual—are tightly keyed to the Student Book. Along with the CD-ROM, these components provide a wealth of practice and an opportunity to tailor the series to the needs of each individual classroom.

AUDIO PROGRAM

All of the Grammar in Context texts and all of the Listening exercises as well as other selected exercises are recorded on cassettes and CDs. The symbol appears next to these activities. The scripts appear in the Teacher's Manual and may be used as an alternative way of presenting these activities.

WORKBOOK

The Workbook accompanying *Focus on Grammar: An Advanced Course for Reference and Practice, Second Edition,* provides a wealth of additional exercises appropriate for self-study of the target grammar of each unit in the Student Book. Most of the exercises are fully contextualized. Themes of the Workbook exercises are typically a continuation or a spin-off of the corresponding Student Book unit themes. There are also ten tests, one for each of the ten Student Book parts. These tests have questions in the format of the Structure and Written Expression section of the TOEFL®. Besides reviewing the material in the Student Book, these questions provide invaluable practice to those who are interested in taking this widely administered test.

TEACHER'S MANUAL

The Teacher's Manual, divided into five parts, contains a variety of suggestions and information to enrich the material in the Student Book. The first part gives general suggestions for each section of a typical unit. The next part offers practical teaching suggestions and cultural information to accompany specific material in each unit. The Teacher's Manual also provides ready-to-use diagnostic and final tests for each of the ten parts of the Student Book. In addition, a complete script of the Listening exercises is provided, as is an answer key for the diagnostic and final tests.

CD-ROM

The *Focus on Grammar* CD-ROM provides individualized practice with immediate feedback. Fully contextualized and interactive, the activities broaden and extend practice of the grammatical structures in the reading, listening, and writing skill areas. The CD-ROM includes grammar review, review tests, and all relevant reference material from the Student Book. It can also be used alongside the *Longman Interactive American Dictionary* CD-ROM.

CREDITS

PHOTOGRAPHS

Grateful acknowledgment is given to the following for providing photographs:

p. 17 Scott Cohen—AP/World Wide Photos; **p. 27** UPI/Corbis; **p. 33** Corbis; **p. 34** Photofest; **p. 70** Atalante/Gamma Sport—Liaison Agency, Inc.; **p. 116** SuperStock, Inc.; **p. 118** Richard E. Hill/Visuals Unlimited; **p. 135** Robert Bores—AP/World Wide Photos; **p. 196** 20th Century Fox—AP/World Wide Photos/Paramount Pictures Corporation, Inc.; **p. 233** AP/World Wide Photos; **p. 244** Corbis; **p. 270** Spencer Grant/Monkmeyer Press; **p. 362** Lou Requena—AP/World Wide Photos; **p. 363** and **p. 374** Paul S. Howell/Liaison Agency, Inc.; **p. 391** AP/World Wide Photos; **p. 405** Art Resource, N.Y.

THE STORY BEHIND THE COVER

The photograph on the cover is the work of **Andy Goldsworthy**, an innovative artist who works exclusively with natural materials to create unique outdoor sculpture, which he then photographs. Each Goldsworthy sculpture communicates the artist's own "sympathetic contact with nature" by intertwining forms and shapes structured by natural events with his own creative perspective. Goldsworthy's intention is not to "make his mark on the landscape, but to create a new perception and an evergrowing understanding of the land."

So, too, *Focus on Grammar* takes grammar found in its most natural context and expertly reveals its hidden structure and meaning. It is our hope that students everywhere will also develop a new perception and an "evergrowing" understanding of the world of grammar.

ACKNOWLEDGMENTS

Writing the SECOND EDITION of this book has been even more fun and challenging than it was the first time around. I'm indebted to many people who helped me in all kinds of different ways. Specifically, though, I want to express my appreciation and gratitude to:

- **My students** over the years.
- **Joanne Dresner**, for her confidence and encouragement.
- **Joan Saslow**, for her perceptive suggestions in the early stages.
- **Sylvia Bloch**, for her research help. She was terrific.
- **Laura McCormick**, for her help with permissions.
- **Irene Schoenberg**, for her friendship and moral support.
- **Robert Ruvo**, for his excellent and sharp-eyed production editing.
- The **CONSULTANTS**, for their invaluable suggestions: **Marcia Edwards Hijaab**, Henrico County Schools, Richmond, Virginia; **Kevin McClure**, ESL Language Center, San Francisco; **Tim Rees**, Transworld School, Boston; **Allison Rice**, Director of the International English Language Institute, Hunter College, New York; **Ellen Shaw**, University of Nevada, Las Vegas. This book wouldn't be what it is without them.
- **Luis Humberto Beze**, **Patricia C. Fleury**, **Luiz Claudio Monteiro**, and other teachers at the Casa Thomas Jefferson in Brasilia, for their many good suggestions for the new edition.
- **Joyce Munn**, International English Language Institute, Hunter College; **John Beesy**, Fordham University ESL Institute; **Eric Glatt**, Center for English Studies, Manhattan; and their students—for their feedback and their valuable suggestions for the new edition.
- **Flo Nyberg** and **Lena Dubinets**, for their help with Russian recipes.
- That genius, whoever he or she is, who came up with the joke about the genie that has been floating around in cyberspace for some time now. Ditto for the unknown authors of the bumper stickers.
- **Greg Stought**, for finding the joke about the girls and the lipstick.
- **Louisa Hellegers**, for her confidence and excellent direction of the whole project. Many thanks.
- **Margo Grant**, for being a topnotch and jolly editor. Sure was fun working with you.
- Above all, to my best friend.

J.M.

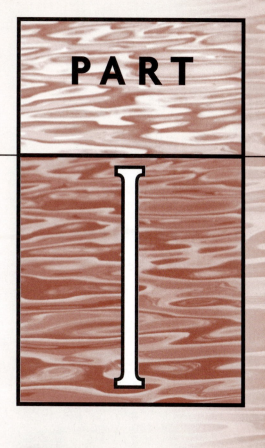

PART

I

TENSE AND TIME

PRESENT AND FUTURE TIME

GRAMMAR IN CONTEXT

QUESTIONS TO CONSIDER

1. Where do you like to travel?

2. Look at the cartoon. When you travel, do you ever bargain to get a better price?

3. Is it fair to try to get a lower price for an item, or is it better to pay the price the seller wants?

 Read an article about learning how to bargain.

W🌐RLD TRAVELER

It's a Bargain
BY TAMMY SAMUELSON

In an open-air market in Turkey, a tourist is admiring the beautiful oriental rugs on display. She finds one she likes and asks the price. "One thousand dollars," the vendor says. She knows she shouldn't pay the full price, so she says "six hundred." "Nine hundred," the vendor counters. The woman throws up her hands in mock frustration and walks away. The vendor goes after her. Not long afterwards both vendor and buyer agree on eight hundred dollars, a 20 percent reduction. Both vendor and customer are smiling and happy. They've just participated in a ritual that has existed for centuries, all over the world: bargaining.

So you're visiting another country this year? You already have your tickets, and you leave next Tuesday at 4 P.M. A week from now you'll be relaxing in the sunshine or visiting famous landmarks. By the end of the summer, you'll have been traveling for several weeks, and it'll be time to think about bringing back some souvenirs for friends and family. Souvenirs cost money, though, so maybe if you do some bargaining, you'll be able to get some good buys. . . . What? You don't know how to bargain? You're afraid to? Relax. In my capacity as *Times* travel editor, yours truly has been making trips abroad since 1995, and bargaining is one thing I've learned how to do. In this week's column I'm going to give you some tips on how to perform this most enjoyable activity.

Many people are used to paying fixed prices for items and are reluctant to bargain. Some may be afraid to hurt the vendor's feelings by offering too low a price. Others are afraid of being assertive. Some may even avoid bargaining because they want to give the impression they can afford anything. Bargaining is not too big a deal in some countries, but even in North America, a certain kind of bargaining goes on whenever someone goes to a yard or garage sale and tries to get the seller to lower the price. In most parts of the world, though, bargaining is a way of life. Vendors expect you to bargain and will be disappointed if you don't. Here are some bargaining tips.

First tip: Find out how much something is worth. When you bargain with someone, the object of the game is not to beat the vendor. It's to pay a fair price for whatever you want to buy. So do some research. Get a good idea of the general price range for an item. That way you'll be able to bargain with confidence.

OK. You've been doing your research. Now you know how much things cost, so you can go shopping.

Second tip: Never accept the first offer. You'll need to make a counter-offer when the vendor announces the price. Remember: The vendor expects this.

Third tip: Treat the vendor with respect. Remember that, while the bargaining experience should not be a competition, it should be a game. Stick to your guns, but have fun with the process. If the vendor insists it's impossible to go any lower on the price, show him or her how much money you have. But be polite.

Fourth tip: Be prepared to walk away if you don't get a fair price. Don't get angry. Just make it clear that you're not going to buy if the vendor doesn't come down. If he doesn't, start to walk away. As soon as you do this, he will most likely come running after you.

The final tip: Be sure to wear sunglasses. For centuries people of many cultures have regarded the eyes as "the windows of the soul." If you're nervous or intimidated, this will show in your eyes. Wear dark glasses to conceal your anxiety. You'll feel more confident if you do.

So, are you persuaded? Feel a little more confident, or at least a little less nervous? If you go home without having experienced bargaining, you'll have missed out on one of life's most interesting experiences. Give it a try. Have a great trip and have no fear! ●

Source: Based on Rich Beattie, "How to Bargain for Anything . . . Anywhere," *Travel Holiday,* September 1998, pp. 56, 58, 60.

UNDERSTANDING MEANING FROM CONTEXT

Circle the letter of the choice closest to the meaning of each italicized word or phrase from the reading.

1. The woman throws up her hands in *mock* frustration and walks away.

   a. pretended   **b.** good   **c.** true

2. They've just participated in a *ritual* that has existed for centuries, all over the world: bargaining.

   a. discussion   **b.** cultural practice   **c.** law

3. Many . . . *are reluctant to* bargain.

   a. really want to   **b.** really love to   **c.** don't really want to

4. *Stick to your guns,* but have fun with the process.

   a. Take your guns with you   **b.** Don't change your position   **c.** Pretend to shoot someone

5. Wear dark glasses to conceal your *anxiety*.

   a. interest   **b.** worry   **c.** anger

GRAMMAR **PRESENTATION**
PRESENT AND FUTURE TIME

PRESENT TIME: IN GENERAL; NOW

SIMPLE PRESENT

Souvenirs **cost** money.

PRESENT PROGRESSIVE			
SUBJECT	**AM / IS / ARE**	**BASE FORM + -ING**	
A tourist	**is**	**admiring**	the beautiful oriental rugs on display.

PAST TO PRESENT TIME: FROM A TIME IN THE PAST UNTIL NOW

PRESENT PERFECT			
SUBJECT	**HAS / HAVE**	**PAST PARTICIPLE**	
This ritual	**has**	**existed**	for centuries.

PRESENT PERFECT PROGRESSIVE			
SUBJECT	**HAS / HAVE BEEN**	**BASE FORM + -ING**	
Yours truly	**has been**	**making**	trips abroad since 1995.

FUTURE TIME: A TIME IN THE FUTURE (GENERAL OR SPECIFIC)

WILL		
WILL	**BASE FORM**	
You**'ll**	**need**	to bring back some souvenirs.

BE GOING TO		
BE GOING TO	**BASE FORM**	
I**'m going to**	**give**	you some tips on bargaining.

FUTURE PROGRESSIVE			
	WILL BE	**BASE FORM + -ING**	
A week from now you	**'ll be**	**relaxing**	in the sunshine.

SIMPLE PRESENT: A SCHEDULE OR TIMETABLE

You **leave** next Tuesday at 4 P.M.

PRESENT PROGRESSIVE: AN ALREADY-ARRANGED ACTION OR EVENT

	AM / IS / ARE	BASE FORM + -ING	
So you	're	traveling	abroad this summer?

TWO ACTIONS IN THE FUTURE

You**'ll need** to make a counter-offer when the vendor **announces** the price.

FUTURE TIME: BEFORE A CERTAIN TIME IN THE FUTURE

FUTURE PERFECT

	WILL HAVE	PAST PARTICIPLE	
You	will have	missed	out on one of life's most interesting experiences.

FUTURE PERFECT PROGRESSIVE

WILL HAVE BEEN		BASE FORM + -ING	
By the end of the summer, you**'ll have been**		traveling	for several weeks.

NOTES

EXAMPLES

1. Use the **simple present** to show actions, events, or states that happen habitually or as a general rule.

- Souvenirs **cost** money.
- Vendors **expect** you to bargain.

We also use the **simple present** to narrate events in sequence.

- A tourist **finds** a beautiful rug and **asks** the price.
- "One thousand dollars," the vendor **says.**

2. Use the **present progressive** to show actions, events, or states that are in progress at the moment (not finished).

- A tourist **is admiring** the beautiful oriental rugs on display.

▶ **BE CAREFUL!** Stative verbs are not usually used in the progressive. These verbs include *have* (= possess), *believe, own, want, like, need, know, love*. See Appendix 2 on page A-2 for a list of common verbs usually used statively. When stative verbs occur in the progressive, they generally have different meanings. Look at the examples in the next column.

- I **have** a blue Toyota Camry. *(possess)*
- We**'re having** dinner now. *(eating)*

3. The **present perfect** and the **present perfect progressive** connect the past and the present. Use them to express states or actions that began in the past and continue until now. Include *for* or *since* and a time expression. Remember that *for* is used to show an amount of time and *since* shows a starting point.

- Bargaining is a ritual that **has existed for** centuries. *(an amount of time)*
- Yours truly **has been making** trips abroad **since** 1995. *(a starting point)*

▶ **BE CAREFUL!** Use the present perfect, not the simple present, for actions or events that began in the past and are continuing now.

- I**'ve been** here for three months now. NOT ~~I'm here for three months now.~~

4. Use *will* to show a future state, action, or event decided on at the moment of speaking.

Will is used in the progressive to describe an action that will be in progress at a certain time in the future.

- You**'ll need** to make a counter-offer when the vendor announces the price.

- A week from now you**'ll be relaxing** in the sunshine or **visiting** famous landmarks.

5. *Be going to* usually shows a planned future. Use it to express a state, action, or event already planned before the moment of speaking.

- In this week's column, I**'m going to give** you some tips on how to perform this most enjoyable activity.

6. We can use both *will* and *be going to* when we say what we think will happen in the future.

- I think I**'ll enjoy** the trip.
- I think I**'m going to enjoy** the trip.

▶ **BE CAREFUL!** Use *will*, not *be going to*, to express an unplanned future action.

- Call me next week. Maybe I**'ll be** free. NOT ~~Maybe I'm going to be free.~~ (*Maybe* shows that the situation is unplanned.)

▶ **BE CAREFUL!** Use *be going to*, not *will*, to talk about a future situation that is already developing.

- Look at those dark clouds! It**'s going to rain**. NOT ~~It will rain.~~

NOTE: Both *will* and *be going to* can be used informally in the progressive to show a planned future action.

- I**'ll be studying** tonight.
- I**'m going to be studying** tonight.

7. You can use the **present progressive** to express a future event or action that has already been arranged.

- So you**'re visiting** another country this year?

8. The **simple present** can be used to show a future state, action, or event that is part of a schedule or timetable.

- You **leave** next Tuesday at 4 P.M.

▶ **BE CAREFUL!** Use the simple present as future <u>only</u> to show something that is part of a schedule.

9. Look at this sentence. It contains an independent clause and a dependent clause.

Many dependent clauses begin with words such as *if, when, before, after, as soon as,* and *until*.

When a dependent clause talks about a future time, use the simple present in the dependent clause and the future with *will* or *be going to* in the independent clause. Both verbs are future in meaning. The simple present shows the first future action, and the future shows the second future action.

independent clause
- You'll need to make a counter-offer
dependent clause
when the vendor announces the price.

dependent clause
- As soon as you **walk** away,
independent clause
the vendor **will** most likely **come running** after you.

▶ **BE CAREFUL!** Don't use the future with *will* or *be going to* in the dependent clause. Use it in the independent clause.

- When we get to Italy, we'll rent a car. NOT ~~When we will get to Italy, we'll rent a car.~~

10. Use the **future perfect** to show a state, action, or event that will happen before a certain time in the future.

- If you go home without having experienced bargaining, **you will have missed out** on one of life's most interesting experiences.

You can also use the **future perfect** in the progressive.

- By the end of the summer, you**'ll have been traveling** for several weeks.

NOTE: The **future perfect** is often used with *by* and *by the time*.

- **By the time** we finish our trip, we**'ll have visited** eighteen countries.

FOCUSED PRACTICE

1 DISCOVER THE GRAMMAR

Part A

1. List the verbs in the first paragraph of It's a Bargain. What verb tense is being used to tell the story? Why do you think that tense is being used?

2. In the last line of paragraph 1, what tense is the verb phrase "has existed"? Why is that tense used in that sentence?

3. In paragraph 2, the future is expressed in three different ways. Underline the verbs and label the ways.

Part B

Look again at some of the sentences from It's a Bargain. *On the lines provided, write the events in the order in which they will happen. Do not include imperatives (commands).*

1. You already have your tickets, and you leave next Tuesday at 4 P.M.

   First: _You already have your tickets._

   Second: _You leave next Tuesday at 4 P.M._

2. Maybe if you do some bargaining, you'll be able to get some good buys.

   First: _____

   Second: _____

3. You'll need to make a counter-offer when the vendor announces the price.

   First: _____

   Second: _____

4. Just make it clear that you're not going to buy if the vendor doesn't come down.

   First: _____

   Second: _____

5. As soon as you do this, he will most likely come running after you.

   First: _____

   Second: _____

6. If you go home without having experienced bargaining, you'll have missed out on one of life's most interesting experiences.

   First: _____

   Second: _____

2 A POSTCARD HOME

Connie Osborne is traveling in Europe. Complete her postcard to her friend Evelyn with the correct forms of the verbs below.

write	visit	shine	stay	love	be	go

London Towers Hotel

Hi Evelyn,   Sunday, July 19

Well, I _____ in
                    1.
London for a week now, and the sun
_____ every day since I got here. What a
       2.
surprise. I _____ my favorite museums
              3.
and all the usual attractions. Went to the British Museum
yesterday and had a great time. Also went to the Tower of
London. I love those guides in their funny hats.

I _____ in a bed and breakfast, which is really
      4.
nice, but it's also pretty expensive, so I _____ to a
                                5.
hostel tonight.

The British people are so friendly and helpful!
And I really _____ the accent.
             6.
I _____ again soon.   Best,
      7.   Connie

To:

Evelyn Nordin
5502 SW 99th St.
Seattle, WA 98136
                    USA

Britain
22p

3 DID YOU DO ANY BARGAINING?

Answer each of the following questions according to your own experience. Then work with another student. Compare your answers.

1. Have you ever traveled to another country?

2. Did you do any bargaining while you were there?

3. Have any of your friends ever given you tips on how to bargain?

Now imagine that you're going to bargain in an open-air market tomorrow.

4. If a vendor does not give you a fair price when you try to bargain, how do you think you'll react?

5. Do you think you'll be nervous or intimidated when you try to bargain? If so, why?

6. When you have been nervous or intimidated in the past, how have you reacted?

④ THE FLEA MARKET

Grammar Notes 1, 2, 4, 5, 9, 10

Work with a partner. Decide which sentences Student A and Student B say. Mark
*the sentences **A** or **B**. Then write them in the order of a dialogue. Read the*
dialogue aloud with your partner.

_____ Take it easy. We'll be there in a few minutes. We'll have arrived as soon as we cross the big bridge coming up. See it?

_____ I'll have developed a splitting headache by the time we get there if you don't stop complaining.

_____ Next time you go to the flea market, I'm staying home!

_____ Well, excuse me for living!

_____ Just stop making all that noise!

_____ We're really late. By the time we get to the flea market, they'll have sold all the best items. Those antique vases I love will be all gone.

_____ Yes. But we're already an hour late. We'll have missed all the best bargains.

_____ Next time we're going to leave home two hours earlier. That way, even if we get lost, we'll still have time to get some good bargains. You know how I love to bargain.

⑤ A WORLD TRAVELER

Grammar Notes 1–4

Read the article about John Clouse. At the time the article was written, Clouse
had visited more countries than anyone else in the world. Complete the passage
by choosing the correct forms of the verbs in parentheses.

TRAVEL   Section 6
_____

This Man's Been Nearly Everywhere

John Clouse _____ the thickest,
     1. (have)
most dog-eared passport in the world. Turn
to page 16 of the *1996 Guinness Book of World
Records* and you _____ the reason.
                   2. (find)
    He _____ the record for traveling
       3. (hold)
to all 192 of the globe's sovereign countries, and
to all but six of the non-sovereign or other
territories that existed in early 1996.

Clouse, who has spent about $1.25 million
roaming from A to Z in the past 40 years, says
he travels for the love of it, not to outrun
anybody else who may be keeping a list. He is
now down to just three remote islands to visit.

    Clouse _____ his journeys since
            4. (continue)
making the record book, and has not only visited
every country in the world, but some two or

three times. Now he _____ on the
                        5. (focus)
remaining three islands.

"Yeah, I'm trying to finagle my way to three

places: the Paracel Islands, owned by China in the

South China Sea," he says. "And on two occasions

the weather has kept me away from reaching

Bouvet, an island in Norwegian Antarctica. No. 3

is Clipperton, a French island about 700 miles west

of Acapulco."

Clouse says he _____ East Africa.
                      6. (love)
"It's one of the most beautiful places in the world,"

he says. "In Kenya and Tanzania the weather is

gorgeous almost every day, and Lake Nyasa must

be what the garden of Eden looked like."

After all his traveling he says, "I

_____ there are evil empires and evil
7. (not believe)
people. Yes, there are some bad leaders in the

world, but seeing people as individuals has taught

me that they are all basically alike. You can be in

some terrible place and someone will extend

hospitality to you."

Clouse _____ light, with a small
           8. (travel)
suitcase, and seldom _____ first class.
                           9. (go)
His complete collection of *National Geographic*

magazines is his main source for research.

Clouse began his traveling adventures just after

World War II when severe frostbite in the war sent

him to England for recovery, then to Paris and

other parts of Europe.

"I thought, boy, this is the life," he says of his

travels then. "And when I got out of law school and

was making a little money, I started to travel."

Years ago he stopped taking photos and now

_____ a journal of his travels.
10. (keep)
He has crossed the Atlantic Ocean at least 100

times, and the Pacific Ocean 40 or 50 times. His

18-year-old son, Chauncey, had visited over 100

countries by the time he was 5 years old. But for

now, it is not "like father like son."

"We _____ about seven miles across
      11. (live)
the river from Kentucky," says Clouse. "My son

would not go those seven miles . . . He'd say, sorry,

Dad, I've got something else to do."

Clouse concludes that the right attitude is

synonymous with the lightness of his suitcase.

"Travel without a lot of mental baggage," he says.

"Try not to go with preconceived notions that the

place _____ dirty or hostile, and if it
        12. (be)
_____, go with the flow and make the
13. (be)
best of it.

"Learn a few words like please and thank you,"

he suggests. "That really _____ people."
                                14. (please)

6 UNDERSTANDING MEANING FROM CONTEXT

Mark the following sentences **True (T), False (F),** *or* **Impossible to know (I)** *based on the reading in Exercise 5.*

Part A

_____ **1.** Clouse will have visited the six remaining territories by the year 2001.

_____ **2.** Clouse has been traveling all these years because he wants to break the world records.

_____ **3.** Clouse's son will accompany him to the last three remote islands.

_____ **4.** Clouse's son has been visiting all the countries with his father.

_____ **5.** Clouse has done all his research on the Internet.

_____ **6.** Clouse has always tried to develop preconceived notions about a place before his visit.

_____ **7.** According to Clouse, if you travel as he has, you will no longer categorize the people of a country as all good or all bad.

Part B

Now look again at these three sentences. Circle the letter of the choice that best explains the meaning of each italicized phrase. Explain the reason for your choice.

1. Clouse *will have visited* the six remaining territories by the year 2001.

    a. visited before the time mentioned   **b.** has already visited before now

_____

2. Clouse's son *has been visiting* all the countries with his father.

    a. visited once   **b.** has visited and is continuing to visit

_____

3. *Clouse has done all his research* on the Internet.

    a. the research is now finished   **b.** the research will be continued

_____

7 BY THIS TIME NEXT YEAR . . .   Grammar Note 10

Tell a partner what new place(s) you will have visited by this time next year. Then tell your partner what you will have accomplished within five years. Use the future perfect.

        EXAMPLE:
        By this time next year, I **will have visited** Mexico City.
        Within five years, I **will have graduated** from college, **gotten** a good job, . . .

8 EDITING

Find and correct the thirteen mistakes in present and future verb usage in the following composition.

 Travel Log

    I am writing these words in English because I ~~am needing~~ need the practice. At this moment I am on an airplane over the Pacific Ocean, on my way to a year of study at New York University in the United States. I am looking forward to being there, but I am also a little afraid. What will I find when I will get to America? Will the Americans be arrogant and violent? Will I make any friends? Am I happy?

    These were the words I wrote in my diary on the airplane last month. But I'm here for a month now, and I've found that things are a lot different from what I expected. I've found that the majority of people here are friendly. They are going out of their way to help you if you need it.

    On television, the news programs are speaking a lot about bad events like accidents, murders, diseases, and fights. But I don't see as much violence in my life as I do on television. I have not been mugged and I no worry all the time about my safety.

    Two of the ideas I had about the United States, however, are seeming to be true. One is that Americans aren't paying much attention to rules. One of my best American friends says, in fact, "Rules are made to be broken." The other idea I had is about the American family. In Japan the family is very important, but some Japanese people are thinking that the family means nothing in the United States. I'm not knowing if this is true or not. But I think it might be true, since my American friends almost never are mentioning their parents or their brothers and sisters. Anyway, I am going to have a chance to see a real American family. I'm going with my roommate Susan to spend Thanksgiving break with her family in Pennsylvania. When I will see her family, I will understand more!

COMMUNICATION PRACTICE

9 LISTENING

The Fosters, a family from England, are traveling in Canada. Listen to their conversation. Then listen again and mark the following sentences **True (T)** *or* **False (F)**.

_____ **1.** Tim is still in bed.

_____ **2.** The Fosters are going to the mall this morning.

_____ **3.** Amy and Tim want to go to the museum.

_____ **4.** Dad thinks the children can learn something at the museum.

_____ **5.** The Fosters are on the tour bus now.

_____ **6.** The Fosters will miss the bus if they don't hurry.

_____ **7.** Amy and Tim like tours.

_____ **8.** Tim thinks it's always important to learn new things.

_____ **9.** Amy and Tim would rather go to the museum by themselves than go on a tour.

_____ **10.** The Fosters will go to the mall before they go on the tour.

10 GROUP GUESSING GAME: A VACATION SPOT

Get into groups of four to six. Choose a vacation spot that you might like to visit. Use the Internet or go to the library to get information about the place. Then talk about your place to the class, describing it and telling what you'll do there, but don't say the name of the place. The rest of the class must guess the vacation spot.

11 ESSAY

Divide into groups of four. Look back at This Man's Been Nearly Everywhere.

Clouse says, "I don't believe there are evil empires and evil people. Yes, there are some bad leaders in the world, but seeing people as individuals has taught me that they are all basically alike. You can be in some terrible place and someone will extend hospitality to you."

Do you agree with Clouse? Why or why not? Give examples to support your viewpoint from your own experiences.

Write a short essay (one or two paragraphs) expressing your response to the quote by Clouse. Give examples from your own experience to support your viewpoint.

12 PICTURE DISCUSSION

Talk with a partner about the picture. What has happened? Do you think the father will have fixed the car by nightfall? Do you think the other car is slowing down in order to help?

2

PAST TIME

GRAMMAR IN CONTEXT

QUESTIONS TO CONSIDER

1. What do you understand by the term "arranged marriage"?

2. Would you rather find your own person to marry or have someone else select that person for you?

3. Do you think an arranged marriage is likely to be a happy marriage?

Read an article about an unusual marriage that took place recently.

LIFESTYLES

A Marriage Made on the Internet?

How many Americans have ever considered asking friends or relatives to select their future spouse for them? Not very many, apparently. Yet this is exactly what David Weinlick did.

Weinlick had apparently been considering marriage and had known for a long time that he was going to get married on June 13, 1998. Where the wedding would take place and who would be invited he already knew. He just didn't know who he would be marrying. You see, he hadn't met his bride yet.

It all started four years ago. Friends would repeatedly ask Weinlick, an anthropology student at the University of Minnesota, when he was going to tie the knot.

He got tired of these questions, so he just picked a date out of the blue: June 13, 1998. As this date kept getting closer and closer, Weinlick, twenty-eight, knew he had to do something. His friend Steve Fletcher came up with the idea of a democratic selection process. Weinlick liked the idea, so he advertised for a bride on the Internet on a Bridal Nomination Committee Web site.

He devised an application form and asked friends and relatives to interview the candidates and select the winner. They did this at a "bridal candidate mixer" before the ceremony on the day of the wedding.

Weinlick's friends and relatives took the request quite seriously.

Internet Marriage

Though Weinlick wasn't sure who his bride would be, he did want to get married. He said he thinks commitment is important and that people have to work at relationships to make them successful. Weinlick's sister, Wenonah Wilms, said she thought that all of the candidates were nice but that she was looking for someone really special. Wilms added that it was important for her brother to marry someone who would fit into family celebrations like at Christmas.

So who won the election? It was Elizabeth Runze, a pharmacy student at the University of Minnesota. Runze hadn't met Weinlick before she picked up a candidate survey on the Monday before the wedding. They talked more when Runze turned in the survey about her career plans and hobbies the next day. After her selection, Runze said the day was the most incredible she had ever experienced.

Weinlick was happy, too. After the selection the groom said the plan turned out almost exactly as he had hoped.

By the time the wedding day rolled around, Weinlick had prepared everything: the rings, the musicians, his tuxedo, and the reception afterwards. The two took their vows at the Mall of America in Minneapolis while about 2,000 shoppers looked on from the upper levels of the mall.

Runze's parents support the marriage. Runze's mother said her daughter was taking the whole event seriously. She predicted the couple's marriage would be long-term.

Weinlick's father wasn't so positive. He said he admired his son's independence and wished him well but wasn't really happy about the wedding, adding that he thought it was a case of treating a serious step too lightly.

From all accounts, the newlyweds are doing well. Weinlick and Runze's union qualifies as an "arranged marriage," a phenomenon which has never had much currency in America. Arranged marriages are common in many other parts of the world, though, or at least they used to be. Maybe they're not such a bad idea.

Sources: Based on information in "A Match Made in the Mall: Minnesota Anthropology Student Weds Bride Chosen by Family and Friends," *Dallas Morning News,* June 14, 1998, p. 7A, copyright: The Associated Press; "Here Come the Bridal Candidates; Society: Friends of 28-year-old will vote to select his mate. As election day nears, Dad is not so sure of the plan," Home Edition, *Los Angeles Times,* June 8, 1998, p. A-19.

UNDERSTANDING MEANING FROM CONTEXT

Make a guess about the meaning of each italicized word or phrase from the reading. Write your guess in the blank provided.

1. Friends would repeatedly ask Weinlick . . . when he was going to *tie the knot.*

_____

2. He got tired of these questions, so he just picked a date *out of the blue.* . . .

_____

3. After the selection, the *groom* said the plan turned out almost exactly as he had hoped.

_____

4. The two *took their vows* at the Mall of America in Minneapolis.

_____

5. Weinlick and Runze's union qualifies as an "arranged marriage," a phenomenon which has never *had much currency* in America.

_____

GRAMMAR **PRESENTATION**
PAST TIME

PAST TIME: A TIME IN THE PAST (GENERAL OR SPECIFIC)

SIMPLE PAST
Weinlick's father **admired** his son's independence and **wished** him well.

PAST PROGRESSIVE			
SUBJECT	WAS / WERE	BASE FORM + -ING	
Weinlick's sister	**was**	**looking for**	someone really special.

USED TO + BASE FORM
Arranged marriages **used to be** common in many parts of the world.

WOULD + BASE FORM
Friends **would** repeatedly **ask** Weinlick when he was going to tie the knot.

PAST TIME: A TIME IN THE PAST (INDEFINITE)

PRESENT PERFECT
How many Americans **have** ever **considered** asking friends or relatives to select their future spouse for them?

PAST TIME: BEFORE A TIME IN THE PAST

PAST PERFECT			
SUBJECT	HAD	PAST PARTICIPLE	
Weinlick	**had**	**known**	for a long time that he was going to get married on June 13, 1998.

PAST PERFECT PROGRESSIVE			
SUBJECT	HAD BEEN	BASE FORM + -ING	
Weinlick	**had** apparently **been**	**considering**	marriage.

PAST TIME: AFTER A TIME IN THE PAST BUT BEFORE NOW

FUTURE IN THE PAST			
	WAS / WERE GOING TO	**BASE FORM**	
Weinlick had known for a long time that he	**was going to**	**get**	married on June 13, 1998.

FUTURE IN THE PAST: *WOULD*			
	WOULD	**BASE FORM**	
He knew where the wedding and who	**would** **would**	**take place** **be**	invited.

FUTURE IN THE PAST: *WOULD BE + -ING*		
	WOULD	**BASE FORM + -ING**
He just didn't know who he	**would**	**be marrying**.

NOTES

EXAMPLES

1. Use the **simple past** to express a state, event, or action at a specific time in the past or a general time in the past.

- Weinlick **liked** the idea, so he **advertised** for a bride on the Internet.

2. Use the **past progressive** to express an action that was in progress (not finished) at a time in the past.

- Weinlick's sister said she **was looking for** someone really special.

3. Use the **present perfect** (*have / has +* past participle) to express a state, event, or action at an indefinite time in the past.

- How many Americans **have** ever **considered** asking friends or relatives to select their future spouse for them?

▶ **BE CAREFUL!** Don't use the present perfect with a past time expression.

- Weinlick **got** married **several months ago**.
  NOT ~~Weinlick has gotten married several months ago.~~

Notice the difference between the simple past and the present perfect. The simple past is the definite past. The present perfect is the indefinite past.	• The two **took** their vows at the Mall of America in Minneapolis. (definite—a specific time) • Arranged marriage **has** never **had** much currency in America. (indefinite—no specific time)

4. Use the **past perfect** (*had* + past participle) to show a state, event, or action that happened before a certain time in the past. Use the **past perfect** with the past tense to show which of two past states, events, or actions happened first. The **past perfect** is often used with *by* or *by the time*.	• Weinlick **hadn't met** his bride yet. *(He had not met her before he set the wedding date.)* • By the time the wedding day rolled around, Weinlick **had prepared** everything. *(First he prepared everything; then the wedding day rolled around.)*

5. Use **used to** + base form to show a habitual state, event, or action that was true in the past but is no longer true.	• Arranged marriages **used to be** common in many countries. *(They're not very common anymore.)*

6. You can also use **would** + base form to express actions or events that occurred regularly during a period in the past. ▶ **BE CAREFUL! Used to** and **would** are similar in meaning when they are used to express past actions. They can be used interchangeably in many situations. However, only **used to** can show past location, state, or possession.	• Friends **would** repeatedly **ask** Weinlick when he was going to get married. • We used to have a summer home. NOT ~~We would have a summer home.~~

7. Use **was / were going to** or **would** + base form to describe a state, event, or action that was planned in the past (before now). Sentences with **was / were going to** or **would** are sometimes called **future in the past**. See Note 5, page 39 for a discussion of sequence of tenses.	• Weinlick had known for a long time that he **was going to get** married on June 13, 1998. • He knew where the wedding **would take place** and who **would be** invited. • He just didn't know who he **would be marrying**.

FOCUSED PRACTICE

1 DISCOVER THE GRAMMAR

Part A

1. *Find three examples of* **would** *+ verb in the unit opener,* A Marriage Made on the Internet? *Do they show a future in the past or a habitual action in the past?*

_____

2. *List the simple past tense irregular verbs in the opener. Write the present form of each one next to the past tense.*

_____

3. *Find a sentence that shows two past actions, one happening before the other. Write the word that says which one happened first.*

_____

Part B

Look again at some of the sentences from A Marriage Made on the Internet?
Write the earlier-occurring state or action on the left and the later-occurring state or action on the right.

1. Weinlick . . . had known for a long time he was going to get married on June 13, 1998.

   earlier   **later**

   Weinlick had known for a long time   he was going to get married on June 13, 1998.

2. He just didn't know who he would be marrying.

   earlier   **later**

   _____

3. Friends would repeatedly ask Weinlick . . . when he was going to tie the knot.

   earlier   **later**

   _____

4. Runze hadn't met Weinlick before she picked up a candidate survey on the Monday before the wedding.

   earlier   **later**

   _____

5. By the time the wedding day rolled around, Weinlick had prepared everything . . .

   earlier   **later**

   _____

❷ DO OPPOSITES ATTRACT?   Grammar Notes 1, 3

Complete the story with the correct past forms of the indicated verbs. Use contractions with pronoun subjects.

Ellen Rosetti and Mark Stevens ___have been married___ for almost a year now. Their
                                                       1. (be married)

marriage almost _____, though. They _____ on a blind date
                             2. (not happen)   **3. (meet)**

when Jennifer's friend Alice _____ two extra tickets for a concert. At first
                                          4. (have)

Jennifer _____ Mark was the most opinionated man she'd ever met. A
                            5. (think)

couple of weeks after the concert, Mark _____ and _____
                                   6. (call up)   **7. (ask)**

Ellen out. Ellen _____ to say no, but something _____ her
                            8. (want)   **9. (make)**

accept. After that, one thing _____ to another. Today Mark says, "Ellen is
                            10. (lead)

unique. I _____ anyone even remotely like her."
        11. (never / meet)

    Ellen says, "At first glance you might have trouble seeing how Mark and I could be

married. In certain ways, we're as different as night and day. I'm an early bird; he's a night

owl. He's conservative; I'm liberal. He loves sports, and I can't stand them. I guess you

might say we're a case of opposites being attracted to each other. But in other ways we're

not so different. For one thing, we both love to travel. We _____ three
                                   12. (take)

fantastic trips since we _____ the knot. The other thing is that we love to
                    13. (tie)

talk. I can't tell you how many fascinating conversations we _____. There
                                             14. (have)

_____ lots of times when we _____ all night talking."
     15. (be)   **16. (stay up)**

    Maybe opposites do attract.

③ THE REST IS HISTORY

This is the story of how Jim Garcia and Jennifer O'Leary met. The sentences are out of order. On a separate piece of paper, rewrite them in a paragraph or two in chronological order, using the past and past perfect as appropriate. Combine sentences as needed. Then compare what you have written with a partner. Here are two possible beginning sentences:

> **A:** Jim Garcia and Jennifer O'Leary got married six months ago.
>
> **B:** Jim Garcia and Jennifer O'Leary had gone to high school together and had been good friends.

About a year ago, both Jennifer and Jim returned to their home town.

Jennifer accepted.

Jim and Jennifer got married six months ago.

Jennifer went away to college.

Jim asked Jennifer for a date.

The rest is history.

Jim Garcia and Jennifer O'Leary had gone to high school together and had been good friends.

Jim and Jennifer graduated and went their separate ways.

Jim went into the military.

Jim and Jennifer ran into each other in the drugstore.

Jim and Jennifer fell in love.

④ BEFORE AND AFTER

Jim Garcia and Mark Stevens both got married fairly recently. Fill in the blanks in their conversation with the correct forms of **used to** *or* **would** *and the indicated verbs. Use* **would** *if possible. Contract* **would** *if it occurs with a pronoun.*

MARK: So, Jim, how does it feel to be an old married man? Been about six months, hasn't it?

JIM: Yep. It feels great. It's a lot different, though.

MARK: Yeah? How so?

JIM: Well, I guess I'd say I ___used to have___ a lot more freedom. Like on Saturdays,
                                 1. (have)

for example. I _____ until eleven or even noon. Then when I got up
                  2. (sleep)

my buddies and I _____ out for breakfast at a restaurant. Now
                  3. (usually go)

Jennifer and I get up at eight at the latest. She's really an early bird. And I either

make her breakfast or she makes it for me. And then on Saturday nights I

_____ on a date and stay out till all hours of the night. Now it's just
         4. (go)

the two of us. Sometimes we go out on Saturday nights, and sometimes we don't.

MARK: Does that bother you?

JIM: You know, it doesn't. Life actually _____ kind of lonely. It's not
                          5. (be)

anymore. What about you? Have things really changed?

MARK: They sure have. For one thing, the neighborhood is totally different. Remember the

apartment I _____ in, right north of downtown? Well, Ellen and I
                6. (live)

just bought a house in the suburbs. That's a trip, let me tell you.

JIM: I'll bet.

MARK: Yeah. My weekends _____ my own. I _____ all day
                7. (be)   **8. (spend)**

Saturday working on my car or going mountain biking. Now I have to cut the grass

and take care of the yard.

JIM: So would you change anything?

MARK: Sure wouldn't. You know how everyone says how great it is to be single? Well, that

_____ my attitude too. Not now. Now I'd say "been there, done that."
         9. (be)

JIM: Me too. I wouldn't change a thing.

5 PLANS AND EXPECTATIONS   **Grammar Note 7**

Before Jim got married, he jotted down some of his plans and expectations. Now
that he's married, he's looking at them. Some of them came true, and some didn't.
Jim is telling Mark about his thoughts. Write Jim's sentences. Use the indicated
future-in-the-past constructions: **was / were going to** + *verb or* **would** + *verb.*

(continued on next page)

Column A

1. "I think it'll be quite a while before we have any children."

2. "I think I'll probably feel just a little bit trapped."

3. "I think that we're going to live in an apartment."

4. "I expect that there won't be as much money to spend."

5. "I hope that we'll be happy."

6. I'm sure that we're going to have a lot of fun together."

7. "I don't think I'll be seeing as much of my buddies."

8. "I figure that we're going to be taking a lot of trips."

Column B

I thought it would be quite a while before

we had any children,

but that's not true. Our first baby is due in four months.

_____

_____

but I haven't felt that way at all.

_____

_____

and we do.

_____

_____

but that's not true. Jennifer really knows how to keep our lifestyle economical.

_____

and we are. Tremendously.

_____

and we do.

_____

and I don't. That's OK, though.

_____

but we haven't taken any, yet.

6 **DEAR ANN**

Read the excerpt from Ann Landers' advice column. Complete the advice column with the correct form of the indicated verbs.

Dear Ann: My husband and I _____ were _____ recently married.
1. (be)
Our wedding _____ beautiful, but there
2. (be)
_____ one problem. We _____ 17 no-shows
3. (be)   4. (have)
and four surprise guests. Two days before the wedding, we

Ann Landers

_____ give the caterers the exact number of guests. After
5. (have to)
that, we _____ billed no matter how many no-shows there
6. (get)
_____. That means we _____ for 13 extra
7. (be)   8. (pay)
meals that nobody _____.
9. (eat)

I understand that sometimes an emergency comes up, but we _____ over $330
10. (waste)
on those no-show dinners. The four extra guests _____ to be no problem because
11. (turn out)
of the no-shows, but generally, surprises are not welcome. What if those 17 people had shown up

and we didn't have enough dinners? It would have been a nightmare.

It is simply good manners to let the hostess know if you are coming or not. And if the number

of people in your party _____, she should be informed about that, too. When you
12. (change)
RSVP, the information you give the hostess is what the cost of the event is based on. Wedding

receptions aren't cheap these days, and paying for no-shows is a terrible waste.

Am I expecting too much from guests? If so, please tell me.   —*San Diego*

Dear San Diego: You are not expecting too much. Letting the hostess know whether you
are coming is no more than common courtesy. Not having enough food because some

inconsiderate people _____ to let you know they were coming is a major
13. (not bother)
embarrassment. A response card and stamped envelope are well worth the extra expense.

I recommend them.

Source: Ann Landers, *Seattle Post-Intelligencer*, October 6, 1998, p. F-2. Permission granted by Ann Landers and Creators Syndicate.

Now discuss the letter with a partner. Do you agree with Ann Landers' advice? Why or why not?

7 EDITING

Read Jennifer Garcia's diary entry. Find and correct the nine errors in verb constructions.

May 20

Dear Diary,

    I just had to write today. It's our six-month anniversary. Jim and I ~~are~~ ^{have been} married six months as of today. So maybe this is the time for me to take stock of my situation. The obvious question is whether I'm happy I get married. The answer is "Absolutely." When I remember what my life has been like before we get married, I realize now how lonely I've been before. Jim is a wonderful guy. Since we both work, we take turns doing the housework. He's really good about that. When we have been dating, I wasn't sure whether or not I'm going to have to do all the housework. But I had not to worry. Today we split everything 50/50. The only complaint I have is that Jim snores at night. When I told him that, he only says, "Well, sweetie, you snore too." I don't believe it. But if this is our only problem, I guess we're pretty lucky.

    Well, Diary, I would have a long and tiring day. It's time to go to sleep. I'll write again soon.

Jennifer

COMMUNICATION PRACTICE

8 LISTENING

Listen to the news broadcast. Then listen again and mark the following sentences **True (T)** *or* **False (F)**.

True **False**

❏ ❏ **1.** According to the broadcast, this is the first parachute wedding that has ever taken place.

❏ ❏ **2.** The bride and groom have known each other for four years.

❏ ❏ **3.** This was the first parachute jump for Yang and Hammer.

❏ ❏ **4.** Yang and Hammer had intended to get married while bungee-jumping.

❏ ❏ **5.** By the time Yang and Hammer landed, they were married.

❏ ❏ **6.** Yang and Hammer were able to find a minister who agreed to marry them while bungee-jumping but decided not to because it was too expensive.

❏ ❏ **7.** This is the most unusual wedding ceremony Reverend Martinez has ever performed.

❏ ❏ **8.** To date, Martinez has made several parachute jumps.

❏ ❏ **9.** Reverend Martinez once married a couple on horseback.

❏ ❏ **10.** Martinez intends to do more parachute jumping.

Do you take this woman to be your lawfully wedded wife?

UNUSUAL WEDDINGS

I now pronounce you husband and wife.

9 INFORMATION GAP: BETTER THAN IT USED TO BE

Working with a partner, complete the text. Each of you will read a version of the same story. Each version is missing some information. Take turns asking your partner questions to get the missing information.

Student A, read the story about Jack Strait. Ask questions and fill in the missing information. Then answer Student B's questions.

Student B, turn to page 32 and follow the instructions there.

EXAMPLE:

A: What kind of company did he use to work for?

B: He used to work for a large, impersonal company.
How long would he be on the road?

A: He would be on the road for two or three weeks at a time.

Jack Strait's life is quite different now from the way it used to be. He used to work for

_____ company. His job required him to do a lot of traveling. He would be on

the road for two or three weeks at a time. It was always the same: As soon as he pulled in

to a town, he would look for _____. The next morning he'd leave his business

card at a lot of different establishments, hoping that someone would agree to see him. If

he'd been lucky enough to arrange an appointment in advance, he'd show them

_____. Occasionally they would buy something; most often they wouldn't.

Jack's marriage began to suffer. He missed his wife a lot, but there wasn't much he

could do about the situation. And when he was on the road, he hardly ever saw his

children. He would try to call them _____ if he had a spare moment, but

usually it was so late that they had already gone to bed. They were growing up without

him. Finally, his wife laid down the law, saying, "Why should we even be married if we're

never going to see each other?" Jack decided she was right. He took a risk. He quit his job

and started his own business. Things were difficult at first, but at least the family was

together.

That was five years ago. Things have changed a lot since then. Jack and his family used

to live in a small apartment. Now they own a house. Life is good.

Compare your story with your partner's. Are they the same? Now discuss these questions: What did Jack's occupation use to be? Is it important to take risks in life as Jack did? Can you think of an example of a risk you have taken in your life?

⑩ ESSAY

Write three or four paragraphs about how marriages used to be arranged and how young people would meet their future mates when your parents were young. Ask an older person you know how it was.

⑪ PICTURE DISCUSSION

With a partner, discuss this picture. Describe the situation. What is happening? Approximately how long do you think these people have been married? Do you think their relationship is less interesting or satisfactory than it used to be, or is it just different? Present your opinions to the class.

Source: Printed by permission of the Norman Rockwell Family Trust. Copyright © 1930 the Norman Rockwell Family Trust.

INFORMATION GAP FOR STUDENT B

Student B, read the story about Jack Strait. Answer Student A's questions. Then ask your own questions and fill in the missing information.

EXAMPLE:

A: What kind of company did he use to work for?

B: He used to work for a large, impersonal company.
How long would he be on the road?

A: He would be on the road for two or three weeks at a time.

Jack Strait's life is quite different now from the way it used to be. He used to work for a large, impersonal company. His job required him to do a lot of traveling. He would be on the road for _____. It was always the same: As soon as he pulled in to a town, he would look for a cheap motel to stay in. The next morning he'd leave _____ at a lot of different establishments, hoping that someone would agree to see him. If he'd been lucky enough to arrange an appointment in advance, he'd show them his samples. _____ they would buy something; most often they wouldn't.

Jack's marriage began to suffer. He missed his wife a lot, but there wasn't much he could do about the situation. And when he was on the road, he hardly ever saw his children. He would try to call them in the evenings if he had a spare moment, but usually it was so late that they had already gone to bed. They were growing up without him. Finally, his wife laid down the law, saying, "Why should we even be married if we're never going to see each other?" Jack decided she was right. He took a risk. He quit his job and started his own business. Things were difficult at first, but at least the family was together.

That was five years ago. Things have changed a lot since then. Jack and his family used to live _____. Now they own a house. Life is good.

Compare your story with your partner's. Are they the same? Now discuss these questions: What did Jack's occupation use to be? Is it important to take risks in life as Jack did? Can you think of an example of a risk you have taken in your life?

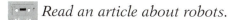
PAST, PRESENT, AND FUTURE

GRAMMAR IN CONTEXT

QUESTIONS TO CONSIDER

1. Would you like to have a personal robot in your home that would work for you?

2. What are some of the advantages and disadvantages of technology around the house?

Read an article about robots.

MY FRIEND THE ROBOT

Technology marches on. What we only dreamed about yesterday is a reality today. What we dream about today will become a reality tomorrow—or, at the rate things are going, maybe this evening. Did you know, for example, that there are now computers that can operate underwater? Soon there will be computers that we can wear. There is now computer-controlled plastic surgery. And then there are robots. Twenty years ago, hardly anyone thought personal computers would become common in the home, but they have. Robots may now be at the stage that personal computers were twenty years ago. The development of the personal robot may be the next big technological advance, and some are predicting that within twenty years, home robots will have become as common as PCs are today.

Robots that looked like vaguely humanoid, walking tin cans used to be the staple of science fiction writers. Czech writer Karel Čapek gave us the word "robot" in his play *R.U.R., Rossum's Universal Robots*, in 1921. Čapek coined the term from *robota*, which means "forced labor" or "drudgery." The robots in Čapek's play eventually destroyed mankind because they had learned to love

continued ▶

MY FRIEND THE ROBOT

and hate. Today, though, most visualize robots not as threatening creatures but as beneficial machines that are helping us with our work, especially unpleasant drudgery.

Computer science professor Gregory Dudek recalls how bulky and awkward computers were when they first appeared and how they've been getting much smaller and more efficient. He predicts the same kind of development for the personal robot, saying, "That's the kind of change we're looking for in the robot industry. I don't think it will happen in the next two years, but in the next five or ten, certainly."

The commercial robot is already a reality. For years, industry has been using robots in factories. Different kinds of robots have started to appear in catalogues and in robot specialty shops. What will the personal robots of the future look like and do? They probably won't resemble humans as much as they do today, and they'll almost certainly be much smaller. Researchers envision small robots that will come out at night to do things like vacuum and mop the floors, eat up dirt and insects, and wash the windows.

However, many researchers see future robots as much more than just mechanical workers that perform the tasks we don't want to do. Many see them as companions. Consider robotic pets, for example. The Sony Corporation has developed a robotic dog that wags its tail, fetches a ball, and responds to human commands. Researchers at the Georgia Institute of Technology have been developing a mobile robot called Pepe, short for

"personal pet." Its makers hope that future users will regard it more as a friend or companion than as a robot. Wouldn't you like to have a robot pet that does what you want, but you wouldn't have to feed it or take it to the vet to get its shots?

Another use of robots is as waiters or servants. Does this sound unbelievable? It isn't. In London's Yo! Sushi restaurant, there are robots that prepare food, serve drinks, warn customers to get out of their way, and make funny statements like, "Life is a never-ending circuit."

Robots will probably never replace humans. Wouldn't it be nice, though, to have companions who will do our drudgery for us, be there when we wish, speak when spoken to, listen attentively to everything we say, and not talk back?

Source: Peter H. Lewis, "And Now, R2D2 for You, Too." *New York Times,* August 6, 1998, p. G1. Copyright © 1998 by the New York Times Co. Reprinted by permission.

UNDERSTANDING MEANING FROM CONTEXT

Circle the letter of the choice closest in meaning to each italicized word or phrase from the reading.

1. Robots that looked like vaguely humanoid, walking tin cans used to be the *staple* of science fiction writers.

   a. main product **b.** mechanical device **c.** home

2. Čapek *coined* the term from "robota," which means "forced labor" or "drudgery."

   a. bought **b.** created **c.** imagined

3. Today, though, most visualize robots not as threatening creatures but as beneficial machines that are helping us with our work, especially unpleasant *drudgery*.

   a. easy, enjoyable work **b.** creative work **c.** boring, difficult work

4. Computer science professor Gregory Dudek recalls how *bulky and awkward* computers were when they first appeared and how they've been getting much smaller and more efficient.

   a. small and easy to handle **b.** expensive and difficult to obtain **c.** large and hard to handle

5. The Sony Corporation has developed a robotic dog that wags its tail, *fetches* a ball, and responds to human commands.

   a. gets and brings back **b.** takes away **c.** chews

GRAMMAR **PRESENTATION**
CONTRASTING TENSES: PAST, PRESENT, AND FUTURE

PAST TIME

SIMPLE PAST: DEFINITE

Czech writer Čapek **gave** us the word "robot" in his play *R.U.R.* in 1921.

PRESENT PERFECT: INDEFINITE

Personal computers **have become** common in the home.

SIMPLE PAST AND PAST PERFECT: TWO PAST ACTIONS

Robots **destroyed** mankind because they **had learned** to love and hate.

PRESENT TIME

SIMPLE PRESENT: IN GENERAL

Technology **marches** on.

PRESENT PROGRESSIVE: NOW

That's the kind of change we**'re looking for** in the robot industry.

PRESENT PERFECT: FROM A TIME IN THE PAST UNTIL NOW

Professor Stern **has worked** at the university all his adult life.

FUTURE TIME

FUTURE WITH *WILL*

Personal robots **won't resemble** humans as much as they do today, and they**'ll** almost certainly **be** smaller.

FUTURE PERFECT: BEFORE A TIME IN THE FUTURE

Some are predicting that within twenty years robots **will have become** as common in the home as PCs are today.

FINISHED ACTION

PRESENT PERFECT			
SUBJECT	*HAS / HAVE*	**PAST PARTICIPLE**	
General Robotics	**has**	**developed**	a robot dog named Pepe.

UNFINISHED ACTION

PRESENT PERFECT PROGRESSIVE			
SUBJECT	*HAS / HAVE* **BEEN**	**PRESENT PARTICIPLE**	
General Robotics	**has been**	**developing**	advanced robots for years.

SIMPLE AND PROGRESSIVE FORMS: ALL OR PART OF AN ACTION

ALL OF AN ACTION: SIMPLE FORM
Sony Corporation has developed a robotic dog that **wags** its tail and **fetches** a ball.

PART OF AN ACTION: PROGRESSIVE FORM
That robot dog **is wagging** its tail.

VERBS USED STATIVELY AND ACTIVELY

STATIVE USE
We **have** a personal robot at our house.
The food **tastes** delicious.

ACTIVE USE
The children **are having** a good time playing with their personal robot.
The chef **is tasting** the stew that he's making.

SEQUENCE OF TENSES

TENSE AND TIME
Most people **visualize** robots as beneficial creatures that **will help** us with our work.
Twenty years ago hardly anyone **thought** personal computers **would be** common in the home.

NOTES	**EXAMPLES**
1. With certain verbs, the **present perfect** and the **present perfect progressive** are similar in meaning. Speakers often use the progressive to suggest a shorter or more temporary action. They often use the simple form to suggest a longer or more permanent action.	• John Brown **has been working** at General Robotics for a year. • Professor Stanley **has worked** for a robotics firm for over twenty years.
If the word *always* is in the sentence, we can only use the simple form.	• Professor Stanley **has always worked** in robotics. NOT ~~Professor Stanley has always been working in robotics.~~
In another use, the progressive and the simple forms are very different in meaning. Only the simple form can be used to describe actions that are finished.	• General Robotics **has developed** a robot dog. (a finished action)
The progressive form is used to describe actions that are still in progress.	• General Robotics **has been developing** advanced robots for years. (an unfinished action)
2. Remember that we use simple forms to describe finished actions or states and actions in general.	• The Sony Corporation has developed a robotic dog that **wags** its tail, **fetches** a ball, and **responds** to human commands. (actions in general)
We use progressive forms to describe actions in progress.	• That's the kind of change we**'re looking for** in the robotics industry. (action in progress)

3. Verbs used **statively** show conditions or situations that exist. Verbs used **actively** show action. Some verbs are basically stative and are rarely used actively (= to depict an action that is happening). Examples of these are *want, need, like, own, know,* and *belong.*

- Professor Stanley **knows** a lot about robots.
  NOT ~~Professor Stanley is knowing a lot about robots.~~

Other verbs are often used statively but are sometimes used actively (= to depict an action happening). When they are used in this way (usually in the progressive), they often take on different meanings. Examples of these are *have* (= eat or drink), *be* (= behave), *think* (= work mentally), and the sense verbs *see, hear, taste, feel,* and *smell.*

- Everyone **will have** a personal robot. *(will possess)*
- We**'ll be having** dinner at a restaurant. *(will be eating)*
- Helen **is** a serious person. (state of being)
- Helen **is being** silly today. *(behaving)*
- The food **tastes** delicious. (state)
- The cook **is tasting** the soup. (action)
- I **think** technology is wonderful. *(My opinion is . . .)*
- Jim **is thinking** carefully. *(working mentally)*

4. Remember that the word *there* shows the **existence** of something. It can be used in the past, present, and future. It is used with simple, not progressive, forms and usually with the verb *be.*

- In a Sushi restaurant in London, **there are** robots that serve drinks.
- **There have been** a lot of technological advances in the last twenty years.
- Didn't **there use to be** a factory on this lot?
- **There were** a lot of people working there.

5. When verbs in the same sentence are in the same general time frame, we usually keep them in the same sequence: past with past; present or present perfect with present or future.

- Twenty years ago, hardly anyone **thought** personal computers **would be** common in the home.
- The Sony Corporation **has developed** a robotic dog that **wags** its tail, **fetches** a ball, and **responds** to human commands. (same general time frame)

When verbs in the same sentence are in different time frames, they are usually not in the same sequence.

- Robots **may** now **be** at the stage that personal computers **were** twenty years ago. (different time frames)

FOCUSED PRACTICE

1 DISCOVER THE GRAMMAR

Part A

1. *Paragraph 1:* Read part of the last sentence in paragraph 1: "within twenty years, home robots will have become as common as PCs are today." Does "will have become" mean *will be in the process of becoming* or *will already be*?

2. *Paragraph 2:* "The robots . . . destroyed mankind because they *had learned* to love and hate." What tense is the verb phrase "had learned"? Why is it used here?

3. *Paragraph 3:* Find and list the simple present tense verbs and the present progressive verbs. Then find the one present perfect progressive verb. Can you explain the difference in meaning among these three different types of verb phrases?

4. *Paragraph 5:* Look at the sentences with "has developed" and "have been developing." What is the difference in meaning between the two sentences?

5. *Paragraph 5:* List the simple present tense verbs. What does this tense signify in these sentences?

Part B

Look again at these sentences from My Friend the Robot. *Then circle* **True (T)** *or* **False (F)**, *according to the meaning of each sentence.*

1. . . . some are predicting that within twenty years, home robots will have become as common as PCs are today.

   (T) F   Home robots will become common before twenty years have passed.

2. The robots in Čapek's play eventually destroyed mankind because they had learned to love and hate.

   T   F   The robots destroyed mankind before they learned to love and hate.

3. Computer science professor Gregory Dudek recalls how bulky and awkward computers were when they first appeared and how they've been getting much smaller and more efficient.

   T   F   They are still getting smaller and more efficient.

4. For years, industry has been using robots in factories.

   T   F   Industry has finished using robots in factories.

5. The Sony Corporation has developed a robotic dog that wags its tail, fetches a ball, and responds to human commands.

   T   F   The company is still developing this robot.

6. Researchers at the Georgia Institute of Technology have been developing a mobile robot called Pepe, short for "personal pet."

   T   F   The company is still developing this robot.

② IN THE YEAR 2012

It is the year 2012. Look at the pictures. Complete the paragraph with the appropriate forms of the verbs in the box.

smell	be	think	have	taste	help

It's almost dinnertime. Herkimer the robot

_____is tasting_____ the soup to see if it's ready.
　　　　1.

Joshua and Jane are hungry. The food

_____ delicious.
　　2.

Mr. and Mrs. Bellotti are relaxing. Mrs. Bellotti

_____ some flowers Mr. Bellotti has just
　　3.

brought home.

The Bellottis _____ dinner. Everyone
4.
_____ the food _____
5. **6.**
delicious.

It's later in the evening. Joshua _____ a
7.
test tomorrow in mathematics. Right now he

_____ trouble finishing his last
8.
homework problem. Herkimer _____
9.
Joshua. He _____ about the solution to
10.
the problem.

Now it's bedtime. Jane _____ usually
11.
very cooperative. Tonight she _____
12.
difficult. Helena the robot _____ a
13.
hard time getting Jane to brush her teeth.

③ WE'VE COME A LONG WAY Grammar Note 4

*Think of a grandparent or an older person you know. Interview that person,
asking these questions. Then record the answers, using* **there** *+ the appropriate
form of the verb* **be** *on the lines below. Share the interview with the class.*

1. In your opinion, what advances in technology have there been in the past fifty years
that you find amazing?

_____

2. What change has there been in your life as a result of these advances in technology?

_____

3. What problems or difficulties did there use to be in your life that no longer exist because of technology?

_____

4. What new inventions do you think there will or might be in our homes fifty years from now?

_____

5. What's the best new invention there ever was, as far as you're concerned?

_____

4 EDITING

Herkimer is one of the new multilingual robots that speak several languages. However, he has problems with English verb tenses. Find and correct the nine errors in verb usage in his journal entry.

April 15; 5:42 P.M.

My owners, Mr. and Mrs. Bellotti, ~~were purchasing~~ *purchased* me a week ago. However, they didn't bring me to their home until yesterday, so I have only been knowing them for one day.

There have been two of us robots in the household, myself and my co-robot, who is named Helena. Helena lived here for several months. She and I are having different responsibilities. Her principal responsibilities are the care of Jane, the daughter, and the household cleaning. My principal responsibilities are the care of Joshua, the son, and the preparation of the family's meals.

So far today I have been preparing breakfast and lunch. The family liked their breakfast very much. They said the food was delicious. For the last hour I have prepared dinner, and it will be ready soon.

Later this evening I will helping Joshua with his mathematics homework. Joshua thinks mathematics is difficult. I'm thinking Joshua needs more self-confidence.

COMMUNICATION PRACTICE

5 LISTENING

Read these questions. Then listen to the news broadcast. Circle **True (T)** *or* **False (F)** *according to the statements in the broadcast.*

T F **1.** Personal robots have not been available until now.

T F **2.** Ready Robotics' new personal robot will be cheaper than previous robots.

T F **3.** Robert the Robot has already gone into production.

T F **4.** Researchers have been working on Robert the Robot for five years.

T F **5.** The company expects to sell a million units of Robert the Robot before the end of the year.

T F **6.** The problem of the woman in Manitoba was that her personal robot ran away.

T F **7.** When Parker found the robot, it was vacuuming the floor.

T F **8.** Parker had washed her dishes before going to bed.

T F **9.** The robot washed the dishes and then mopped the floor.

T F **10.** The robot that Parker found was friendly.

6 INFORMATION GAP: RENEGADE ROBOTS

Working with a partner, complete the following newspaper article. Each of you will read a version of the article. Each version is missing some information. Take turns asking your partner questions to get the missing information.

Student A, read the article below. Ask questions and fill in the missing information. Then answer Student B's questions.

Student B, turn to page 46 and follow the instructions there.

EXAMPLE:

A: What happened to Marsha Jacobs at four o'clock in the morning?

B: She was awakened at four o'clock in the morning. Where did she think she was?

A: She thought she was in the Twilight Zone.

DALLAS MORNING NEWS   Section 3

Robots Answer Mystery Summons

BY MARILYN SCHWARTZ
STAFF WRITER

DALLAS—Marsha Jacobs _____ at four o'clock in the morning. She thought she was in the Twilight Zone.

"It was like _____," Mrs.

Jacobs explained. "There was this funny, shuffling noise. I looked up and couldn't believe what I was seeing.

"The inflatable robot we got for Christmas _____. The scary part was that the remote control that operates the unit was in the den. That robot _____."

The incident didn't end at the Jacobs' north Dallas home. All over the city, inflatable butler robots _____.

"I got a call at midnight last week," explained Jesse Summers. "It was my sister's security patrol company. My sister _____, and they had my number to call in case of an emergency."

The sister's burglar alarm was ringing. Summers met the security men and _____ to check the problem.

"I didn't know whether to laugh or scream," said Summers. "There was no intruder, just my sister's inflatable robot walking around. I mean it was eerie."

One of the security men gave him a disgusted look. He told Summers that was the second time in a month a robot had set off an alarm system.

Jim Smith of Plano, Texas, says his robot _____ during Christmas dinner.

"I thought my son was playing a trick with the remote control," Smith said. "He thought _____. We stopped laughing when we discovered the remote control was turned off in the den."

So who are you going to call when a robot comes to life?

Source: Marilyn Schwartz, "Robots Answer Mystery Summons," *The Dallas Morning News.* Reprinted with permission of *The Dallas Morning News.*

7 ESSAY

Overall, would it be positive or negative to have a household robot? Write an essay of two or three paragraphs, expressing your opinion about what you think might or might not happen if household robots become common.

8 PICTURE DISCUSSION

With a partner, talk about the cartoon. Explain the meaning of each statement. What has already happened? Will the man be able to defeat his robot friend in the next game?

WHAT IF YOUR ROBOT PAL IS SMARTER THAN YOU ARE?

ROBOTMAN © NEA. Reprinted by permission.

INFORMATION GAP FOR STUDENT B

Student B, read the article below. Get information from Student A. Ask questions and fill in the missing information. Answer Student A's questions.

EXAMPLE:

A: What happened to Marsha Jacobs at four o'clock in the morning?

B: She was awakened at four o'clock in the morning.
Where did she think she was?

A: She thought she was in the Twilight Zone.

DALLAS MORNING NEWS   Section 3

Robots Answer Mystery Summons

BY MARILYN SCHWARTZ
STAFF WRITER

DALLAS—Marsha Jacobs was awakened at four o'clock in the morning. She thought she was in _____.

"It was like a bad movie or a nightmare," Mrs. Jacobs explained. "There was this funny, shuffling noise. I looked up and couldn't believe _____.

"The inflatable robot we got for Christmas was heading straight for our bed. The scary part was that the remote control _____ was in the den. That robot was walking by itself."

The incident didn't end at the Jacobs' north Dallas home. All over the city, inflatable butler robots seemed to be coming to life.

"I _____ at midnight last week," explained Jesse Summers. "It was my sister's security patrol company. My sister was out of town, and they had my number to call in case of an emergency."

The sister's burglar alarm _____. Summers met the security men and entered the house to check the problem.

"I didn't know whether to laugh or scream," said Summers. "There was no intruder, just my sister's inflatable robot walking around. I mean it was eerie."

One of the security men gave him a disgusted look. He told Summers that was the second time in a month _____.

Jim Smith of Plano, Texas, says his robot just walked into his dining room during Christmas dinner.

"I thought my son _____ with the remote control," Smith said. "He thought I was doing the same thing. _____ when we discovered the remote control was turned off in the den."

So who are you going to call when a robot comes to life?

Source: Marilyn Schwartz, "Robots Answer Mystery Summons," *The Dallas Morning News.* Reprinted with permission of *The Dallas Morning News.*

Review or SelfTest

I. *Sherry, Akiko, and Lisa are spending the school year in an international exchange program in Spain. Complete their conversation with their friends, using* **would** *or* **will** *and correct forms of* **be going to** *(was / were going to or is / are going to). Use* **will** *or* **would** *if* **be going to** *is not specified.*

SHERRY: I wonder where Jaime and Demetrios are. Demetrios said

_____*they'd be*_____ here by 12:30. It's already 12:45.
      1. (they / be)

AKIKO: Well, when I talked to Jaime this morning he told me he

_____ stop at the post office to mail a package. That's
    2. (be going to)

the only thing I can think of.

LISA: These men! They can never be anywhere on time. We

_____ miss the train if they don't come soon.
    3. (be going to)

SHERRY: What about lunch? Did Jaime say _____ bring
                        4. (he / be going to)

sandwiches?

AKIKO: No, he says _____ at a restaurant near the castle.
             5. (we / eat)

. . . Oh, here they come. . . . At last! Where have you guys been?

_____ a new leaf and not be late anymore?
6. (you / be going to / turn over)

That's what you said.

JAIME: Well, we promised that _____ not to always be late!
                        7. (we / try)

We're working on it. Oh, by the way, Igor is coming after all. He says

_____ a later train and meet us at three o'clock. OK,
   8. (he / take)

ladies, time's a-wasting. Let's get on the train!

II. *Complete the conversations with* **used to** *or* **would***. Use* **would** *if possible.*

1. A: _____*Didn't you use to smoke*_____ ?
          a. (not / you / smoke)

  B: Yeah, I _____ , but I quit six months ago.
             b.

47

A: Good. I _____ smoke, too. It was terrible. When I was a
　　　　　　　　　　c.

serious smoker, I _____ smoke two packs a day. I'm glad
　　　　　　　　　　　　d.

I stopped.

2. A: When I was a child, my family spent every summer at a lake in the mountains.

We kids _____ a hike every morning. In the afternoon, we
　　　　　　e. (take)

_____ swimming.
　　f. (go)

B: Yeah, our summers were like that, too. My parents _____ a
　　　　　　　　　　　　　　　　　　　　g. (own)

cottage on the beach. They sold it after we grew up, but when I was ten and eleven,

we _____ every July there. Ah, those were the good old days!
　　　h. (spend)

Life _____ carefree. Now it's just hectic.
　　　i. (be)

III. *The Mendozas are visiting Italy as part of a tour. Today is the morning of July 20.*
Look at their itinerary. Then complete the sentences, using the correct verb tense
forms and pronouns.

Fred and Alice Mendoza	**Itinerary**	**Italy Trip, July 15–23**

July 15: Arrive at Rome airport; check in at hotel in Rome

July 16: Tour Vatican City, including the Sistine Chapel

July 17: Day trip to Pompeii; return to Rome to spend
　　　　 the night

July 18: Visit other attractions in Rome: the Colosseum, the
　　　　 Forum, the Trevi Fountain; stay in Rome that night

July 19: Take train to Venice; arrive in Venice late afternoon

July 20: Take walking tour of Venice in the morning;
　　　　 take gondola ride in the afternoon; tour
　　　　 St. Mark's Cathedral; take evening train to
　　　　 Florence; arrive early morning

July 21: Tour Florence

July 22: Another day touring
　　　　 Florence; late afternoon:
　　　　 take train to Pisa; spend
　　　　 the night there

July 23: Tour Pisa. Return to Rome
　　　　 late afternoon; take 9:00
　　　　 P.M. evening flight to
　　　　 return home

1. The Mendozas _____have been_____ in Italy since the night of July 15.
　　　　　　　　　　(be)

2. They _____ the first four nights in Rome.
　　　　　　(stay)

3. On their first full day in Rome, _____ Vatican City.
　　　　　　　　　　　　　　　　　　　(tour)

4. Since arriving in Italy, _____ Pompeii, the Colosseum, the Trevi Fountain,
　　　　　　　　　　　(also see)
the Forum, and some of Venice.

5. Right now it's 11:00 A.M. _____ around Venice since 9:00 this morning.
　　　　　　　　　　　　　(walk)

6. _____ a gondola ride yet.
　　(take)

7. Tonight _____ the train to Florence.
　　　　　　(take)

8. _____ in Florence early tomorrow morning.
　　(arrive)

9. _____ two days in Florence and one night in Pisa.
　　(spend)

10. By late afternoon on July 23, _____ to Rome.
　　　　　　　　　　　　　　　(return)

11. _____ home at 9:00 P.M. on the twenty-third.
　　(fly)

IV. *Look at the pictures. Complete each pair of sentences with a simple verb form in one sentence and a progressive verb form in the other. Use the verbs* **develop**, **taste**, **be**, **have**, *and* **write**.

1. Mr. Schoenberg's students _____ usually
　　　　　　　　　　　　　　　　　　a.
well behaved. Today, for some reason, they
_____ difficult.
　　b.

2. Amy Tanaka is a novelist. She _____ five
　　　　　　　　　　　　　　　　　　　a.
novels. She _____ a sixth novel since last
　　　　　　　　　　b.
October and expects to complete it in July.

3. The employees of Excelsior Computer

_____ their annual holiday party
a.

this evening. They always _____ it
b.

sometime in December.

4. Excelsior Computer _____ an
a.

amazing new software program since last

summer and expects to release it in four months.

In the past ten years the company

_____ fifteen major software
b.

programs.

5. Helen Hammond _____ the stew
a.

she's been making. It _____ terrible.
b.

V. *Circle the letter of the one word or phrase that is <u>not</u> correct.*

1. Just before the telephone <u>rang</u>, I <u>was hoping</u> someone <u>called</u> to   A B Ⓒ D

A   B   C

<u>suggest</u> going somewhere.

D

2. Igor <u>doesn't go</u> with us to Toledo today; <u>he's</u> <u>staying</u> home because he   A B C D

A   B   C

<u>has to</u> finish a term paper.

D

3. By the time <u>you'll</u> <u>get</u> to Manila, <u>I'll</u> <u>have returned</u> to Barcelona.   A B C D

A   B   C   D

4. After I <u>got up</u> this morning, I <u>went</u> out, <u>was doing</u> the shopping, and   **A B C D**
           A   B   C

     <u>cleaned</u> up the apartment.
        D

5. I <u>hope</u> dinner <u>is going to</u> <u>be</u> ready soon. <u>It's smelling</u> delicious!   **A B C D**
      A   B   C   D

6. <u>I didn't even think</u> there <u>would be</u> a party. Akiko and Jaime   **A B C D**
          A   B

     <u>have done</u> a great job of <u>organizing</u> last night's get-together.
       C   D

7. The plane <u>has</u> just <u>taken off</u> when I <u>realized</u> that I <u>had given</u> my   **A B C D**
            A   B   C   D

     parents the wrong arrival date.

8. Demetrios <u>was</u> surprised when he <u>received</u> an "A" on the exam   **A B C D**
           A   B

     because he <u>thought</u> he <u>will fail</u> it.
            C   D

9. When the professor <u>asked</u> me where my homework <u>was</u>, I <u>told</u> him   **A B C D**
                 A   B   C

     <u>I already turned</u> it in.
         D

10. We <u>haven't</u> <u>been visiting</u> Venice for more than a year, so I <u>think</u>   **A B C D**
        A   B   C

     <u>we'll be going</u> there.
       D

VI. *Go back to your answers to Part V. Write the correct form for each item that you believe is incorrect.*

1.   would call   **6.** _____

2. _____   **7.** _____

3. _____   **8.** _____

4. _____   **9.** _____

5. _____   **10.** _____

▶ ***To check your answers, go to the Answer Key on page 56.***

FROM GRAMMAR TO WRITING THE SENTENCE

In English a sentence must have at least one **independent**, or **main**, clause. A main clause must have a subject and its verb—a verb that shows person, number, and time. Only one type of main clause has no subject: an imperative sentence. In imperative sentences, the subject *you* is understood. (Note that *Let's dance* is a kind of imperative sentence. *You* is understood to be included in the meaning of *Let's*.)

A main clause does not depend on another clause to be fully understood.

Other clauses are said to be **dependent**. Dependent clauses have a subject and a verb, but they are dependent on another clause to be fully understood.

Look at the following sentences. The complete subjects are underlined once and the complete verbs twice.

EXAMPLES:

Sherry and her friends are students.

They are spending a year studying in Spain in an exchange program.

All the students in the program arrived a month ago.

Most of them will stay for the entire year.

Sherry's sister Martha has received three letters from her.

The letters were written over a period of three months.

Write soon.

Are exchange programs good learning experiences?

The following word groups are not sentences.

Sherry sitting and writing a letter. (no verb)

Were taking the train to Barcelona. (no subject)

Such an exciting year. (no subject or verb)

Because she was afraid of heights. (dependent clause)

Which was a beautiful building. (dependent clause)

1 *On the line below each of the following word groups, write* **sentence** *if the group is an independent clause. If the word group is not a sentence, write* **not a sentence** *and explain why by writing* **no subject**, **no verb**, **no subject and no verb**, *or* **dependent clause**.

1. Sherry at the library doing research.

　　 not a sentence—no verb

2. All afternoon.

3. Akiko and Lisa were at home.

4. Has been an exciting year.

5. A worthwhile experience meeting students from many nations.

6. They would do it again.

7. Which they had always wanted to do.

8. Think about this question.

2 *Read the following paragraph. You will find eight sentences and nine groups of words that are not sentences. On the lines provided, write the eight sentences.*

In late December. Sherry, Akiko, and Lisa took a one-day trip to Barcelona. Not knowing anyone there. They stayed in a youth hostel for a very reasonable price. On their one day in the city. They visited the Sagrada Familia, Gaudí's famous cathedral. Which was unfinished when Gaudí died and is still unfinished. All three girls were impressed by the cathedral's beauty. And decided to climb to the top instead of taking the elevator. Nearing the top, Akiko began to feel vertigo and had to start down again. Sherry and Lisa continued climbing. Even Sherry, who had done a great deal of mountain climbing in Canada. Felt nervous and unprotected at the summit. Both she and Lisa agreed that the view was magnificent. And the climb worth it. The three decided to return to Barcelona. As soon as they could.

(continued on next page)

1. Sherry, Akiko, and Lisa took a one-day trip to Barcelona.

2. _____

3. _____

4. _____

5. _____

6. _____

7. _____

8. _____

The first word of a sentence begins with a capital letter. A sentence ends with some punctuation, most commonly a period, a question mark, or an exclamation point. Sometimes a sentence ends with a semicolon or colon. When one sentence ends with a semicolon or colon, the first word of the next sentence does not need to be capitalized. In sentences containing quotations, quotation marks come <u>after</u> commas and periods.

EXAMPLES:

Who knows the answer?

French food is very delicious**;** it is known all over the world.

That's Don's problem**:** he never wants to do anything adventurous.

"When you're traveling in England,**"** our travel agent said, **"**I recommend staying in bed and breakfasts.**"**

3 *Read and study the following paragraph. It contains seventeen sentences. Find the seventeen sentences and insert initial capitalization and end punctuation in the appropriate places. Do not add or eliminate any commas.*

Last summer when my wife and I were traveling in Morocco, we had one of the most interesting bargaining experiences ever. we were in an open air market in Rabat, and I really wanted to buy a Moroccan jilaba, a long, heavy, ankle-length garment there were several different shops where jilabas were sold, but Helen and I were drawn to one shop in particular, why I don't know I tried one jilaba on it fit perfectly, and I knew it was the one I wanted, so I asked the merchant how much it was he said it was $200 now I've always been intimidated by the prospect of bargaining, so I was ready to pay his price Helen took me aside, however, and said, "That's too much he expects you to bargain" when I said I couldn't bargain, she told me that bargaining was part of the game and that I should offer him $100 I sighed, tried to swallow the lump in my throat, and croaked "$100" he smiled and said "$150," whereupon I said "$110" he looked offended and shook his head Helen grabbed my hand, and we started walking away I thought that was going to be the end of the experience, but then the merchant came running after me, saying "$125, Sir" I ended up buying the jilaba for that amount, and I still have it since then I've never been afraid to bargain

4 **APPLY IT TO YOUR WRITING**

One of the best ways to avoid sentence fragments is to read what you have written aloud, for your voice will usually tell you where one sentence ends and another begins. Write a paragraph or two about an experience you have had while traveling. Read your paragraph aloud to discover whether you have any sentence fragments. Then work with a partner. Your partner will read your paragraph aloud, and you will read your partner's. Try to discover and correct any sentence fragments.

REVIEW OR SELFTEST
ANSWER KEY

NOTE: In this answer key, where the contracted verb form is given, it is the preferred form, though the full form is also acceptable. Where the full verb form is given, it is the preferred form, though the contracted form is also acceptable.

I.
2. was going to
3. 're going to
4. he was going to
5. we'll eat
6. Weren't you going to turn over
7. we'd try
8. he'll take

II.
b. used to
c. used to
d. 'd
e. would take
f. 'd go
g. used to own
h. 'd spend
i. used to be

III.
2. stayed
3. they toured
4. they've also seen
5. They've been walking
6. They haven't taken
7. they're taking
8. They'll be arriving / They'll arrive
9. They're spending / They're going to spend / They'll be spending
10. they'll have returned
11. They fly / They're flying

IV.
1. a. are
   b. 're being
2. a. has written
   b. has been writing
3. a. are having
   b. have
4. a. has been developing
   b. has developed
5. a. is tasting
   b. tastes

V.
2. A
3. A
4. C
5. D
6. C
7. A
8. D
9. D
10. B

VI.
2. isn't going (to go)
3. you
4. did
5. It smells
6. did
7. had
8. would fail / was going to fail / had failed
9. I'd (I had) already turned
10. visited

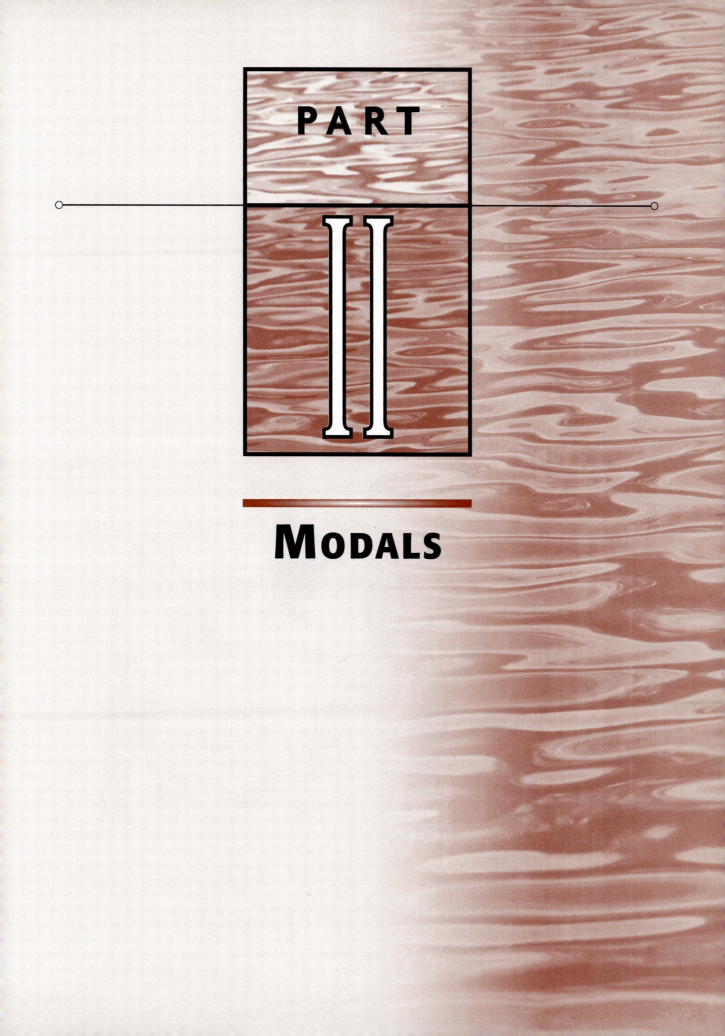

PART

II

MODALS

MODALS: NECESSITY

GRAMMAR **IN CONTEXT**

QUESTIONS TO CONSIDER

1. Look at the cartoon. What is the mother telling her son to do? Is this a practice in your culture?

2. What are some things that should and shouldn't be done in your culture?

What We **Should** and **Shouldn't** Have Done

BY TRAVEL EDITOR TIM LARSON

SIX MONTHS AGO my company sent me to work at our branch office in Japan. My Japanese co-workers have been friendly and gracious, and last week one of them invited my wife and me to his house for dinner. We were honored to be invited, and the food was delicious. But even though Masayuki and Yukiko, his wife, were most polite and friendly and never gave an indication that anything was wrong, we felt a bit uncomfortable about the evening. I decided to ask my friend Junichi about it. He's lived both in Japan and Canada, so he knows the differences between the two cultures. He gave me a lot of pointers. Now we know what we should and shouldn't have done.

The first tip was about taking off our shoes. We knew that you're supposed to take off your shoes when you enter a Japanese home, so we did. We didn't know we were supposed to arrange them so they'd be pointing toward the door when we left so that we'd be able to put them on without having to turn around. But this wasn't a big mistake, Junichi said.

The second pointer was about gifts. Helen and I knew you're supposed to take a gift to a Japanese home. Masayuki and Yukiko seemed a little shocked, though, when we pulled the present out of a plastic bag and said, "We thought you'd like this Canadian CD. It's rock and roll." Junichi chuckled and said, "Well, you should have wrapped the CD. It's OK to bring it in a plastic bag, but the gift itself has to be wrapped. And you mustn't say anything about it. Just give it to your hosts. The main problem, though, was the gift itself."

"You mean we should have taken something different?"

"Yes. A rock and roll CD isn't really an appropriate gift."

"Well, what should we have taken?"

"Maybe a box of chocolates. Or you could have taken some flowers."

After that I told Junichi about what happened before dinner. Masayuki and Yukiko had invited us to sit down for some tea and snacks. The tea was delicious, but we had trouble eating the raw sushi. I was able to finish mine, but Helen couldn't finish hers. Masayuki and Yukiko seemed a little puzzled. Junichi chuckled again and said, "Well, in Japan, it's considered impolite to leave half-eaten food on a plate."

> *"Well, in Japan, it's considered impolite to leave half-eaten food on a plate."*

"You mean you've got to eat everything that's offered to you?" I asked.

"You don't have to. But if you take something, you must finish it."

After we ate, Helen asked Yukiko if she could help her in the kitchen. This is the way we do things back in Canada, but Junichi says you shouldn't in Japan. According to the rules of

(continued on next page)

59

Japanese culture, visitors aren't allowed to go into the kitchen. The other thing you probably shouldn't do, he says, is praise pictures or ornaments in the house. If you do, your Japanese hosts might feel they have to give the object to you. Fortunately, we didn't do that.

At the end of the evening, Masayuki asked us if we'd like to have another drink. We thought it wouldn't be polite to say no, so we accepted and stayed for another half hour. Finally we felt that we absolutely had to leave, so when Masayuki invited us to have another drink, I said, "We'd really like to, but it's late. We'd better get going, or we won't be able to get up in the morning." Masayuki and Yukiko seemed relieved.

Junichi said, "That's what you should have done in the first place. When a Japanese host invites you to have a drink at the end of the evening, you should refuse gently. Otherwise you could be there all night."

I asked what he thought we might do to rectify the situation. "Shall we invite them over?" I asked. He said, "Yeah, you ought to do that. Just remember all the things I've told you. But don't invite them to an informal, western-style party with a lot of loud music. Just make it a simple dinner for the four of you."

Good advice, I thought. What really struck me is how much we all have to learn about other cultures.

Source: Based on information in Rex Shelley, *Culture Shock: Japan* (Portland, OR: Graphic Arts Publishing, 1993).

UNDERSTANDING MEANING FROM CONTEXT

Make a guess about the meaning of each italicized word or phrase from the reading. Write your guess in the blank provided.

1. He gave me a lot of *pointers*.

_____

2. The other thing you probably shouldn't do is *praise* pictures or ornaments in the house.

_____

3. I asked what he thought we might do to *rectify* the situation.

_____

4. What really *struck* me is how much we all have to learn about other cultures.

_____

GRAMMAR **PRESENTATION**
MODALS: NECESSITY

DEGREE OF NECESSITY

ABSOLUTELY NECESSARY; OBLIGATORY

If you take something, you absolutely **must finish** it.

The gift itself **has to be** wrapped.

If you express admiration for objects in the house, your hosts might feel they **have to give** the object to you.

You mean you**'ve got to eat** everything that's offered to you?

You **don't have to take** everything that's offered to you.

And you **mustn't say** anything about it.

Finally we felt that we absolutely **had to leave**.

EXPECTED

We knew that you**'re supposed to take off** your shoes when you enter a Japanese home, so we did.

We didn't know we **were supposed to arrange** them so they'd be pointing toward the door when we left.

STRONGLY ADVISED

We**'d better get going**, or we won't be able to wake up in the morning.

ADVISED

You probably **shouldn't praise** pictures or ornaments in the house.

Yeah, you **ought to do** that.

You **should have wrapped** the CD.

Shall we **invite** them over?

SUGGESTED

Then Helen asked Yukiko if she **could help** her in the kitchen.

I asked what he thought we **might do** to rectify the situation.

Or you **could have taken** some flowers.

NOTES	EXAMPLES
1. *Can, could, shall, should, may, might, will, would, must, ought to,* and *had better* are **modals**. They are special auxiliary verbs that behave differently from other verbs.	• Helen asked Yukiko if she **could help** her in the kitchen. • You **mustn't say** anything about it. • **Shall** we **invite** them over?
2. In general, modals are restricted in their use. There are **modal-like expressions** with similar meanings to replace them. Note these: *must* *have to* *should* *be supposed to* *can / could* *be able to* *may* *be allowed to*	 • You **must finish** everything on your plate. / You **have to finish** everything on your plate. • You **should take** a gift. / You**'re supposed to take** a gift. • Helen **couldn't finish** her sushi. / Helen **wasn't able to finish** her sushi. • You **may not enter** the kitchen. / You**'re not allowed to enter** the kitchen.
3. The modals and modal-like expressions *must, have to, have got to, had better, be supposed to, should, ought to, might,* and *could* show degrees of **necessity**, with *must* as the strongest and *could* as the weakest.	• You **must finish** everything on your plate. (very strong—a rule) • You **should take** a gift. (less strong—a good idea) • You **could take** some flowers. (even less strong—It would be a nice action, but there are other possibilities.)

4. *Must, have to,* and *have got to* are similar in meaning. *Must* is more formal. Use it to show very strong **obligations** that can't be escaped.

Have to is used in all tenses and situations.

Have got to is informal and is used mostly in conversation. It is rarely used in the negative. *Have to* is used instead.

Note the two negatives of *must.* They are very different in meaning. *Mustn't* means "necessity not to do something." *Don't / doesn't have to* means "no necessity to do something."

Use *will have to* to show **future necessity**.

Use *had to* to show **past necessity**.

▶ **BE CAREFUL!** Don't use *must have* + participle to show past necessity. Use *had to* instead.

- If you take something on your plate, you **must** finish it.

- Your hosts might feel that they **have to give** you the object.

- You mean you**'ve got to eat** everything that's offered to you?
- No, you **don't have to**.

- When you present a gift, you **mustn't say** anything about it. (*It's necessary not to do this.*)
- You **don't have to eat** everything that's offered to you. (*It's not necessary to do this.*)

- We**'ll have to invite** them over to our house.

- We felt we **had to leave**. (*We felt it was necessary.*)

- We **had to leave**.
  NOT ~~We must have left.~~

5. *Should* and *ought to* are similar in meaning and are equivalent in most situations. They mean "it would be a good idea if . . ." Use them to offer advice. *Should* is more theoretical. *Ought to* is used more to offer a specific suggestion that may be followed. *Ought to* is rare in questions and negatives, where it is usually replaced by *should*.

- You **should refuse** gently. (*a good idea in theory*)
- You **ought to invite** them over. (*an actual suggestion that I am making for you to follow*)

6. Note the difference in meaning between *should* and *must*. Use *must* (or *have to* or *have got to*) to express an obligation that can't be escaped. Use *should* (or *ought to*) to give advice. Remember that advice is a good idea but does not have to be followed.

- You **must take off** your shoes when you enter a Japanese house. *(a rule of Japanese culture)*
- You **should take** candy or flowers as a gift. *(a good idea, but these are not the only two things that can be taken)*

7. *Had better* is stronger than *should* and *ought to*. Use it to show a warning that something bad or negative will happen if the advice isn't followed.

▶ **BE CAREFUL!** Since *had better* is a strong expression, it can seem rude or impolite if not used correctly. It is usually used by people who have authority over other people or with people we know very well.

- We**'d better get going**, or we won't be able to wake up in the morning.

- Jim, if you're going to the Carlsens' house for dinner, you**'d better take** a gift of some sort.

  OK, Mom. Good suggestion.

8. Use *be supposed to* to show a **strong expectation**. *Be supposed to* is used only in the present and past. In the past, the affirmative suggests that the expectation didn't happen. The negative suggests that the expectation did happen.

- We knew that you**'re supposed to take off** your shoes when you enter a Japanese home, so we did.
- We didn't know we **were supposed to arrange** them so they'd be pointing toward the door when we left. *(We didn't do this.)*
- We **weren't supposed to mention** the gift we'd brought. *(We did mention it.)*

Notice the difference in meaning between *be supposed to* and *have to / had to*.

Be supposed to shows an expectation, but *have to / had to* shows an obligation.

- We **were supposed to take** flowers. *(That was the expectation, but we didn't do it.)*

- We **had to leave** when he offered us a second drink. *(That was the obligation. We did.)*

9. Use *should have* and *ought to have* + past participle to express **advice** about past situations. *Should have* and *ought to have* suggest that the action did not happen. *Shouldn't have* suggests that it did.

- That's what you **should have done** the first time. *(That's what you **ought to have done** the first time.)*

10. Use *might* or *could* to talk about polite, not-too-strong **suggestions**.

- I asked what we **might do** to rectify the situation. *(I asked what we **could do** to rectify the situation.)*

11. Use *might have* and *could have* + past participle to make polite **suggestions** about a **past opportunity**. They are similar in meaning. In this sense, *might have* and *could have* in an affirmative sentence mean that the action didn't happen.

- You **could have taken** some flowers. *(This is my suggestion. It was an opportunity, but it didn't happen.)*

12. *Shall* is sometimes used in questions to ask about another person's **opinion** about a course of action. It is used only with *I* or *we*. When *shall* is used with *we*, it is often followed by a sentence with *let's*. In this meaning, *shall* is somewhat similar to *should*.

This is the only common use of *shall* in North American English.

- **Shall** we **invite** them over? *(What's your opinion about this idea?)*

13. Use *could* to show **past ability**. Don't use it in the affirmative to talk about a single (finished) action in the past. Use *was / were able to* instead.

In the negative, *was / were able to* and *could* are interchangeable.

- I **was able to finish** my sushi. Not ~~I could finish my sushi.~~

- Helen **couldn't finish** her sushi.
  OR
- Helen **wasn't able to finish** her sushi.

FOCUSED PRACTICE

1 DISCOVER THE GRAMMAR

Look again at some of the sentences from What We Should and Shouldn't Have Done. *Each sentence can be said in a similar way. Circle the letter of the choice that is similar in meaning.*

1. We knew that you're supposed to take off your shoes when you enter a Japanese home, so we did.
   a. You should take off your shoes when you enter a Japanese home.
   b. You could take off your shoes when you enter a Japanese home.

2. "Well, you should have wrapped the CD."
   a. You might have wrapped the CD.
   b. You were supposed to wrap the CD.

3. "Or you could have taken some flowers."
   a. You might have taken some flowers.
   b. You should have taken some flowers.

4. "You mean you've got to eat everything that's offered to you?" I asked.
   a. You mean you're supposed to eat everything that's offered to you?
   b. You mean you have to eat everything that's offered to you?

5. After we ate, Helen asked Yukiko if she could help her in the kitchen.
   a. Helen asked Yukiko if she might help her in the kitchen.
   b. Helen asked Yukiko if she should help her in the kitchen.

6. According to the rules of Japanese culture, visitors aren't allowed to go into the kitchen.
   a. Visitors may not go into the kitchen.
   b. Visitors would not go into the kitchen.

7. And you mustn't say anything about it.
   a. You don't have to say anything about it.
   b. You had better not say anything about it.

8. If you do, your Japanese hosts might feel they have to give the object to you.
   a. Japanese hosts might feel they must give the object to you.
   b. Japanese hosts might feel they should give the object to you.

9. When a Japanese host invites you to have a drink at the end of the evening, you should refuse gently.
   a. You must refuse gently.
   b. You ought to refuse gently.

10. "Shall we invite them over?" I asked.

    a. Should we invite them over?

    b. Will we invite them over?

11. He said, "Yeah, you ought to do that."

    a. You're supposed to do that.

    b. You should do that.

2   **SHOULD WE LEAVE A TIP?**   Grammar Notes 1, 2, 3

Masako, a visiting exchange student, is talking to her American friend Jane.
Complete their conversation with items from the box. Use each item once.

could have left	should we have left	don't have to leave	had to worry
should you leave	you're supposed to do	were supposed to leave	expected to do
I ought to leave	~~are you supposed to leave~~		

JANE: Hi, Masako. How are things going?

MASAKO: Really well. But there's something I wanted to ask you about.

JANE: OK. What?

MASAKO: Tipping. I just don't understand it. <u>Are you supposed to leave</u> a tip everywhere
                                              1.

    you eat? This is really bothering me. I've never _____
                                                    2.

    about this before. We don't tip in Japan.

JANE: You don't?

MASAKO: No. You're not really _____ that. It's all included in the
                                            3.

    service charge.

JANE: Tell me more. Have you had a problem with this?

MASAKO: Yeah. Last week a Chinese friend of mine and I had dinner at a restaurant. We

    knew we _____ a tip, but we didn't know how much.
                            4.

JANE: How much did you leave?

MASAKO: About twenty-five percent. _____ more?
                                      5.

JANE: Wow! Twenty-five percent. That's a lot. The service must have been really good.

MASAKO: Actually, it wasn't. The waiter was pretty rude . . . and slow.

(continued on next page)

JANE: Well, if you're really not satisfied with the service, you

_____ anything.

   6.

MASAKO: So how much _____ if you're satisfied?

   7.

JANE: Between fifteen and twenty percent. Fifteen is the usual.

MASAKO: Hmm. OK. Now here's another question. I'm confused about what

_____ if you're sitting at a lunch counter instead of at a

   8.

table. Do you leave anything?

JANE: It's a nice gesture. Why do you ask?

MASAKO: Yesterday I had lunch at a cafeteria counter. There was a waitress who was really

nice and polite. I felt like _____ her something.

   9.

JANE: Did you?

MASAKO: No.

JANE: Well, you _____ something. Maybe five to ten percent.

   10.

MASAKO: Oh. OK. Next time I will.

---

③ SHOULDS AND SHOULDN'TS   Grammar Notes 2, 3, 5, 6

Look again at What We Should and Shouldn't Have Done. *Write seven sentences about what Bob and Helen* should have done *and* shouldn't have done.

> **EXAMPLE:**
> They should have wrapped the CD.

1. _____

2. _____

3. _____

4. _____

5. _____

6. _____

7. _____

4 **DEAR MISS MANNERS** Grammar Notes 4, 5, 11, 12

Part A

Read Miss Manners' advice column. As you read, take note of the italicized expressions.

MISS MANNERS RESCUES CIVILIZATION

❧Christmas Presents❧

DEAR MISS MANNERS,

This year, my company sent me a gift box containing, among other things, ham, bacon, and sausage. Last year, I received a whole smoked turkey. I have been a vegetarian for over four years and am offended even by the sight of such frivolous expense of life. But I don't want to offend my company superiors, and I know that all employees receive the same gift, so it might not be fair to make exceptions for just me. But how can I prevent this from happening next year, and what *do I do* with the corpses in the freezer? *Should I send* a thank you note?

GENTLE READER,

Unless you work for a grocery wholesaler, it seems foolish of your employer to spend money on presents which *could have been put* into a Christmas bonus. This being a business relationship, not a friendship, the company can hardly be expected to know what would please each individual, as demonstrated by the fact that even a conventional food item was offensively unsuitable in your case.

It seems equally futile to try to explain your individual preferences in the minimal thank you note appropriate for an impersonal gesture. If you *must, Miss Manners suggests you thank them* for the food "which, as a vegetarian, I do not eat, but which I have donated to the homeless." Just don't count on this being remembered next year, when someone else may be assigned to send out silly presents.

Source: From **MISS MANNERS RESCUES CIVILIZATION: FROM SEXUAL HARASSMENT**, FRIVOLOUS LAWSUITS, DISSING AND OTHER LAPSES IN CIVILITY by Judith Martin. Copyright © 1996 by Judith Martin. Reprinted by permission of Crown Publishers, Inc.

Now rewrite each of the italicized phrases with a modal or modal-like expression having a similar meaning. Go over the answers as a class. Then discuss possible answers to questions 1 and 2.

1. What *do I do* with the corpses in the freezer?

   What should I do with the corpses in the freezer?

2. *Should I send* a thank you note?

   _____

3. It seems foolish of your employer to spend money on presents that *could have been put* into a Christmas bonus.

   _____

4. If you *must* . . .

   _____

5. *Miss Manners suggests that you thank them* for the food . . . [Hint: Eliminate "Miss Manners." Use "you" as the subject.]

   _____

Part B

Discuss the letter with a partner. Do you agree or disagree with Miss Manners'
suggestions?

5 EDITING

Read the letter that Jason, who is traveling in East Africa, sent to his sister. Find
and correct the eleven errors in modals or modal-like expressions.

May 15

Dear Emily,

    I know I should ~~write~~ *have written* sooner, but I just won't be able to find the time. This package deal that
Steve and I got was so cheap, and we've been so many places! We've been having some
amazing adventures. We climbed Mount Kilimanjaro! Yes, really! It took five days. We went to a
hotel in Arusha, Tanzania, and hired a group of Tanzanian men to take us up to the top and
down again. That's the only way anyone is allowed climb the mountain these days. You can't
just go up on your own. It takes three days to climb up and two to come back down.

    We stayed in a little cabin each night. On the third night, we were at 15,000 feet, and it
was really cold. We went to bed at sunset so that we can get up at 2 A.M. to attempt the
summit. I was so cold I must put on all my clothes in my sleeping bag. I was glad to get up so I
could have gotten warm.

    It took three hours to climb to the top, and both Steve and I had our own guide. I could make
it to the top, but Steve wasn't able to because he had altitude sickness. Too bad. But what an
experience it was to be at the top! I felt like I was the king of the world. Anyway, we couldn't
meet any nicer guys than the ones who carried our stuff. I heard that you're suppose to tip
them if you feel they've given you good service, so of course we were glad to do that.

    After Kilimanjaro we took a bus to Ngorongoro Crater. We rode a Land Rover down into the
crater to see the animals. We were able see lions, rhinos, giraffes, and hundreds of zebras.
Fantastic. You and Jennifer ought to have come next summer if you can save up the money.
Maybe you can get a special deal like we did.

    Well, enough for now. We're flying to Nairobi tonight,
and then it's on to Cairo and then Turkey. I'll write again
when I have time. Love to Mom and Dad.

Love,

Jason

COMMUNICATION PRACTICE

6 LISTENING

Listen to the telephone conversation.

Now listen again. Then circle the item that correctly completes each statement.

1. Jason (sent / didn't send) his parents a postcard.

2. Jason and Steve (went / didn't go) to Cairo.

3. Jason and Steve (were able to / were not able to) get another flight to Cairo a few days later.

4. It (was necessary / wasn't necessary) to leave early to get to the airport.

5. Emily thinks Jason (should / shouldn't) go to the embassy.

6. Jason (wrote down / didn't write down) his passport number.

7. You (must have / don't have to have) identification to get a new passport.

8. The embassy (has been able to / hasn't been able to) prove Jason's identity.

9. Jason (wants / doesn't want) Emily to fax him a copy of his passport application.

7 INFORMATION GAP: WHY WON'T THEY WAIT ON US?

Working with a partner, complete the story. Each of you will read a version of the same story. Each version is missing some information. Take turns asking your partner questions to get the missing information.

Student A, read the story below. Ask questions and fill in the missing information. Then answer Student B's questions.

Student B, turn to page 75 and follow the instructions there.

EXAMPLE:

A: Where were the married couple traveling?

B: They were traveling in eastern Europe.
What was the first problem?

A: The first problem was finding accommodations.

A married couple were traveling in _____. Up until they had entered this particular country, they had been having a wonderful time. Now, however, everything seemed to be going wrong. The first problem was finding accommodations. They were supposed to stay at _____, but when they arrived at the hotel, they discovered that there was no record of their reservation, so they had to spend their first night at the train station. The next day, after several hours of looking, they

(continued on next page)

were finally able to get a room at a hotel _____. There were
two rooms available: one very expensive room with one king-sized bed, and another
inexpensive one with only one small twin bed. Since they were on a tight budget, they
decided they'd better take the inexpensive room.

The second problem had to do with communication. In other countries they had been
able to use _____. Here very few people were able to speak
those languages. Since the couple didn't speak the native language of the country, it was
hard to make themselves understood.

The third problem involved food. After spending hours finding accommodations, they
were starving, so they went into an elegant restaurant. They sat down at a table and were
soon brought menus. When they looked at them, however, _____
_____. The husband said he thought they should have at
least brought along a phrase book. They hadn't done that, though, so they didn't know
what to order.

Time passed. Other people were being served, but none of the waiters would
_____. They began to get quite frustrated. They noticed that
a boy about ten years old seemed to be listening to their conversation. Just when they were
at their wits' end, the boy got up and came over to their table. "Excuse me," he said. "I
couldn't help hearing you talk about your problem. No one has come and taken your order
because you have to _____. Then they'll take your order." The
husband and the wife were both astonished but grateful to the boy. The wife asked, "How
is it that your know our language? You speak it very well." The boy said, "Oh, I lived in
your country for three years. I learned it there." Then the boy asked, "Shall I help you
order? I can translate the menu for you." The couple were even more grateful and thanked
the boy heartily.

When they got back to their own country, their friends asked them what they had liked
best about the trip. The wife said, "Well, we both think _____
_____. Everything went wrong at first,
but the whole thing is engraved in our memories. We won't forget it. At some point,
everybody should have the kind of trip where things don't go right. That's when you learn
things. Maybe that's what people mean when they say travel is broadening."

8 SMALL GROUP DISCUSSION: IS IT OK IN YOUR CULTURE?

Divide into groups of four. Decide individually whether each of the following behaviors is required, advised, or allowed in your culture or another culture you are familiar with. Check the appropriate boxes. Then discuss the results with the others in your group.

	must	should	mustn't	shouldn't	don't have to
a. take a gift when invited to someone's house	☐	☐	☐	☐	☐
b. ask how old someone is	☐	☐	☐	☐	☐
c. smoke without asking permission	☐	☐	☐	☐	☐
d. hug friends when you see them	☐	☐	☐	☐	☐
e. shake hands when you meet someone	☐	☐	☐	☐	☐
f. take off your shoes when you enter a house	☐	☐	☐	☐	☐
g. offer to pay your share when someone invites you to a restaurant	☐	☐	☐	☐	☐
h. ask how much someone weighs	☐	☐	☐	☐	☐
i. ask what someone does (as an occupation)	☐	☐	☐	☐	☐
j. leave a tip in a restaurant	☐	☐	☐	☐	☐
k. call people by their first name	☐	☐	☐	☐	☐

❾ ESSAY

Write a short essay (two to three paragraphs) about a situation that you had to deal with or are still facing—a problem like Jason's in the dialogue. Tell what you should *or* could *have done (past) or what you* should, could, *or* ought *to do (future).*

❿ PICTURE DISCUSSION

With a partner, discuss this picture, saying as much as you can. Describe the situation. How must the woman and her children be feeling? Consider the family from another country. What do you think they should or shouldn't have done? How should they be behaving? What could they do to reduce the discomfort of the woman and her children?

INFORMATION GAP FOR STUDENT B

Student B, read the story below. Answer Student A's questions. Then ask your own questions and fill in the missing information.

EXAMPLE:

A: Where were the married couple traveling?

B: They were traveling in eastern Europe.
What was the first problem?

A: The first problem was finding accommodations.

A married couple was traveling in a small country in Europe. Up until they had entered this particular country, they had been having a wonderful time. Now, however, everything seemed to be going wrong. The first problem was _____.
They were supposed to stay at the Grand State Hotel, but when they arrived at the hotel, they discovered that there was no record of their reservation, so they had to spend their first night at _____. The next day, after several hours of looking, they were finally able to get a room at a hotel far from the center of town. There were two rooms available: one very expensive room with one king-sized bed, and another inexpensive one with only one small twin bed. Since they were on a tight budget, they decided they'd better _____.

The second problem had to do with communication. In other countries they had been able to use French, German, and Spanish. Here _____ were able to speak those languages. Since the couple didn't speak the native language of the country, it was hard to make themselves understood.

The third problem involved food. After spending hours finding accommodations, they were starving, so they went into an elegant restaurant. They sat down at a table and were soon brought menus. When they looked at them, however, they could hardly understand a word. The husband said he thought they should have at least brought along
_____. They hadn't done that, though, so they didn't know what to order.

Time passed. Other people were being served, but none of the waiters would come and take their orders. They began to get quite frustrated. They noticed that a boy about ten years old seemed to be listening to their conversation. Just when they were at their wits' end, the boy got up and came over to their table. "Excuse me," he said. "I couldn't help

(continued on next page)

hearing you _____. No one has come and taken your order because you have to go and pay for your meal first. Then they'll take your order." The husband and the wife were both astonished but grateful to the boy. The wife asked, "How is it that your know our language? You speak it very well." The boy said, "Oh, I lived in your country for three years. I learned it there." Then the boy asked, "_____? I can translate the menu for you." The couple were even more grateful and thanked the boy heartily.

When they got back to their own country, their friends asked them what they had liked best about the trip. The wife said, "Well, we both think the most memorable part was visiting that little country. Everything went wrong at first, but the whole thing is engraved in our memories. We won't forget it. At some point, everybody should have _____ _____. That's when you learn things. Maybe that's what people mean when they say travel is broadening."

MODALS: CERTAINTY

GRAMMAR **IN CONTEXT**

QUESTIONS TO CONSIDER

1. Why don't cats like to swim?

2. Why are baby boys usually dressed in blue and girls in pink?

3. Why are there so few women pilots?

 Read the following essay.

THE REALLY IMPORTANT QUESTIONS IN LIFE

A couple of weekends ago I had a dinner party at my house, and the after-dinner conversation time was the perfect opportunity for Sally to tell us all about the new things she'd learned. Sally is one of those people who collect all kinds of information that's certainly interesting but may not be very useful. True to form, Sally announced, "Guess what I found out?"

We all groaned, for we knew what was coming next.

"What, Sally? " I said tolerantly.

"Well, I've been reading this fascinating book called *Imponderables*. You know, puzzling questions that you can't explain precisely but that we all wonder about? I found out some really neat things. Want to hear about them?"

"Everybody'd better get themselves some soda and a snack," I said. "This could take a while."

"OK. Here's the first thing I learned. Now, I'm going to ask you these questions, and we'll see how many you can answer. Ready?"

"Ready!" we all chorused.

"OK. First question. Why don't cats like to swim?"

(continued on next page)

"They must be afraid of water," Scott said. "Or at the very least, they must not like it much."

"That can't be the reason," Nan said. "It's too obvious."

"Nan's right," Sally answered. "Everyone thinks cats are afraid of water. But that's not it."

"It might be because they're lazy. They know they'll have to clean their coats," Mary volunteered.

"Right on, Mary!" Sally said. "That's pretty much it. Cats are fanatics about keeping themselves clean. And they *are* basically lazy. They don't like to swim because they know it'll take too long to get their coats clean and dry."

"OK," I said. "Not bad. What's your next question?"

"Next question: Why in some cultures do people dress baby boys and baby girls in different colors? And why boys in blue and baby girls in pink? You've got to go back in history to answer this one."

"Hmm," Marilyn mused. "I don't know about why pink and blue specifically, but they might have started using different colors just to tell boys and girls apart."

"That's absolutely right. They did," Sally answered. "And so what about blue and pink?"

"Well," said Jim, "They may have thought that certain colors were luckier than others. Is that part of it?"

"Yep. People thought that babies needed to be protected from evil spirits. And they thought blue was the strongest color because it was the color of the sky, and the sky was associated with heaven."

"But," Jim said, "why did boys get the blue?"

"That's easy enough to answer," Nan said. "They must have felt boys had more status, so they got the strongest color. They really couldn't have chosen any other color if blue was the strongest."

"That's it," said Sally. "As for girls, it's not so clear. But people in those times must not have thought that evil spirits would bother girls, because it was several centuries before girls got their own color. When girls did get a color, it was because legend taught that girls were born inside of pink roses."

"Very interesting," said Bob. "What else, Sally?"

"Why are there so few women pilots on commercial airplanes?"

"There may not be enough jobs to go around," I said.

"No, that's not it. There are lots of jobs."

"Easy," said Marilyn. "It's got to have something to do with gender stereotypes. People have traditionally thought that women aren't capable of flying airplanes."

"That's part of it," Sally said. "But there's more to it than that."

"Could it have something to do with military experience?" Jim queried. "Back when they started, there might not have been enough women with the right training."

"Yes," Sally answered. "In the early days of commercial airlines, a lot of pilots were hired because they had military flying experience, especially in combat. Women didn't have combat experience, so very few of them were chosen. If they were chosen, they had to have experience in flight school."

Nan said, "But now that a lot more women are in the military, that should change, right? I mean, women can go into combat now."

"Right," said Sally. "In fact, some experts think that women actually have an advantage over men because they make better pilots. It may take a while, but it'll change."

"You know, Sally," Nan asked, "I think I want to read this book. Where can I get hold of it?"

"You ought to be able to find it at that big bookstore downtown. Or you might even find it in the supermarket. But I'll lend you my copy if you can't."

"Great," Nan said.

Source: Based on information in David Feldman, *Imponderables: The Solution to the Mysteries of Everyday Life* (New York: William Morrow, 1986, 1987).

UNDERSTANDING MEANING FROM CONTEXT

Circle the letter of the choice closest in meaning to each italicized word or phrase from the reading.

1. *True to form,* Sally announced, "Guess what I found out?"

   a. Telling the truth   **b.** Speaking formally   **c.** As she usually does

2. We all groaned, *for* we knew what was coming next.

   a. because   **b.** although   **c.** besides

3. "They don't like to swim because they know it'll take too long to get their *coats* clean and dry."

   a. paws   **b.** fur   **c.** surroundings

4. "Women didn't have *combat* experience, so very few of them were chosen."

   a. military   **b.** supervisory   **c.** fighting

GRAMMAR **PRESENTATION**
MODALS: CERTAINTY

DEGREE OF CERTAINTY: PRESENT AND PAST

SPEAKER IS ALMOST CERTAIN			
It	must has to 's got to	have	something to do with cultural stereotypes.
They	must not	like	it much.
That	can't	be	the reason.
They	must have	felt	boys had more status.
People	must not have	thought	spirits would bother girls.
They	can't have couldn't have	chosen	any other color if blue was the strongest.

SPEAKER IS LESS CERTAIN			
It	may might could	take	a while, but it'll change.
He	could	be	wondering when things will change.
There	may not might not	be	enough jobs to go around.
They	may have	thought been	that certain colors were luckier than others. wondering what colors were luckier.
	might have	started	using different colors just to tell boys and girls apart.
There	may not have might not have	been	enough women with military training.

DEGREE OF CERTAINTY: FUTURE

SPEAKER IS QUITE SURE
But now that a lot more women are in the military, that **should change**, right?
You **ought to be able to** find it at that big bookstore downtown.

SPEAKER IS LESS SURE BUT CONSIDERS SITUATION POSSIBLE			
It	**may** **might** **could**	take	a while, but it'll change.

NOTES

EXAMPLES

1. The modals and modal-like expressions *must, have to, have got to, may, might, can't, couldn't, should,* and *ought to* express degrees of **certainty**. They are used when a speaker is speculating about something based on logic and facts as understood by the speaker.

- This information is interesting but **may not be** very useful. (a degree of certainty)

Remember that models are used in progressive as well as simple forms.

- They may have been wondering which colors were luckier.

When we want to state a fact we are absolutely—100 percent—sure of, we don't use modals.

- This information is interesting but **is not** useful. (certainty—no use of modals)

2. Use *must* when you are speculating and are almost sure.

- Cats **must be** afraid of water.
- They **must have felt** boys had more status.

Have to and *have got to* are also used to show **near certainty**.

- It**'s got to have** something to do with gender stereotypes.

3. Use *can't, can't have, couldn't,* and *couldn't have* when you feel that it is **impossible** to conclude otherwise.

- That **can't** be the reason.
- They **couldn't have used** any other color besides blue.

4. Use *may, might,* or *could* when you are less sure but think that a situation is at least possible.

- There **may not be** enough jobs to go around.
- It **might be** because they're lazy.
- **Could it have** something to do with military experience?
- There **might not have been** enough women with the right training.

5. Use *should, ought to, may, might,* and *could* to express **future probability**. *Should* and *ought to* express a greater degree of certainty. *May, might,* and *could* express a lesser degree.

- But now that a lot more women are in the military, that **should change**, right?
- You **ought to be able to find** it at that big bookstore downtown.
- Or you **might** even **find** it in the supermarket.

6. Note the two different meanings of *could have* + participle.

- They **could have started** using different colors just to tell boys and girls apart.
  (*It's possible they did this. I'm not sure.*)
- You **could have called** me.
  (*You didn't—a missed opportunity.*)

FOCUSED PRACTICE

1 DISCOVER THE GRAMMAR

Look again at some of the sentences from The Really Important Questions in Life. *For each item, circle the letter of the choice that is similar in meaning.*

1. "This could take a while."

   a. This may take a while.

   b. This should take a while.

2. "That can't be the reason."

   a. That couldn't be the reason.

   b. That must not be the reason.

3. "It might be because they're lazy."

   a. It could be because they're lazy.

   b. It must be because they're lazy.

4. ". . . they might have started using different colors just to tell boys and girls apart."

   a. They could have started using different colors . . .

   b. They must have started using different colors . . .

5. "They may have thought that certain colors were luckier than others."

   a. They might have thought that certain colors were luckier than others.

   b. They must have thought that certain colors were luckier than others.

6. "But people in those times must not have thought that evil spirits would bother girls . . ."

   a. It's probable that they thought this.

   b. It's possible that they thought this.

7. "It's got to have something to do with gender stereotypes."

   a. It might have something to do with gender stereotypes.

   b. It must have something to do with gender stereotypes.

8. "You ought to be able to find it at that big bookstore downtown."

   a. You might be able to find it there.

   b. You should be able to find it there.

9. "Or you might even find it in the supermarket."

   a. You may be able to find it there.

   b. You should be able to find it there.

❷ WHERE'S HARRY?

Read the conversation. Complete it with modal constructions from the box.

must have	might be	may have had to	should be
must have been visiting	could be working	~~could have gotten~~	might be meeting

BLAKE: I wonder what's keeping Harry. He's usually on time for office parties. I

suppose he _____could have gotten_____ stuck in traffic.
                        1.

SAMANTHA: Yeah, that's a possibility. Or he _____ work late. I've never
                                                        2.

known him to be late to a party.

BLAKE: You know, I've always felt there's something a little puzzling—or even

mysterious—about Harry.

SAMANTHA: What makes you say that?

BLAKE: Well, he never says much about his past. He's really an interesting guy, but I

don't know much about him. For all I know, he _____ an
                                                            3.

international spy.

SAMANTHA: I think I know what you mean. Or he _____ as a
                                                        4.

government agent.

BLAKE: Something tells me this is a case of *cherchez la femme*.

SAMANTHA: What does that mean?

BLAKE: It means "look for the woman." I figure he _____ a
                                                            5

girlfriend that he doesn't want us to know about.

SAMANTHA: Yeah, maybe so. You know, now that I think of it, he always leaves work early

on Friday afternoons. I see him go to the parking garage about 4:00, and it

always seems like he's trying not to be seen. He _____ his
                                                        6.

secret love somewhere.

[*The doorbell rings.*]

BLAKE: Oh, wait a minute. There's the doorbell. Everyone else is here. That

_____ him.
        7.

HARRY: Hi, folks. Sorry I'm late. Had some business to take care of.

SAMANTHA: Business, huh. You mean romantic business?

HARRY: Romantic business? What are you talking about?

BLAKE: We figure you _____ your lady love. After all, we see you
8.
leave early every Friday afternoon.

HARRY: Pretty funny. Well, there is a lady, and I love her. But it's not what you think.

SAMANTHA: What is it, then?

HARRY: My mother. She's eighty-eight years old and she lives in a retirement center.

I go and see her every Friday.

3 **THE TUNGUSKA EVENT**   Grammar Notes 1, 2, 5

Read about a strange occurrence in Siberia in 1908.

THE TUNGUSKA EVENT

On June 30, 1908, in the Tunguska area of central Siberia, a momentous event took place, the cause of which remains unexplained to this day. The calm of the summer morning was suddenly destroyed by an object which plowed erratically through the sky and crashed into the ground, exploding on impact with a force of 10 to 15 megatons of energy. Eyewitnesses in the nearby town of Vanovara said the explosion of the object, whatever it was, left an illuminated trail in the sky many kilometers in length and a mushroom-shaped cloud over the scene. In the town of Kansk, 800 kilometers away, an engineer stopped his train because he thought some of the train cars had exploded. The shock wave from the explosion was recorded as far away as London. The impact caused immense devastation: Most of the trees within 20 kilometers of the point of impact were knocked down, and in the vicinity of the impact point, windows were broken and roofs torn off houses. The Angara, a major river of the area, flooded. Villages and herds of reindeer, along with 500,000 acres of pine forest, were obliterated.

a momentous event took place, the cause of which remains unexplained to this day

One would assume that scientists, government officials, and other interested parties would have made it a high priority to investigate the explosion. It wasn't until 1927, though, that an official investigation was conducted. One of the most puzzling facts to emerge from the investigation was that no crater was discovered at the impact site. Researchers theorized that there had been a crater and that it was now simply buried beneath a swamp.

Twenty years later, a geologic expedition ascertained that no crater in fact existed, suggesting that the blast hadn't been caused by the impact of a meteor. The expedition recorded further evidence of the great devastation wrought by the blast, including the fact that toppled trees were discovered radiating outward from the center of the explosion. However, there were still trees standing at the center of the blast area, indicating that the

(continued on next page)

explosion had taken place from immediately above. Tests made on botanical specimens from the area showed great and quick tree growth, perhaps caused by radiation. To some investigators, this suggested the same kind of nuclear explosion as took place in Hiroshima during World War II.

Today there are a number of explanations given as to the possible cause of the Tunguska Event. The most widely accepted one is that a 10,000-ton remnant of Encke's Comet entered the earth's atmosphere at a very high speed, burned up during entry, and crashed onto the earth's surface, causing a fireball and a shock wave but not creating a crater. Other explanations include the possibility of the impact of an errant black hole or the crashing of an alien space ship. The jury is still out.

Source: Based on information in www.kent/net/paranormal/places/tungus/index.html.

Now look back at the article. Write sentences with past modals about the Tunguska blast, using the prompts given. Choose the more appropriate modal in each case.

1. People who observed the blast ____must have been____ astonished.
(should / must) be

2. The blast _____ people and animals living near the impact point.
(must / might) kill

3. Because they found no crater, scientists assumed that it _____ a
(should / could) not be

meteor that caused the blast.

4. Today, a widely accepted explanation is that a comet _____ over the
(must / should) explode

earth's surface.

5. Another explanation is that a black hole _____ the earth.
(must / might) hit

6. Still another explanation is that an alien space ship _____ in
(may / ought to) crash and explode

the blast area.

7. Some people wonder if the Tunguska blast _____ a nuclear explosion.
(could / must) be

4 EDITING

Read the following student essay. Find and correct the nine errors in the use of modals.

Why We Itch

           might
One ~~must~~ think that with all the scientific progress that has been made in the last

century, researchers would be able by now to answer this very simple question: Why do

we itch? Unfortunately, scientists can't answer this question with any certainty. They

simply don't know.

There are some clear cases involving itching. If a patient goes to her doctor and complains of terrible itching and the doctor finds hives or some other kind of rash, the doctor might say that she must eaten something that didn't agree with her—or that she might been stung or bitten by some insect. This kind of case can be easily diagnosed. Most itching, however, does not have obvious causes.

Here's what scientists do know. Right under the surface of the skin there are sensory receptors that register physical stimuli and carry messages to the brain. These receptors detect pain and let the brain know about it. If there is a high level of physical stimulation to the body, this stimulation might reported it to the brain as pain. If the level of physical stimulation is low, the sensors might be report it as itchiness.

There has been a lot of speculation about the function of itching. Some researchers theorize that the function of itching may to warn the body that it is about to have a painful experience. Others theorize that early humans might developed itching as a way of knowing that they needed to take vermin and insects out of their hair. Still others believe that itching could a symptom of serious diseases such as diabetes and Hodgkin's disease.

One of the most interesting aspects of itching is that it may have be less tolerable than pain. Research has shown, in fact, that most people tolerate pain better than itching. Many will allow their skin to be painfully broken just so they can get rid of an itch.

Source: Based on information in David Feldman, *Imponderables: The Solution to the Mysteries of Everyday Life.* (New York: William Morrow, 1986, 1987).

COMMUNICATION PRACTICE

5 LISTENING

Listen to a discussion in a biology class. Then listen to certain sentences again. Circle the letter of the sentence that gives the correct information about what each speaker says.

1. a. It's impossible that it was me on the tape.

   b. It's possible that it was me on the tape.

2. a. There's probably a mistake.

   b. There's possibly a mistake.

3. a. The students might have had this experience before.

   b. It's almost certain that the students have had this experience before.

4. a. According to Professor Stevens, it would be a good idea for the students to figure out the answer.

   b. According to Professor Stevens, the students will probably be able to figure out the answer.

5. a. Allison thinks it's probably because we hear the sound in different ways.

   b. Allison thinks it's possibly because we hear the sound in different ways.

6. a. Bart thinks it's possibly because the sound travels through different substances.

   b. Bart thinks it's almost certainly because the sound travels through different substances.

7. a. Kathy believes that it's certain that it's a combination of the two things.

   b. Kathy believes that it's possible that it's a combination of the two things.

8. a. Darren thinks the sound others hear must be the real sound.

   b. Darren thinks the sound others hear could be the real sound.

9. a. Kathy thinks the sound we hear should be the real sound.

   b. Kathy thinks the sound we hear has to be the real sound.

10. a. Professor Stevens is sure that internal hearing is more real than external hearing.

   b. Professor Stevens is almost certain that internal hearing is more real than external hearing.

6 SOLVE THE PUZZLE

Work with a partner to solve these riddles. Using past modals, suggest several possible solutions to each puzzle—from most likely to least likely—and label them accordingly.

1. On November 22, 1978, an eighteen-year-old thief broke into a lady's house and demanded all her money. She gave him all she had: $11.50. The thief was so angry that he demanded she write him a check for $50. Two hours later the police caught the thief. Why?

2. A dog owner put some food in a pan for her cat. Then, because she didn't want her dog to eat the cat's food, she tied a 6-foot rope around his neck. Then she left. When she came back, she discovered that the dog had eaten the cat's food. What happened?

3. A young girl named Michelle decided to ride her bicycle from her own town to a town 10 kilometers away. After a while she reached a crossroads where she had to change direction. She discovered that the signpost with arrows pointing to different towns in the area had blown down. She didn't know which road was the right one. Nevertheless, she was able to figure out which road to take. What do you think she did?

4. Roy Sullivan, a forest ranger in Virginia, had seven experiences in his life in which he was struck by a powerful force. Two times his hair was set on fire. He had burns on his eyebrows, shoulder, stomach, chest, and ankle. Once he was driving when he was hit and was knocked 10 feet out of his car. What do you think happened to him?

*Sources: For riddle 1: Eric Elfman, *Almanac of the Gross, Disgusting, and Totally Repulsive* (New York: Random House, 1994); for riddles 2 and 3: Louis G. Cowan, *The Quiz Kids, Questions and Answers* (Akron, Ohio: Saalfield Publishing, 1941); for riddle 4: Ann Elwood and Carol Orsag Madigan, *The Macmillan Book of Fascinating Facts* (New York: Macmillan, 1989).*

7 SMALL GROUP DISCUSSION

Form groups of four. Look back at The Tunguska Event. *Which explanation do you think is the most likely? Which do you like best? Discuss your opinions with your partners. Report your opinions to the class.*

8 ESSAY

Write a paragraph or two in which you attempt to answer one of the following questions. You can make your paragraphs serious or humorous.

- Why don't we ever see baby pigeons?
- Why do we cry at happy endings?
- Why do women wear such uncomfortable shoes?
- Why are cities warmer than their outlying areas?

*Source of topics: David Feldman, *Imponderables: The Solution to the Mysteries of Everyday Life* (New York: William Morrow, 1986, 1987).*

9 PICTURE DISCUSSION

With a partner, discuss this picture. Describe the situation, saying as much as you can. Why do you think the house is such a mess? Where do you think the teenagers' parents are? Have they been gone a short time or a long time? Do you think the parents will be back soon?

REVIEW OR SELFTEST

I. *Complete the letter to a columnist and the columnist's response with the correct tense forms of the indicated modals and modal-like expressions. Make the modals negative where necessary, and include necessary subject pronouns.*

Dear Pamela:

My wife, Jeaninne, and I invited a Japanese colleague to dinner last week.

We had invited her before, but she'd _____had to decline_____ because of other
                                        1. (have to / decline)

commitments. Finally, _____. Things were going well at
                            2. (be able to / come)

first. Yoko, my co-worker, seemed a little nervous, but that was

understandable. I thought she was probably trying to remember how

_____ when you visit an American home. She brought a
   3. (be supposed to / act)

beautifully wrapped present, which my wife just _____ right
                                      4. (have to / open)

away. Yoko _____ that very much, because she looked upset.
               5. (must / like)

I thought maybe in Japan _____ the paper. Maybe
                          6. (be supposed to / tear)

_____ it off gently and fold it, or something. Anyway, my
   7. (be supposed to / take)

wife tore it off with a flourish and pulled out a box of excellent chocolates.

She _____ until after dinner, but she insisted on passing
               8. (could / wait)

them around and having everyone eat some of them. Before dinner! Yoko was

embarrassed. She said she _____ something else for a gift.
                     9. (should / bring)

Pamela, what went wrong? It think it was all Jeaninne's fault.

                                        Puzzled in Pittsburgh

Dear Puzzled:

You _____ anybody for this problem. It's a clear case
          10. (have to / blame)

of cultural misunderstanding. What you _____ is that
                                 11. (must / understand)

in Japan when someone takes a gift to a friend's house, the friend

_____ it in front of the visitor. It is more polite to wait until
  12. (should / open)

(continued on next page)

later to open it, so it _____ something of a shock to your Japanese friend
                        13. (may / be)

to see your wife make such a big scene. That's not what one _____ in
                                                            14. (be supposed to / do)

Japan.

Don't be too concerned about it. I'm sure your friend will understand when you explain

to her and apologize.

Pamela

II. *Read the story. Replace each underlined expression with a modal or modal-like
expression having the same or a similar meaning. Write your answers on the lines
below.*

One of the most puzzling experiences I've ever had happened last winter. It was one of

those typical dark and stormy nights that you read about in mystery novels. Sitting on the

sofa in the living room, I <u>could hear</u> thunder and see an occasional flash of lightning.
                            1.

It <u>had to have been</u> at least 1:00 A.M. I was reading a mystery novel that was so exciting
   2.

I <u>couldn't put it down</u>. Suddenly the phone rang, startling me out of my wits. I picked up
   3.

the receiver, muttering to myself something like, "Who <u>can that be</u> at this hour of the night?
                                                             4.

<u>Someone probably died</u>." But no. There were a few seconds of silence; then a low,
5.

disembodied voice said, "Help me. Help me." "Who are you?" I asked. "Who is this?" No

answer. The phone went dead.

The next morning it all seemed like a bad dream. I was troubled enough by the

experience to tell my friend Josh about it. "It <u>may have just been</u> a crank call," he said.
                                                  6.

"Or it <u>might have been</u> one of your friends playing a joke on you."
       7.

"What <u>do you think I should do</u>?"
       8.

"Do? Why do anything? It won't happen again."

It did happen again, though, the following night. At precisely 1:12 A.M. (I looked at my

watch this time) the phone rang again, waking me out of a sound sleep. The same deep,

disembodied voice was on the other end of the line. I responded in the same way, but the

voice just said, "Help me, help me." Then there was silence, and the line went dead as

before.

The next day I told Josh about it again. "I still say <u>it's got to be</u> some friend of yours
_{9.}
playing a joke. Don't you recognize the voice?"

"Not at all," I said. "It <u>can't be</u> anyone I know."
_{10.}

"Well, call the phone company. <u>They'll probably have</u> an idea about what to do."
_{11.}

I never did call the phone company, for some reason. This experience went on for the
next five nights. At precisely 1:12 A.M., the phone would ring, and I would pick it up, only
to hear the same thing. "Help me, help me." After that, it stopped. Since then I haven't
stopped wondering if I <u>should have called</u> the police.
_{12.}

I wonder if it <u>could really have been</u> someone who needed help. Or was it just a
_{13.}
trickster? <u>Maybe I'll never find out</u>.
_{14.}

1. __was able to hear__

2. _____

3. _____

4. _____

5. _____

6. _____

7. _____

8. _____

9. _____

10. _____

11. _____

12. _____

13. _____

14. _____

III. *Look at the pictures. Write a sentence using the suggested modal or modal-like
expression to describe each situation, making sure to put the verbs in the correct
tense.*

1.

(should)

__They should all be__

__wearing their seat belts.__

2.

(must)

_____

_____

(continued on next page)

3.

(had better)

_____

4.

(be supposed to)

_____

5.

(might)

_____

6.

(could)

_____

7.

(may)

_____
_____

8.

(should)

_____
_____

IV. *Circle the letter of the one word or phrase in each sentence that is <u>not</u> correct.*

1. I think we <u>ought</u> <u>look into</u> a nice guided tour—that is, if we <u>can find</u>
        A   B   C

    one that <u>won't bankrupt</u> us.
             D

(A) B C D

2. Fortunately, I <u>could get</u> a scholarship to attend college; otherwise,   **A B C D**
            A
    I never <u>could have</u> <u>afforded</u> <u>to go</u>.
                B   C   D

3. You <u>had better</u> <u>to set</u> your alarm if you expect to <u>be able to</u> <u>wake up</u>   **A B C D**
          A   B   C   D
    on time.

4. The only thing I <u>can think</u> of as to why Joe isn't here is that he   **A B C D**
                  A
    <u>might have</u> <u>have to</u> <u>work</u> late.
       B   C   D

5. Do you think I <u>shall</u> <u>take</u> a gift to the party today, or do you think   **A B C D**
                A   B
    I <u>might</u> <u>be able to wait</u> until Saturday?
        C   D

6. They <u>might not</u> <u>had</u> <u>been</u> injured in the accident if they had been   **A B C D**
          A   B   C
    <u>wearing</u> their seatbelts.
      D

7. We <u>ought to</u> <u>take</u> some extra cash along on the trip, but we absolutely **A B C D**
        A   B
    <u>don't have to</u> <u>forget</u> our passports.
         C   D

8. Joe called to say that he <u>won't</u> <u>be able to</u> make it by seven o'clock, but **A B C D**
                         A   B
    he <u>must</u> <u>manage to get</u> here by eight.
       C   D

9. <u>You'll be</u> <u>supposed to</u> to fertilize your rose bushes if <u>you expect</u> them **A B C D**
     A   B   C
    <u>to produce</u> any flowers.
       D

10. I suppose Amy <u>could have</u> <u>had to</u> stay late at the office, but she told   **A B C D**
                A   B
    me she <u>didn't</u> <u>had to</u> work tonight.
         C   D

V.   *Go back to your answers to Part IV. Write the correct form for each item that you believe is incorrect.*

1.   *ought to* _____   **6.** _____

2. _____   **7.** _____

3. _____   **8.** _____

4. _____   **9.** _____

5. _____   **10.** _____

▶ **To check your answers, go to the Answer Key on page 99.**

PART II

FROM GRAMMAR TO WRITING TOPIC SENTENCES

A common way of organizing an essay or other piece of writing in English is to begin with a topic sentence. A topic sentence is a general sentence which covers the content of the entire paragraph. All the supporting examples and details of the paragraph must fit under this sentence. It is usually the first sentence in the paragraph. Look at this paragraph from the essay "The Tunguska Event":

> Today there are a number of explanations given as to the possible cause of the Tunguska Event. The most widely accepted one is that a 10,000-ton remnant of Encke's Comet entered the earth's atmosphere at a very high speed, burned up during entry, and crashed onto the earth's surface, causing a fireball and a shock wave but not creating a crater. Other explanations include the possibility of the impact of an errant black hole or the crashing of an alien space ship. The jury is still out.

The topic sentence for this paragraph is "Today there are a number of explanations given as to the possible cause of the Tunguska Event." This sentence tells the reader what to expect in the paragraph: some explanations about the causes of the Tunguska explosion.

 Look at this paragraph. It contains many supporting details but no topic sentence. Read the paragraph. Then circle the letter of the best topic sentence for the paragraph.

> For one thing, you should always remove your shoes when you enter a Japanese home, and you should leave them pointing toward the door. Another suggestion is to make sure that you bring a gift for your Japanese hosts, and to be sure to wrap it. A third recommendation is to be appreciative of things in a Japanese house, but not too appreciative. Finally, remember that when you sit down to eat, you do not have to accept every kind of food that you are offered, but you are expected to finish whatever you do put on your plate.

Choices

   a. Visiting a Japanese home is very enjoyable.

   b. Taking a gift is very important when you visit a Japanese home.

   c. There are a number of things to keep in mind when you visit a Japanese home.

   d. When you visit a Japanese home, be sure not to eat too much.

2 *Read the following paragraph. Then look at the four variations of possible topic sentences. Which one is the best? Why? What is wrong with each of the other choices?*

> One reason is that when commercial flights began, all pilots were male. Men were hired because they had flight experience obtained in combat. Women, not having been in combat, had no flight experience. A second reason is simply prejudice: The powers in the airline industry presumably believed the stereotype that there are certain jobs that women cannot do as well as men. A third reason is inertia and the status quo—flying has mostly been a male-dominated profession since it began, and it takes time to change things. Eventually we will see more and more female commercial airline pilots, but for the present, old ideas die hard.

Choices

   a. Why there are so few women commercial pilots today.

   b. There are three principal reasons why there are so few women commercial pilots today.

   c. Women pilots in aviation.

   d. Men are still prejudiced about women's capabilities.

3 *Look at each of the following sets of details. For each set, write an appropriate topic sentence.*

   1. _____

     a. For one thing, there's almost always a traffic jam I get stuck in, and I'm often late to work.

     b. Also, there's not always a parking place when I do get to work.

     c. Worst of all, I'm spending more money on gas and car maintenance than I would if I took public transportation.

   2. _____

     a. One is that I often fall asleep when watching the TV screen, no matter how interesting the video is.

     b. Another is that watching movies is basically a social experience, and I'm usually alone when I watch videos.

     c. The main reason is that the TV screen, no matter how large it is, diminishes the impact that you get when watching a movie on the big screen.

(continued on next page)

3. _____

    a. Nothing spontaneous usually happens on a guided tour, but I've had lots of spontaneous things happen when I've charted my own vacation course.

    b. Tour guides present you with what they think is interesting, whereas when you are in charge of your own vacation, you do what you think is interesting.

    c. Unplanned vacations can often be cheaper than guided tours.

4. _____

    a. Cats don't bark and wake up the neighbors or bite the mailman.

    b. Dogs have to be walked at least two times a day, but cats handle their own exercise.

    c. Cats eat a lot less than dogs.

    d. You can't leave your dog at home when you take a vacation, but you can leave your cat if a friend or neighbor will come and feed it.

4 APPLY IT TO YOUR WRITING

Write a paragraph of several sentences about one of the following topics, a similar topic that interests you, or a topic suggested by your teacher. Make sure that your paragraph has a topic sentence. Then share your work with three or four other students. Read each others' paragraphs. Point out strengths and offer suggestions.

Topics
- an annoying habit
- the best part of the day
- night owls vs. early birds
- the ideal vacation
- a societal problem
- expectation vs. reality

REVIEW OR SELFTEST
ANSWER KEY

I.
2. she was able to come
3. you're supposed to act
4. had to open
5. must not have liked
6. you're not supposed to tear
7. you're supposed to take
8. could have waited
9. should have brought
10. don't have to blame
11. must understand
12. shouldn't open
13. may have been
14. is supposed to do

II.
2. must have been
3. wasn't able to put it down
4. could that be
5. Someone must have died
6. It might have just been / It could have just been
7. may have been / could have been
8. do you think I ought to do / shall I do
9. it has to be / it must be
10. couldn't be
11. They should have / They ought to have
12. ought to have called
13. might really have been / may really have been
14. I may never find out / I might never find out

III. Possible Answers:
2. They must have forgotten to put gas in the tank.
3. They'd better slow down.
4. Drivers are supposed to carry their driver's license with them.
5. Jerry might have missed his flight. / Jerry might have decided to take a different flight.
6. Jerry could have called his parents to tell them what he was going to do.
7. It may rain.
8. They should have brought their raincoats and umbrellas. / They shouldn't have tried to play tennis today.

IV.
2. A	5. A	8. C
3. B	6. B	9. A
4. C	7. C	10. D

V.
2. was able to get
3. set
4. had to
5. should / ought to
6. have
7. mustn't
8. should
9. You're
10. have to

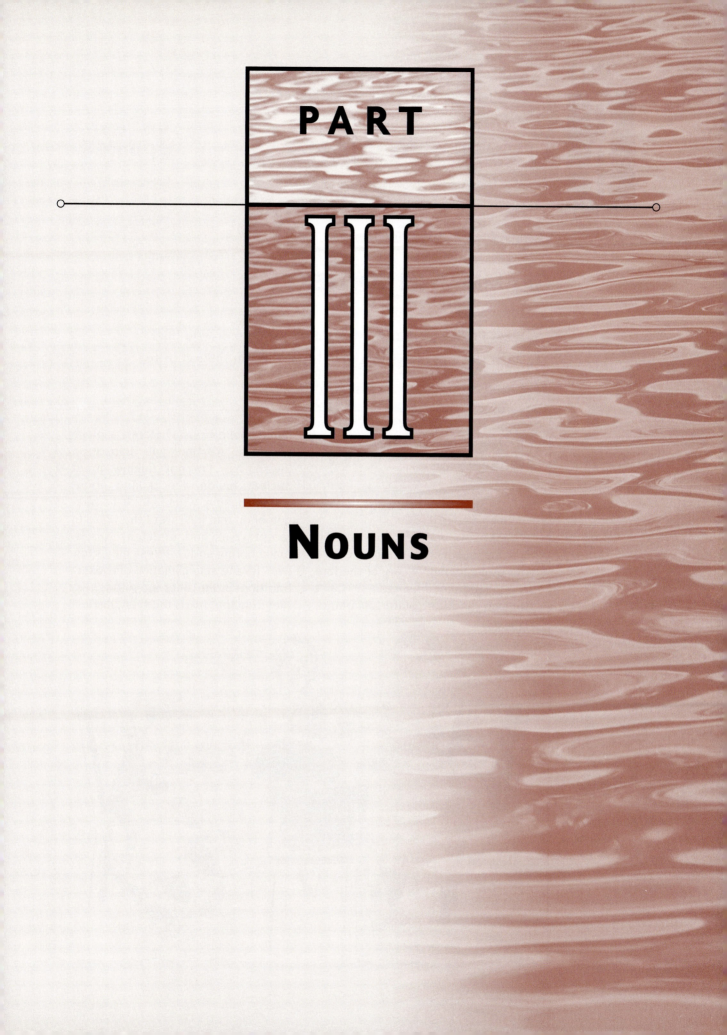

PART

III

NOUNS

6 COUNT AND NON-COUNT NOUNS

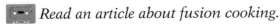

GRAMMAR **IN CONTEXT**

QUESTIONS TO CONSIDER

1. What foods of cultures other than your own do you like?

2. What are some ways that people use food in their culture?

Read an article about fusion cooking.

TIME FOR FUSION

Think, now. Are you tired of the same old meals, tired of eating your own cooking? Weary of the fare at fast-food establishments? Can't stomach another plate of bland, home-cooked pasta? Here's a piece of advice: It's time you discovered fusion. No, I'm not talking about nuclear fusion. I'm talking about fusion cooking. What is it? It's a phenomenon that has swept the world in recent years and threatens to displace boring and tasteless meals forever. It's the amalgamation of cooking traditions from different cultures—a blending that takes the best, tastiest

EAT YOUR VEGETABLES.

elements of one culture's cooking and mixes them with the best elements of others.

There are many kinds of fusion cooking, of course, but Pacific Rim fusion, or East–meets–West, is paramount. In her *Terrific Pacific Cookbook,* Anya Von Bremzen, an authority in the field of cuisine, talks about Pacific Rim fusion. According to Von Bremzen, "The great culinary traditions of Europe and Asia, long distant and remote, each exotic to the other, have blended, fused, and overlapped—sometimes with seismic effects. The heartland of this new cuisine is a great loop of countries strung like a necklace around the edges of the seemingly endless Pacific Ocean." Foods and flavors which would have been unheard of in the past—coconut, ginger, lemon grass, curry, tropical fruit—are fast becoming the norm in the American home kitchen. However, the movement is not all in one direction. While Americans have gotten more into such things as noodles and curry, Asian people are beginning to embrace pasta and enchiladas. With a little effort, you can learn to bring your meals out of the dull and commonplace and into the realm of the exciting and delicious.

But wait a minute, you say. It takes a lot of work to prepare good, tasty Asian food, doesn't it? Not really. Fusion meals can be prepared easily. In a matter of minutes, a little bit of work will transform your meal into a work of art.

Nowhere is this fusion more apparent than in Hawaii, which, appropriately enough, is one of those crossroad places that bridge cultures. Hawaiians have taken elements of the food traditions of the peoples of Polynesia, Japan, China, Portugal, Okinawa, Korea, Southeast Asia, and even New England and have created a new cuisine known simply as "Local Food." In Hawaii, no one group sets the cultural tone. The population is one-third Pacific Islander, one-third Asian, and one-third Caucasian, and Local Food is a synthesis of the favorites of these groups. Established as a phenomenon after World War II, Local Food usually has rice as the center of the meal, more meat than Asians usually eat, and fewer fruits and vegetables. It's the kind of food you can get at lunch wagons and small eateries—not what you would find at a classy restaurant. A common meal might include Japanese white rice topped by several different meats, such as beef teriyaki, Chinese pork, or curry, perhaps accompanied by macaroni salad and some kind of vegetable.

Rachel Laudan, an authority on Hawaiian cuisine, is amazed by the ways in which Hawaiian people use food. It brings people together and helps them communicate. "Laudan describes Local Food, along with the local pidgin language, as the glue that holds the diverse ethnic groups together and sets them apart from outsiders," says writer Judith Pierce Rosenberg.

Hawaiian Local Food may be a microcosm of the future. We're surely going to see more of fusion cooking in the new millennium. Not only does it allow us to escape from the monotony of choices at fast-food restaurants, but it also allows us to eat more healthfully. And perhaps fusion cooking symbolizes something more than just tastier meals. Perhaps it represents the advent of the shrunken world and the world culture whose outlines we are just beginning to be able to recognize. ⏱

Sources: Based on Anya Von Bremzen, *Terrific Pacific Cookbook* (New York: Workman Publishing, 1995); Judith Pierce Rosenberg, "Hawaii's 'Local Food': A Fusion of Ethnic Flavors," *Christian Science Monitor,* June 3, 1998, p. 14.

UNDERSTANDING MEANING FROM CONTEXT

Part A

Make a guess about the meaning of each italicized word or phrase from the reading. Write your guess in the blank provided.

1. *Weary* of the fare at fast-food establishments?

   _____

2. Weary of the *fare* at fast-food establishments?

   _____

3. With a little effort, you can learn to bring your meals out of the dull and commonplace and into the *realm* of the exciting and delicious.

   _____

4. Hawaiian Local Food may be a *microcosm* of the future.

   _____

Part B

Answer the questions about other vocabulary from the reading.

5. The word *cuisine* is used many times in the reading, along with its more common synonym. What word is a synonym of *cuisine*?

   _____

6. Look at this sentence from the reading:

   > It's the amalgamation of cooking traditions from different cultures—a blending that takes the best, tastiest elements of one culture's cooking and mixes them with the best elements of others.

   The word *amalgamation* has a synonym in this sentence. What word means something similar to *amalgamation*?

   _____

GRAMMAR **PRESENTATION**
COUNT AND NON-COUNT NOUNS

NON-COUNT NOUNS IN "COUNTABLE" FORM	
NON-COUNT NOUN	**"COUNTABLE" FORM**
I'll have **tea**.	I'll have **a cup of tea**.
You need **advice**.	Let me give you **a piece of advice**.
We're having **meat** for dinner.	There are **several different meats** in this dish.
Fruit is nutritious.	Hawaiian food has **fewer fruits** and vegetables than Asian food.
Let's play **tennis**.	Let's play **a game of tennis**.

USES OF NON-COUNT NOUNS	
NON-COUNT NOUNS IN "MASS" USE	**NON-COUNT NOUNS IN "COUNT" USE**
It takes **work** to prepare a meal.	Your meal is **a work** of art.
I want some **coffee**.	Please bring us **two coffees**.
Wine is produced in France.	Chablis is **a** white **wine**.
This food needs some **spice**.	Turmeric and cardamom are **two spices** that originated in India.
The sun provides **light**.	She saw **two lights** shining in the sky.

NOTES

EXAMPLES

1. Nouns are names of persons, places, and things. There are two types of nouns: **proper nouns** and **common nouns**. **Proper nouns** are names of particular persons, places, or things. They are usually unique.

- Akira Kurosawa, São Paulo, the Golden Gate Bridge

Common nouns refer to people, places, or things but are not the names of particular individuals.

- book, courage, heart, rhinoceros, vegetable, water

2. There are two types of common nouns: **count nouns** and **non-count nouns**. **Count nouns** name things that can be counted.

- one woman, nine planets

Non-count (or **mass**) **nouns** name things that cannot be counted in their normal sense because they exist in a "mass" form. Non-count nouns in their normal meaning are not preceded by *a* or *an*, though they are often preceded by *some* and *the*.

- I bought rice.
  NOT ~~I bought a rice.~~
- Let me give you **some advice**.
  NOT ~~Let me give you an advice.~~

A **non-count noun** is normally followed by a **singular verb**.

- **Corn is** grown there.
  NOT ~~Corns are grown there.~~
- **Rice feeds** millions.
- **Physics seems** complicated.

3. Notice the following categories of non-count nouns and examples of them. See Appendix 5 on page A-4 for a more complete list of non-count nouns.

Abstractions	• advice, behavior, chance, energy, evil, fun, good, happiness, honesty, love
Activities	• bowling, dancing, football, hiking, soccer, tennis
Diseases	• AIDS, cancer, malaria, measles
Elements	• gold, magnesium, plutonium, silver
Foods	• beef, fruit, meat, rice, wheat
Gases	• air, carbon dioxide, oxygen, smoke
Liquids	• coffee, gasoline, soda, water, wine
Natural phenomena	• aurora borealis, cold, electricity, ice, light, lightning, rain, snow, thunder
Occupations	• construction, nursing, teaching
Particles	• dust, pepper, salt, sand, sugar
Subjects	• astronomy, business, English, history, Japanese, physics, science, Spanish
Others	• choice, equipment, furniture, news

4. We frequently make **non-count nouns countable** by adding a phrase that gives them a form, a limit, or a container. See Appendix 6 on page A-5 for a more complete list of phrases for counting non-count nouns.

NON-COUNT NOUN	**"COUNTABLE STATE"**
furniture	• a piece of furniture
lightning	• a bolt (*flash*) of lightning
meat	• a piece of meat
rice	• five grains of rice
sand	• a grain of sand
tennis	• a game of tennis
thunder	• a clap (*bolt*) of thunder
water	• a cup of water

5. Many non-count nouns are used in a countable sense without the addition of a phrase (such as "a piece of"). When they are, they can be preceded by *a / an* and can occur in the plural. Compare the following **non-count nouns** in **mass use** and **count use**.

MASS USE	**COUNT USE**
I ate **meat** for dinner.	• Different **meats** are available at the supermarket. (*types of meat*)
We need to take **water** along on the camping trip.	• There are carbonated and uncarbonated mineral **waters**. (*brands of mineral water*)
TV is both good and bad.	• Yesterday we bought **a TV**. (informal for *television set*)
Too much **salt** in the diet can be unhealthful.	• The mixture contains **a salt**. (*a type of chemical compound*)
I drink **coffee** every morning.	• Please bring us **three coffees**. (informal for *three cups of coffee*)
France produces **wine**.	• Cabernet Sauvignon is **a wine** produced in France.

(continued on next page)

It takes **work** to prepare an elegant meal.

Light is essential for the growth of crops.

Many events seem governed by **chance**.

I have no **money**.

- Your meal is **a work** of art.
- There's **a light** in the window.
- I had **a chance** to talk with Sarah. (*an opportunity*)
- The state will use tax **moneys** to fund the project. (*amounts of money from different tax sources*)

---

6. BE CAREFUL! When non-count nouns occur alone or are preceded by *some*, they denote things that don't have any particular boundaries.

When non-count nouns are preceded by *a* or *an*, they acquire a boundary and are limited in some sense. A discrete amount or limit is suggested.

- I drank **some soda**. (*no particular amount*)
- **Work** can be exhausting. (*work in general*)
- I drank **a soda**. (*a discrete amount— probably a can or glass*)
- *Don Quixote* is **a literary work**. (*a single literary work, contained in a book*)

---

7. Study the following **non-count nouns ending in -s** and **irregular plural count nouns**. See Appendix 4 on page A-4 for a list of irregular plurals.

- **mathematics, economics, physics** (non-count nouns ending in *-s*)
- **criterion, phenomenon, nucleus** (singular count nouns)
- **criteria, phenomena, nuclei** (irregular plural forms)
- **cattle** (a plural form only; no singular form exists)

---

8. BE CAREFUL! In its normal usage, the word *people* is a **plural**, denoting "more than one person." In this meaning, it does not have a singular form. The word *people* meaning a particular group of human beings or particular groups of human beings can have a singular and a plural form.

The word *cattle* (= a group of cows) is a collective plural. There is no singular form.

- Hawaiian **people** use food in unusual ways. (*Hawaiian people in general*)
- Hawaiians have taken elements of the food traditions of many **peoples** and have created a new cuisine. (*many different ethnic groups*)

- Ranchers raise **cattle**. (*cows*)

FOCUSED PRACTICE

1 DISCOVER THE GRAMMAR

Look again at these two paragraphs from Time for Fusion. *You will find thirteen non-count nouns and twenty-three count nouns. Circle the count nouns and underline the non-count nouns as used in the exercise. Do not include proper nouns (any words capitalized). Count usages of words only once.*

There are many (kinds) of fusion <u>cooking</u>, of course, but Pacific Rim fusion, or East–meets–West, is paramount. In her *Terrific Pacific Cookbook*, Anya Von Bremzen, an authority in the field of cuisine, talks about Pacific Rim fusion. According to Von Bremzen, "The great culinary traditions of Europe and Asia, long distant and remote, each exotic to the other, have blended, fused, and overlapped—sometimes with seismic effects. The heartland of this new cuisine is a great loop of countries strung like a necklace around the edges of the seemingly endless Pacific Ocean." Foods and flavors which would have been unheard of in the past—coconut, ginger, lemon grass, curry, tropical fruit—are fast becoming the norm in the American home kitchen. However, the movement is not all in one direction. While Americans have gotten more into such things as noodles and curry, Asian people are beginning to embrace pasta and enchiladas. With a little effort, you can learn to bring your meals out of the dull and commonplace and into the realm of the exciting and delicious.

But wait a minute, you say. It takes a lot of work to prepare good, tasty Asian food, doesn't it? Not really. Fusion meals can be prepared easily. In a matter of minutes, a little bit of work will transfer your meal into a work of art.

2 BLENDING
Grammar Notes 3, 5

Part A

Read more about fusion cooking. Complete the article with words from the box.

menu	rolls	foods	ways	rules	century
~~food~~	cuisines	chefs	spices	flavoring	

COPLEY NEWS SERVICE, SAN DIEGO, CA   AUGUST 5, 1998   F5

"Fusion" Cooking Melds Cultures and Tastes
BY CHARLYN FARGO

Fusion _____*food*_____ can be called the blending of flavors and _____ as completely
              1.   **2.**

and effectively as the melding of America, and it is a celebration of the country's multiculturism.

Under the old French _____ of cooking, certain _____ were always
                                        3.   **4.**

prepared certain ways. Those rules have been changed. Egg _____ don't have to include only
                                                          5.

Chinese cabbage and shrimp. Plum sauce isn't just used in Chinese cuisine but to give the foods an

Asian _____.   *(continued on next page)*
      6.

And not just Asian. Mexican, Caribbean, Cuban—they all work to influence regional cuisine in

_____ not previously considered. On the West Coast, the cuisine of East and West have
      7.

flourished side by side for more than a _____, since the California gold rush propelled
           8.

San Francisco's first significant Asian immigration.

But it's only in the past two decades that inventive _____ have begun to blend the
          9.

cooking styles of East and West.

Norman Van Aken, chef and owner of Norman's in Miami and the author of *Norman's New World*

Cuisine, is credited as the father of "new world" cuisine and with coining the term "fusion cuisine."

For Van Aken fusion cuisine began more than ten years ago when he was working in Key West, Florida.

He began drawing on tropical flavorings along with _____ and seasonings from Cuba,
          10.

the Bahamas, and the Old South for his food. His _____ was filled with items such as
          11.

lobster enchiladas, rum and pepper-painted grouper (the sauce includes rum, peppercorns, cloves, and

soy sauce) and yucca-stuffed crispy fish.

His new world cuisine—with the flavors of the Bahamas and Cuba melded with Florida's

produce—is just one of many cuisines considered fusion.

Source: Charlyn Fargo, "Fusion Cooking Melds Cultures and Tastes," Copley News Service (San Diego, CA),
August 5, 1998, p. F5.

Part B
Work with a partner to answer these questions.

1. Could "foods" be a correct answer for item 1 in Part A? Why or why not?

_____

2. Could "food" be a correct answer for item 4 in Part A? Why or why not?

_____

3. Could "flavorings" be a correct answer for item 6 in Part A? Why or why not?

_____

4. Could "spice" be a correct answer for item 10 in Part A? Why or why not?

_____

❸ COMMUNITY BULLETIN BOARD

The new interactive websites on the Internet give people information about entertainment, cultural events, and the weather. Fill in the blanks in the bulletin board messages, choosing from the forms given. Refer to Appendices 5 and 6 on pages A-4 and A-5 for help in completing this exercise if necessary.

Community Bulletin Board for August 25, 2002

_____Rain_____ is in the forecast for this afternoon and early evening. Don't worry,
1. (Rain / A rain)

though; it will be light rain, not at all like the heavy _____ which have been
2. (rains / rain)

falling in the Midwest this week.

Community Bulletin Board for August 25, 2002

Poet Jefferson Saito will give _____ of his poetry tonight in the Burlington
3. (reading / a reading)

Civic Center. He describes his latest book of poems as _____ in
4. (work / a work)

_____ .
5. (progress / a progress)

Community Bulletin Board for August 25, 2002

On Tuesday afternoon at four o'clock at City Hall, Professor Helen Hammond, who has

written _____ of the space program, will lead _____ on the
6. (history / a history)   **7. (talk / a talk)**

exploration of _____ in the twenty-first century at _____ when
8. (space / a space)   **9. (time / a time)**

we seem to be running out of funding for the space program.

(continued on next page)

Community Bulletin Board for August 25, 2002

If you haven't made reservations for the annual Labor Day picnic, _____ is

                                    10. (a time / time)

running short. _____ on the remodeling of Patton Pavilion, where the picnic will

        11. (Work / A work)

be held, is almost complete. All residents of Burlington are of course invited, but you must have a

ticket, which will cover the price of dinner. The menu will include fish, meat, and pasta as

possible main courses. _____ and _____ are complimentary.

           12. (Soda / A soda)   **13. (milk / a milk)**

Adult participants may purchase _____, including Columbia Merlot,

                    14. (wine / a wine)

_____ produced in the eastern part of the state.

15. (a red wine / red wine)

Community Bulletin Board for August 25, 2002

On Friday evening at 8:00 P.M. in the Civic Auditorium, Professor Mary Alice Waters will present

a program on the Xhosa, _____ of southern Africa. Professor

        16. (indigenous people / an indigenous people)

Waters will show _____ about marriage customs of the Xhosa and other

        17. (a film / film)

_____ of the southern third of the African continent.

18. (people / peoples)

---

4 A WORK OF ART   Grammar Notes 4–6, 8

*Work with a partner. Take turns asking questions using items in the box. Each
partner asks and answers six questions.*

a work of art	fruits	a game of . . .	a piece of advice
spices	pieces of furniture	a TV	a wine
tax moneys	peoples	a people	cuisines

EXAMPLES:

PARTNER A: Tell me something that you consider **a work of art**.

PARTNER B: I consider Van Gogh's painting *Starry Night* **a work of art**.

PARTNER B: How many pieces of furniture . . . ?

PARTNER A: There are eight . . .

5 EDITING

Find and correct the eleven errors involving count and non-count nouns in the letter.

⁓ Sugar Loaf Mountain   Rio de Janeiro, Brazil ⁓

April 15

Dear Kids,

   Your mom and I are having a wonderful time in Brazil. We landed in Rio de Janeiro on Tuesday as scheduled and made it to our hotel without any problems. On Wednesday we walked and sunbathed on Copacabana and Ipanema beaches. The only problem was that I dropped my camera and got ~~sands~~ *sand* in it, and now it's not working. Actually, there's one other problem: we don't have enough furnitures in our hotel room. There's no place to put anything. But everything else has been great. We went to a samba show, and even though it was geared for tourist, it was a lot of fun.

   The Brazilian people is very friendly and helpful. On Friday we had a flight to São Paulo scheduled for 9:00 A.M., and we missed the bus and couldn't get a taxi. But we were saved by one of the hotel employee, who gave us a ride to the airport. We got there in the nick of time. Now we're in São Paulo. It's an exciting place, but I can't get over the traffics. It took two hours to get from our hotel to the downtown area. Yesterday we had lunch at a famous restaurant where they serve feijoada, a typical Brazilian foods. It had so many spice in it that our mouths were on fire, but it was delicious. Tonight we are going to have dinner at another restaurant where they serve all kinds of meat. They raise a lot of cattles in Brazil, and meat is very popular. This restaurant is one of the most famous ones.

   The other thing about Brazil that's really interesting is the amount of coffee the Brazilians drink. They have little cups of coffees several times a day—called caffezinho. We tried it; it's very strong and sweet.

   That's all for now. Your mom hasn't had a time to go shopping yet, which is good. You know how much I hate shopping.

Love,
Dad

COMMUNICATION PRACTICE

6 LISTENING

Read these statements. Then listen to the cooking show.

1. Flo's pelmeni is a _____ dish. (national origin)

2. The principal meat ingredient of pelmeni is _____. (type of meat)

3. Other types of meat that can be used in making pelmeni are _____.

4. The meat mixture is contained in balls made of _____.

5. Pelmeni generally contains only one vegetable: _____.

6. The meat mixture contains _____. (part of eggs)

7. Pelmeni balls are cooked by _____. (method of cooking)

8. The pelmeni balls are finished cooking when _____.

9. At banquets in the home country, _____ are made. (number of individual balls of pelmeni)

10. One person can easily eat at least _____ pelmeni balls. (number)

Now listen again. Complete the sentences above.

7 INFORMATION GAP: A GRAIN OF SAND

Student B, turn to page 117 and follow the instructions there. Student A, read statements 1–6 aloud. Student B will read the best completion for each statement, including a phrase from the box below in each statement. Then reverse the process for items 7–12.

a speck of	a piece of	a grain of	a bolt of / a flash of	a branch of
an article of	a clap of	a game of	a current of	a herd of

Student A's statements

1. An individual particle of a cereal grown in warm and wet areas is called . . .

2. A collection of bovine mammals is called . . .

3. A continuing flow of electrons is termed . . .

4. A small piece of a very fine, sometimes powdery material is termed . . .

5. A particular staging of an athletic competition played on an outdoor field and using a round ball is called . . .

6. A subcategory of that science which deals with the study of planets, stars, and galaxies is called . . .

Student A's completions

g. thunder

h. jewelry

i. sand

j. lightning

k. furniture

l. advice

Dictation

 Now listen to the sentences. On a separate sheet of paper, write each sentence in full.

8 ESSAY

Write an essay of two or three paragraphs about the best or worst meal experience you have ever had. Your essay can be serious or funny. Describe the kind of meal it was and what was good or bad about it.

9 PICTURE DISCUSSION

Working with a partner, look carefully at this photograph for a few minutes. Talk to your partner about all the foods you see. Then close your books and together try to remember as many details as possible. Compare your findings with those of other students.

INFORMATION GAP FOR STUDENT B

Listen as Student A reads each statement (1–6). Read aloud the best completion for each statement including a phrase from the box below. Then read statements 7–12. Student A will read the best completion for each statement.

| a speck of | a piece of | a grain of | a bolt of / a flash of | a branch of |
| an article of | a clap of | a game of | a current of | a herd of |

Student B's completions

a. soccer

b. astronomy

c. rice

d. cattle

e. electricity

f. dust

Student B's statements

7. A statement of recommended behavior is . . .

8. An individual particle of a material produced by the disintegration of stone and rocks is called . . .

9. A single discharge of electrical current between clouds or between clouds and the earth is . . .

10. A single movable structure on which one sits or sleeps is called . . .

11. A decorative object worn on the body or the clothes is called . . .

12. An instance of loud sound usually accompanying lightning is . . .

7

Definite and Indefinite Articles

GRAMMAR IN CONTEXT

QUESTIONS TO CONSIDER

1. What is an example of an environmental problem that you consider serious?

2. Do you think people exaggerate the seriousness of hazards to the environment?

3. How can serious environmental problems be remedied?

Read the story and think about the environmental issues raised.

Once Upon a Time . . .

ONCE UPON A TIME there was a green and beautiful planet. It was the third planet out from a yellowish sun in a stellar system in a relatively remote part of the galaxy. Members of the Galactic Council knew that the planet was between 4 and 5 billion years old, but no one was sure exactly how long life had existed there.

The Galactic Council had been watching Green, as they called it, for millennia. It was a responsibility of the Council to observe and monitor all planets that harbored life in an effort to predict which ones might destroy themselves. Thus the Council could intervene if it had to. Each planet had

its own watcher, and Planet Green's was Ambassador Gorkon. His job was to visit Green and investigate thoroughly. On this occasion Gorkon was making his report to Mr. Xau, the president of the Galactic Council.

President Xau said, "Well, Gorkon, you're late getting back. There must have been something serious happening to keep you on Green for so long."

Gorkon responded, "Yes, sir. I had to stay longer to be absolutely sure of my calculations. Affairs are not going well there. I'm afraid that if Green doesn't change its ways immediately, the planet won't be able to support life, and life won't endure there. Green is now on a destructive path. There used to be clean air and water, but now there's pollution everywhere. The acid rain that's caused by the pollution in the atmosphere has killed plants and some animals. In some large cities you can hardly see the sky, and the land is full of garbage and toxic waste dumps. They're cutting down beautiful rain forests in the southern hemisphere. They've been releasing some very dangerous chemicals—fluorocarbons, we would call them—into the atmosphere, and a hole in the ozone layer has developed over the southern polar cap. You're aware how dangerous ultraviolet radiation can be. If something isn't done, the amount of radiation in the atmosphere will be very dangerous and even lethal within twenty or thirty years. It could happen even sooner."

The president looked sad and asked, "Is that the only serious problem?"

Gorkon responded, "Unfortunately not. Several individual nations on Green have developed the bomb and other deadly weapons. So far they've avoided using the weapons against each other, and right now there's a sort of uneasy peace, but there's no guarantee it's going to last. The saddest thing that's happening on Green, though, is the extinction of species. Some have already died off entirely, and many more species are endangered—like wolves and tigers. Environmentalists are making efforts to save the whale and the panda, but it's mostly a case of too little too late. You know what happens to a planet when its species start to die off."

"Yes, of course," said the president. "We've got to stop that. Well, shall I call the Council into executive session?"

"Yes, Mr. President," said Gorkon. "Right away. I'm afraid we're going to have to interfere. If we don't, Green may not last much longer. We wouldn't want to see them suffer the same fate as Earth did."

UNDERSTANDING MEANING FROM CONTEXT

Read each sentence and study the italicized word or phrase. Then answer the vocabulary questions.

1. It was a responsibility of the Council to observe and monitor all planets that *harbored* life in an effort to predict which ones might destroy themselves.

   What verb in the fourth paragraph has the same general meaning as

   harbored? _____

2. I'm afraid that if Green doesn't change its ways immediately, life won't be able to *endure* there.

   What word in the final paragraph has a similar meaning to *endure?*

   _____

3. If something isn't done, the amount of radiation in the atmosphere will be very dangerous and even *lethal* within twenty or thirty years.

   What verb in the same paragraph is closest in general meaning to

   lethal? _____

4. The saddest thing that's happening on Green, though, is the *extinction* of species.

   What verb in the same paragraph has the same general meaning as

   extinction? _____

5. I'm afraid we're going to have to *interfere.*

   What verb in the second paragraph has a similar meaning to *interfere?*

   _____

6. We wouldn't want to see them *suffer the same fate* as Earth did.

   What is the meaning of the phrase *suffer the same fate as?*

   _____

GRAMMAR **PRESENTATION**
ARTICLES

THE: DEFINITE ARTICLE

FOR COUNT NOUNS

Members of **the Galactic Council** knew that **the planet** was between 4 and 5 billion years old.

Several individual nations on Green have developed **the bomb**.

FOR NON-COUNT NOUNS

The acid **rain** that's caused by **the pollution** in the atmosphere has killed plants and some animals.

A / AN: INDEFINITE ARTICLE

FOR SINGULAR COUNT NOUNS

Green is now on **a** destructive **path**.

It was **a responsibility** of the Council to observe and monitor all planets that harbored life in **an effort** to predict which ones might destroy themselves.

ZERO ARTICLE

FOR PLURAL COUNT NOUNS

The land is full of garbage and toxic waste **dumps**.

They're cutting down beautiful rain **forests** in the southern hemisphere.

FOR NON-COUNT NOUNS

. . . but now there's **pollution** everywhere.

You're aware how dangerous ultraviolet **radiation** can be.

FOR PROPER NOUNS

The Galactic Council had been watching **Green**, as they called it, for millennia.

President Xau said, "Well, **Gorkon**, you're late getting back."

Planet Green's [watcher] was **Ambassador Gorkon**.

NOTES	**EXAMPLES**
1. A **noun** or **noun phrase** is **definite** when the speaker and listener both know which specific person, place, or thing is being talked about. Use the **definite article**, *the*, with singular and plural count and non-count nouns that are definite for you and your listener.	• They're cutting down beautiful rain forests in **the southern hemisphere**. • So far they've avoided using **the weapons** against each other.
2. A noun is also definite when it represents something that is **unique**.	• There is a hole in **the ozone layer**. (*There is only one ozone layer.*) • **The president** needs to do something. (*There is only one president.*)
3. An adjective can often make a noun represent something unique. Some examples of such adjectives are *right*, *wrong*, *first*, *only*, and the comparative and superlative forms of adjectives.	• Is that **the only** serious **problem**? • **The saddest thing** that's happening on Green is the extinction of species.
4. A noun or noun phrase can be made definite by context.	• In some large cities you can hardly see the sky, and **the land** is full of garbage and toxic waste dumps.
5. When a speaker or listener does not have a particular person, place, or thing in mind, the noun representing it is indefinite. Use the **indefinite article**, *a / an*, with indefinite singular count nouns.	• You know what happens to **a planet** when its species start to die off. (*any planet—no particular planet in mind*)

6. A noun is often indefinite the first time a speaker mentions it. It is usually definite after the first mention.

- Several individual nations on Green have developed the bomb and other lethal **weapons**.
- So far they've avoided using **the weapons** against each other. (second mention of *weapons*)

7. Use **zero article** (= no article) with plural count nouns and non-specific non-count nouns.

- **Affairs** are not going well there. (*affairs in general*)
- . . . now there's **pollution** everywhere.

8. Use zero article before the names of people or their titles.

- **Gorkon** was making his report to **Mr. Xau**.
- **President Xau** said, "Well, **Gorkon**, you're late getting back."
- Planet Green's [watcher] was **Ambassador Gorkon**.

9. A noun is **generic** when it represents all members of a class or category of persons, places, or things. Generic nouns can be singular or plural count nouns. Note these three ways of using count nouns generically. These patterns are approximately the same in meaning *when used to classify or define* something.

- Many more species are endangered—like **wolves** and **tigers**. (zero article + count noun)

  OR

- Many more species are endangered—like **the wolf** and **the tiger**. (definite article + singular count noun)

  OR

- Many more species are endangered—like **the wolves** and **the tigers**. (definite article + plural count noun)

Non-count nouns can also be used generically.

- You're aware how dangerous ultraviolet **radiation** can be. (zero article + non-count noun)

(continued on next page)

10. BE CAREFUL! In statements where you are <u>not</u> classifying or defining with a generic noun, you may <u>not</u> use *a / an* in front of the noun.

- Environmentalists are making efforts to save **the whale** and **the panda**.

  OR

- Environmentalists are making efforts to save **the whales** and **the pandas**.

  OR

- Environmentalists are making efforts to save **whales** and **pandas**.
  NOT ~~Environmentalists are making efforts to save a whale and a panda.~~

11. The definite article, *the*, is used with the names of some countries and many geographical features or regions.

See Appendices 7 and 8 on pages A-5 and A-6 for lists of these countries and regions.

- There are environmental problems in **the United States**.
- Camels are native to **the Middle East**.

FOCUSED PRACTICE

 DISCOVER THE GRAMMAR

Look again at some of the sentences from Once Upon a Time *on page 118. Circle the letter of the sentence that describes the meaning of each sentence from the text.*

1. It was the third planet out from a yellowish sun.

   a. We know how many suns there are.

   b. We don't know how many suns there are.

2. Members of the Galactic Council knew that the planet was between 4 and 5 billion years old.

   a. There was one Galactic Council.

   b. There was more than one Galactic Council.

3. It was a responsibility of the Council to observe and monitor all planets that harbored life.

   a. The Council had one responsibility.

   b. The Council had many responsibilities.

4. They're cutting down beautiful rain forests in the southern hemisphere.

   a. They're cutting down some of the rain forests in the southern hemisphere.

   b. They're cutting down all of the rain forests in the southern hemisphere.

5. A hole in the ozone layer has developed over the southern polar cap.

   a. There is one ozone layer.

   b. There is more than one ozone layer.

6. A hole in the ozone layer has developed over the southern polar cap.

   a. There is one polar cap.

   b. There is more than one polar cap.

7. Several individual nations on Green have developed the bomb.

   a. They have developed one particular type of bomb.

   b. They have developed bombs in general.

8. Environmentalists are making efforts to save the whale and the panda.

   a. They're trying to save a particular whale and a particular panda.

   b. They're trying to save all whales and all pandas.

9. You know what happens to a planet when its species start to die off.

   a. This sort of thing can happen to all planets.

   b. This sort of thing can happen to one planet only.

2 JULY BREAKS RECORD   Grammar Notes 1–7, 10

Part A

*Read the article. Insert **a**, **an**, or **the** where necessary. If no article is needed, leave a blank.*

USA TODAY, Sunday, August 2, 1998   Section 9

July Breaks Worldwide Temperature Record

🌐 Global Warming   BY TRACI WATSON

WASHINGTON—July was __the__ world's
 1.
warmest month on record, and 1998 is on

track to become _____ planet's hottest
                  2.
known year, data reported Monday shows.

_____ temperatures in each of the
 3.
past 15 months have broken global highs

for that month. But July was distinctive in

another way: Its average of 61.7 degrees

Fahrenheit was more than half a degree

higher than that of July 1997, the planet's

previous warmest month, according to the

National Climatic Data Center in Asheville,

North Carolina. Scientists say the increase,

0.6 degrees, is unusually large.

"It would be hard to ignore that some-

thing's going on—and that something is

global warming," Vice President Gore said

Monday in announcing the data.

Last year was the hottest year mea-

sured since reliable data collection began

in the late 1800s.

Gore has held _____ series of news
                         4.
conferences to focus _____ attention on
                      5.
_____ global warming, one of his pet
 6.
causes. And the weather is working in his

favor.

_____ heat wave slammed North
 7.
Texas with 29 consecutive days of triple-

digit temperatures in July and August.

_____ heat is blamed for 126 deaths in
 8.
the state.

Heat in _____ Middle East has killed
            9.
52 people and sickened hundreds, accord-

ing to The Associated Press. Even Egyptians,

used to toiling in the desert, have taken to

working at night to avoid 100-degree day-

time heat that has persisted for three

weeks. Temperatures have hit 122 degrees

in Kuwait, where pools have equipment to

chill the water.

Temperatures soared to 100 in Paris on

Monday, and even higher elsewhere in

USA TODAY, Sunday, August 2, 1998

France. Locals and _____ tourists splashed
10.
in fountains near the Eiffel Tower and the
Louvre.

Some scientists suspect that the new
records are due partly to the El Niño
weather phenomenon and partly to global
warming. But a few say the higher temperatures are part of the normal climate cycle.

Most scientists agree that global warming, the gradual rise in worldwide temperature over the past century, is caused by so-
called greenhouse gases. These gases are
emitted by _____ cars, factories, and
11.
power plants. They rise into _____
12.
atmosphere and trap heat.

Some climate experts predict that

continued global warming could bring
more floods, more droughts, and higher sea
levels that would inundate coastal areas.

But scientists caution that it is impossible to link global warming to any given
abnormal weather event.

Gore has long been one of the most
prominent voices calling for action against
global warming. He was the primary supporter in the White House of an international treaty to slow global warming that
was written in December 1997 in Kyoto,
Japan.

That treaty has been greeted with skep-
ticism in the Senate, which must ratify it for
_____ United States to take part.
13.

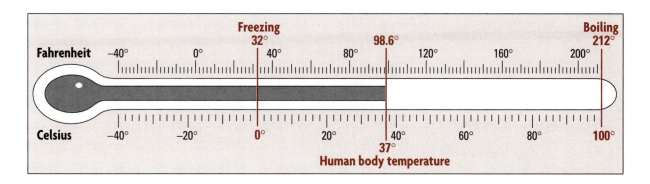

Part B

Work with a partner. Partner A, explain the reasons for your choices in items 2–7.
Partner B, explain the reasons for your choices in items 8–13.

3 **DISASTERS**

Here are some notable environmental disasters that have occurred in this century.
Insert **a**, **an**, *or* **the**, *where necessary. Leave a blank where no article is required.*

Disaster at Sea: Many Lives Lost

APRIL 16, 1912. ___The___ Titanic, _____
         1.   **2.**

British steamer, sank in _____ North
                     3.

Atlantic last night after hitting _____
                          4.

iceberg, disproving its builders' claims that

it couldn't be sunk.

Chernobyl Damage Wider Than Previously Reported

DETAILS ARE FINALLY EMERGING. On April 26, 1986,

_____ fires and explosions following _____
 17.   **18.**

unauthorized experiment caused _____ worst accident
                            19.

in _____ history of nuclear
   20.

power at the nuclear power plant in Chernobyl, Ukraine.

At least thirty-one people were killed in _____ disaster
                                21.

itself, and _____ radioactive material
        22.

was released into the atmosphere. Approximately 135,000

people were evacuated from _____ vicinity. Scientists
                        23.

warned of _____
     24.

Partial Meltdown at Three Mile Island

On March 28, 1979, _____ worst
                5.

nuclear accident ever to occur in

_____ United States took place at
  6.

the Three Mile Island nuclear reactor

in Pennsylvania. _____ causes
             7.

were _____ equipment failure and
    8.

_____ human error, leading
 9.

to a loss of coolant in _____
                10.

reactor and _____ partial
      11.

meltdown of _____ reactor's
       12.

nuclear core. _____
      13.

meltdown of _____ nuclear
       14.

core could have been total. If

_____ coolant hadn't been
 15.

lost, _____ accident might
    16.

not have happened.

MASSIVE OIL SPILL IN ALASKA

MARCH 24, 1989. _____ oil tanker *Exxon Valdez* struck Bligh Reef in
              26.

Prince William Sound, Alaska, tonight, causing _____ worst oil spill in
                                      27.

_____ U.S. history. More than 10 million barrels of _____ oil were
 28.   **29.**

spilled, causing the death of _____ many animals and resulting in
                        30.

_____ great environmental damage. _____ captain of _____
 31.   **32.**   **33.**

Valdez was said to have been drinking in his cabin at _____ time of
                                34.

_____ accident, with _____ ship being piloted by _____ first
 35.   **36.**   **37.**

mate, who was inexperienced. Exxon agreed to pay for _____ cost of
                                  38.

cleaning up _____ spill. It was determined that _____ captain, rather
        39.   **40.**

than _____ first mate, should have been piloting _____ vessel.
     41.   **42.**

Source: Some information taken from *The World Almanac and Book of Facts 1999* (Mahwah, NJ: Primedia Reference, 1998), pp. 228, 236.

④ EDITING

Read the following composition about genetic engineering and the environment.
It contains twelve errors in the use of articles. Find and correct the errors. Some
of the errors are made more than once.

Genetic Engineering and the Environment

People say we are now able to perform genetic engineering. I am
against this for several reasons. First, it is dangerous to tamper with
~~the~~ nature because we don't know what will happen. We could upset
the balance of the nature. For example, people are against the
mosquito because it carries a malaria. Suppose we change the DNA of
the mosquito so that it will die off. That will stop a malaria, but it will
upset the balance of the nature because certain other species depend
on the mosquito. If we destroy it, these other species won't be able to
survive. This will have serious effect on environment.

Second, genetic engineering will take away people's control over their
own lives. Suppose scientists develop the capability to isolate gene for
violent behavior and they eliminate this gene from future generations.
This may eliminate violence, but I believe that behavior is matter of
choice, and this type of genetic engineering will eliminate choice. It will
make people behave as someone else has determined, not as they have
determined, and it will take away an individual responsibility.

Third, genetic engineering will remove chance from our lives. Part
of what makes the life interesting is unpredictability. We never know
exactly how someone, or something, is going to turn out. It's fun to
see what happens. As far as I am concerned, we should leave genetic
engineering to Creator.

COMMUNICATION PRACTICE

5 LISTENING

Read these statements. Then listen to the conversation between a husband and a wife.

1. **a.** The Indian tribe wants to kill all whales.
   b. The Indian tribe wants to kill some whales. *(circled)*

2. **a.** The standoff is between all environmentalists and all Indians.
   b. The standoff is between some environmentalists and some Indians.

3. **a.** The newspaper article supports the environmental point of view in general.
   b. The newspaper article supports a particular environmental point of view.

4. **a.** The husband supports all Indians.
   b. The husband supports a particular group of Indians.

5. **a.** The husband thinks the Indians should be able to kill all whales.
   b. The husband thinks the Indians should be able to kill some whales.

6. **a.** The wife believes in saving some whales.
   b. The wife believes in saving all whales.

7. **a.** The wife thinks it's cruel to hunt all whales.
   b. The wife thinks it's cruel to hunt some whales.

8. **a.** Some cattle are domestic animals.
   b. All cattle are domestic animals.

9. **a.** The wife thinks all whales are intelligent.
   b. The wife thinks some whales are intelligent.

10. **a.** The husband thinks we should consider the viewpoint of all Indians.
    b. The husband thinks we should consider the viewpoint of a particular group of Indians.

Now listen again. Then circle the letter of the sentence that correctly conveys the information in the conversation.

6 INFORMATION GAP: YOUR ENVIRONMENTAL QUOTIENT

*Work with a partner to find out your Environmental Quotient (EQ). How much
do you know about the environment and the world of nature? Student B, turn to
page 134 and follow the instructions there. Student A, read the five sentence
beginnings below. Student B will read aloud the best completion for each
statement. Then reverse the process. Where necessary, circle the choice that uses
the correct article or zero article.*

Student A's prompts

1. (The environment / Environment) is . . .

2. A primate is . . .

3. A cetacean is . . .

4. A marsupial is . . .

5. (The ozone layer / An ozone layer) is . . .

Student A's completions

*Student A, read the best completion for each sentence aloud. Circle the correct
article or zero article where necessary.*

f. a tailless Australian marsupial living in and feeding on (a eucalyptus tree / the
eucalyptus tree).

g. compounds of (fluorine and carbon / the fluorine and carbon) used industrially
to lubricate and refrigerate.

h. (a member / the member) of an order of animals that bear their young alive.

i. a form of oxygen with (the distinctive odor / a distinctive odor).

j. the upper portion of (atmosphere / the atmosphere) above 11 kilometers.

Now determine your EQ and your partner's EQ.

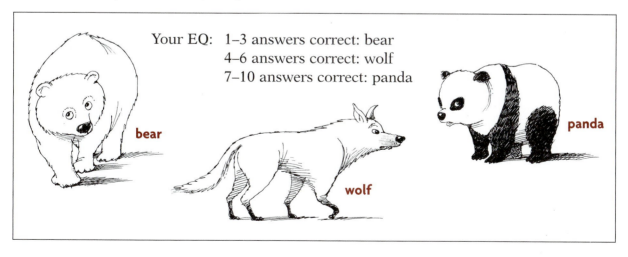

Your EQ: 1–3 answers correct: bear
4–6 answers correct: wolf
7–10 answers correct: panda

bear

wolf

panda

7 ESSAY

Choose an environmental issue that you consider important, and write an essay of two or three paragraphs on it. Say why you think the issue is important and what should be done about it. Choose one of these issues or your own idea.

Possible Issues

- saving endangered animals
- improving air quality
- improving water quality
- getting rid of nuclear weapons
- disposing of garbage
- ensuring the supply of clean water

8 PICTURE DISCUSSION

Examine the chart of geologic time on page 133. With a partner, choose one period of time that interests you and research that period on the Internet (if you have access to a computer, or in printed resource materials if you don't). One informative website you may wish to visit is www.ucmp.berkeley.edu. You can specify a particular period that you want information about:

www.ucmp.berkeley.edu./paleozoic

www.ucmp.berkeley.edu./mesozoic

www.ucmp.berkeley.edu./cenozoic

Then prepare a short lecture about the period you chose (with illustrations, if possible) to present to the class.

Outline of the earth's history

This geological time scale outlines the development of the earth and of life on the earth. The earth's earliest history appears at the bottom of the chart, and its most recent history is at the top.

Period or epoch and its length			Beginning (years ago)	Development of life on the earth	
Cenozoic Era	Quaternary Period	Holocene Epoch $11\frac{1}{2}$ thousand years	$11\frac{1}{2}$ thousand	Human beings hunted and tamed animals; developed agriculture; learned to use metals, coal, oil, gas, and other resources; and put the power of wind and rivers to work.	Cultivated plants
		Pleistocene Epoch 2 million years	2 million	Modern human beings developed. Mammoths, woolly rhinos, and other animals flourished but died out near the end of the epoch.	Human beings
	Tertiary Period	Pliocene Epoch 3 million years	5 million	Sea life became much like today's. Birds and many mammals became like modern kinds and spread around the world. Humanlike creatures appeared.	Horses
		Miocene Epoch 19 million years	24 million	Apes appeared in Asia and Africa. Other animals included bats, monkeys, and whales, and primitive bears and raccoons. Flowering plants and trees resembled modern kinds.	Apes
		Oligocene Epoch 10 million years	34 million	Primitive apes appeared. Camels, cats, dogs, elephants, horses, rhinos, and rodents developed. Huge rhinoceroslike animals disappeared near the end of the epoch.	Early horses
		Eocene Epoch 21 million years	55 million	Birds, amphibians, small reptiles, and fish were plentiful. Primitive bats, camels, cats, horses, monkeys, rhinoceroses, and whales appeared.	Grasses
		Paleocene Epoch 10 million years	65 million	Flowering plants became plentiful. Invertebrates, fish, amphibians, reptiles, and mammals were common.	Small mammals
Mesozoic Era		Cretaceous Period 80 million years	145 million	Flowering plants appeared. Invertebrates and amphibians were plentiful. Many fish resembled modern kinds. Dinosaurs with horns and armor became common. Dinosaurs died out.	Flowering plants
		Jurassic Period 68 million years	213 million	Cone-bearing trees were plentiful. Sea life included shelled squid. Dinosaurs reached their largest size. The first birds appeared. Mammals were small and primitive.	Birds
		Triassic Period 35 million years	248 million	Cone-bearing trees were plentiful, as were fish and insects. The first turtles, crocodiles, and dinosaurs appeared, as did the first mammals.	Dinosaurs
Paleozoic Era		Permian Period 38 million years	286 million	The first seed plants—cone-bearing trees—appeared. Fish, amphibians, and reptiles were plentiful.	Seed plants
	Carboniferous Period	Pennsylvanian Period 39 million years	325 million	Scale trees, ferns, and giant scouring rushes were abundant. Fish and amphibians were plentiful. The first reptiles appeared. Giant insects lived in forests where coal later formed.	Reptiles
		Mississippian Period 35 million years	360 million	Trilobites had nearly died out. Crustaceans, fish, and amphibians were plentiful. Many coral reefs were formed.	Amphibians
		Devonian Period 50 million years	410 million	The first forests grew in swamps. Many kinds of fish, including sharks, armored fish, and lungfish, swam in the sea and in fresh waters. The first amphibians and insects appeared.	Fish
		Silurian Period 30 million years	440 million	Spore-bearing land plants appeared. Trilobites and mollusks were common. Coral reefs formed.	Corals
		Ordovician Period 65 million years	505 million	Trilobites, corals, and mollusks were common. Tiny animals called graptolites lived in branching *colonies* (groups).	Graptolites
		Cambrian Period 39 million years	544 million	Fossils were plentiful for the first time. Shelled animals called trilobites, and some mollusks, were common in the sea. Jawless fish appeared.	Trilobites
Precambrian Time Almost 4 billion years (?)			$4\frac{1}{2}$ billion (?)	Coral, jellyfish, and worms lived in the sea about 1,100 million years ago. Bacteria lived as long ago as $3\frac{1}{2}$ billion years. Before that, no living things are known.	Bacteria

Source: From *THE WORLD BOOK ENCYCLOPEDIA,* © 2000, World Book, Inc. By permission of the publisher.

INFORMATION GAP FOR STUDENT B

Student B, read aloud the best completion for each sentence that Student A reads. Circle the correct article or zero article where necessary. Then read the sentence beginnings below.

Student B's completions

   a. (the member / a member) of an order of mammals including dolphins, porpoises, and whales.

   b. the part of the atmosphere that normally has high ozone content and that blocks ultraviolet radiation from entering the lower atmosphere.

   c. the collection of physical, biological, and climatological surroundings in which earth organisms live.

   d. (member / a member) of a higher order of mammals which includes apes and human beings.

   e. a member of a group of lower mammals having (a pouch / the pouch) on the abdomen.

Student B's prompts

Student B, read the next five prompts aloud.

   6. Fluorocarbons are . . .

   7. (A stratosphere / The stratosphere) is . . .

   8. Ozone is . . .

   9. A koala is . . .

   10. A mammal is . . .

MODIFICATION OF NOUNS

GRAMMAR **IN CONTEXT**

QUESTIONS TO CONSIDER

1. What is the difference between hoping for something to happen and expecting it to happen? Discuss this with your classmates.

2. In your experience, does what you expect to happen usually happen? Give an example.

3. How can expectations be a negative force? How can they be a positive force?

Read an article about expectations from Pocket Digest.

The Expectation Syndrome
I Hope for It,
but I Don't Expect It
by JESSICA TAYLOR

PICTURE THE SCENE: It's the seventeenth Winter Olympics in Lillehammer, Norway. Dan Jansen, a famous American speed skater, is about to compete in the 500-meter race. This is the fourth Olympics he has participated in. In the first three races, he failed to win any medals. This will be his last Olympic competition, so the pressure is on. About halfway through the 500, one of Dan's skates catches a rough spot on the ice, and this slows him down. He wins no medal at all. Three days later Dan competes in the 1000-meter race. Everyone knows this is his last chance for a medal. Some observers have already written him off. Dan starts off well. As he is coming around a turn, though, his skate again hits a rough spot on the ice, and he almost falls. Will the outcome be the same? He says to himself that he's just going to keep skating and let what happens happen. In effect, he "casts his fate to the winds" and ceases to worry about the outcome. The result? Dan sets a world record and wins the gold medal. ▶

speed skater Dan Jansen

Picture another situation: Your two best film-buff friends have seen the reissued *Star Wars*, but you haven't seen it yet. They rave about its superb color photography and awesome special effects. They applaud its basically serious and even profound treatment of the age-old conflict between good and evil. They say it's the best American movie of the last half of the century. When you go to see it, though, you're disappointed. You don't find it as excellent as everyone has been saying. In fact, you consider it just another action-adventure flick.

These situations illustrate what we might call "the expectation syndrome," a condition in which events do not turn out as we feel they ought to. Children often do not meet their parents' career expectations of them. Athletes do not always win what people expect them to win. Great literature doesn't always seem as good as it should. I asked psychiatrist Robert Stevens whether there is an actual scientific basis for the negativity of expectations or whether this is merely a philosophical question, an unpleasant, frustrating irony of the human condition.

STEVENS: Well, what we're really talking about here, I think, is the immense power of the mind. For example, there is a documented medical phenomenon called "focal dystonia," which is an abnormal muscle function caused by extreme concentration. Somehow, when athletes are concentrating too hard, they "short circuit" certain brain functions and miss the basket, don't hit the ball, or lose the race. In effect, they're letting their expectations control them. So there's a physiological counterpart to what the mind manifests.

POCKET DIGEST: Have you ever had any experience with this phenomenon in your personal, everyday life?

STEVENS: Yes, I think I have. We're learning more about the human brain all the time. It seems that the mind has immense power for both positive and negative things. Let me give you an example from skiing. There are days when, as a cautious, high-intermediate skier, I stand at the top of a steep, icy slope, plotting my every move down the course, fearing that I'll fall. Sure enough, I do fall. Other days I feel different. My expectations are miles away. I ski well and don't fall. When we focus excessively on goals, our expectations tend to take over and our mind places us outside the process. On the other hand, when we concentrate on the process instead of the goal, we're often much more successful. Have you heard the phrase "trying too hard"?

POCKET DIGEST: Very interesting. What would be your recommendation about expectations, then?

STEVENS: Well, all I've been able to come up with so far is that it's better to hope for things than to expect them.

> In effect, they're **letting their expectations control them.**

UNDERSTANDING MEANING FROM CONTEXT

Circle the letter of the choice closest in meaning to each italicized word or phrase from the reading.

1. Your two best *film-buff* friends have seen the reissued "Star Wars."

   a. film producer   **b.** film lover   **c.** film star

2. They *rave about* its superb color photography and awesome special effects.

   a. report about   **b.** are crazy about   **c.** talk enthusiastically about

3. In effect, he *"casts his fate to the winds"* and ceases to worry about the outcome.

   a. trusts that the winds will be favorable   **b.** waits for favorable winds   **c.** just takes his chances

4. So there's a *physiological* counterpart to what the mind manifests.

   a. emotional   **b.** physical   **c.** psychological

5. So there's a physiological counterpart to what the mind *manifests*.

   a. discloses   **b.** conceals   **c.** maintains

GRAMMAR **PRESENTATION**
MODIFICATION OF NOUNS

ADJECTIVE MODIFIERS		
	MODIFIER(S)	**HEAD NOUN**
Dan Jansen is	a **famous American** speed	skater.
He won in in	a **gold*** the **1000**-meter the **seventeenth** Winter	medal race Olympics.

NOUN MODIFIERS		
	MODIFIER(S)	**HEAD NOUN**
Dan Jansen is	a famous American **speed**	skater.
He won in in	a **gold*** the 1000-**meter** the seventeenth **Winter**	medal race Olympics.

ADJECTIVE AND NOUN MODIFIERS OF THE SAME HEAD NOUN		
	MODIFIER(S)	**HEAD NOUN**
Your	**two best film-buff**	friends have seen the reissued *Star Wars*.
They rave about its and	**superb color** **awesome special**	photography effects.

*The word *gold* can be considered a noun or an adjective, depending on whether it refers to the material or the color.

NOTES	EXAMPLES

1. Nouns can be modified both by adjectives and by other nouns. **Adjective and noun modifiers** usually come before the noun they modify. The noun that is modified is called the **head noun**.

- Dan Jansen, a **famous American speed** skater, is . . .

  adjective modifier — **famous American**
  noun modifier — **speed**

2. When there is more than one modifier, the modifiers generally occur in a fixed order. The following list shows the order that adjectives most often follow*. This order is not invariable and can be affected or changed by the emphasis a speaker wishes to give to a particular adjective. It is unusual for head nouns to have more than three modifiers.

POSITION	TYPE OF MODIFIER	
1	determiners	• a, an, the, this, that, these, those, my, your, Allison's
2	possessive amplifier	• own
3	sequence words	• first, second, tenth, next, last
4	quantifiers	• one, two, few, little, much, many, some
5	opinions or qualities	• ugly, beautiful, dull, interesting, intelligent, wonderful, disgusted, interested
6	size, height, or length	• big, tall, long, short
7	age or temperature	• old, young, hot, cold
8	shapes	• square, round, oval
9	colors	• red, blue, pink, purple
10	nationalities, social classes, or origins	• American, Brazilian, Japanese, eastern, upper-class, lower-middle-class, scientific, historic, mythical
11	materials	• wood, cotton, denim, silk, glass, stone

*Although many authors have developed lists explaining the order of modifiers, the author wishes to acknowledge particularly Thomas Lee Crowell, *Index to Modern English* (New York: McGraw-Hill, 1964).

3. The examples in the right-hand column illustrate modifier order as listed in Note 2. When a noun has two or more modifiers from the same category, their order is difficult to prescribe.

determiner	sequence word	quantifier	head noun
• **the**	**first**	**three**	competitions

determiner	opinion or quality	age	
• **that**	**interesting**	**old**	lady

determiner	size	shape	color	
• **a**	**big**	**round**	**red**	ball

determiner	opinion or quality	age	origin	
• **that**	**beautiful**	**old**	**Russian**	vase

determiner	opinion or quality	age	material	
• **those**	**fragile**	**old**	**porcelain**	vases

4. Noun modifiers always come before the nouns they modify.

When there are both adjective and noun modifiers, the noun modifiers come closest to the head noun.

- A **house guest** is a guest who is visiting and staying in someone's house.
- A **guest house** is a small house for guests to stay in.
- Jansen is a **famous American speed** skater.

5. Compound modifiers are constructed of more than one word. Here are two common kinds of compound modifiers.

a. number + noun

- She has a **ten-year-old** daughter.
  (*She has a daughter who is ten years old.*)

b. noun + past participle

- It's a **crime-related** problem.
  (*It's a problem related to crime.*)

When compound modifiers precede a noun, they are always hyphenated.

▶ **BE CAREFUL!** Note how the plural word in this phrase becomes singular when it comes before the noun.

- It's a race of 500 **meters**.
- It's a 500-**meter** race.
  NOT ~~It's a 500-meters race.~~

6. When a noun has **two or more modifiers**, commas separate only those of equal importance. To decide whether modifiers are of equal importance, place **and** between them. If the meaning of the new phrase is logical, the adjectives are equally important and need to be separated by a comma. If the meaning with **and** is not logical, the adjectives are not equally important and are not separated by a comma.

- a **cautious, high-intermediate** skier
  (A *cautious and high-intermediate skier* sounds logical.)

- an **abnormal muscle** function
  (An *abnormal and muscle function* does not sound logical.)

7. BE CAREFUL! In written English, it is generally recommended to have no more than two nouns together. Using too many nouns together can be confusing. Look at the examples. Is Jerry a student who won an award for painting portraits? Is Jerry a painter who won an award for painting students? Is the award given by the students?

- Jerry Jones won the **student portrait painter** award.

To avoid confusing sentences like this, break up the string of nouns with prepositional phrases or rearrange the modifiers in some other way.

- Jerry Jones won the award for painting portraits of students.

  OR

- Student Jerry Jones won the award for painting portraits.

There is no similar problem with adjective modifiers.

- The clever little brown-and-white fox terrier impressed us all.
  (All the adjectives clearly modify *fox terrier*.)

FOCUSED PRACTICE

1 DISCOVER THE GRAMMAR

*Examine the following sentences from the article that opens this unit or related to the article. Circle all head nouns that have noun or adjective modifiers. Underline adjective modifiers once and noun modifiers twice. Underline only those modifiers that come before the noun. Do not underline determiners in this exercise (**a, an, the, this, that, my, your**, etc.).*

1. It's the <u>seventeenth</u> <u>Winter</u> (Olympics) Lillehammer, Norway.

2. Your two best film-buff friends have seen the reissued *Star Wars*.

3. They rave about its superb color photography and awesome special effects.

4. They applaud its basically serious and even profound treatment of the age-old conflict between good and evil.

5. Children often do not meet their parents' career expectations of them.

6. I asked Robert Stevens whether there is an actual scientific basis for the negativity of expectations.

7. There is a documented medical phenomenon called "focal dystonia," which is an abnormal muscle function caused by extreme concentration.

8. Can we generalize this phenomenon beyond the sports arena into common, everyday occurrences?

9. I stand at the top of a steep, icy slope, plotting my every move down the course.

10. This skiing example illustrates the basic problem of expectations.

11. Right now we're really in the elementary stages of biological and psychiatric brain research.

2 READING ALOUD   Grammar Notes 5, 6

Pam and Alan Murray have taken their son Joshua to Charles Tanaka, a reading specialist, because Joshua cannot read aloud in class. Complete the sentences in their conversation with compound modifiers, using the phrases in parentheses to create a hyphenated phrase.

DR. TANAKA: Joshua, tell me about your problems with reading.

JOSHUA: Well, I get frustrated in my reading class. It's only

<u>   a fifty-minute period   </u>, but to me it seems like a year. This
         1. (a period that lasts fifty minutes)

semester our teacher gives us oral reading assignments every day. She used to call on me to read aloud and I would freeze up, even if it was only

_____. Now she doesn't call on me anymore.
2. (an assignment that is one paragraph long)

DR. TANAKA: But you don't have any problem with silent reading?

JOSHUA: Nope. I can read _____ in a day or two. I love to
3. (a book that is 300 pages long)

read to myself.

PAM: And his reading comprehension is excellent!

DR. TANAKA: Uh-huh. Pam and Alan, how long has this been going on?

ALAN: Since Josh started the first grade—he's twelve now, so it's been

_____ for him and for us.
4. (an ordeal that has lasted six years)

DR. TANAKA: Any idea how this started?

PAM: Well, I definitely think it's _____. Joshua lisped
5. (a problem related to stress)

when he started school. He pronounced all his "s" sounds as "th" sounds.

That might have had something to do with it.

JOSHUA: Yeah! The other kids would laugh at me when I tried to read aloud and get

the "s" sounds right. It just got worse and worse until I couldn't read

anything out loud.

DR. TANAKA: Uh-huh. There is another possibility. Maybe this is just

_____. You might need glasses. Let's test your
6. (a problem related to eyesight)

vision. Look at that eye chart on the wall and say the letters on the fifth line.

JOSHUA: *[reads]* X-Z-Q-A-M-W.

DR. TANAKA: OK. Now the seventh line.

JOSHUA: *[reads]* P-S-R-B-N-F.

DR. TANAKA: Hmm. OK, now the bottom two lines. Look carefully. They make a sentence.

JOSHUA: *[reads]* "Night was falling in Dodge City. The gunslinger walked down the

street wearing _____."
7. (a hat that holds ten gallons)

DR. TANAKA: Very good! I think I understand. It sounds like you have what we call

_____. You're anxious about being asked to
8. (anxiety induced by performance)

perform, and you expect to read poorly aloud, so you do. But you just

(continued on next page)

showed me you can read fine out loud when you're not thinking about it. I

distracted you when I told you I wanted to test your eyes.

JOSHUA: Wow! No kidding?

DR. TANAKA: That's right. It's not going to be that hard to help you, either. I've got

_____ that should have you reading perfectly—if

     9. (a program that takes two months)

you're game to try it. What do you think?

JOSHUA: I sure am. When can we start?

3 **PARTY EXPECTATIONS**   Grammar Notes 2, 3, 5, 6

Bill and Nancy, a young married couple, are going to attend a party at the home
of Nancy's new boss. They are trying to dress for the occasion and aren't sure
what is expected, and Nancy is very worried about making a good impression.
Unscramble the sentences in their conversation.

BILL: This is _____ a formal office party _____, isn't it? What if I wear

     1. (party / office / formal / a)

_____ ?

     2. (tie / my / silk / new)

NANCY: That's fine, but don't wear _____ with it.

     3. (shirt / purple / ugly / that / denim)

People will think you don't have _____ .

     4. (clothes / any / suitable / dress-up)

BILL: So what? Why should I pretend I like to dress up when I don't?

NANCY: Because there are going to be _____ , and I have

     5. (people / business / a lot of / important / there)

to make _____ . It's my job, remember? I don't

     6. (impression / a / intelligent / , / good)

want people to think I have _____ for a

     7. (dresser / unstylish / a / , / sloppy)

husband, which of course you're not. Humor me just this once, OK, Sweetie?

Hmm . . . I wonder if I should wear _____ or

     8. (round / my / earrings / sapphire / blue)

_____ .

     9. (green / oval / ones / emerald / the)

[Later, at the party]

NANCY: Hi, Paul. This is Bill, my husband.

PAUL: Welcome. Bill, I'm glad to know you. You two are

_____ to arrive. Help yourselves to snacks.

     10. (guests / two / first / our)

There are _____. Please make
      11. (sandwiches / excellent / some / tomato and fresh mozzarella cheese)

yourselves at home. You know, Nancy, I'm sorry I didn't make it clear that this isn't

_____. You two really look great, but I hope you
    12. (elegant / party / dress-up / , / an)

won't feel out of place.

BILL: Thanks. By the way, Paul, I really like _____
                                         13. (beautiful / shirt / purple / denim / that)

you're wearing. Where did you get it?

④ EDITING

Every week or two, medical student Jennifer Yu writes in her computer diary.
Find and correct the thirteen modification errors here.

Dear Diary:

    It's 12:00 midnight, the end of ~~day a long~~ *a long day*. My two first weeks of school medical are

over, and I'm exhausted but exhilarated! I'm so glad I decided to go to medical school. It was

definitely right the decision. I'm not completely sure yet, but I think I want to go into

psychiatry child clinical because I love working with children.

    Yesterday our child psychology class visited a hospital local where disturbed children

many go for treatment. I expected to see a lot of boys and girls acting out, but most of them

were pretty quiet and relaxed. They just looked like they needed some personal attention.

    Today in our class medical surgery we had a teacher student, male young a intern who

was filling in for professor our usual. It was really interesting to get viewpoint a student

on things.

    Only the thing I don't like about medical school is the tasteless cafeteria food! I'm going

to have to start taking lunch my own brownbag.

    Well, Diary, it's time for me to get some sleep. I hope this new computer program works

correctly. I'll write again soon.

COMMUNICATION PRACTICE

⑤ LISTENING

Joshua Murray is working on his reading program with Dr. Tanaka. Listen to their conversation.

Comprehension

Mark **True**, **False**, *or* **I don't know** *for each sentence.*

	True	False	I don't know
1. The first session will last only thirty minutes.	❑	❑	❑
2. Joshua likes his own voice.	❑	❑	❑
3. A growth spurt often occurs during adolescence.	❑	❑	❑
4. Joshua is thirteen years old.	❑	❑	❑
5. Joshua is afraid of reading orally.	❑	❑	❑
6. The phrase that Joshua will say to distract himself will not be difficult to remember.	❑	❑	❑
7. In the story Joshua reads, people feel lonely.	❑	❑	❑
8. The people in the story have three dogs.	❑	❑	❑
9. Large, warm, and furry dogs can keep you warm on a cold night.	❑	❑	❑

Optional Dictation

Now listen again and fill in the blanks. Place commas between adjectives when the speaker pauses, and be sure to hyphenate compound modifiers.

1. Our first meeting is only going to be <u>a thirty-minute session</u> .

2. We don't want to make this _____.

3. I feel like _____.

4. And I feel like I have _____.

5. You're just going through _____.

6. It happens to _____.

7. The key to getting you over this _____

is to distract you from thinking about how well you're doing.

8. Let's think of _____

that you can keep in the back of your mind.

9. "It was _____."

10. "It promised to be one of _____."

11. What's _____?

12. It's a night that's so cold that you need _____

to sleep with to keep you warm.

---

6 **TAPE DISCUSSION**

1. How does Joshua feel at the end of the conversation?

2. How can developmental problems like Joshua's affect a person's life? Do you know any examples you can share with the class?

3. If you had a friend with a similar problem, what advice would you give?

---

7 **INFORMATION GAP: BASEBALL**

Work with a partner.

Student A: Add a noun or adjective modifier to each definition and read it to Student B. Student B has ten seconds to identify what you are referring to. If Student B doesn't understand, repeat your sentence. Then listen to Student B's definitions.

Student B, turn to page 151 and follow the instructions.

> **EXAMPLE:**
> **STUDENT A:** They can throw a baseball at _____high_____ speeds.
> **STUDENT B:** Baseball pitchers.

Definitions

1. He hits the ball with a _____, smooth stick.

2. He wears a _____ mask to protect his face.

3. Mark McGwire holds the record for hitting the most of these in _____

season.

4. To hit a home run, a batter has to run around the _____ bases and land

on this.

5. This is _____ name for a baseball field.

(continued on next page)

Answers

1. the batter

2. the catcher

3. home runs

4. home plate

5. the diamond

8 A POEM

Read and think about the poem. Think particularly about how the poem deals with the question of expectations.

CASEY AT THE BAT

By Ernest L. Thayer

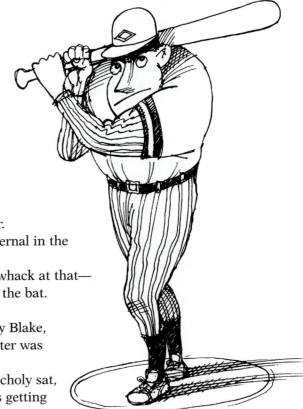

The outlook wasn't brilliant for the
  Mudville nine that day;
The score stood four to two, with but
  one inning more to play;
And so, when Cooney died at first, and
  Barrows did the same,
A sickly silence fell upon the patrons
  of the game.

A straggling few got up to go in deep despair.
The rest clung to that hope which springs eternal in the
  human breast;
They thought, if only Casey could but get a whack at that—
We'd put up even money now, with Casey at the bat.

But Flynn preceded Casey, as did also Jimmy Blake,
And the former was a pudding, while the latter was
  a fake;
So upon that stricken multitude grim melancholy sat,
For there seemed but little chance of Casey's getting
  to the bat.

But Flynn let drive a single, to the wonderment of all,
And Blake, the much despised, tore the cover off the ball;
And when the dust had lifted, and men saw what had occurred,
There was Jimmy safe at second and Flynn a-hugging third.

Then from the gladdened multitude went up a joyous yell;
It bounded from the mountain-top, and rattled in the dell;
It struck upon the hillside, and recoiled upon the flat,
For Casey, mighty Casey, was advancing to the bat.

There was ease in Casey's manner as he stepped into his place,
There was pride in Casey's bearing, and a smile on Casey's face.
And when, responding to the cheers, he lightly doffed his hat,
No stranger in the crowd could doubt 'twas Casey at the bat.

Ten thousand eyes were on him as he rubbed his hands with dirt,
Five thousand tongues applauded when he wiped them on his shirt;
Then while the writhing pitcher ground the ball into his hip,
Defiance gleamed in Casey's eye, a sneer curled Casey's lip.

And now the leather-covered sphere came hurtling through the air,
And Casey stood a-watching it in haughty grandeur there;
Close by the sturdy batsman the ball unheeded sped.
"That ain't my style," said Casey. "Strike one," the umpire said.

From the benches, black with people, there went up a muffled roar,
Like the beating of the storm-waves on a stern and distant shore;
"Kill him! Kill the umpire!" shouted someone in the stand.
And it's likely they'd have killed him had not Casey raised his hand.

With a smile of Christian charity great Casey's visage shone;
He stilled the rising tumult; he bade the game go on;
He signalled to the pitcher, and once more the spheroid flew,
But Casey still ignored it, and the umpire said "Strike two."

"Fraud!" cried the maddened thousands, and the echo answered, "Fraud!"
But a scornful look from Casey, and the audience was awed;
They saw his face grow stern and cold, they saw his muscles strain,
And they knew that Casey wouldn't let that ball go by again.

The sneer is gone from Casey's lip, his teeth are clenched in hate,
He pounds with cruel violence his bat upon the plate;
And now the pitcher holds the ball, and now he lets it go,
And now the air is shattered by the force of Casey's blow.

Oh, somewhere in this favored land the sun is shining bright,
The band is playing somewhere, and somewhere hearts are light;
And somewhere men are laughing, and somewhere children shout;
But there is no joy in Mudville—mighty Casey has struck out.

Source: Historybuff.com/library

Discussion

1. What does this poem show about expectations?

2. Why do you think Casey struck out?

9 ESSAY

Have you ever expected something to happen and it didn't? You didn't win the game, get an A, win the election, and so on. Write two or three paragraphs telling what happened. Try to explain why it happened. Did it have anything to do with the expectation syndrome?

10 PICTURE DISCUSSION

Select one student who likes to draw to go to the board. (This person does not look at the picture.) Then study the picture of the dining room and describe it in as much detail as you can to the student standing at the board. The student at the board draws the dining room, based on your descriptions. When that student has finished drawing, discuss what is out of place or unusual about what the student at the board has drawn.

INFORMATION GAP FOR STUDENT B

Listen to Student A read the definitions. You have ten seconds to guess the items your partner is referring to. If you do not understand, Student A will repeat the definition.

Add a noun or adjective modifier to each definition and read it to Student A. Student A has ten seconds to identify what you are referring to. If Student A doesn't understand, repeat your sentence.

EXAMPLE

STUDENT B: This _____keen-eyed_____ person stands behind the catcher and decides whether or not the ball thrown is a strike.

STUDENT A: The umpire.

Definitions

1. This is a _____-member group of players.

2. This happens when a batter takes a _____ swing and misses the ball.

3. This is the name for a one-_____ hit.

4. This is the name for a two-_____ hit.

5. This is the name for a three-_____ hit.

Answers

1. a baseball team

2. a strike

3. a single

4. a double

5. a triple

9

QUANTIFIERS

GRAMMAR **IN CONTEXT**

QUESTIONS TO CONSIDER

1. Do you pay for most things with cash or with credit cards?
2. What would be the advantages and disadvantages of living in a cashless society?

Read an article about money.

What's Happening to Ca$h?

A major event took place on January 1, 1999. The Euro made its debut in most of the countries of the European Union. What is the Euro? It's a single currency that, by the year 2002, will replace most of the individual European currencies—like the German mark, the French franc, and the Spanish peseta. The debut of the Euro seems destined to accelerate a trend that has been developing for many years now: the movement toward the cashless society.

Not all of the countries of the European Union are using the Euro. Britain, Sweden, and Denmark, for the time being at least, are maintaining their own currencies. Even so, the Euro will have a great many significant effects not only on European finance but also on that of the world in general. There won't be any Euro coins and bills for a

DO YOU TAKE ANY CREDIT CARDS?

while, but people will be able to use either checks or debit and credit cards to make a lot of their purchases. The European phenomenon will accelerate the trend worldwide to use less cash and more "electronic" money. Is this positive or negative? Or is it just neutral, neither a good nor a bad thing?

Are there any advantages to cash? Yes, of course. Suppose, for example, that you are walking down a street and you remember that you need to buy some flowers. You see a flower vendor, and you suddenly decide that this is the time to buy a dozen roses. So what do you do? Write a check, or pull out your debit or credit card? At this writing, few flower vendors take checks, and even fewer take plastic. Most of them prefer cold, hard cash. If you've got a little money with you, you simply pull out a few bills, hand them to the vendor, and happily walk away with your flowers. Pretty easy, huh? It wouldn't be that easy without cash.

Or suppose you're at an athletic event—a soccer match, a basketball game, or a volleyball tournament. Suddenly you realize you're hungry. You walk out to the concession stand to buy a couple of hot dogs. How would that work in a cashless society? Can you imagine pulling out a credit or debit card to pay for a hot dog? So cash has its advantages.

Of course, cash has a good many disadvantages as well. For one thing, it's easy to be robbed. For another, cash is heavy. Carrying a lot of coins can make holes in your pockets. It's inconvenient to take a great deal of money with you to pay for large purchases. Imagine trying to carry enough cash to pay for a house, or a car—or even a sofa.

Now there are also a number of advantages to electronic money. Think about it. You're traveling in Europe. Anyone who did this in the past knows that it was a bit of a pain to have to learn a new money system every time you crossed a border. Now, however, Euro prices are standardized, and you don't have to worry about whether a certain amount of your money will bring a different rate each time it's changed into a different local currency. What if things were that way everywhere? Wouldn't it be simpler?

Then there's the matter of bill paying. Traditionally, most people in North America have paid their bills with checks. Recently, however, a trend has developed to have bills paid automatically. Japanese people have been doing this for years. In Japan, payment for such things as heat, electricity, and water is handled by automatic electronic deduction from a bank account. It's much easier than having to write several different checks to several different agencies. And since it's automatic, people don't have to worry about whether they've forgotten to pay their bill.

Of course, there are certain disadvantages to electronic money, too. Some people have little use for plastic cards, saying that using them encourages us to live beyond our means. Others say that using electronic money places too much control of our personal finances in the hands of strangers. Mistakes are easily made.

The jury is still out on whether the trend toward less and less use of cash is good or bad. What seems clear is that it's definitely on its way.

UNDERSTANDING MEANING FROM CONTEXT

Circle the letter of the choice closest in meaning to each italicized word or phrase from the reading.

1. The Euro *made its debut* in most of the countries of the European Union.

    a. had a significant effect
    b. made its first appearance
    c. was proposed

2. The debut of the Euro *seems destined to* accelerate a trend that has been developing for many years now.

    a. it's possible that it will
    b. it's probable that it will
    c. it's unfortunate that it will

3. You walk out to the *concession stand* to buy a couple of hot dogs.

    a. food and drink stand
    b. vending machine
    c. restaurant

4. Some people have little use for plastic cards, saying that using them encourages us to *live beyond our means*.

    a. spend more money than we have
    b. spend money responsibly
    c. spend very little

5. *The jury is still out on* whether the trend toward less and less use of cash is good or bad.

    a. There are court cases to decide
    b. It's obvious
    c. It's not yet clear

GRAMMAR **PRESENTATION**
QUANTIFIERS OF NOUNS

QUANTIFIERS USED WITH SINGULAR COUNT NOUNS

It was a bit of a pain to have to learn a new money system **every** time you crossed a border.

. . . whether a certain amount of your money will bring a different rate **each** time it's changed into a different local currency . . .

You can use **either** currency in this country.

Or is it just neutral, **neither** a good nor a bad thing?

QUANTIFIERS USED WITH PLURAL COUNT NOUNS

. . . you simply pull out **a few** bills . . .

. . . **few** flower vendors take checks . . .

. . . and even **fewer** take plastic.

. . . a trend that has been developing for **many** years now . . .

. . . the Euro will have **a great many** significant effects . . .

Of course, cash has **a good many** disadvantages as well.

It's much easier than having to write **several** different checks to **several** different agencies.

Now there are **a number of** advantages to electronic money.

You walk out to the concession stand to buy **a couple of** hot dogs.

. . . you suddenly decide that this is the time to buy **a dozen** roses.

People will be able to use **either** checks or credit and debit cards to make some of their purchases.

Of course, there are **certain** disadvantages to electronic money, too.

QUANTIFIERS USED WITH NON-COUNT NOUNS

If you've got **a little** money with you . . .

Some people have **little** use for plastic cards . . .

The European phenomenon will accelerate the trend to use **less** cash and **more** electronic money.

It's inconvenient to take **a great deal of** money with you to pay for large purchases.

Others say that using electronic money places too **much** control of our personal finances in the hands of strangers.

. . . it was **a bit of** a pain to have to learn a new money system every time you crossed a border.

QUANTIFIERS USED WITH NON-COUNT NOUNS AND PLURAL COUNT NOUNS

NON-COUNT NOUNS

I've got **a lot of** (**lots of**) cash on me.

She has **no** money at all.

The European phenomenon will accelerate the trend worldwide to use **less** cash and **more** electronic money.

The children have already spent **most of** their allowance.

I need **some** financial advice.

I've got **plenty of** plastic but no cash.

None of the work is finished.

Did you save **any** money?

All of the cash has been spent.

Imagine trying to carry **enough** cash to pay for a house, or a car . . .

PLURAL COUNT NOUNS

Carrying **a lot of** (**lots of**) coins can make holes in your pockets.

I have **no** credit cards with me.

We made **more** purchases on this year's vacation than last year's.

The Euro made its debut in **most of** the countries of the European Union.

. . . you remember that you need to buy **some** flowers.

Plenty of us are credit card junkies.

None of the bills have been paid.

Do you take **any** credit cards?

Not **all** (**of**) the countries of the European Union are using the Euro.

I have **enough** financial problems to see a consultant.

NOTES	EXAMPLES
1. Quantifiers state precisely or suggest generally the amount or number of something. English has many expressions to quantify nouns and pronouns. These are comprised of phrases or single words that come before the noun or pronoun.	• You suddenly decide that this is the time to buy **a dozen** roses. • Are there **any** advantages to cash?
2. Certain quantifiers are used with singular count nouns; others are used with plural count nouns; others are used with non-count nouns; and still others are used with count and non-count nouns.	
a. *Each, either, every,* and *neither* are used with singular count nouns.	• It was a pain to learn a new money system **every** time you crossed a border. • Or is it **neither** a good nor a bad thing?
b. *Both (of), a bunch (of), a couple (of), either of, neither of, a few (of), fewer (of), a great many (of), a good many (of), many (of), a number of,* and *several (of)* are used with plural count nouns.	• It's much easier than having to write **several** different checks to **several** different agencies. • The Euro will have **a great many** significant effects.
c. *A bit of, a great deal of, less, little (of), a little (of),* and *much (of)* are used with non-count nouns.	• It was **a bit of** a pain to have to learn a new money system every time you crossed a border.
d. *All (of), any (of), enough (of), half (of), a lot of, lots of, most of, no, none, none of, some (of),* and *(ten) percent (of)* are used with non-count nouns and plural count nouns.	• Not **all (of)** the countries of the European Union are using the Euro. • I spent **all (of)** my money. • The Euro made its debut in **most of** the countries of the European Union. • My son spent **all (of)** his allowance.

(continued on next page)

3. Many quantifiers appear in phrases with the preposition *of*. The *of* is used when the speaker or writer is specifying particular persons, places, things, or groups.

When speakers or writers make general statements, having no particular persons, places, or things in mind, they use quantifiers without *of*.

- **Most of** the countries of the European Union are using the Euro.
  (*The speaker has in mind a group of countries.*)

- **Most people** don't really understand finance.
  (*people in general—no specific group*)

4. In **spoken affirmative sentences**, native speakers usually prefer *a lot of* or *lots of* to *much* and *many*, which sound more formal. However, *much* and *many* are often used in negative sentences and in questions.

- Carrying **a lot of coins** can make holes in your pockets.
- Do you have **much cash** with you?
- Do you have **many** credit **cards**?

5. Note the characteristics of *some* and *any*. Use *some* with plural count nouns and non-count nouns in affirmative statements.

Use *any* with plural count nouns and non-count nouns in negative statements.

Use both *some* and *any* in questions. *Any* is generally preferred in negative questions.

- You need to buy **some flowers**.
- We need to take **some money** with us.

- There won't be **any** Euro **coins**.
- I don't have **any cash** on me.

- Are there **any** advantages to cash?
- Are there **some** advantages to cash?

6. Note that when *any* is used in affirmative statements it doesn't quantify. It refers to an unspecified person, place, or thing.

- **Any** of these currencies can be used in Europe.

7. Note the difference between *less* and *fewer* and between *amount* and *number*. *Less* and *amount* are used with non-count nouns, while *fewer* and *number* are used with count nouns.

- The European phenonmenon will accelerate the trend to use **less cash** and more electronic money.
- Even **fewer [vendors]** take plastic.
- . . . whether a certain **amount of** your **money** will bring a different rate each time it's changed . . .
- Now there are also **a number of** advantages to electronic money.

8. Note the difference between *a few* and *few*, *a little* and *little*.

- You simply pull out **a few** bills.
  (You pull out some bills.)
- **Few** vendors take checks.
  (Not many vendors take checks.)
- If you've got **a little** money with you . . .
  (If you've got some money with you . . .)
- Some people have **little** use for plastic cards.
  (Some people don't have much use for plastic cards.)

9. BE CAREFUL! The quantifiers *some of, any of, most of, half of, (ten) percent of,* and *none of* can be followed by a singular or a plural verb, depending on the noun before the verb.

- **Most of** the money **has** been spent.
- **Most of** the European Union countries **are** using the Euro.

FOCUSED PRACTICE

1 DISCOVER THE GRAMMAR

Look again at some of the sentences from What's Happening to Cash? *In each case, say whether or not the word in parentheses could be used to replace the italicized word or phrase without changing the meaning or creating an incorrect sentence. If not, explain why.*

1. Even so, the Euro will have *a great many* significant effects. (many)

2. There won't be *any* Euro coins and bills for a while. (some)

3. Are there *any* advantages to cash? (some)

4. You remember that you need to buy *some* flowers. (any)

5. At this writing, *few* flower vendors take checks . . . (a few)

6. . . . and even *fewer* take plastic. (less)

7. If you've got *a little* money with you . . . (little)

8. . . . you simply pull out *a few* bills. (few)

9. Of course, cash has *a good many* disadvantages as well. (a great many)

10. Carrying *a lot of* coins can make holes in your pockets. (many)

11. Some people have *little* use for plastic cards. (a little)

12. The jury is still out on whether the trend toward *less and less* use of cash is good or bad. (fewer and fewer)

2 SAVING FOR A TRIP   Grammar Notes 2–5, 7, 9

Married couple Ron and Ashley Lamont are trying to save money for a trip to Europe. They are examining their budget. Fill in the blanks in their conversation with expressions from the box. You will use each expression once.

some	the amount of	plenty of	most of
both of	~~a lot of~~	the number of	fewer
less	one of	both	much
neither one of	many	every	

ASHLEY: Honey, we're still spending ___*a lot of*___ money on things we don't really
1.

need. After I pay the bills, we're going to have _____ cash left over
2.

than we did last month. And we were supposed to be saving for the trip to

Europe, remember? If we don't start saving more money, we won't be able to go.

RON: What have we bought that we don't need?

ASHLEY: That new exercise machine, for one thing. _____ us has used it more
3.
than two or three times since we bought it. We could get a year's membership at
the athletic club for _____ money that it cost and still have money
4.
left over.

RON: You mean _____ us could get a membership?
5.

ASHLEY: No, _____ us could. That's what I'm saying. The machine cost $300,
6.
and memberships are $100 each. Let's sell the thing and start going to the athletic
club.

RON: Hmm . . . maybe you're right. What else?

ASHLEY: Well, we're spending more than ten dollars a month extra on those premium
cable channels. We'd have _____ channels to choose from if we cut
7.
back to the basic coverage, but we don't watch _____ TV anyway.
8.

RON: Yeah, you're right. . . . And based on _____ times we've actually used
9.
it, I'd say we could get rid of call waiting on the phone. Even though it hasn't
happened very _____ times, _____ my friends say they
10.   11.
hate it when they call and then another call comes in while we're talking.

ASHLEY: Uh-huh. Let's cancel it, then. And one more suggestion. We should

_____ start taking a brownbag lunch to work instead of going out at
12.
noon. If we did these four things, we'd have _____ money left over
13.
_____ month that could go into our trip fund.
14.

RON: Oh, no! Not my lunches with the boys! Lunchtime is when I get to see them.

ASHLEY: Invite the boys over to play _____ volleyball. Then think of Paris.
15.

❸ THE EURO

Read the following article about the Euro. Then work with a partner. Together, complete the text with appropriate quantifiers. Discuss your selections.

TRAVEL GUIDE

TRAVELERS WILL BENEFIT FROM EURO

LONDON (AP)—Trying to keep track of expenses while traveling around Europe can feel like a never-ending math test, converting every price into dollars. Make a mistake, and you might get fleeced like a Shetland sheep.

The creation of the Euro, a common currency for _____*eleven*_____ European nations,
1.
will bring short-term headaches to travelers, but _____ long-term benefits.
2.

The headaches stem from the fact that _____ actual Euro notes or coins
3.
will be available until 2002, even though the Euro will officially exist in bank accounts beginning January 1.

You should be able to charge purchases on your credit card in Euros in _____
4.
places, especially tourist destinations, but _____ cash transactions will have
5.
to be made in local currencies.

Two Prices

During the three-year transition before the Euro fully takes over, travelers will see _____ goods with two prices, one
6.
in local currency and the equivalent in Euros.

More math mayhem? Perhaps not.

You'll still have to fork over francs to get what you want in France, but the Euro number can be useful for comparing prices across borders and for figuring out dollar equivalents.

Because the eleven currencies will have permanently fixed rates against the Euro, you no longer have to keep track of eleven exchange rates, just one: the dollar–Euro rate. No more dividing _____ price by
7.
1,600 in Italy and 5.6 in France.

What's more, the Euro's value is expected to be fairly close to the dollar's, meaning a lot _____ long division and a welcome
8.
relief for the mathematically challenged.

Comparison Shopping

Comparison shopping across the borders will be a snap. A hotel room in Paris for 850 francs might seem like a bargain compared with one that costs 225,000 lire in Rome. But not when you see that the Paris room is 130 Euros vs. 115 Euros for the one in Italy.

Some people who travel frequently to Europe are already looking forward to the Euro, even if it means seeing double on _____ price tags for three years.

9.

Richard Schroeter, an agricultural trade consultant based in Washington, says the Euro should be "a real plus" for frequent travelers to Europe such as himself.

"It gets very confusing figuring out how _____ things cost. Trying to go from

10.

shopping in Belgium to shopping in Italy is quite a change," Schroeter said. "Now, it's as if you were traveling through the United States and every state had a different currency."

Source: The Associated Press, *CBS Market Watch Report,* December 30, 1998.

4 EDITING

Read the following excerpt from the president's speech to the nation. Find and correct the eight errors in his speech which the proofreader did not find.

 "MY FELLOW CITIZENS. We're at a time in our history when we need to make some real sacrifices. Recent presidents have made a great many pledges they didn't keep. You may not like everything I tell you tonight, but you deserve to hear the truth. On the economy, we've made ˄*a* little progress, but we still have a great deal more to do, so there are several things I'm proposing. First, I want to raise taxes on the very wealthy because a few of them are really paying their share. Second, the amount of middle-class people shouldering an unfair share of the tax burden is too great, so I'm asking for a tax cut for the middle class. If I'm successful, most of you in the middle class will be paying ten percent less in taxes next year, though few of you in the higher-income brackets might see your taxes rise little. How do I intend to make up the lost revenue? The problem with the national income tax is that there are much loopholes in the current law which allow any people to avoid paying any taxes at all. My additional plan is to replace the lost revenue with a national sales tax, which is fairer because it applies to all people equally. Third, we have no money to finance health care reform, and we've made a little progress in reducing pollution and meeting clean air standards. Therefore, I am asking for a fifty-cent-a-gallon tax on gasoline. With a great many more people using mass transit, and with the amount of additional revenue, we will be able to finance our new health care program and help the environment at the same time."

COMMUNICATION PRACTICE

5 LISTENING

Jack Andrews, who is three months behind on his loan payments, is talking on the telephone with Nancy Grant, the loan officer at his bank. Listen to their conversation.

Comprehension

*Now listen again and respond **True (T)** or **False (F)** to the following statements.*

_____ **1.** Jack can't pay the bank right away.

_____ **2.** Jack has always made his payments on time.

_____ **3.** Jack will earn more money in his new job than he did in his old job.

_____ **4.** At first, Nancy doesn't want to recommend an extension of Jack's time to pay.

_____ **5.** Jack has to pay something right away, or Nancy will turn his account over to a collection agency.

_____ **6.** Nancy says Jack has to make his full payment immediately.

_____ **7.** Jack asks for a lot of time to come up with some money.

_____ **8.** Nancy can help Jack a lot even if he doesn't make a payment.

Optional Dictation

Now listen once more and fill in the blanks in the text.

(telephone rings)

GRANT: United Central Bank. This is Nancy Grant speaking. May I help you?

ANDREWS: Hello, Ms. Grant? This is Jack Andrews.

GRANT: Oh, yes, hello, Mr. Andrews. What can I do for you?

ANDREWS: I wanted to ask if I could have _____a little more time_____ on this month's
                                                              1.
payment.

GRANT: OK. Let me just look at your file. Hmm . . . well, we've received

_____ for three months, and your file shows that
           2.

_____ have been made on time since you took out the loan.
           3.

I'm sorry, but I can't recommend _____.
                                              4.

ANDREWS: I know, Ms. Grant, but I just started a new job. I'll be earning

_____ than I did in my last position, but I won't be getting
        5.

paid for a month.

GRANT: Well, Mr. Andrews, we try to be helpful here, but we do have

_____ that we have to uphold. There's _____
        6.   **7.**

I can do at this point. In fact, I'm going to have to turn your account over to a

collection agency if you don't pay at least _____ on your
        8.

outstanding balance.

ANDREWS: Could I have just _____ to try to come up with
        9.

_____? I'm sure I can arrange something if I can have just
        10.

_____.
        11.

GRANT: _____ would you need?
        12.

ANDREWS: How about ten days?

GRANT: All right, Mr. Andrews. If you can make a payment within ten days, we'll reopen

your account. I can't do _____ for you otherwise.
        13.

ANDREWS: Thank you, Ms. Grant.

❻ THE NUMBERS GAME

*Look at the exchange chart. Play in teams of four to six students. Team B, turn to
page 167. Team A asks Team B the six questions that appear on page 166. Then
Team B asks Team A six questions. Score points.*

CURRENCY LAST TRADE	U.S. $ N / A	Aust $ Jan 8	U.K. £ Jan 8	Can $ Jan 8	DMark Jan 8	FFranc Jan 8	¥en Jan 8	SFranc Jan 8	Euro Jan 8
U.S. $	1	0.6348	1.645	0.6614	0.5929	0.1768	0.009013	0.7195	1.159
Aust $	1.575	1	2.591	1.042	0.934	0.2785	0.0142	1.133	1.826
U.K. £	0.608	0.386	1	0.4021	0.3605	0.1075	0.00548	0.4375	0.7049
Can $	1.512	0.9598	2.487	1	0.8964	0.2673	0.01363	1.088	1.753
DMark	1.687	1.071	2.774	1.116	1	0.2981	0.0152	1.214	1.955
FFranc	5.657	3.591	9.304	3.742	3.354	1	0.05099	4.07	6.559
¥en	111	70.43	182.5	73.38	65.78	19.61	1	79.83	128.6
SFranc	1.39	0.8823	2.286	0.9192	0.824	0.2457	0.01253	1	1.611
Euro	0.8625	0.5475	1.419	0.5705	0.5114	0.1525	0.007774	0.6206	1

Team A's Questions:

1. Andrew has 10,000 pounds in his savings account. Roberta has 10,000 dollars in hers. In terms of absolute value, who has less money?

2. The Euro is currently trading at $1.16 to the dollar. Will it take fewer dollars or fewer Euros to purchase something?

3. A tourist from France and another tourist from Germany both want to buy the same item. Will it take more francs or more marks to make the purchase?

4. A tourist from Canada wants to buy something in the United States. She has $400 Canadian. The price is $350 U.S. Will she have enough money?

5. Will it take fewer Swiss francs or French francs to purchase an item?

6. A tourist from Japan is traveling in Europe and has only traveler's checks in denominations of 1,000 yen. He wants to buy something that costs one Euro. How much money will he have to change?

 **ESSAY**

Have you ever had a problem figuring out the currency when you visited another country? Did you perhaps tip the waiter $10 instead of $1 by mistake? Did something amusing happen? Something not so funny? Write two or three paragraphs telling your story.

8 PICTURE DISCUSSION

Talk with a partner. Explain what is happening. What is the problem? What would you do if you were in this situation?

THE NUMBERS GAME FOR TEAM B

Look at the exchange chart. Play in teams of four to six students. Team A asks Team B six questions. Then Team B asks Team A six questions. Score points.

CURRENCY LAST TRADE	U.S. $ N/A	Aust $ Jan 8	U.K. £ Jan 8	Can $ Jan 8	DMark Jan 8	FFranc Jan 8	¥en Jan 8	SFranc Jan 8	Euro Jan 8
U.S. $	1	0.6348	1.645	0.6614	0.5929	0.1768	0.009013	0.7195	1.159
Aust $	1.575	1	2.591	1.042	0.934	0.2785	0.0142	1.133	1.826
U.K. £	0.608	0.386	1	0.4021	0.3605	0.1075	0.00548	0.4375	0.7049
Can $	1.512	0.9598	2.487	1	0.8964	0.2673	0.01363	1.088	1.753
DMark	1.687	1.071	2.774	1.116	1	0.2981	0.0152	1.214	1.955
FFranc	5.657	3.591	9.304	3.742	3.354	1	0.05099	4.07	6.559
¥en	111	70.43	182.5	73.38	65.78	19.61	1	79.83	128.6
SFranc	1.39	0.8823	2.286	0.9192	0.824	0.2457	0.01253	1	1.611
Euro	0.8625	0.5475	1.419	0.5705	0.5114	0.1525	0.007774	0.6206	1

Team B's Questions

1. A tourist has 100 Canadian dollars and 100 Australian dollars. He wants to change them into French francs. Will he get more francs for the Canadian money or for the Australian money?

2. In a duty-free shop at an airport, a tourist sees two items she would like to buy. One costs two French francs, and the other costs two Swiss francs. Which item costs less?

3. Two tourists came back from a trip to Europe. One had 100 German marks. The other had 100 Australian dollars. In terms of absolute value, who had more money?

4. A tourist had only 1,000 yen. He wanted to buy something that cost 20 U.S. dollars. Did he have enough money?

5. Will it take fewer British pounds or U.S. dollars to purchase something?

6. A German tourist wants to buy something that costs 10 Australian dollars. He has only traveler's checks in denominations of 10 marks each. How many traveler's checks will he have to change?

REVIEW OR SELFTEST

I. *Complete each item with* **a / an** *or* **the**. *Leave a blank if no article is needed.*

CYCLONES

According to ___the___ National Weather Service, _____ cyclones
        1.   **2.**

are _____ areas of circulating winds that rotate counterclockwise in
    3.

_____ Northern Hemisphere and clockwise in _____ Southern
4.   **5.**

Hemisphere. They are generally accompanied by some kind of _____
                                           6.

precipitation and by _____ stormy weather. _____ tornadoes and
             7.   **8.**

_____ hurricanes are _____ types of cyclones, as are _____
9.   **10.**   **11.**

typhoons, which are _____ storms that occur in _____ western
            12.   **13.**

Pacific Ocean.

_____ hurricane is _____ cyclone that forms over _____
14.   **15.**   **16.**

tropical oceans and seas and has _____ winds of at least seventy-four
                          17.

miles _____ hour. _____ hurricane rotates in _____ shape
     18.   **19.**   **20.**

of _____ oval or _____ circle. _____ hurricanes can cause
   21.   **22.**   **23.**

_____ great environmental damage. _____ Hurricane Andrew,
24.   **25.**

which hit _____ coasts of Louisiana and southern Florida in August
        26.

1992, caused _____ extreme devastation. In terms of _____
        27.   **28.**

environmental damage, _____ Hurricane Andrew is one of _____
              29.   **30.**

most devastating hurricanes ever to hit _____ United States. Fourteen
                        31.

people died because of _____ Andrew's effects.
           32.

II. *Each of the following sentences contains one error in the use of articles. Correct each sentence by rewriting each incorrect phrase.*

1. One of the best things we can do to help the environment is to encourage the recycling.

   <u>. . . to encourage recycling.</u>

2. Bats are mammals, not the birds.

   _____

3. An orangutan is anthropoid ape dwelling in the jungles of Borneo and Sumatra.

   _____

4. The Mesozoic era was third of the four major eras of geologic time.

   _____

5. Jurassic period was the period of the Mesozoic era when dinosaurs were present and birds first appeared.

   _____

6. The Milky Way galaxy is galaxy to which the sun and the solar system belong.

   _____

7. The meltdown is an inadvertent melting of a nuclear reactor's core.

   _____

8. The movie *The China Syndrome* dramatizes a theoretical disaster hypothesizing the meltdown of nuclear reactor so total that the earth would be penetrated by radioactive material.

   _____

9. Rain forests in South America are being cleared to make fields for raising the cattle.

   _____

10. The acid rain is rain with higher-than-normal acidity caused by pollution.

    _____

III. *Look at the pictures. Write a sentence under each picture, in which the indicated noun is used in a count sense, either with **a / an** or in the plural.*

1. (light)

There's a light in the window.

2. (furniture)

3. (work)

4. (advice)

5. (people)

6. (spices)

7. (lightning)

_____

_____

8. (wine)

_____

_____

IV. *Complete the conversations by putting the noun modifiers in the correct order.*

1. A: It feels like _____a sweltering summer day_____ here, even though it's spring.
   a. (sweltering / a / day / summer)

   What's the weather like where you are?

   B: Here it feels like _____. I envy you.
   b. (chilly / day / a / winter / late)

2. A: What do you think of _____?
   a. (satin / pink / new / my / tie)

   B: It makes you look like _____.
   b. (European / young / handsome / a / businessman)

3. A: We were finally able to build _____. It's just
   a. (brick / own / our / new /house)

   what we've always wanted.

   B: It sounds great. Maybe we could do the same. We feel like we're living in

   _____.
   b. (hovel / little / dirty / old / a)

V. *Complete the conversations with the correct quantifiers, choosing from the items given.*

1. A: Let's get off this freeway. There's just too _____much_____ traffic.
   a. (much / many)

   B: Yeah, let's. The _____ of people driving is incredible. I've never seen
   b. (amount / number)

   this _____ cars.
   c. (much / many)

2. A: Can you bring soda to the picnic? I don't have _____.
   a. (some / any)

   B: Yeah, I think I've got _____ left over from the party.
   b. (some / any)

3. A: How do you feel about your new job? Do you have as _____
                                               a. (much / many)

    responsibilities as you used to?

  B: The job is great. I have about the same _____ of work
                                        b. (amount / number)

    to do as before, but I have _____ stress and _____
                              c. (less / fewer)   **d. (less / fewer)**

    problems.

4. A: How do you think you did on the test? I think I did _____ better
                                    a. (little / a little)

    than last time—maybe even _____ better. What about you?
                          b. (a lot / many)

  B: Well, I think I probably made _____ mistakes, but I have the feeling
                                c. (few / a few)

    I did well overall.

5. A: Mr. President, do you think _____ of your proposed legislation will
                                 a. (much / many)

    be passed by Congress during this session?

  B: Yes, I think _____ of our proposals will be approved. We're
               b. (a great deal / a great many)

    not taking _____ for granted, though. We still have
            c. (nothing / anything)

    _____ work to do.
    d. (a great deal of / a great many)

  A: The polls say that there's _____ support nationwide for your
                     e. (little / a little)

    military program. Isn't that going to hurt you?

  B: Not in the long run, no. _____ of the voters actually support the
                  f. (Few / A few)

    military system the way it is now. I think we'll be successful.

VI. *Circle the letter of the one word or phrase in each sentence that is <u>not</u> correct.*

1. <u>The journey</u> from Los Angeles to San Diego is <u>a</u> <u>three-hours</u> trip if   **A**   **B**   **Ⓒ**   **D**
      A   B   C
    <u>the traffic</u> isn't heavy.
    D

2. <u>The chief executive officer</u> of <u>the company</u> I work for lives in   **A**   **B**   **C**   **D**
             A   B
    <u>beautiful condominium</u> in <u>a ten-story building</u>.
    C   D

3. <u>Plan</u> to build <u>a comprehensive monorail system</u> is <u>a</u>   **A**   **B**   **C**   **D**
    A   B   C
    <u>citizen-initiated proposal</u>.
    D

4. One of <u>the most famous inventions</u> in <u>the history</u> of <u>humankind</u> is
                A   B   C

  <u>a wheel</u> .
   D
                          A   B   C   D

5. <u>The</u> <u>two first</u> films shown in last weekend's film series were   **A   B   C   D**
  A   B

  <u>the most popular ones</u> in <u>the series</u>.
         C   D

6. <u>The extinction</u> of <u>the dinosaurs</u> is still <u>a matter</u> of debate in   **A   B   C   D**
    A   B   C

  <u>scientific community</u>.
      D

7. Vancouver, <u>the largest city</u> in <u>Canadian Southwest</u>, is   **A   B   C   D**
          A   B

  <u>the closest major Canadian port</u> to <u>the Far East</u>.
         C   D

8. When Sarah was a child, she disliked <u>peas</u>, <u>carrots</u>, <u>bean</u>, and   **A   B   C   D**
                         A   B   C

  <u>most other vegetables</u>.
     D

9. <u>The Wheelers'</u> <u>ten-years-old daughter</u>, Melanie, was born in   **A   B   C   D**
    A   B

  <u>the city of Rotterdam</u> in <u>the Netherlands</u>.
         C   D

10. Ralph is in <u>the intensive care ward</u> of <u>the city hospital</u> after being **A   B   C   D**
             A   B

  struck by <u>a lightning</u> on <u>a camping trip</u>.
         C   D

VII. *Go back to your answers to Exercise VI. Write the correct form for each item that you believe is incorrect.*

1.   <u>three-hour</u>   5. _____   8. _____

2. _____   6. _____   9. _____

3. _____   7. _____   10. _____

4. _____

▶ *To check your answers, go to the Answer Key on page 180.*

PART III

FROM GRAMMAR TO WRITING
AGREEMENT

When we speak of agreement in English, we are referring to agreement in number and gender. Agreement in number is the matching of singulars with singulars and plurals with plurals. Agreement in gender is the matching of masculine with masculine and feminine with feminine. There are two types of agreement: subject-verb agreement and pronoun-antecedent agreement.

Every sentence in English can be divided into two parts: the subject and the predicate. The subject is a person, place, or thing about which a statement is made. The predicate is the statement, and it always contains the verb. Subjects and verbs of English sentences must agree in number. In the following sentences, the complete subject is underlined once and the complete predicate is underlined twice.

Birds chirp.

Koalas live in Australia.

The men at Ron's office like to play volleyball.

Nadia and Phil López are trying to save money.

The danger of credit cards is that they encourage us to live beyond our means.

To determine the complete subject of a sentence, ask a *who* or *what* question. The answer to that question will be the complete subject.

The man on the train reminded Penny of her father.

Who reminded Penny of her father? **The man on the train**. (complete subject)

The increasing extinction of plant and animal species is alarming.

What is alarming? **The increasing extinction of plant and animal species**. (complete subject)

1 *Underline the complete subject in each of the following sentences.*

1. <u>Five of my best friends</u> are coming over tonight to play volleyball.

2. The Siberian tiger and the blue whale are endangered species.

3. That man who is sitting at the mahogany desk is our loan officer.

4. Relatively few adults or teenagers are able to handle credit cards wisely.

5. The expectation that we will like well-known works of art, literature, or music can detract from our appreciation of them.

There is one word in the complete subject that controls the verb (or auxiliary) in the sentence. To determine this main subject, find the word that the other words modify. In the following sentences, the main subject is underlined.

My blue silk <u>necktie</u> is gorgeous.

Our first three <u>attempts</u> were unsuccessful.

Notice that the main subject of a sentence is never located in a prepositional phrase (a phrase beginning with a preposition and ending with a noun or pronoun—e.g., *on the table*). In the following sentences the prepositional phrases are underlined, the main subject is circled, and an arrow is drawn between the simple subject and the verb.

(One) <u>of my best friends</u> has five credit cards.

(Both) <u>of my brothers</u> are behind on their car payments.

The (fate) <u>of the blue whale</u> is unclear.

(Either) <u>of the plans</u> is worthwhile.

(None) <u>of the proposals</u> has much merit.

(Neither) <u>of the skaters</u> is expected to win a gold medal.

2 *Circle the main subject in each of the following sentences, and draw an arrow between it and the verb.*

1. A (list) of available jobs was posted on the office bulletin board.

2. Much of what you were told was inaccurate.

3. Neither of those two politicians is in favor of cutting taxes.

4. None of the work has been completed satisfactorily.

5. Very little of this work can be done by one person working alone.

6. The singing of that famous Australian opera star is uplifting.

Be careful with the word *there*. Even though *there* is often the grammatical subject of a sentence, it is linked to a word later in the sentence that controls the verb. In the following sentences, an arrow connects the word *there* and the noun it is linked to. Note the underlined verb.

There ~~are hundreds of animals on the~~ Endangered Species list.

There ~~have been many en~~vironmental disasters in the last twenty years.

There <u>is</u> a large, fierce dog guarding the house.

3 *Choose the correct verb to complete each sentence.*

1. There _____has_____ never been an environmental disaster of this magnitude.
(has / have)

2. There _____ many reasons why I am against the use of nuclear power.
(is / are)

3. There _____ always a rational explanation for his behavior.
(isn't / aren't)

4. There _____ been fewer business mergers this year than last.
(has / have)

5. There _____ a lot of demonstrators present at the environmental rally.
(was / were)

6. There _____ any elegantly dressed people at the party. Everyone was
(wasn't / weren't)
wearing blue jeans.

Compound subjects are those in which the subject is composed of more than one item. They are often connected by *and*.

Ron and Ashley are going to join a health club. (two subjects—*Ron, Ashley*)

The blue whale, **the timber wolf**, **and the whooping crane** need our protection. (three subjects: *whale, wolf, crane*)

Sometimes words appear to be compound subjects, but they really constitute a single phrase made up of two items acting as a unit. These take a singular verb.

Bacon and eggs is a high-cholesterol but nourishing meal.
(*Bacon and eggs is a single dish.*)

The owner and manager of the bank is Mr. Bates.
(*Mr. Bates is one person who has two roles.*)

Choose the correct verb to complete each sentence.

1. Both the whale and the grizzly bear _____*need*_____ federal protection.
(needs / need)

2. Bipolar disorder and schizophrenia _____ two serious mental disorders.
(is / are)

3. The director and star of the film _____ Robert Redford.
(was / were)

4. Liver and onions _____ a meal detested by many children.
(is / are)

5. Mathematics _____ often considered a difficult subject.
(is / are)

Pronoun agreement is similar to subject-verb agreement. In formal English, pronouns agree in number and gender with their antecedents.

> All the **students** brought **their** books to class on the first day. (*Their* agrees with *students*.)

> **Jack** ate **his** lunch quickly. (*His* agrees with *Jack*.)

> **Martha** stopped by to see **her** mother after class. (*Her* agrees with *Martha*.)

> Each of **us** needs to bring **our** own ideas to the meeting. (*Our* agrees with *us*.)

In informal English, usage is somewhat different. The words *everyone / everybody, anyone / anybody, someone / somebody, no one / nobody,* and *a person* are often used with plural forms. Look at these examples.

Formal	**Informal**
Everyone drove **his** (**her / his or her**) car to the picnic.	**Everyone** drove **their** own car to the picnic.
If you see **anyone** from our office, tell **him** (**her / him or her**) to see me.	If you see **anyone** from our office, tell **them** to see me.
All the **employees** came, didn't **they**?	**Everybody** came, didn't **they**?

BE CAREFUL! Use these plural forms only in informal (conversational) English. Use the correct singular forms in writing and formal speech.

Sometimes it is possible to make a sentence correct for formal English by changing the subject to the plural:

> **Everyone** brought **their** own lunch.   All the **employees** brought **their** own lunch.

5 Complete each of these sentences with correct forms for formal and for informal English.

Formal	**Informal**
1. Does everyone have _____ **1.** book with him?	Does everyone have _____ **2.** book with them?
2. No one knows _____ own **3.** destiny.	No one knows _____ own **4.** destiny.
3. If any of the performers shows up, send _____ to my office. **5.**	If any of the performers show up, send _____ to my office. **6.**
4. A person needs to have _____ priorities straight. **7.**	A person needs to have _____ priorities straight. **8.**

Subjects connected by *either / or* and *neither / nor* behave differently from compound subjects. The subject that is closer to the verb determines whether the verb is singular or plural.

Either the **president** or his cabinet **members are** responsible for this environmental policy. (two subjects: *president, members; members* is closer to the verb and forces the plural verb *are*)

Neither the **members** of the city council nor the **mayor supports** more real estate development. (two subjects: *members, mayor; mayor* is closer to the verb and forces the singular verb *supports*)

Note that if we reverse the order of the above sentences, the verb changes.

Either the cabinet **members** or the **president is** responsible for this environmental policy.

Neither the **mayor** nor the **members** of the city council **support** more real estate development.

Pronouns whose antecedents are nouns connected by *either / or* and *neither / nor* behave in the same way. The noun closer to the pronoun determines the correct pronoun.

Neither **Susan** nor **the Johnsons** enrolled **their** children in that school. (*The Johnsons* is closer to the pronoun and forces *their*.)

6 Choose the correct verb or pronoun in the following sentences.

1. Either Bob Ashcroft or the Mendozas _____*are*_____ going to host this year's party.
(is / are)

2. Neither pollution nor other atmospheric phenomena _____ thought to be
(is / are)
related to the unusual weather we've been having.

3. Neither the local environmentalists nor the mayor _____ a plan that will
(has / have)

satisfy everyone.

4. Either major credit cards or a check _____ an acceptable means of payment.
(is / are)

5. Neither Venus nor the outer planets _____ a breathable atmosphere.
(has / have)

6. Neither my daughters nor my son owns _____ own car.
(their / his)

---

 *The following letter to the editor of a newspaper has twelve errors in
subject-verb agreement and pronoun-antecedent agreement. Find and
correct the errors. Use forms that are correct for formal English.*

Editor, The Times

    Many parts of our once-beautiful city ~~is~~ *are* starting to look like mini garbage dumps.
You will recall that legislation requiring recycling within the city limits were passed last
year, and the mayor and other local politicians encourages us to recycle, but in my
apartment complex there is no bins for recycling. The result is that people take no
responsibility for his own actions, and everyone tosses their trash and recyclables
(glass, plastic bottles, cans, etc.) right in with the food that is being thrown away.
Neither the manager of the complex nor the owners of the building has bought any
new containers for the items that are supposed to be recycled. So what else can
everyone do but mix their trash together? Either the manager or the owners is
responsible for breaking the law here. Not us! Meanwhile, trash cans in the downtown
area is overflowing with garbage, and vacant lots all around the city is littered with
soda cans, broken glass, and paper. The owner and publisher of your newspaper,
Stanford Black, have always been a supporter of a clean environment. I urge your
paper to take leadership in solving this problem.

---

8 **APPLY IT TO YOUR WRITING**

*Interview someone about his or her family or some close friends. Ask about
brothers, sisters, children, activities, and so on. Then write a paragraph of
five or six sentences summarizing what the person said. Make sure that you
have correct subject-verb and pronoun-antecedent agreement. Write the
paragraph twice: once for those forms correct in formal English, and once
for forms used in informal English. Exchange papers with a partner. Edit
each other's paragraphs. Then rewrite your paragraphs, if necessary, and
submit them to your teacher.*

I.

2. no article	**18.** an
3. no article	**19.** A
4. the	**20.** the
5. the	**21.** an
6. no article	**22.** a
7. no article	**23.** no article
8. no article	**24.** no article
9. no article	**25.** no article
10. no article	**26.** the
11. no article	**27.** no article
12. no article	**28.** no article
13. the	**29.** no article
14. A	**30.** the
15. a	**31.** the
16. no article	**32.** no article
17. no article	

II.

2. . . . not birds.

3. An orangutan is an anthropoid ape . . .

4. The Mesozoic era was the third . . .

5. The Jurassic Period . . .

6. The Milky Way galaxy is the galaxy . . .

7. A meltdown is . . .

8. . . . hypothesizing the meltdown of a nuclear reactor.

9. . . . raising cattle.

10. Acid rain is . . .

III. Possible Answers

2. Several pieces of furniture are for sale.

3. *A Thousand Cranes* is a work of literature by Yasunari Kawabata.

4. The mother is giving her son a piece of advice.

5. The Shan are a people of Myanmar.

6. Curry, rosemary, oregano, and thyme are spices.

7. The tree was hit by a bolt of lightning.

8. Rioja is a wine produced in Spain.

IV.

1. b. a chilly late-winter day

2. a. my new pink satin tie

b. a handsome young European businessman

3. a. our own new brick house

b. a dirty little old hovel

V.

1. b. number	**b.** a lot
c. many	**c.** a few
2. a. any	**5. a.** much
b. some	**b.** a great many
3. a. many	**c.** anything
b. amount	**d.** a great deal of
c. less	**e.** little
d. fewer	**f.** Few
4. a. a little	

VI.

2. C	**5.** B	**8.** C
3. A	**6.** D	**9.** B
4. D	**7.** B	**10.** C

VII.

2. a beautiful condominium

3. The plan

4. the wheel

5. first two

6. the scientific community

7. the Canadian Southwest

8. beans

9. ten-year-old daughter

10. lightning / a bolt of lightning

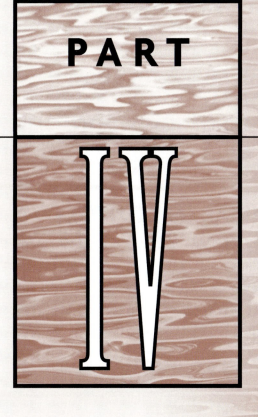

PART

IV

ADJECTIVE CLAUSES AND PHRASES

ADJECTIVE CLAUSES: REVIEW AND EXPANSION

GRAMMAR **IN CONTEXT**

QUESTIONS TO CONSIDER

1. If you could select one adjective that best describes your personality, what adjective would it be?

2. Is there anything to be gained by classifying people into personality types or placing yourself in a personality category? If so, what?

Read an article about personality types.

WHAT TYPE ARE YOU?

Suppose you attend a party where there are several people you know well. The hosts have a new party game. They ask everyone to take five minutes and compare each person to a flower. Which flower would you choose for each person? For that matter, which flower would you choose for yourself? Are you the kind of person who resembles a sunflower, open to the world most of the time? Or are you more like a four o'clock, someone who only opens up at special moments?

This may sound like just a fun activity, something which is suitable only for get-togethers or for amusing yourself. But there is actually a science of identifying personality types. Personality identification grew out of the work of Swiss psychologist Carl Jung and the studies of two American women, Katharine Briggs and her daughter, Isabel Briggs Myers. After considerable study of Jung's work, Briggs and her daughter developed a system in which they formulated four personality dimensions and sixteen different personality types. This test, which has been refined many times over the decades, has been validated by the millions of people who have taken it. What follows is a brief description of what has come to be known as the Myers-Briggs test. Take a look at it. As you're reading about these categories, try to place yourself into one or more of them.* You may learn something about your friends, co-workers, and loved ones, and yourself.

The first dimension is a familiar one: extrovert or introvert. This category has to do with the way in which people direct their energy. An extrovert is basically a person whose energies are activated by being with others. An introvert is basically a person whose energies are activated by being alone. Mary is a good example of an extrovert. She's the kind of person whom others consider shy, but there's no correlation between shyness and either introversion or extroversion. At a party, once Mary meets some people she feels comfortable with, she starts to open up and get energized. Her friend Bill is the opposite. Bill isn't shy at all, but after he's been at a party for a while, he's weary and ready to go home. He finds the conversation interesting enough but is just as likely to be imagining a time when he was hiking alone in the mountains.

The second dimension of personality is sensor or intuitive. This category has to do with the kind of information we notice and remember easily. Sensors are practical people who notice what is going on around them. They rely on past experiences to make determinations. Intuitives are more interested in relationships between things or people. They tend to be imaginative and to focus on what could be. Jack and Barbara, who have been married for years, are good examples of these types. At a party, Jack, whose parents own a sofa company, notices immediately that their hosts have bought a new sofa and asks the hosts where they bought it. Barbara is much less interested in the sofa and more interested in the strained way their hosts are talking with each other. Did they have a fight? Jack is the sensor and Barbara the intuitive here.

The third personality dimension is thinker or feeler. This category has to do with the way in which we come to conclusions. Thinkers are those who tend to make decisions objectively and impersonally on the basis of what makes sense and what is logical. Feelers make decisions based on their own personal values and how they feel about choices. Helen and Gary are good examples. They've just gone to a bank to apply for a loan. The loan officer tells them that they owe too much on their credit cards and that they'll have to pay off their debt before they can borrow money. This makes perfect sense to Helen, which leads us to classify her as a thinker. Gary's reaction is quite different. The loan officer, by whom Gary feels criticized, is only trying to do his job. Gary takes his comments personally, which is why he is to be considered a feeler.

The fourth category is judger or perceiver. This dimension has to do with the kind of environment that makes us feel most comfortable. Judgers are people who prefer a structured and predictable environment. They like to make decisions and have things settled. Perceivers are more interested in keeping their options open, preferring to experience as much of the world as possible. Tim and Samantha are good examples of these types. Tim, who always has a plan for everything, gets impatient with Samantha when he calls and asks

*To learn more about personality type and to determine your type, visit *www.personalitytype.com.*

(continued on next page)

WHAT TYPE ARE YOU?

her for a date. Tim wants things to be nailed down; Samantha wants to keep her options open and flexible.

So now we're left with this question: What good is the ability to pigeonhole people, or ourselves, for that matter? It certainly doesn't give us any magic powers or tools for dealing with people. But it can give us insight. It can help us understand others better, and perhaps minimize or at least reduce conflict. Best of all, it can help us to understand ourselves.

Source: Adapted from "What's Your Personality Type?" *New Woman.* August 1998, pp. 68–71, by Barbara Barron-Tieger and Paul D. Tieger, authors of *Do What You Are, Nurture by Nature,* and *The Art of SpeedReading People.*

UNDERSTANDING MEANING FROM CONTEXT

Make a guess about the meaning of each italicized word or phrase from the reading. Write your guess in the blank provided.

1. This test, which has been *refined* many times over the decades, has been validated by the millions of people who have taken it.

   _____

2. Barbara is much less interested in the sofa and more interested in the *strained* way their hosts are talking with each other.

   _____

3. Tim wants things to be *nailed down*; Samantha wants to keep her options open and flexible.

   _____

4. What good is the ability to *pigeonhole* people, or ourselves, for that matter?

   _____

5. But it can give us *insight*.

   _____

GRAMMAR **PRESENTATION**
ADJECTIVE CLAUSES: REVIEW AND EXPANSION

IDENTIFYING ADJECTIVE CLAUSES

WHO

Are you the kind of person **who resembles a sunflower**, open to the world most of the time?

THAT

This dimension has to do with the kind of environment **that makes us feel more comfortable**.

WHOM

She's the kind of person **whom others consider shy**.

WHEN

He is likely to be imagining a time **when he was hiking alone in the mountains**.

WHERE

Suppose you attend a party **where there are several people you know well**.

WHICH

This may sound like just a fun activity, something **which is suitable for get-togethers**.

WHOSE

An introvert is basically a person **whose energies are activated by being alone**.

PREPOSITION + *WHICH*

This category has to do with the way **in which people direct their energy**.

PREPOSITION + *WHOM*

He finds the people **with whom he's talking** interesting.

DELETED RELATIVE PRONOUN

Suppose you go to a party where there are several people **(whom / that) you know well**.

NONIDENTIFYING ADJECTIVE CLAUSES

WHO

Jack and Barbara, **who have been married for many years**, are examples of these types.

WHOM

The loan officer, **by whom Jack feels criticized**, is only trying to do his job.

WHICH

This test, **which has been refined many times over the decades**, has been validated by the millions of people who have taken it.

WHOSE

Jack, **whose parents own a sofa company**, notices immediately that his hosts have bought a new sofa.

NONIDENTIFYING ADJECTIVE CLAUSE MODIFYING AN ENTIRE PRECEDING IDEA

This makes perfect sense to Helen, **which is why we can classify her as a thinker**.

NOTES

1. Adjective clauses are **dependent clauses** that modify nouns and pronouns. They are introduced by the relative pronouns *who, whom, whose, that,* and *which,* or by *when* and *where.* Sentences with adjective clauses can be seen as a combination of two sentences.

2. Adjective clauses that are used to identify (distinguish one person or thing from another) are called **identifying** (also called **restrictive, defining,** or **essential**).

EXAMPLES

- Sensors are persons. Sensors are practical and notice what is going on around them.
- Sensors are persons **who are practical and notice what is going on around them**.

- Judgers are people **who prefer a structured and predictable environment**. (The clause *who prefer a structured and predictable environment* identifies which kind of people are judgers.)

3. An adjective clause that is not used to identify something but simply adds extra information is called **nonidentifying** (or **nonrestrictive**, **nondefining**, or **nonessential**).

- Jack and Barbara, **who have been married for years**, are good examples of these types. (The clause *who have been married for years* doesn't identify the people we are talking about. The names *Jack* and *Barbara* do that. This clause simply adds extra information about Jack and Barbara.)

Punctuation note: Nonidentifying adjective clauses are enclosed by commas. Identifying adjective clauses have no commas around them.

Pronunciation note: When spoken, identifying adjective clauses have no pauses before or after them. Nonidentifying clauses do have pauses when spoken.

- The man who is sitting in the first row is married to Barbara. (identifying—no pauses)
- Jack, who is sitting in the first row, is married to Barbara. (nonidentifying—pauses)

See From Grammar to Writing after Part IV, page 214, for more information about punctuation of adjective clauses.

4. Like all clauses, adjective clauses contain subjects and verbs. The **relative pronouns** *who*, *which*, and *that* are used as subjects.

- Are you **someone who only opens up at special moments**? (*Who* is the subject of the clause verb *opens*.)
- This may sound like just a fun activity, something **which is suitable only for get-togethers**. (*Which* is the subject of the clause verb *is*.)
- This dimension has to do with the kind of environment **that makes us feel most** comfortable. (*That* is the subject of the clause verb *makes*.)

▶ **BE CAREFUL!** Do not use a double subject pronoun in an adjective clause.

- Judgers **are people who prefer a structured and predictable environment**.
  NOT ~~Judgers are people who they prefer a structured environment.~~

(continued on next page)

5. The **relative pronouns** *whom*, *that*, and *which* are used as objects in adjective clauses.

- She's the kind of person **whom others consider shy.** (*Whom* is the direct object of the verb *consider*.)

- Once Mary meets some people **that she feels comfortable with**, she starts to open up. (*That* is the object of the clause preposition *with*.)

- This category has to do with the way **in which people direct their energy**. (*Which* is the object of the clause preposition *in*.)

▶ **Be careful!** It is common in conversation to omit the relative pronoun *who, whom, which,* or *that*. This can only be done, however, if the relative pronoun is an object. You cannot omit the relative pronoun if it is the subject of a clause.

- Once Mary meets some people
  may be omitted
  (that) she feels comfortable with . . .

  may not be omitted
- Sensors are people **who are practical and notice what is going on around them**.
  Not ~~Sensors are people are practical and notice what is going on around them.~~

---

6. *Who* and *whom* are used to refer to persons, not things. *That* can be used to refer to both persons and things and is considered more informal than *who* or *whom* when it is used to refer to people. *Which* is used to refer only to things.

Which and *that* are used interchangeably in identifying clauses.

In **nonidentifying clauses**, only *which* is usually used.

- Thinkers are those **who / that tend to make decisions objectively and impersonally**.
  Not ~~Thinkers are those which tend to make decisions objectively and impersonally.~~

- This dimension has to do with the kind of environment **that / which makes us feel most comfortable**.

- This test, **which has been refined many times over the decades**, has been validated by the millions of people who have taken it.
  Not ~~This test, that has been refined . . .~~

---

7. *Whom* is considerably more formal than *who* and is appropriate for formal writing and careful speech. *Who* is appropriate elsewhere. (Although *who* is used as a subject in adjective clauses, it is often used as an object in conversational speech.)

- She's the kind of person **whom others consider shy.** (formal)

- She's the kind of person **who others consider shy.** (less formal, conversational—*who* is used as an object)

8. In conversation and informal writing, native speakers commonly place the preposition in an adjective clause at the end of the sentence, and they often omit the relative pronoun.

- Once Mary meets some people **she feels comfortable with** . . . (informal, conversational)
- Once Mary meets some **people that she feels comfortable with** . . . (slightly more formal)
- Once Mary meets some people **who she feels comfortable with** . . . (a bit more formal)
- Once Mary meets some people **whom she feels comfortable with** . . . (even more formal)
- Once Mary meets some people **with whom she feels comfortable** . . . (the most formal)

9. The **relative pronoun *whose*** is used to introduce an adjective clause in which a possessive is needed. *Whose* does not appear without a following noun in an adjective clause.

- An extrovert is basically a person **whose energies are activated by being with others**.

10. Adjective clauses can be introduced by ***when*** and ***where***. Adjective clauses with *when* describe a time; adjective clauses with *where* describe a place.

- He is just as likely to be imagining a time **when he was hiking alone in the mountains**.
- Suppose you attend a party **where there are several people you know well**.

11. The **relative pronoun *which*** can be used informally to introduce a clause that modifies an entire preceding idea. In this situation, *which* must be preceded by a comma. This type of sentence is used in conversation and informal writing but not generally in formal writing. In formal writing, a noun is added before *which*.

- This makes perfect sense to Helen, **which leads us to classify her as a thinker**. (The clause *which leads us to classify her as a thinker* modifies the entire preceding idea: that "this makes perfect sense to Helen.")
- This makes perfect sense to Helen, **a fact which leads us to classify her as a thinker**.

FOCUSED PRACTICE

1 DISCOVER THE GRAMMAR

Part A

Look again at the following sentences adapted from What Type Are You? *In each case, say whether or not the italicized relative pronoun could be rewritten according to the suggestion in parentheses without creating a different meaning or an incorrect sentence. Explain why or why not.*

1. Are you the kind of person *who* resembles a sunflower, open to the world most of the time? (that)

2. This may sound like just a fun activity, something *which* is suitable only for get-togethers or for amusing yourself. (who)

3. She's the kind of person *whom* others consider shy . . . (delete the relative pronoun)

4. He finds the conversation interesting enough but is just as likely to be imagining a time *when* he was hiking alone in the mountains. (where)

5. This category has to do with the kind of information we notice and remember easily. (add the relative pronoun *that* before *we*)

6. Sensors are people *who* are practical and notice what is going on around them. (whom)

7. Jack and Barbara, *who* have been married for years, are good examples of these types. (that)

8. Jack takes the comment personally, wondering what he did wrong, *which* is why he would be classified as a feeler. (that)

9. Tim, *who* always has a plan for everything, gets impatient with Samantha when he calls and asks her for a date. (that)

10. In the decades since, this test has been refined many times and has been validated by the millions of people *who* have taken it. (delete the relative pronoun)

Part B

Find three sentences in the reading in which the relative pronoun has been deleted. How could these sentences be said with a relative pronoun?

1. _____

2. _____

3. _____

2 PEOPLE IN THE OFFICE Grammar Note 11

Dolores Atwood, a personnel officer for a publishing company, is writing an evaluation of the employees in her department who are being considered for promotion. Write adjective clauses with **which** *to modify entire preceding ideas.*

LOOK BOOKS Personnel Evaluation CONFIDENTIAL

Elaine Correa has only been with us for a year but is definitely ready for promotion,

___which is not surprising___ given the glowing recommendations she got from her last employer.
    1. (not / be surprising)

Burt Drysdale has proven himself to be a team player, _____
                        2. (I / find / somewhat amazing)

considering the fact that he rubbed everyone the wrong way at first. I do recommend him for promotion.

    Alice Anderdoff, on the other hand, is not performing up to expectations,

_____ because I was the one who recruited her. I don't believe she
        3. (bother / me)

should be considered for promotion at this time.

    Mel Tualapa is a very congenial employee, _____ , but he can't
                4. (be / what everyone / like / about him)

be promoted yet because he's only been with us for six months.

    Lately, Tom Curran has often been ill and consistently late to work, _____
                        5. (be / mystifying)

because he was such a model employee at first. I don't recommend him at this time.

---

3 FORMAL AND INFORMAL Grammar Notes 1, 2, 4–8, 11

Read the following two descriptions. The first is a spoken report by a head attorney to her team of lawyers. The second contains the same information but is a formal written description. Complete the spoken report with informal adjective clauses, omitting the relative pronoun if possible and using contractions. Put the verbs in the correct tenses. Complete the written report with formal adjective clauses. Do not omit the relative pronoun, and put prepositions at the beginning of clauses in which they occur. Do not use contractions.

Spoken Report

Our client is a guy ____who's been in trouble____ for minor offenses, but I don't think he's a
        1. (have / be / in trouble)

murderer, _____ I feel comfortable defending him. He served time
    2. (be / why)

in the penitentiary from 1997 to 1999, and according to all the reports he was a person

_____ . Since he got out of jail in 1999, he's had a good employment
3. (the other prisoners / look up to)

(continued on next page)

record with Textrix, an electronics company _____. The
                                4. (he / be working / for)

psychological reports on him show that when he was in prison he was a person

_____ well balanced and even tempered, _____
5. (the psychiatrists / consider)   **6. (be / why)**

I don't think he's guilty.

Written Report

Our client is a man _____ for minor offenses, but I do not believe
                    7. (have / be / in trouble)

that he is a murderer, _____ feel comfortable in defending him.
                      8. (a fact / make me)

He served time in the penitentiary from 1997 to 1999, and according to all the reports

he was a person _____. Since he was released from prison in
                    9. (the other prisoners / respect)

1999, he has had a good employment record with Textrix, an electronics company

_____. His psychological profile suggests that when he was in
     10. (for / he / be working)

prison he was a person _____ well balanced and even tempered,
                      11. (the psychiatrists / consider)

_____ believe that he is not guilty.
     12. (evidence / make me)

④ EDITING

*Read the letter from a college student to his parents and correct the eight errors in
relative pronouns in adjective clauses.*

Dear Mom and Dad,   September 28

    Well, the first week of college has been hectic, but it's turned out OK. My advisor is a lady
who
~~she~~ is also from Winnipeg, so we had something who we could talk about. Since I haven't

decided on a major, she had me take one of those tests show you what you're most interested

in. She also had me do one of those personality inventories that they tell you what kind of

person you are. According to these tests, I'm a person whom is an extrovert. I also found out

that I'm most interested in things involve being on the stage and performing in some way, who

doesn't surprise me a bit. I always liked being in school plays, remember? I signed up for two

drama courses. Classes start on Wednesday, and I'm getting to know the other guys which live

in my dormitory. It's pretty exciting being here.

    Not much else. I'll call in a week or so.

                                         Love,
                                         Al

COMMUNICATION PRACTICE

5 LISTENING 1

Listen to the conversation. Then listen again and circle the letter of the sentence which correctly describes what you heard.

1. **a.** Bob took the job because it pays well.
   b. Bob took the job because he likes the work.

2. **a.** Paperwork makes Bob angry.
   b. The fact that Bob has been assigned to do a lot of paperwork makes him angry.

3. **a.** Bob is irritated because his co-worker is a passive-aggressive type of person.
   b. Bob is irritated because he wasn't consulted before being assigned to his co-worker.

4. **a.** Jennifer is surprised that Bob is disgruntled.
   b. Jennifer is surprised that Bob took the job.

5. **a.** His feelings about his co-workers are making Bob wonder about himself.
   b. The fact that Bob didn't investigate the company is making him wonder about himself.

6 TAPE DISCUSSION

How can you deal with a co-worker you are not getting along with? Talk with a partner. Share your views with the class.

7 LISTENING 2

Read and listen to the following excerpts from a telephone conversation that Al had with his parents. Then circle the letters of the sentences that correctly describe the meanings of certain sentences that you heard.

1. **a.** There is one supervisor.
   b. There is more than one supervisor.

2. **a.** All of Al's roommates are from Canada.
   b. Some of Al's roommates are from Canada.

3. **a.** Al has one English class.
   b. Al has more than one English class.

4. **a.** Al has one history class.
   b. Al has more than one history class.

(continued on next page)

5. a. There is one group of girls.

   b. There is more than one group of girls.

6. a. Al has one advisor.

   b. Al has more than one advisor.

⑧ INTERACTION

Work with a partner. On a separate piece of paper, complete this questionnaire, once for yourself and once in relation to the personality traits you perceive your partner to have. Then compare your answers.

1. I would rather spend Friday or Saturday night

   a. at a party with a group of people.   **b.** at home alone.

2. I am basically

   a. outgoing.   **b.** reserved or shy.

3. In general I'd say I am

   a. easy to get to know.   **b.** not so easy to get to know.

4. In general, I am closer to being

   a. a creative person.   **b.** a practical person.

5. In general, I

   a. appreciate constructive criticism.   **b.** dislike constructive criticism.

6. I think it's more important to

   a. always tell the truth, no matter the consequences.   **b.** avoid telling the whole truth if necessary to keep from hurting someone's feelings.

7. Basically, I prefer

   a. to be the leader.   **b.** to let someone else be the leader.

8. I usually

   a. take a long time to make a decision.   **b.** make a decision quickly.

⑨ ESSAY

Consider again the personality categories which have been mentioned in this unit, and choose the one which you believe fits you the best. Write an essay of three or four paragraphs showing why you fit the category. Include several examples from your own experience.

OR

Visit the Keirsey Web site at http://www.keirsey.com/cgi-bin/keirsey/newktsa.cgl *and take the Keirsey Temperament Sorter II test online. Then study the results. Write an essay in which you explain why you feel the test is accurate or inaccurate regarding your personality.*

⑩ PICTURE DISCUSSION

Look at this picture as a reflection of a time and a place. What was it like? How are the people dressed? How do they relate to each other? Describe the picture, using adjective clauses whenever appropriate.

Georges Seurat, French, 1859–1891, *A Sunday on La Grande Jatte*—1884–86.
Oil on canvas, 1884–86, 207.6 × 308 cm. Helen Birch Bartlett Memorial Collection, 1926.224.
Photograph ©1999, The Art Institute of Chicago, All Rights Reserved.

EXAMPLE:
The woman **who is standing in the center of the picture** is holding her daughter's hand very tightly.

ADJECTIVE CLAUSES WITH QUANTIFIERS; ADJECTIVE PHRASES

GRAMMAR **IN CONTEXT**

QUESTIONS TO CONSIDER

1. Do you like movies? What do you look for in a movie? Do you see movies primarily for entertainment, or do you want a film to be something more?

2. Which kind of movie do you like better—one in which you already know what is going to happen, or one in which you don't know what is going to happen?

Read the movie review.

THE TITANIC

TITANIC

by Dartagnan Fletcher

All the fanfare surrounding James Cameron's blockbuster movie *Titanic* was rubbing this reviewer the wrong way. When *Titanic* had first been released I'd resisted seeing it because, to be frank, I just didn't feel like watching 1,500 people drown. I was even more turned off when I heard James Cameron accept his Academy Award for Best Direction: "Tonight I'm the king of the world." "How arrogant can a person be?" I wondered. The next day at my desk at the newspaper, I jotted down ten reasons why I shouldn't have to see *Titanic* and write a review of it, all of which I eventually threw away when my wife dragged me to the picture. It's a good thing she did. Arrogance aside, Cameron, director of many well-known movies, including *Terminator I* and *II* and *True Lies*, has done it again. I was quite pleasantly surprised. My advice to you is this: Go and see it. Anyone interested in cinema should experience this film.

Titanic, said to have cost at least $200 million to make, is well on its way to becoming the highest-grossing movie of all time. Before seeing the picture I was aware that many people have gone back again and again to see it, and I wondered why. "It must be because of the special effects," I said to myself. There's much more to *Titanic* than special effects, however. What really makes the picture work is the story-within-the-story framework. As the film opens, we focus on a modern-day treasure hunter who has mounted an expedition in which divers will attempt to recover a famous and very valuable necklace reported to have gone down with the *Titanic* when it sank on April 16, 1912. The expedition just happens to be televised, and the telecast just happens to be watched by a 101-year-old woman who not only was on the *Titanic* but who has the necklace. Before we know it, the woman and her granddaughter have joined the expedition, at which time they proceed to tell everyone what it was really like the night of the disaster. Once the old lady begins telling her tale, the film proceeds in flashbacks of her recollections.

One of *Titanic's* strengths is its full panoply of actors, most of whom distinguish themselves. Leonardo DiCaprio plays Jack Dawson, the young man on the ship who meets and rescues Rose DeWitt Bukater (a young woman played by Kate Winslett) from an impending marriage about which she is despairing. There's an interesting chemistry between DiCaprio and Winslett. Gloria Stewart does a wonderful job of playing Winslett's character at the age of 101. Particularly effective is Kathy Bates, who plays the role of Molly Brown of unsinkable Molly Brown fame. But the real standout for this reviewer is Billy Zane, who plays to perfection the role of Rose's incredibly arrogant and stuffy fiancé whom, of course, Rose does not marry in the end.

(continued on next page)

TITANIC (continued)

Watching a movie like this, one is faced with the inevitable question that has been asked many times: Is it more suspenseful to know the end of a story or not to know the end of it? I come down on the side of the former. We all know what happened when the *Titanic* sank: 1,500 people died. Somehow, knowing the outcome makes the suspense greater. Once we have gotten to know the characters, our knowledge of their ultimate fate makes the experience of watching their story play out all the more poignant. Still, if you're James Cameron making a blockbuster movie, the fact remains that 1,500 people died in the disaster, in which case you've got to figure out how not to make the film a downer. I mean, you can't just end it with 1,500 dead people slipping beneath the water, can you? Cameron had to find a way to end *Titanic* in an uplifting fashion, and he did. I'll leave it to you to find out how he does it.

By the way, I must assure my readers that I will not be a member of that group responsible for destroying the pleasure of many moviegoers by divulging the secret of what happens to the necklace. Find out for yourself by going and seeing the movie. Rumor has it, though, that with *Titanic's* reissue, the lines to get in are long, in which case you might want to take along a sleeping bag and a picnic lunch. The wait will be worth it. Rating: $3\frac{1}{2}$ stars out of a possible ★★★★.

UNDERSTANDING MEANING FROM CONTEXT

Circle the letter of the choice closest in meaning to the italicized word or expression from the reading.

1. All the *fanfare* surrounding James Cameron's blockbuster movie *Titanic* was rubbing this reviewer the wrong way.

   a. confusion   **b.** celebration   **c.** music

2. All the fanfare surrounding James Cameron's blockbuster movie *Titanic* was *rubbing this reviewer the wrong way*.

   a. irritating this reviewer   **b.** helping this reviewer   **c.** puzzling this reviewer

3. One of *Titanic's* strengths is its full *panoply* of actors . . .

   a. collection   **b.** impressive arrangement   **c.** acting ability

4. Billy Zane . . . plays to perfection the role of Rose's incredibly arrogant and *stuffy* fiancé . . .

   a. interesting   **b.** boring   **c.** intelligent

5. Once we have gotten to know the characters, our knowledge of their ultimate fate makes the experience of watching their story play out all the more *poignant*.

   a. annoying   **b.** difficult to comprehend   **c.** emotionally powerful

GRAMMAR **PRESENTATION**
ADJECTIVE CLAUSES WITH QUANTIFIERS; ADJECTIVE PHRASES

ADJECTIVE CLAUSES WITH QUANTIFIERS
One of *Titanic's* strengths is its full panoply of actors, **most of whom distinguish themselves**.
The next day at my desk at the newspaper, I jotted down ten reasons why I shouldn't have to see *Titanic* and write a review of it, **all of which I eventually threw away** when my wife dragged me to the picture.
Rumor has it, though, that the lines to get into *Titanic* are long, **in which case you might want to take along a sleeping bag and a picnic lunch**.

ADJECTIVE PHRASES
Anyone **interested in cinema** should experience this film.
Titanic, **said to have cost at least $200 million to make**, is well on its way to becoming the highest-grossing movie of all time.
Cameron, **director of many well-known movies, including *Terminator I* and *II* and *True Lies***, has done it again.

NOTES

EXAMPLES

1. Certain **nondefining adjective clauses** follow the pattern quantifier + preposition + relative pronoun *whom* or *which*. These relative pronouns refer to an earlier head noun.	• One of *Titanic's* strengths is its full panoply of actors, **most of whom distinguish themselves**. (*Whom* refers to the head noun *actors*.)

2. Another adjective clause of this type is made with just a preposition and a relative pronoun. Sentences with *of whom* and *of which* are rather formal and more common in writing than in speech.	• Jack Dawson meets and rescues Rose DeWitt Bukater from an impending marriage **about which she is despairing**.
Sometimes a noun can appear instead of a quantifier.	• Cameron has directed many famous movies, **examples of which** are *Terminator I* and *II* and *True Lies*.
▶ **BE CAREFUL!** Remember that we use *whom* to refer to people and *which* to refer to things.	• One of *Titanic's* strengths is its full panoply of actors, **most of whom** distinguish themselves. NOT ~~most of which distinguish themselves.~~

3. The adjective phrase *in which case* is used to introduce a clause. Use this phrase when you could restate the phrase by saying *in that case, in that situation, if that is the case,* or *if that happens.* The relative pronoun *which* refers to an idea described earlier in the sentence.

- Rumor has it that lines to get into the movie are long, **in which case** you should take along a sleeping bag and a picnic lunch. (*In which case* can be restated as "If it is the case that the lines are long . . .")

4. Remember that a **phrase** is a group of words which doesn't have a subject and a verb. Adjective clauses, both defining and nondefining, are commonly reduced to adjective phrases. Speakers and writers do this when they want to achieve an economy of language while maintaining clarity of meaning.

- Anyone **who is interested in cinema** should experience this film.
- Anyone **interested in cinema** should experience this film. (The relative pronoun *who* and the verb *is* are deleted, leaving a defining phrase modifying *anyone.*)

5. There are two ways of reducing an adjective clause to an adjective phrase.

   a. If the adjective clause contains a form of the verb *be*, delete the relative pronoun, the form of *be*, and any accompanying auxiliaries.

- I will not be a member of that group [that is] **responsible for destroying the pleasure of many moviegoers by divulging the secret of what happens to the necklace**.
- *Titanic*, [which is] **said to have cost at least $200 million to make**, is well on its way to becoming the highest-grossing movie of all time.

   b. If the adjective clause does not contain a form of the verb *be*, delete the relative pronoun and change the verb to its present participial form.

- *Titanic*, **which stars** Leonardo DiCaprio and Kate Winslett, is on its way to becoming the highest-grossing movie of all time.
- *Titanic*, **starring** Leonardo DiCaprio and Kate Winslett, is on its way to becoming the highest-grossing movie of all time.

FOCUSED PRACTICE

 DISCOVER THE GRAMMAR

Part A

*Look again at the movie review. Find three adjective clauses containing **which** and one containing **whom** and write them on the lines provided. Then write the noun referred to by each of these relative pronouns.*

1. which I eventually threw away. noun: reasons

2. _____

3. _____

Part B

*On the lines provided, write six adjective phrases which have been reduced from adjective clauses by deleting the verb **be**. Then write each phrase as a clause by restoring the verb **be**.*

1. all of the fanfare surrounding James Cameron's blockbuster movie.

all of the fanfare that is surrounding James Cameron's blockbuster movie.

2. _____

_____

3. _____

_____

4. _____

_____

5. _____

_____

6. _____

_____

Part C

*Look at this sentence. Rewrite it as two sentences by changing the adjective phrase with **including** to a separate sentence.*

Cameron is the director of many well-known movies, including *Terminator I* and *II*.

_____

_____

② FILM TRIVIA

*Complete the following statements about movies, writing adjective clauses in the
form* **quantifier + preposition + relative pronoun**.

1. Mel Gibson and Danny Glover, ___both of whom starred in the Lethal Weapon movies___,
    (both / star / in the *Lethal Weapon* movies)
also acted together in *Maverick*.

2. Sean Connery, Roger Moore, and Timothy Dalton,

_____, come from Britain, while
    (all / have / play / the role of James Bond)
Pierce Brosnan, the newest Bond, is Irish.

3. *Star Wars, The Empire Strikes Back,* and *Return of the Jedi,*

_____, are the middle three films in a
    (all / have / earn / over $100 million)
projected nine-part series.

4. *Saving Private Ryan* and *Schindler's List,*

_____, have been critical as well as
    (both / direct / by Steven Spielberg)
financial successes.

5. Walt Disney's animated productions,

_____, are known worldwide.
    (most / be / loved by children)

6. Roberto Benigni and Wim Wenders,

_____, are both highly regarded
(neither / be / very / very well-known to mass American audiences)
European film directors.

③ POPULAR MOVIES

*Complete each sentence with a nonidentifying adjective phrase for each film
mentioned.*

1. *E.T.,* _____directed by Steven Spielberg_____, was the top-earning film
    (direct / by / Steven Spielberg)
until it was toppled by the reissued *Star Wars* and by *Titanic*.

2. *Jurassic Park,* _____, is the fourth-
    (base / on / Michael Crichton's novel)
biggest moneymaking film of all time.

3. *The Sound of Music,* _____ , is the

(star / Julie Andrews and Christopher Plummer)

top-grossing nonanimated musical film.

4. *Dances with Wolves,* _____ , is the

(direct and produce / by / Kevin Costner)

top-grossing western film.

5. *Star Wars, The Empire Strikes Back,* and *Return of the Jedi,*

_____ , were conceived, written, and

(feature / Harrison Ford, Carrie Fisher, and Mark Hamill)

produced by George Lucas.

---

4 **MOVIE GENRES**   Grammar Notes 2–5

*Combine each pair of sentences about types of movies into a single sentence with
an adjective clause or phrase.*

1. Many recent science fiction films have been huge financial successes. They include
Jurassic Park, Independence Day, and *Men in Black.*

Many recent science fiction films, including Jurassic Park, Independence Day, and

Men in Black, have been huge financial successes.

2. Comedies have continued to be extremely popular and very successful financially.
Recent examples of them are *There's Something about Mary, Mrs. Doubtfire,* and
Liar, Liar.

_____

_____

3. Musical animated films have also become very popular. They include *The Lion King,
Pocahontas,* and *The Hunchback of Notre Dame.*

_____

_____

4. It looks as though sequels to big movie hits may lose their appeal. In that case,
moviemakers will be forced to become more creative.

_____

_____

5 EDITING

Read the letter and correct the ten errors involving adjective clauses and phrases. Delete verbs or change relative pronouns where necessary, but do not change punctuation or add relative pronouns.

Malibu Manor
BED AND BREAKFAST

July 15

Dear Eric,

Diana and I are having a great time in Los Angeles. We spent the first day at the

beach in Venice and saw where *Harry and Tonto* was filmed—you know, that movie

a few years ago ~~starred~~ Art Carney and an orange cat? Yesterday we went to

Universal Studios and learned about all the cinematic tricks, most of them I wasn't

aware of. Amazing! The funny thing is that even though you know that an illusion

is presented on the screen is just an illusion, you still believe it's real when you see

the movie. Then we took the tram tour around the premises and saw several actors

working, some of them I recognized. I felt like jumping off the tram and shouting

"Would everyone is famous please give me your autograph?" In the evening we

went to a party at the home of one of Diana's friends, many of them are connected

with the movie business. I had a really interesting conversation with a fellow works

in the industry who claims that a lot of movies are made these days are modeled

conceptually after amusement park rides. Just like the rides, they start slowly and

easily, then they have a lot of twists and turns are calculated to scare you to death,

and they end happily. Pretty fascinating, huh? What next?

Sorry to babble on so much about the movies, but you know what an addict

I am. Anyway, I may be coming back a day early, in that case I'll call and let you

know so that you can pick me up at the airport.

Love you lots,

Jean

COMMUNICATION PRACTICE

⑥ LISTENING

 *Listen to the TV film reviewer give her weekly review. Then listen again to certain of the reviewer's sentences. For each numbered item, respond **T (True)** or **F (False)** to indicate if it correctly restates the sentence that you heard.*

_____ 1. The film festival can be seen this holiday weekend.

_____ 2. None of these great movies has been shown in more than a decade.

_____ 3. *Fargo* is based on a murder case created by director Joel Coen.

_____ 4. *Fargo* is about a car salesman who is kidnapped because of his debts.

_____ 5. The reviewer believes that it was right for *Forrest Gump* to win the award for best picture.

_____ 6. *Forrest Gump* makes the reviewer cry.

_____ 7. The reviewer thinks that you shouldn't see *Evita* if you don't like musicals.

_____ 8. *Evita* was directed by Madonna.

_____ 9. Michael J. Fox was responsible for launching *Back to the Future*.

_____ 10. The reviewer says black-and-white movies are not pretty.

_____ 11. All who regard themselves as serious movie junkies must see *Casablanca*.

⑦ A REVIEW OF *THE LION KING*

Read this capsule movie review.

> ## ◨ MOVIE REVIEW
> ## The Lion King
> (1994) C-88m.
>
> **Rating:** ★★★   **Directors:** Roger Allers, Rob Minkoff.
> **Voices of:** Jonathan Taylor Thomas, Matthew Broderick, James Earl Jones, Jeremy Irons, Moira Kelly, Miketa Calame, Ernie Savella, Nathan Lane, Robert Guillaume, Rowan Atkinson, Madge Sinclair, Whoopi Goldberg, Cheech Marin, Jim Cummings.
>
> A lion cub raised to take his father's place someday as king of the jungle is sabotaged by his evil uncle—and lives in exile until he realizes his rightful place in the circle of life. With distant echoes of BAMBI, this entertaining Disney cartoon feature (highlighted by a chart-topping and Oscar-winning music score by Hans Zimmer) has dazzling scenics, some show-stopping animation, and outstanding voice work—but drama so intense (and comedy so hip) it's not really for very young viewers. [G]

Source: "The Lion King," copyright © 1997 by Leonard Maltin, from LEONARD MALTIN'S TV MOVIES AND VIDEO GUIDE by Leonard Maltin. Used by permission of Dutton Signet, a division of Penguin Putnam, Inc.

Discussion

Is violence in children's movies and / or literature appropriate? Violence and threatening situations are part of the world of children's literature—consider Little Red Riding Hood, Jack and the Beanstalk, *and so on. Why do you think this is so? Discuss as a class.*

8 INFORMATION GAP: A MOVIE REVIEW

Working with a partner, complete the text. Each of you will read a version of a review of the film Schindler's List. *Each version is missing some information. Take turns asking your partner questions to get the missing information.*

Student A, read the review of Schindler's List. *Ask questions and fill in the missing information. Then answer Student B's questions.*

Student B, turn to the Information Gap on page 208 and follow the instructions there.

EXAMPLE:

A: Whom did Schindler save?

B: He saved more than 1,000 Polish Jews.
Whom did they manufacture crockery for?

A: For the German army.

 MOVIE REVIEW
Schindler's List
(1993) **C/B&W-195m.**

Rating: ★★★★   **Director:** Steven Spielberg.
Starring: Liam Neeson, Ben Kingsley, Ralph Fiennes, Caroline Goodall, Jonathan Sagalle, Embeth Davidtz, Malgoscha Gegel, Shmulik Levy, Mark Ivanir, Beatrice Macola.

Staggering adaptation of Thomas Keneally's best-seller about the real-life Catholic war profiteer who initially flourished by sucking up to the Nazis, but eventually went broke saving the lives of more than 1,000 _____ by employing them in his factory, manufacturing _____ for the German army. Filmed almost entirely on location in Poland, in gritty b&w, but with a pace to match the most frenzied Spielberg works, this looks and feels like nothing Hollywood has ever made before. The three central characters rate—and receive—unforgettable performances: Neeson, who's towering as _____; Kingsley, superb as his Jewish accountant (and conscience); and Fiennes, who's frightening as the odious _____. Outstanding screenplay by Steven Zaillian and _____ by Janusz Kaminsky. Spielberg's most intense and personal film to date. Seven _____ include Best Picture, Director, Adapted Screenplay, and Original Score (John Williams).®

---

9 GROUP DISCUSSION

Divide into groups of six to eight and discuss the pros and cons of one of the following issues. For the first item (the rating system), prepare carefully for the discussion by doing some research, either by going to the library or by using the Internet. For the second item, you can speak from your own experience. Share the main points of your discussion with the class as a whole.

1. The rating system for films should be strengthened / should be left as it is.

2. Movies have / have not become too violent.

10 ESSAY

Write your own movie review in an essay of three or more paragraphs. Choose a film that you liked or disliked, but try to be objective in your review. Read your review to the class and answer any questions your classmates might ask about the movie.

11 PICTURE DISCUSSION

Talk with a partner. What is happening here? Why are the teenagers protesting? What is the theater policy? What do you think the reporter is saying? Write her statements.

_____

_____

_____

INFORMATION GAP FOR STUDENT B

Student B, read the review of Schindler's List. *Answer Student A's questions.*
Then ask your own questions and fill in the missing information.

EXAMPLE:

A: Whom did Schindler save?

B: He saved more than 1,000 Polish Jews.
   Whom did they manufacture crockery for?

A: For the German army.

 **MOVIE REVIEW**
Schindler's List
(1993) **C/B&W-195m.**

Rating: ★★★★   **Director:** Steven Spielberg.
Starring: Liam Neeson, Ben Kingsley, Ralph Fiennes, Caroline
Goodall, Jonathan Sagalle, Embeth Davidtz, Malgoscha
Gegel, Shmulik Levy, Mark Ivanir, Beatrice Macola.

Staggering adaptation of Thomas Keneally's best-seller about the real-life Catholic war

profiteer who initially flourished by sucking up to the Nazis, but eventually went broke

saving the lives of more than 1,000 Polish Jews by employing them in his factory, manufacturing

crockery for _____. Filmed almost entirely on location in

_____, in gritty b&w, but with a pace to match the most frenzied

Spielberg works, this looks and feels like nothing Hollywood has ever made before. The three

central characters rate—and receive—unforgettable performances: Neeson, who's towering as

Oskar Schindler; Kingsley, superb as _____ (and conscience); and

Fiennes, who's frightening as the odious Nazi commandant. Outstanding

_____ by Steven Zaillian and cinematography by Janusz Kaminsky.

Spielberg's most intense and personal film to date. Seven Oscars include Best

_____, Director, Adapted Screenplay, and Original Score

(John Williams).®

Source: "Schindler's List," copyright © 1997 by Leonard Maltin, from *LEONARD MALTIN'S TV MOVIES AND VIDEO GUIDE* by
Leonard Maltin. Used by permission of Dutton Signet, a division of Penguin Putnam, Inc.

REVIEW OR SELFTEST

I. *Read the paragraphs and underline all of the adjective clauses.*

Recently at work I had an experience <u>that proved to me the truth of that old adage: Things may not be what they seem</u>. The experience involved two people I work with in my secretarial job. The first, whom I'll call "Jennifer," is one of those sunny types who always greet you in a friendly manner and never have an unkind word to say. The second, whom I'll call "Myrtle," is the type who rarely gives compliments and can sometimes be critical. Between the two of them, I thought Jennifer was the one who was my friend. Myrtle never seemed to care much for me, which is why I didn't seek out her friendship. I learned, though, that I had been reading them wrong.

About two months ago, some money was stolen from someone's purse in the office. It happened on an afternoon when all three of us, Jennifer, Myrtle, and I, were working together. Our boss, who tends to jump to conclusions, questioned the three of us and said that someone whose name he wouldn't reveal had implicated me in the theft. Jennifer, whom I expected to stand up for me, hemmed and hawed and said she didn't know where I'd been at the time of the theft, which was a lie. Myrtle, however, spoke up and said she knew I couldn't have been the one who had stolen the money because she and I had been working together all afternoon. The boss accepted her statement, and that ended the unpleasantness, and it also ended my friendship with Jennifer. I found out later that she wanted my job. I don't know whether or not she was the one who took the money, but I do know that the old proverb that tells us not to judge a book by its cover has some truth in it. Myrtle and I have been friends ever since.

II. *Read the sentences, which form a narration. Circle the correct relative pronoun for each sentence.*

1. John and Kathleen Carter, (that / (who)) got married about a year ago, recently bought a new house.

2. The neighborhood (that / in which) they have been living is a somewhat dangerous one.

3. The neighborhood (that / who) they are moving into is much safer.

4. Their new house, (that / which) they bought quite cheaply, does need some fixing up.

5. However, they will be receiving some help from their neighbors, most of (who / whom) they like.

6. The Ibarguens, (who / whom) live next door to them, have volunteered to lend their tools.

7. The Travantis, (who / whom) live across the street from John and Kathleen, have promised to help them put in a new lawn.

8. The Ibarguens, (who / whose) daughter is the same age as Mackenzie, John and Kathleen's daughter, are helping Mackenzie make new friends.

9. Kathleen, (that / who) works for a county hospital, will still have to commute to work.

10. John, (whom / whose) company is nearby, will be able to walk to work.

III. *Read the sentences, which form a narration. Put the relative pronoun in parentheses if it can be omitted. Do not omit relative pronouns if they are subjects.*

1. On our trip to Europe last summer, we met a lot of people (whom) we liked.
2. One of the most interesting was a young man from Italy who was named Cosimo.
3. We were hitchhiking outside Florence. Cosimo, who was on his way home from Pisa, stopped and picked us up.
4. The car that he was driving was a 1982 Volkswagen.
5. Cosimo took us to his house, which was not far from downtown Pisa, and invited us to stay for a few days.
6. He also introduced us to a group of people that we felt very comfortable with.
7. We were scheduled to go to Switzerland next, so Cosimo gave us the address of a cousin of his who lived in Bern.
8. We had such a wonderful time in Italy and Switzerland that we decided to go back next year, which will cost money but will be worth it.

IV. *Complete each sentence with a nonidentifying* **which-** *clause that modifies the first clause. Add necessary pronouns and verbs.*

1. Frannie needs to stay home to reenergize herself,

   which is why she can be considered an introvert.   .
   (why / an introvert)

2. Jonathan becomes energized when he is around other people,

   _____ .
   (why / an extrovert)

3. Sensors are practical people who notice what is going on around them,

_____.

(why / past experiences to make determinations)

4. Intuitives are interested in relationships between things or people,

_____.

(the fact that / what could be than what is)

5. Judgers are people who prefer a structured and predictable environment,

_____.

(preference for making decisions and having things settled)

V. *Write a sentence containing an adjective clause describing the indicated people. Punctuate the clauses correctly, paying attention to whether the clauses are identifying or nonidentifying. Use* **who**, **whom**, **whose**, **that**, **which**.

1. The man _who is talking with the receptionist has brought his daughter to the dentist_.

2. The girl _____.

3. The boy _____.

4. The man _____.

5. The poster _____.

6. The poster _____.

7. The woman _____.

8. The woman _____.

VI. *Circle the letter of the one underlined word or phrase which is not correct in each sentence.*

1. George Lucas, <u>whose</u> work <u>including</u> *Star Wars*, *The Empire Strikes*
             A   B
   Back, and *Return of the Jedi* and <u>who</u> <u>has become</u> a world-famous
                               C   D
   movie director and producer, is directing more *Star Wars* films.

       A Ⓑ C D

2. Previously married couple Kenneth Branagh and Emma Thompson,

   <u>both</u> <u>of which</u> are well-known internationally, appeared together
    A   B
   while still married in films <u>directed</u> by Branagh, <u>including</u> *Henry V*
                      C   D
   and *Peter's Friends*.

       A B C D

3. Police <u>in Charleston</u> are investigating a crime <u>that</u> <u>was committing</u>
           A   B   C
   yesterday evening between 11:00 P.M. and midnight at the city art
   museum, <u>which</u> is located on Fifth Avenue.
            D

       A B C D

4. Detective Amanda Reynolds, <u>who</u> is the chief investigating officer in the
                        A
   case, says <u>that</u> the police have no suspects yet but are focusing on tips
           B
   <u>suggest</u> <u>that</u> the theft may have been an inside job.
    C   D

       A B C D

5. Al, <u>whom</u> is a freshman at the university, is pleased with his college
       A
   living situation because he likes <u>the people</u> <u>he</u> is rooming <u>with</u>.
                                B   C   D

       A B C D

6. His courses, <u>none</u> <u>of which</u> are easy, are all classes <u>requiring</u> a
            A   B   C
   considerable amount of study, <u>that</u> is why he has joined a study group.
                            D

       A B C D

7. Textrix, <u>the company</u> <u>for that</u> Alex works, tends to employ people
            A   B
   <u>who are</u> self-starters and <u>who have</u> at least ten years of experience in
    C   D
   the field.

       A B C D

8. Alicia, <u>an extrovert loves</u> working with people and <u>who can</u> also work
           A   B
   independently, had many accomplishments in her last job, <u>which is</u> why
                                           C
   I think she's <u>the person we should hire</u>.
                  D

       A B C D

9. The lines <u>to get into</u> *Star Wars: The Phantom Menace,* <u>a movie</u> <u>directed</u>   **A**   **B**   **C**   **D**
           A   **B**   **C**

   by George Lucas, may be long, <u>in that case</u> I would recommend going
                                                D

   to a matinee screening.

10. Jaime, <u>who</u> has been employed for ten years at a company <u>that</u> stresses   **A**   **B**   **C**   **D**
             A   **B**

   team-building and cooperative effort, is a person <u>who</u> has learned to
                                                C

   value <u>the people with he works</u>.
                 D

VII. *Go back to your answers to Exercise VI. Write the correct form for each item that you believe is incorrect.*

1.   includes _____   **6.** _____

2. _____   **7.** _____

3. _____   **8.** _____

4. _____   **9.** _____

5. _____   **10.** _____

▶ *To check your answers, go to the Answer Key on page 217.*

FROM GRAMMAR TO WRITING
PUNCTUATION OF ADJECTIVE CLAUSES

Remember that the two types of adjective clauses are identifying and nonidentifying. Identifying adjective clauses identify or give essential information. Nonidentifying clauses give additional or nonessential information.

EXAMPLES:

I saw three movies last week. The movie that I liked best was *You've Got Mail*.

The adjective clause **that I liked best** is identifying because it says which movie I am talking about. If the clause were removed, the sentence would not make complete sense.

The movie was *You've Got Mail*.

Therefore, the clause is essential for the sentence's meaning.

Casablanca, **which contains the famous song** "As Time Goes By," is considered a film classic.

The nonidentifying clause **which contains the famous song "As Time Goes By"** adds more information about *Casablanca*. This clause, however, is not used to identify. If it were removed, the sentence would still make sense.

Casablanca is considered a film classic.

In speech, identifying clauses have no appreciable pauses before or after them. Therefore, they are not enclosed in commas when written. Nonidentifying clauses, on the other hand, do have pauses before and after them. Therefore, they are enclosed in commas.

EXAMPLES:

A person who needs others to become energized is an extrovert. (identifying; no commas)

James, who comes alive when he feels comfortable with the people around him, is an extrovert. (nonidentifying; commas)

If you are unsure whether a clause is identifying or nonidentifying, try reading it aloud. The natural pauses made by your voice will help you to determine whether or not the clause needs to be enclosed in commas.

Punctuate the following sentences containing adjective clauses. They form a narration.

1. Tom and Sandra who have been married for more than twenty-five years are both outgoing people.

2. Tom who is clearly an extrovert loves meeting new people.

3. Sandra who is very quick to make friends loves to have friends over for dinner.

4. Tom and Sandra have two married sons both of whom live abroad.

5. The son who is older lives with his family in Britain.

6. The son who is younger lives with his family in southern Italy.

7. Tom and Sandra own a house in the city and one in the country. The one that they spend most of their time in is in the city.

8. The house that they spend summers in is located in Vermont.

Like clauses, adjective phrases are also identifying or nonidentifying, depending on whether they add essential or extra information.

EXAMPLES:

The postwar director most responsible for putting Italian cinema on the map is Federico Fellini. (identifying; no commas)

Federico Fellini, the director of such classics as *8 1/2*, died in 1994. (nonidentifying; commas)

 Punctuate the following sentences containing adjective phrases.

1. A film produced by George Lucas is almost a guaranteed success.

2. A film directed by Steven Spielberg is likely to be a blockbuster.

3. *Life Is Beautiful* directed by Roberto Benigni and starring Benigni and his wife has become well known all over the world.

4. Many Canadians including Donald Sutherland and Michael J. Fox are major international film stars.

5. The Universal Studios located in California was established decades ago.

6. The Universal Studios located in Florida was established much more recently.

3 *Punctuate the following letter containing adjective phrases and clauses.*

September 30

Dear Mom and Dad,

Thanks for bringing me down here to the University last Sunday. Classes didn't start until Wednesday, so I had a few days to get adjusted. I'm signed up for five classes: zoology, calculus, English, and two history sections. It's a heavy load, but they're all courses that will count for my degree. The zoology class which meets at 8:00 every morning is going to be my hardest subject. The history class that I have in the morning is on Western Civilization; the one in the afternoon is on early United States history. Calculus which I have at noon every day looks like it's going to be easy. Besides zoology, the other class that's going to be hard is English. We have to do a composition a week.

I like all of my roommates but one. There are four of us in our suite including two girls from Texas and a girl from Manitoba. Sally who is from San Antonio is great; I feel like I've known her all my life. I also really like Anne the girl from Manitoba. But Heather the other girl from Texas is kind of a pain. She's one of those types of people who never tell you what's bothering them and then get hostile. All in all, though, it looks like it's going to be a great year. I'll write again in a week or so.

Love,
Vicky

4 **APPLY IT TO YOUR WRITING**

Bring to class a detailed photograph from a magazine, a newspaper, or your own collection. In class, write a paragraph of eight to ten sentences describing the picture. Include a number of adjective clauses in your paragraph, making sure to use at least one identifying and one nonidentifying adjective clause. Exchange your paper with a partner. Read each other's paragraphs aloud and make suggestions if necessary. Check for correct punctuation.

REVIEW OR SELFTEST
ANSWER KEY

I. I work with in my secretarial job

whom I'll call "Jennifer"

who always greet you in a friendly manner and never have an unkind word to say

whom I'll call "Myrtle"

who rarely gives compliments and can sometimes be critical

who was my friend

which is why I didn't seek out her friendship

when all three of us, Jennifer, Myrtle, and I, were working together

who tends to jump to conclusions

whose name he wouldn't reveal

whom I expected to stand up for me

which was a lie

who had stolen the money

who took the money

that tells us not to judge a book by its cover

II.
2. in which
3. that
4. which
5. most of whom
6. who
7. who
8. whose
9. who
10. whose

III.
2. no change
3. no change
4. (that)
5. no change
6. (that)
7. no change
8. no change

IV. Possible Answers:
2. which is why he can be termed an extrovert
3. which is why they often rely on past experiences to make determinations
4. which is indicated by the fact that they tend to focus more on what could be than on what is
5. which is shown by their preference for making decisions and having things settled

V. Possible Answers:
2. The girl, whose father is talking to the receptionist, doesn't want to visit her dentist.
3. The boy, whose mother is reading him a story, is named Jerry.
4. The man who is looking at one of the posters has a bad toothache.
5. The poster that is to the left of the receptionist's desk is about gum disease.
6. The poster that is to the right of the receptionist's desk is about brushing properly.
7. The woman who is reading a story to her son is wearing an enormous hat.
8. The woman who is reading a magazine has her dog with her.

VI.
2. B
3. C
4. C
5. A
6. D
7. B
8. A
9. D
10. D

VII.
2. of whom
3. was committed
4. suggesting
5. who
6. which
7. for which
8. an extrovert who loves
9. in which case
10. the people with whom he works / the people he works with

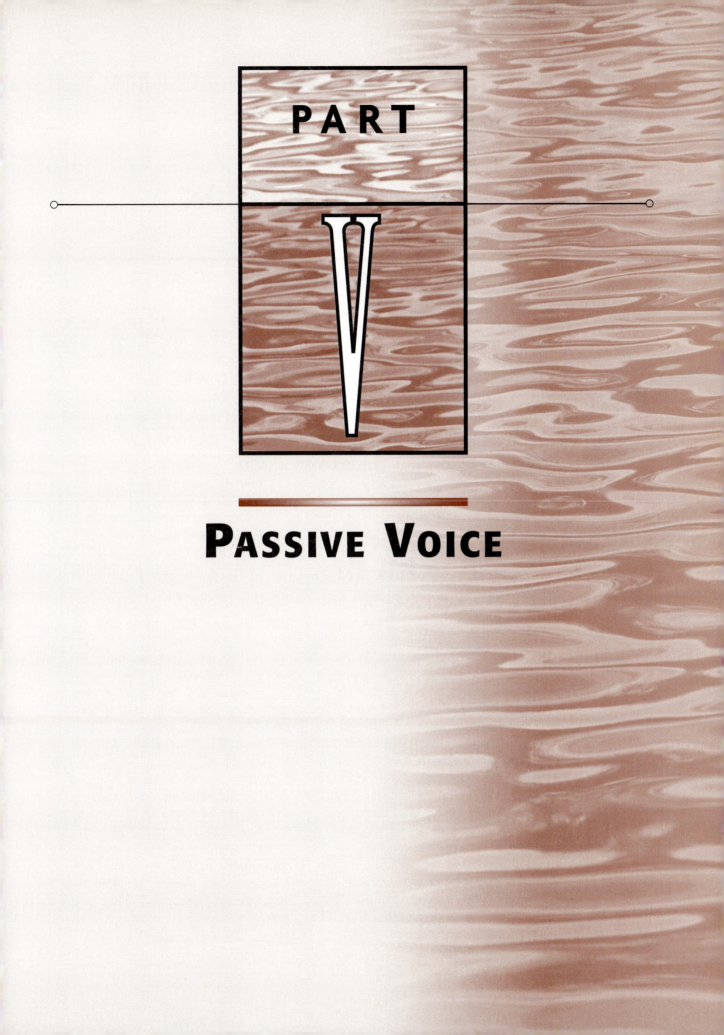

PART

V

PASSIVE VOICE

12

THE PASSIVE: REVIEW AND EXPANSION

GRAMMAR IN CONTEXT

QUESTIONS TO CONSIDER

1. Many people find unsolved mysteries fascinating. Do you enjoy hearing about them? Why? Do you know of any unsolved mysteries?

2. Some people think there is a need for mystery in life, for things to remain unexplained. Do you agree or disagree?

3. Why do people sometimes sympathize with criminals and want them to get away with their crimes?

Read the article Did He Get Away with It?

DAILY NEWS

Did He Get Away with It?

A lot of crimes never get solved. The case of Dan Cooper is one that hasn't been. It was the evening before Thanksgiving, late November 1971. On a short flight between Portland and Seattle, a flight attendant was handed a note by a mysterious middle-aged man dressed in a dark suit. The flight attendant thought he was making a romantic advance, so she slipped the note into her pocket. The man leaned closer to her, saying, "Miss, you'd better look at that note. I have a bomb." A bit later he opened his briefcase so that she could see several red cylinders and a lot of wires within. The man, who used the alias "Dan Cooper," was demanding $200,000, four parachutes, and a plane that would fly him to Mexico.

The plane proceeded to Seattle with none of the other passengers even aware that it was being hijacked. The other passengers got off the plane, and "Cooper" got what he was demanding. He received the $200,000, all in twenty-dollar bills that had been photo-copied by FBI agents so that they could easily be identified later. Then the plane was refueled and took off for Mexico.

A few minutes later, Cooper ordered the flight attendant to go to the cockpit and stay there. As she was leaving, she noticed him trying to tie something around his waist— presumably the bag of money. Then he opened the plane's rear stairway and jumped out of the plane. The crew felt pressure bumps which were probably caused by Cooper's jumping off the stairway. When Cooper jumped, into wind and freezing rain, the air temperature was seven degrees below zero. He was wearing no survival gear and only loafers on his feet.

Cooper has not been seen or heard from since that night. Who was Cooper? Did he get away with his escapade? Or did he get killed in the process of trying to commit the perfect crime?

Authorities speculate that Cooper landed near Ariel, a small town near the Columbia River north of Portland. Only one real clue has been discovered. Eight and a half years later, in 1980, an eight-year-old boy who was digging in a sandbank unearthed $5,800 of Cooper's loot. The money was only a few inches below the surface of the earth, but it had been eroded so badly that only the picture and the serial numbers on the bills were visible. Rotting rubber bands were found along with the money, indicating that the cash must have been deposited there before the bands fell apart. Since then, the area has been searched thoroughly, but no trace of Cooper has been found.

So what really happened? Many investigators believe that Cooper had to have been killed by the combination of the weather conditions and the impact of his fall. If this is true, though, why have none of the man's remains ever been discovered? Is more information known about this case than has been released? Have knowledgeable people been prevented from discussing the case? Is Cooper's body lost in some inaccessible area of the wilderness area into which he jumped, or is he living a luxurious life under an alias in some unknown location and driving a Rolls-Royce? Did he have the $5,800 buried by an accomplice in order to throw authorities off the track? Or did he bury it himself? In Ariel, the small town near where he might have landed, Cooper has become a legend. His story has been depicted in books and articles and even a movie. Patrons of a tavern in Ariel still celebrate the anniversary of the hijacking every year. The bar's owner, Dona Elliot, says, "He did get away with it . . . so far." Others don't think so. Jerry Thomas, a retired soldier who has been working independently on the case, thinks Cooper didn't survive the fall and that eventually his body will be found. "I know there is something out here," he says. "There has to be."

The mystery goes on.

Sources: Based on information in Mark McGwire, "15 Minutes of Fame," *Biography Magazine,* September 1998; and Richard Severn, "D. B. Cooper: Perfect Crime or Perfect Folly?" *Seattle Times,* November 17, 1996.

UNDERSTANDING MEANING FROM CONTEXT

Read each sentence. Think about the meaning of each italicized word or expression. Then answer each question.

1. The man, who used the *alias* "Dan Cooper," was demanding $200,000, four parachutes, and a plane that would fly him to Mexico.

   Was "Dan Cooper" the man's real name or a false name?

   _____

2. Did he *get away with his escapade?*

   Does the question ask whether Cooper succeeded in his plan or

   abandoned his plan? _____

3. Eight and a half years later, in 1980, an eight-year-old boy who was digging in a sandbank *unearthed $5,800 of Cooper's loot.*

   Did the boy find the money above ground or below ground?

   _____

4. *Rotting* rubber bands were found along with the money, indicating that the cash must have been deposited there before the bands fell apart.

   What was the condition of the rubber bands found along with the

   money? _____

GRAMMAR **PRESENTATION**
THE PASSIVE: REVIEW AND EXPANSION

SIMPLE PRESENT		
SUBJECT	**BE (OR GET)**	**PAST PARTICIPLE**
Some mysteries	**are**	**solved** easily.
A lot of crimes never	**get**	**solved**.

PRESENT PROGRESSIVE

Cooper's case **is** still **being investigated**.

SIMPLE PAST		
SUBJECT	**BE (OR GET)**	**PAST PARTICIPLE**
Some think Cooper	**was**	**killed** when he jumped from the plane.
Some think Cooper	**got**	**killed** when he jumped from the plane.

PAST PROGRESSIVE

The plane proceeded to Seattle with none of the other passengers even aware that it **was being hijacked**.

PRESENT PERFECT

Cooper has **not been seen or heard from** since that night.

PAST PERFECT

He received the $200,000, all in twenty-dollar bills that **had been photocopied** by FBI agents.

FUTURE

Jerry Thomas thinks Cooper didn't survive the fall and that eventually his body **will be found**.

MODALS AND MODAL-LIKE EXPRESSIONS

Rotting rubber bands were found along with the money, indicating that the cash **must have been deposited** there before the bands fell apart.

Many investigators believe that Cooper **had to have been killed** by the combination of the weather conditions and the impact of his fall.

PASSIVE CAUSATIVE

Did he **have** the $5,800 **buried** by an accomplice in order to throw authorities off the track?

NOTES	EXAMPLES
1. Passive sentences are formed with the verbs *be* (*am, are, is, was, were, be, been, being*) or *get* (*get, gets, got, gotten, getting*) plus a past participle.	• The plane **was refueled** and took off for Mexico. • A lot of crimes never **get solved**.
▶ **BE CAREFUL!** Only **transitive verbs**, those that take one or more objects, can be made passive. **Intransitive verbs** (verbs which do not take objects) cannot be made passive.	• People **have found** no trace of Cooper. (transitive—can be made passive) • No trace of Cooper **has been found**. (passive) • The plane **proceeded** to Seattle. (intransitive—cannot be made passive)

2. In general, the **active voice** is considered stronger than the **passive voice**. Writers often prefer the active to the passive voice. In academic writing, however, the passive is frequently used. In writing and speaking, there are three instances in which the passive voice is recommended.	
a. When we don't know or don't care who performed the action.	• Then the plane **was refueled** and took off for Mexico.
b. When we want to avoid mentioning who performed the action.	• **Have** knowledgeable people **been prevented** from discussing the case?
c. When we want to focus on the receiver instead of the performer of the action.	• Cooper **had to have been killed** by the combination of the weather conditions and the impact of his fall.

3. We often omit the *by* phrase in passive sentences if we consider it undesirable or unnecessary to mention the performer.	• Why **have** none of the man's remains ever **been discovered**?

4. Most commonly, the **direct object** in an active sentence becomes the subject in a passive sentence.

- Cooper **hijacked the plane**.
  active   direct object
- **The plane was hijacked** by Cooper.
  passive

However, it is common for an **indirect object** to be the subject of a passive sentence.

- Cooper **handed** a note **to the attendant**.
  direct object / indirect object
- **The attendant was handed** a note by Cooper.

5. The passive with *get* is more informal than the passive with *be*. It is conversational and is characteristic of informal writing.

- If Cooper survived, will he ever **get caught**?

The *get*-passive sometimes is used to emphasize action and to focus on what happens to someone or something.

- Did Cooper **get killed** when he jumped from the plane?

6. *Get* and *have* are used to form the **passive causative**. Use the passive causative to talk about services that people arrange for someone else to do.

- Perhaps Cooper **got** his hair **dyed** before the hijacking to disguise himself.

The **passive causative** can occur with or without a *by* phrase, but we often omit the *by* phrase.

- **Did** Cooper **have** the $5,800 buried by an accomplice?

7. Review the formation and use of the passive in modal constructions.

- The 20-dollar bills had been photocopied by FBI agents so that they **could** easily **be identified** later.

FOCUSED PRACTICE

1 DISCOVER THE GRAMMAR

Part A

Look again at the opening reading, Did He Get Away with It? *You will find 24 passive constructions. Underline them. Then look at Grammar Note 2 on page 224. Write* **a***,* **b***, or* **c** *above each passive construction to show what kind of passive it is.*

1. <u>get $\overset{a}{\text{solved}}$</u>

Part B

 Listen to the excerpt from the radio mystery show "Phantasma." Then listen again as you read the "Phantasma" script. Circle all passive constructions with **be** *or* **get***.*

Midnight. Earlier the city (was blanketed) by a nearly impenetrable mist, the perfect environment for a crime to be committed. Now the streets are getting pelted by violent raindrops. No one is about. On the sixty-seventh floor of a massive office building, the door to an executive suite of offices lies ajar. Inside, the main room is dimly lit. A man's body lies crumpled near the windows. An hour ago he got hit by a heavy object. The carpet around him is slowly getting stained by blood. A perfect crime has been committed. Or has it? A spark of life remains in the man. His life can be saved if help arrives soon. The perpetrator is now far from the scene, sure that he is going to be paid handsomely for his work. He is certain that the man was killed by the blow to his head, and he is convinced that his murderous actions were not noticed. He believes that his whereabouts are unknown. He is wrong! Phantasma knows who the perpetrator is and where he is. Phantasma knows all! Ha ha ha ha ha ha ha!

Part C

Complete the "Phantasma" story. Write an ending of three or four sentences. Use at least one passive in your ending. Read your ending to the class.

_____

_____

_____

_____

_____

② THREE FAMOUS MYSTERIES Grammar Notes 1–4

*Fill in the blanks in the following article with passive constructions with **be** and the indicated verbs in the correct tenses.*

Three Unsolved Mysteries Continue to Fascinate

So you think there are no more mysteries, that all mysteries __are solved__
1. (solve)
in time? Think again. The pages of history teem with mysteries that _____ .
2. (never crack)
Consider, for example, the case of the brigantine ship *Mary Celeste*. The ship had left New York for Italy in 1872 and _____
3. (later sight)
floating erratically east of the Azores. No one _____ on board, though
4. (find)
everything else on the ship _____
5. (determine)
to be in order, and there was no indication why the *Mary Celeste* _____ . In
6. (abandon)
fact, tables _____ for afternoon
7. (apparently set)
tea. One theory speculates that the ship _____ by an impending explo-
8. (threaten)
sion that _____ by fumes from
9. (cause)
her cargo of alcohol. That theory, however,

_____ .
10. (never prove)

A second perplexing mystery is that of Amelia Earhart, the famous aviator who in the twenties and thirties _____
11. (consider)
the quintessential example of the rugged

female individual. Earhart flew across the Atlantic with two males in 1928 and set a record for a cross-Atlantic flight in 1932. In 1937 she embarked on her most ambitious plan, a flight around the world. Earhart began her flight in Miami in June and _____ only by Fred
12. (accompany)
Noonan, her navigator. They reached New Guinea and left for Howland Island in the South Pacific on July 1. After that, no radio reports or messages of any kind _____ . No remains of her plane
13. (receive)
_____ by naval investigators.
14. (locate)
Did she simply attempt the impossible? _____ when her
15. (she and Noonan / simply kill)
plane ran out of fuel and crashed in the Pacific? Or could something else have happened? No one really knows.

A third unsolved mystery has to do with monsters—lake monsters, that is. Everyone knows about Nessie, the famous creature that is supposed to inhabit Loch Ness in Scotland.

(continued on next page)

Not too many people are yet aware, however, of the monster who is said to live in the Great Lake at Ostersund in central Sweden. This mystery _____. Over four
16. (still investigate)
thousand sightings _____ of
17. (report)
Nessie, the Scottish beast, but the resident of the Great Lake, if he exists, _____
18. (only spot)
175 times in 400 years. The monster, who _____ Storsjoeodjuret in Swedish,
19. (name)
_____ as being 15 to 20 feet long,
20. (describe)
gray, green, or red in color, with a head like a dog or fish. In 1998, the lake

_____ in a search for clues.
21. (comb)
Storsjoeodjuret _____, but Adrian
22. (not see)
Shine, the noted investigator of the Loch Ness monster, is optimistic, saying about the search that "It was inconclusive but encouraging." More investigations _____
23. (undertake)
in the future.

For the time being, at least, the riddle of the *Mary Celeste*, the fate of Amelia Earhart, and the existence of the Swedish lake monster will have to remain mysterious.

Sources: Adapted from Kenneth C. Davis, *Don't Know Much About History* (New York: Avon Books, 1990) and "Swedish Lake Monster Eludes Search Party," *Dallas Morning News*, August 17, 1998, p. 14A.

3 **JOYCE'S DIARY**   Grammar Note 5

Read the following diary entry. Fill in the blanks with forms of the **get***-passive.*

March 15

Dear Diary,

This has been a strange day. I __got woken up__ by a phone call at five o'clock this
1. (wake up)
morning. When I answered the phone, I heard music in the background, and there

was just the click of someone hanging up. I wouldn't think anything of it except that

this is the fifth time I've _____ out of bed like this. It has me worried.
2. (roust)

Am I just _____ by some "friend" with a weird sense of humor, like my
3. (harass)

friend Harriet? She _____ periodically by practical jokers. Or am I
4. (bother)

going to _____ by someone who's been watching me and my apart-
5. (rob)

ment? Tomorrow I'm going to _____ on the doors just in case. I'm also
6. (the locks / change)

going to call the telephone company. I just hope I don't _____ again
7. (disturb)

tomorrow morning. I need a good night's sleep.
                                                        Joyce

4 EDITING

Read the following script for a radio bulletin about a hit-and-run accident. In order to strengthen the writing, change all the sentences except the ones that are underlined from passive to active or from active to passive. Write the sentences in the order that makes the most sense.

A hit-and-run accident occurred this evening at approximately 8:45 P.M. The intersection of Fourth and Madison was being crossed by an eight-year-old boy.[1] A blue Toyota Corolla hit him.[2] Massive injuries were sustained by the boy.[3] Paramedics took him to Harborview Medical Center.[4] They are caring for him in the intensive care ward.[5] His condition is critical. The sheriff asks anyone with information about the accident to contact the sheriff's office at 444-6968.[6] They are offering a reward.[7]

1.   An eight-year-old boy was crossing the intersection of Fourth and Madison.

2.   _____

3.   _____

4.   _____

5.   _____

6.   _____

7.   _____

COMMUNICATION PRACTICE

5 LISTENING

Some animals have been stolen from the city zoo. Listen to the conversation between police detective Harry Sadler and zoo administrator Lane Akimura. Then listen again. Circle the letter of the sentence that gives correct information about what happened.

1. a. The janitor found the keeper.

  b. The keeper found the janitor.

2. a. Akimura examined the keeper.

  b. A physician examined the keeper.

3. a. The keeper had been drugged.

  b. The keeper had been hit.

4. a. It takes two weeks to see turtles.

  b. Two turtles were taken two weeks ago.

5. a. The police were notified about the first theft.

  b. The police weren't notified about the first theft.

6. a. The zoo expansion has been completed.

  b. The zoo expansion hasn't been completed.

7. a. Voters haven't yet approved the zoo expansion.

  b. Voters have already approved the zoo expansion.

8. a. First the animals eat. Then the food preparation area is cleaned.

  b. First the food preparation area is cleaned. Then the animals eat.

9. a. Detective Sadler will check the janitor's references himself.

  b. Detective Sadler will ask someone else to check the janitor's references.

6 INFORMATION GAP: A MYSTERY ENTITY

Student A, read clues 1–4 to Student B. Student B will complete the clues. Switch roles after item 4. Then put the clues in the correct order and decide what the mystery item is.

Student B, turn to page 233 and follow the instructions there.

Student A's Prompts

1. I was born, or maybe I should say I was created . . .

2. An all-night card game . . .

3. I was created by . . .

4. The "hero" type of me gets its name . . .

Student A's Conclusions

5. . . . have been known by my name since then.

6. . . . some slices of meat between two slices of bread.

7. . . . is shaped like a submarine.

8. . . . so he ordered a snack to be delivered to the gambling table.

9. . . . that I'm being eaten somewhere in the world this very minute.

7 "RAFFLES" GANG HITS PALACES OF VENICE

Read the London Daily Telegraph *account of a contemporary unsolved mystery.*
Then respond **True (T)**, **False (F)**, *or* **Don't Know (DK)**.

LONDON DAILY TELEGRAPH

"Raffles" Gang Hits Palaces of Venice

EUROPEAN WIRE SERVICE—
A gang of thieves is stripping Venice's finest palaces of paintings and artifacts worth millions of rands. The gang, known as the "Raffles of the Rialto," appears to have inside knowledge of which palaces are equipped with burglar alarms and which are unoccupied at any particular time.

In the biggest of a string of heists so far, the gang made off just over a week ago with the only oil painting still in private hands by the Venetian Old Master Canaletto, estimated to be worth about R11.35 million.

The 65m by 13m signed canvas, *Il Fonteghetto dela Farina*, was spirited away from the collection of the late Count Alvise Guistiniani. It was the most celebrated work in the collection.

The thieves also took a valuable map of Venice and other treasures from a palace in the Dorsoduro when the Count's adopted daughter was out. The palace had no alarm.

Before departing, the robbers added insult to injury by drinking the owner's champagne in antique Murano glasses.

The Canaletto was reportedly not even insured. Days before it was stolen, the thieves paid a visit to the house next door belonging to Italy's ambassador to London, Paolo Galli, which cost his family dearly.

On this occasion, the gang emptied the entire first floor of the palace, taking the family silver valued at about R946,000. The break-in was discovered by his daughter Francesca when she returned from a holiday.

Two other similar robberies took place in September,
(continued on next page)

"Raffles" Gang

including one in Palazzo Mocenigo. The palace was once the ancestral home of Count Alvise di Robilant, the former Sotheby's director bludgeoned to death in an unsolved case early last year, and was where Lord Byron lived when he wrote *Don Juan*.

Investigators piecing together the clues last week said they believed they could be dealing with a group of professionals who were working on commission and knew the city "to perfection." "These people are too clever and too well informed for words," an investigator said. "It's as though they had a plan of Venice where every palace minus an alarm was clearly indicated."

Source: © Telegraph Group Limited, London, 1999.

Comprehension

_____ **1.** "Raffles" is the Italian word for "gang."

_____ **2.** Priceless paintings and other art works are being cleaned out of Venice's finest palaces.

_____ **3.** The thieves were daring enough to drink brandy in antique glasses at one of the palaces.

_____ **4.** The palaces that were robbed were all outfitted with new alarm systems.

_____ **5.** One of the palaces that were robbed was the home of Sotheby's director, who was murdered in an unsolved case last year.

_____ **6.** The work of the thieves led police to call them amateurs.

Small Group Discussion

In groups of four, discuss these questions.

1. Why do you think the Canaletto was not insured?

2. Why do you think the palace from which the painting was stolen had no alarm?

3. How could the gang who stole the painting have such complete knowledge of Venice and knowledge of which palaces were unoccupied and without alarms?

8 ESSAY

Write an essay describing an unsolved mystery in the area where you live. It could be a murder, someone's disappearance, or some strange natural phenomenon. Describe what the mystery is and how it might have been caused. Offer some possible solutions to the mystery.

❾ PICTURE DISCUSSION

This is a photograph of one group of crop circles which have been found in grain fields in England. There is still no officially accepted explanation of how these circles were made, or by whom. Form groups of four. Describe the circles in as much detail as possible. Then speculate as to how they might have been made. Use the passive whenever appropriate.

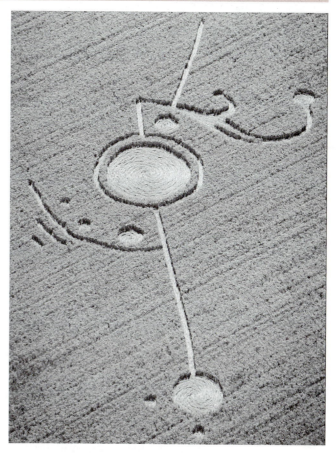

EXAMPLE:
The grass in the circles **has been flattened** by some force.

INFORMATION GAP FOR STUDENT B

Choose one of the phrases 1–4 to complete each clue that Student A reads. Switch roles after item 4. Then put the clues in the correct order and decide what the mystery item is.

Student B's Conclusions

1. . . . because of the hero-sized appetite that's needed to eat me.

2. . . . at 5 o'clock in the morning on August 6, 1762.

3. . . . was being played at a gambling table.

4. . . . an Englishman named John Montagu, the fourth earl of the place I was named after.

Student B's Prompts

5. The snack ordered by my creator was composed of . . .

6. It's almost certain . . .

7. My creator was hungry but too busy to leave the game, . . .

8. Two slices of bread with a filling between them . . .

9. And the submarine type of me . . .

13 REPORTING IDEAS AND FACTS WITH PASSIVES

GRAMMAR **IN CONTEXT**

QUESTIONS TO CONSIDER

1. Look at the illustration. What does it show? What is happening here?
2. What do you think the illustration means? Discuss your answer with a partner before you read the story.

Read an article about an unusual tribe of people.

THE SHRINE ROOM

The Strangest of Peoples

For decades anthropologists have been studying strange and unusual peoples all over the world. One of the strangest peoples of all is a group called the Nacirema, a legendary tribe living in North America.

The territory of the Nacirema is located between the Canadian Cree and the Tarahumare of Mexico. On the southeast their territory is bordered by the Arawak of the Caribbean. Relatively little is known of the origin of this people, though they are said to have come from somewhere east. In fact, the Nacirema may be related to certain European peoples.

Nacirema people spend a great deal of time on the appearance and health of their bodies. In Nacirema culture the body is generally believed to be ugly and likely to decay. The only way this decay can be prevented is through participation in certain magical ceremonies. In every Nacirema house there is a special shrine room dedicated to this purpose. Some Nacirema houses have more than one shrine room. In fact, it is felt in Nacirema culture that the more shrine rooms a family has, the richer it is.

What is in the shrine room? The focal point is a box built into the wall. Inside the box is a large collection of magical potions, medicines, and creams. Below the box is a small font from which water is obtained. Every day each member of the Nacirema family enters the shrine room, bows to the chest, and receives magic, holy water from the fountain.

Women whose heads have been baked are regarded as beautiful.

Several rituals in Nacirema culture are performed by one sex or the other, but not by both. Every morning, for example, a Nacirema man places a magic cream on his face and then scrapes and even cuts his face with a sharp instrument. A ritual performed only by women involves a barbaric ceremony in which the women bake their heads in small ovens for an hour or so. Women whose heads have been baked are regarded as beautiful.

In Nacirema culture, the mouth is considered one of the most important parts of the body. The Nacirema are fascinated by the mouth and believe that its condition has an important and supernatural effect on all social relationships. The daily body ritual involves an activity which would be considered disgusting in some cultures. It is reported that the Nacirema actually insert into their mouths a stick on one end of which are animal hairs covered with a magical paste! They then move these sticks back and forth in their mouths in highly ritualized gestures.

Among the most important individuals in the culture are practitioners named "holy-mouth-people." Naciremans visit these practitioners once or twice a year. The holy-mouth-people possess excellent sharp instruments for performing their magic ceremonies. They place these instruments in the mouths of the Naciremans. If there are any holes in the teeth, they are enlarged by the use of these tools. Then a supernatural substance is placed in each hole. It is said that the purpose of this practice is to prevent decay in the teeth and to help the Nacirema people to make friends and find spouses.

Another very important person in Nacirema culture is the "listener," a witch doctor who has the power to get rid of the devils in the heads of people who have been bewitched. Naciremans believe that parents bewitch their own children, especially while teaching them the secret toilet rituals, and that the listeners must "unbewitch" them. It is also believed that the secret to getting rid of these devils in their heads is simply to talk about them, usually while reclining on a sofa.

Much more research is needed in order to understand this strange people.

Clearly, the Nacirema are a magic-inspired tribe. Much more research is needed in order to understand this strange people.

Source: Adapted from Horace Miner, "Body Ritual among the Nacirema," *American Anthropologist* 58:3, June 1956.

UNDERSTANDING MEANING FROM CONTEXT

Circle the letter of the choice closest in meaning to the italicized word or phrase from the reading.

1. In every Nacirema house there is a special *shrine room* dedicated to this purpose.
   - **a.** place for doing work
   - **b.** place for practicing religious ceremonies
   - **c.** place for relaxing

2. Below the box is a small *font* from which water is obtained.
   - **a.** body of water
   - **b.** source of water
   - **c.** container of water

3. They then move these sticks back and forth in their mouths in highly *ritualized* gestures.
   - **a.** ceremonial
   - **b.** energetic
   - **c.** athletic

4. Naciremans believe that parents *bewitch their own children* . . .
   - **a.** criticize their own children
   - **b.** teach their own children
   - **c.** place their children under magical control

COMPREHENSION

1. Is this article serious, or is it supposed to be funny?

2. On what does the author seem to think too much of the Nacirema people's time is spent?

3. What are the magical ceremonies that are practiced by the Nacirema?

4. What is the special ritual that is performed by the Nacirema man every morning?

5. What is the special ritual that is performed by the woman?

6. Is the description of the shrine room amusing to you? Why is it funny?

7. What is your response to the author's descriptions of the Nacirema's tribal customs?

8. Pick out a few details of the descriptions that are particularly funny to you. Share them with the class to see if they are seen as humorous by everyone.

9. By whom is the story told? What do you think that person's culture might be like? Would it be different from that of the Nacirema?

GRAMMAR **PRESENTATION**
REPORTING IDEAS AND FACTS WITH PASSIVES

PASSIVE

In Nacirema culture the body **is** generally **believed** to be ugly and likely to decay.

STATIVE PASSIVE

The territory of the Nacirema **is located** between the Canadian Cree, the Tarahumare of Mexico, and the Arawak of the Caribbean.

REDUCED PASSIVE

One of the strangest peoples of all is a group **called** the Nacirema, a legendary tribe living in North America.

NOTES

EXAMPLES

1. There are two types of **passive constructions**: action passives and non-action passives. Action passives show actions. Non-action passives show ideas, beliefs, opinions, findings, and facts.

- A supernatural substance
  action passive
  is placed in each hole.
  non-action passive
- The mouth **is considered** one of the most important parts of the body.

2. Non-action passives are often used in reporting the news and in academic discourse. We use them to create an impartial and objective impression by removing the speaker or writer somewhat from the idea.

- Little **is known** about the origin of this strange people.

3. Speakers and writers can create an even greater distance between themselves and the idea by starting the sentence with *It*.

- **It is felt** that the more shrine rooms a family has, the richer it is.

4. Non-action passives are made from *be* + past participle. They are not made from *get*.

- The Nacirema people **are said** to have come from somewhere east.

5. Non-action passives frequently used to report ideas, beliefs, and opinions include *think, consider, regard, say, allege, believe, claim,* and *suggest*.

These passives can take a *by* phrase.

Passive sentences of this type can be converted to the active voice.

- Women whose heads have been baked **are regarded** as beautiful.

- Women whose heads have been baked **are regarded by Naciremans** as beautiful.

- **Naciremans regard** women whose heads have been baked as beautiful.

6. Passive sentences that express the opinions and beliefs of others are often followed by infinitives.

- In Nacirema culture the human body **is** generally **believed to be** ugly and likely to decay.

7. Stative passives are a kind of non-action passive. They are often used to report facts. Examples of stative passives include *be located* (*in, at,* etc.), *be found* (*in, at,* etc.), *be made up of, be divided* (*into, by,* etc.), *be related to*.

Stative passives cannot take a *by* phrase and cannot be converted to the active voice. There is no performer of an action.

- The Nacirema territory **is located** between the Canadian Cree, the Tarahumare of Mexico, and the Arawak of the Caribbean.

- The Nacirema **may be related to** certain European peoples. (no *by* phrase or active sentence possible)

8. Notice how some passive constructions can be reduced from full passives by deletion of *be* and the relative pronouns *who, which,* or *that*.

- One of the strangest peoples of all is a group **(that is) called** the Nacirema.

FOCUSED PRACTICE

 DISCOVER THE GRAMMAR

Part A

Look again at the opening reading, The Strangest of Peoples. *Find five action passives and five non-action passives. Write them in the blanks provided.*

Action Passives	Non-Action Passives
can be prevented	is located

Part B

Look at these two sentences from The Strangest of Peoples. *Could they be rewritten with a* **by** *phrase? Could they be rewritten in the active voice? Why or why not? Explain on the lines provided.*

1. In Nacirema culture, the mouth is considered one of the most important parts of the body.

   _____

2. In fact, the Nacirema may be related to certain European peoples.

   _____

Part C

Look again at The Strangest of Peoples. *Find the six reduced passives and rewrite them as full passives.*

1. a group called the Nacirema / a group that is called the Nacirema

2. _____

3. _____

4. _____

5. _____

6. _____

2 **MYTH, LEGEND, OR REALITY?**

Read the following article about past cultures. Complete the sentences with passive constructions, using the indicated verbs.

W RLD REVIEW

Where do we draw the lines among myth, legend, and reality? How much is true and how much invented? What happens to groups or cultures when they disappear? What happens to their people? We decided to explore some of these questions.

First let's consider the saga of the ancient pueblo people of the U.S. Southwest. They ___are called___ the Anasazi by the Navajo
1. (call)
people, a term which means "ancient ones," and though their origin _____,
2. (not know)
they _____ to have settled about
3. (think)
A.D. 100 in the Four Corners area, where today the corners of the states of Arizona, Utah, Colorado, and New Mexico come together. They _____ to have
4. (know)
developed subsistence agriculture and to have built impressive cities and spectacular cliff dwellings. About the year 1300, however, something happened to the Anasazi.

They abandoned their dwellings and migrated to other locales such as the Rio Grande Valley in New Mexico and the White Mountains in Arizona.

Today it _____ by many
5. (assume)
anthropologists that the Anasazi are the forebears of present-day pueblo peoples in the Southwest. The question remains, however: What brought an end to their flourishing culture? Drought? Incursions by unfriendly tribes? Can certain present-day Native Americans of the Southwest _____ as the descendants of
6. (regard)
the Anasazi? Or did the Anasazi actually disappear?

Next, let's turn our attention to the story of Atlantis, the famed "lost continent" which _____ to have existed in the
7. (say)
Atlantic Ocean. Supposedly Atlantis _____ west of the Strait of
8. (locate)
Gibraltar, which _____ the
9. (call)

Pillars of Hercules by the Greeks. Is Atlantis a myth, or does it have a basis in reality? Plato wrote about Atlantis in two of his dialogues, describing it as a fabulous island larger than Libya and Turkey put together. Atlantis _____ by Plato to have
10. (believe)
existed about nine thousand years before his era. The Atlanteans _____ to
11. (repute)
have conquered many lands around the Mediterranean and _____ to
12. (say)
have become evil and greedy in the process. Their island or continent _____
13. (suppose)
to have sunk into the sea after being hit by earthquakes. Was there really an Atlantis? Were the survivors of the catastrophe really the ancestors of the present-day Basques, as

_____ by certain twentieth-
14. (claim)

century tale-spinners? Is the Atlantis story just an entertaining legend invented by Plato? Or, if Atlantis was real, is the problem simply that it existed so long ago that wisps of its memory are all that remain? The legend of Atlantis _____ by many present-
15. (think)
day scholars to have been influenced by reports of the disaster on the island of Thira, north of Crete in the Mediterranean Sea. Thira was destroyed about 1500 B.C. by volcanic eruptions and accompanying earthquakes, which also devastated civilization on nearby Crete. Is the Thira disaster the basis for the Atlantis legend, or do the descendants of Atlanteans walk among us? The answer

_____.
16. (not / yet / know)

3 EDITING

Read the following student essay about a creature that may or may not be real. Find and correct the ten errors in passive constructions. Some passive constructions have more than one error.

The Snowman

Every area of the world has its own legends, and Asia is no different. One of the most famous is the Abominable Snowman, or yeti, of the Himalayas. Is yeti just a legend that is ~~believe~~ ^{believed} because people want strange things to be real, or does he really exist?

Yeti said to be a huge creature—perhaps as tall as eight feet. His body is suppose to be covered with long, brown hair. He said to have a pointed head and a hairless face that looks something like a man's. And it is claiming that he lives near Everest, the highest mountain in the world.

Sightings of yeti have reported for centuries, but he was made know to the rest of the world only in 1921. In that year, members of an expedition to climb Mt. Everest saw very large tracks in the snow that looked like prints of a human foot. No conclusive evidence of Yeti's existence was found during that expedition, but interest stimulated. Other expeditions were made. In 1951, explorer Eric Shipton led a search in which some gigantic, human-appearing tracks were found. One again, yeti himself was not seen. In 1969, Sir Edmund Hillary, who along with Tenzing Norkay first climbed Mt. Everest, mounted another expedition, this time with the intention not only of seeing yeti but of capturing him. Once again, tracks were discovered, but that was all. Hillary apparently decided eventually that the tracks might simply be normal animal tracks enlarged by the daytime melting of the snow. In 1964, Boris F. Porshev, a Russian scientist, said that he believed that yeti actually existed. He theorized that yeti is a surviving descendant of Neanderthal man, a creature who thought to have lived 25,000 to 75,000 years ago. Porshev has never been able to see an actual yeti, however.

The mystery continues. Does yeti really exist, or do people just want to believe he exists? It seems to me that there must be more to this mystery than just melted tracks. Centuries of reports by Himalayan sherpas must mean something. Besides, other yeti-type creatures have reported—most notably, Bigfoot in North America. Time will tell, but in the meantime, perhaps we shouldn't be so quick to dismiss the Abominable Snowman as nothing more than an entertaining story.

Source: Based on information in Kenneth B. Platnick, "Yeti," in *Great Mysteries of History* (New York: Dorset Press, 1971).

COMMUNICATION PRACTICE

❹ LISTENING 1

Listen to the news bulletin. Then listen again and mark the following statements **True, False,** *or* **I don't know** *based on what you heard on the news bulletin.*

	True	False	I don't know
1. The earthquakes are said to have registered a nine on the Richter scale.	❏	❏	❏
2. The epicenter of the quakes was located in the Pacific Ocean.	❏	❏	❏
3. The exact number of drowned people is known.	❏	❏	❏
4. It is certain that severe flooding has occurred inland.	❏	❏	❏
5. The citizens of the country should head for low areas.	❏	❏	❏
6. The country struck by earthquakes is very large.	❏	❏	❏
7. The citizens of this country are calm, gentle, and law-abiding.	❏	❏	❏
8. The time is the present day.	❏	❏	❏

❺ LISTENING 2

Listen to the TV quiz game.

Comprehension

Now listen again. Match these items to complete each statement.

_____ **1.** Homer

_____ **2.** Siddartha Gautama

_____ **3.** Simón Bolívar

_____ **4.** Anastasia Romanova

_____ **5.** Plato

a. was thought to have been murdered in the 1917 Russian revolution.

b. is thought to have created the story of Atlantis.

c. is known as the father of Buddhism.

d. is considered the father of South American democracy.

e. is thought to have been the author of the *Iliad* and the *Odyssey*.

Optional Dictation

🔊 *Now listen again, completing the sentences with passive constructions.*

He _____was called_____ the Liberator and _____ the father of South
          1.   2.
American democracy.

He _____ the author of the *Iliad* and the *Odyssey*. However, it
          3.

_____ for certain whether he was one specific person or a composite of
          4.
many people.

His *Dialogues* _____ today all over the world. He _____ in
                    5.   6.
Greece in 427 B.C. Some people say that the myth of Atlantis _____ by him.
                                                                  7.

Born in India, he _____ as the father of Buddhism, a religion that
                    8.

_____ by many people in Asia.
          9.

She _____ in the 1917 revolution. It _____ persistently
          10.

_____ that this one daughter somehow survived the assassination attempt
          11.
and eventually made her way to America.

⑥ GROUP GUESSING GAME

*Divide into groups of four to six. Using passive
constructions, prepare five or more statements about any
famous figure you choose: a political or religious leader,
an author, an explorer, an inventor, and so on. The other
students in your group will try to guess who the figure is.
Make the first statements less obvious than the later ones.*

> **EXAMPLES:**
> 1. He **was called** "great soul" by his followers
>   and admirers.
> 2. In his time, he **was revered** for, among
>   other things, his efforts in favor of the
>   untouchables.
> 3. He **is known** today as the father of the
>   nonviolent movement called passive
>   resistance.

4. He **is regarded** as the principal force behind the achievement of India's independence.

5. In the world today he **is considered** one of the greatest religious leaders of all time.

Answer: Mohandas (Mahatma) Gandhi

 THE NACIREMA

Read more about the Nacirema.

The focal point of the shrine is a box or chest which is built into the wall. In this chest are kept the many charms and magical potions without which no native believes he could live. These preparations are secured from a variety of specialized practitioners. The most powerful of these are the medicine men, whose assistance must be rewarded with substantial gifts. However, the medicine men do not provide the curative potions for their clients, but decide what the ingredients should be and then write them down in an ancient and secret language. This writing is understood only by the medicine men and by the herbalists who, for another gift, provide the required charm.

The charm is not disposed of after it has served its purpose, but is placed in the charm-box of the household shrine. As these magical materials are specific for certain ills, and the real or imagined maladies of the people are many, the charm-box is usually full to overflowing. The magical packets are so numerous that people forget what their purposes were and fear to use them again. While the natives are very vague on this point, we can only assume that the idea in retaining all the old magical materials is that their presence in the charm-box, before which the body rituals are conducted, will in some way protect the worshipper.

The focal point of the shrine is a box or chest which is built into the wall.

Source: Horace Miner, "Body Ritual among the Nacirema," *American Anthropologist*, 58:3, June 1956.

Now, with a partner, decide what these items really represent:

the charm-box   herbalists
the medicine men   magical packets

 ESSAY

Imagine that you are writing a description like the Nacirema story about the people of your own country. Write two or three paragraphs. Describe some habits that you think other people would find amusing, or describe them in an amusing way as in the Nacirema story. Have fun!

9 PICTURE DISCUSSION

Divide into several groups and study this map of the East Asian region. Discuss what you know about the history, culture, peoples, and geography of this area. Then, as a group, prepare a set of questions with passive voice about some of the facts you discussed. Each group should take a turn asking questions of the other groups. Score points.

REVIEW OR SELFTEST

I. *Complete the conversations with* **be** *or* **get** *passive forms and the indicated verbs. Use* **be** *unless* **get** *is specified.*

1. **A:** Where _____was the missing child found_____ ?
       <u>a. (the missing child / find)</u>

   B: She _____ walking barefoot along
            <u>b. (discover)</u>
   Stinson Beach.

2. **A:** How do you think the team is going to do this year?

   B: Pretty well, except that I'm sure they'll

       _____ by Central University.
            <u>(get / beat)</u>

3. **A:** What happened to your car?

   B: It _____ by a truck—a small one,
            <u>(get / hit)</u>
   fortunately.

4. **A:** Mary, _____ for six months.
            <u>a. (we / getting / overcharge)</u>

   B: I think we ought to _____ . I've heard the
                  <u>b. (have / the company / investigate)</u>
   same complaint from the neighbors.

5. **A:** Why are these floors so dirty? _____
                                  <u>a. (they / not / clean)</u>
   every day?

   B: Normally, yes, but somehow the cleaning

       _____ this morning.
            <u>b. (not / get / do)</u>

6. **A:** Please don't give food to the animals. They

       _____ on a special diet.
            <u>a. (feed)</u>

   B: OK. Will we be able to see the animals

       _____ while we're here at the zoo?
            <u>b. (getting / feed)</u>

   A: Yes. _____ at four o'clock today.
                  <u>c. (they / will / feed)</u>

II. *Read the newspaper article. Rewrite the six numbered sentences, changing passive verb forms to the active and active verb forms to the passive. Eliminate all **by** phrases in passive sentences. Do not change intransitive verbs, and do not change the quotation.*

<u>It is said by local citizen Ronald Mason that his lesson has been learned by him</u>. On
1.

Tuesday, Mason was in a hurry to get to a job interview. <u>His motorcycle was parked by</u>
2.

<u>him in a handicap parking space</u>. <u>When Mason came out of the interview, it was</u>
(2. continued) **3.**

<u>discovered by him that someone had removed his motorcycle from the handicap spot</u>.
(3. continued)

<u>Someone had placed it upside down in the pool of the adjacent fountain</u>. <u>People had</u>
4. **5.**

<u>noticed no one in the area</u>. <u>After recovering his motorcycle, it was said by Mason, "I'll</u>
(5. continued) **6.**

never do that again. I deserved what I got."

1. <u>Local citizen Ronald Mason says that he has learned his lesson.</u>

2. _____

3. _____

4. _____

5. _____

6. _____

III. *Fill in the blanks in the paragraph with passive forms of the indicated verbs.*

Consider the situation of the mysterious "lost colony" established by Sir Walter Raleigh

in 1585 on the Outer Banks of what is now North Carolina. It _____is felt_____
1. (feel)

today that the plan for the settlement, which _____ on Roanoke Island,
2. (locate)

was ill conceived from the start. Geographical conditions were not favorable, and the local

tribes were not friendly. In 1590 all of the colonists _____ by explorers to
3. (find)

have vanished, leaving behind only some refuse and the word *Croatoan*, the name of a

nearby island, written on a tree. What happened to the colonists? No one knows for sure,

but today they _____ to have been killed or carried away by neighboring
4. (assume)

peoples.

Today it _____ by some that at least a few of the colonists were
      5. (believe)
absorbed into local tribes. In fact, descendants of the original native inhabitants of the

area claim Raleigh's colonists as their ancestors. If this is true, the people of the lost

colony _____ lost at all, for their genes live on in those descendants.
   6. (not / should / consider)

Source: Adapted from Kenneth C. Davis, *Don't Know Much About History?* (New York: Avon Books, 1990), pp. 13–14.

IV. *Look at the pictures. For each picture, write a passive sentence with* **be** *or* **get**.
Use **be** *unless* **get** *is specified, using the suggested prompts.*

1.

Mrs. O'Reilly (get / catch)

Mrs. O'Reilly is going to get

caught for speeding if

she doesn't slow down.

2.

Mrs. O'Reilly (get / stop)

_____

_____

_____

3.

Two months ago (tear down)

_____

_____

_____

4.

Now (build)

_____

_____

_____

5.

Mrs. Platt (have / repair)

_____

_____

_____

6.

Once a month / Mr. Platt
(get / cut and trim)

_____

_____

_____

7.

The yeti / the Himalaya Mountains
(think / live)

_____

_____

_____

8.

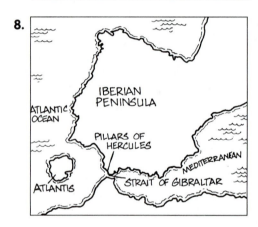

The lost continent of Atlantis /
Atlantic Ocean / Strait of Gibraltar
(say / be located)

_____

_____

_____

V. *Read the sentences in the news broadcast. Circle the letter of the one underlined word or phrase that is <u>not</u> correct.*

This is news to the hour on KXYZ.

1. The Hawaiian island of Kahoolawe <u>has</u> just <u>being</u> <u>hit</u> <u>by</u> a tsunami,
                                 A   B   C D

or tidal wave.

                 A **(B)** C   D

2. The tsunami <u>were</u> <u>caused</u> <u>by</u> an earthquake <u>centered</u> in the Pacific   A B C D
     A   B   C   D
Ocean south-southeast of Midway Island.

3. Damage on Kahoolawe <u>is</u> <u>say</u> <u>to</u> <u>be</u> extensive.   A B C D
                    A   B   C D

4. In Central Africa, a breakthrough <u>is</u> <u>being</u> <u>report</u> involving resumption   A B C D
                          A   B   C
of the <u>stalled</u> peace talks.
        D

5. These talks <u>were</u> <u>been</u> <u>held</u> last week <u>between</u> the leaders of Tintoria   A B C D
              A   B   C   D
and Illyria.

6. They <u>have been</u> <u>broken off</u> <u>when</u> the president of Illyria <u>stormed</u> out   A B C D
        A   B   C   D
of the first face-to-face meeting.

7. The Secretary-General of the United Nations <u>says</u>, "We <u>must</u> <u>get</u> these   A B C D
                                      A   B   C
talks <u>start</u> again."
       D

8. In fact, it <u>is</u> <u>rumored</u> that the talks <u>are be</u> <u>resumed</u> next week in   A B C D
             A   B   C   D
Switzerland.

9. The new space station that <u>is being</u> <u>sponsored</u> by the seven-nation   A B C D
                         A   B
consortium <u>will</u> <u>launch</u> next week from Woomera Field in Australia.
            C   D

10. The station <u>will</u> <u>be</u> <u>staff</u> by astronauts from each of the seven   A B C D
                A   B   C
<u>participating</u> nations.
   D

That's news to the hour from KXYZ.

VI. *Go back to your answers for Exercise V. Write the correct answer for each item you believe to be incorrect.*

1. _been_____   **6.** _____

2. _____   **7.** _____

3. _____   **8.** _____

4. _____   **9.** _____

5. _____   **10.** _____

▶ **To check your answers, go to the Answer Key on page 256.**

FROM GRAMMAR TO WRITING
PARALLELISM

Parallelism (also called parallel structure) is an important feature of English that makes our speaking, and especially our writing, easier to understand. To make speech or writing parallel, put all items in a series in the same grammatical form.

EXAMPLES:

Over the weekend I **bought a new car**, **painted the living room**, and **planted a garden**. (All three verbs in the predicate are in the simple past and in the active voice.)

The prisoner **was arrested**, **taken** to the police station, and **booked** and **fingerprinted**. (All three verb phrases are in the passive voice.)

My favorite hobbies are **skindiving**, **reading**, and **playing the guitar**. (All three subject complements are gerunds or gerund phrases.)

Children in this program are not allowed **to watch television** or **to eat junk food**. (The two complements are infinitive phrases.)

We will concentrate in this unit on parallelism with nouns and articles and with active or passive voice. See *From Grammar to Writing* after Part VII, page 342, for a discussion of parallelism with gerunds and infinitives.

In writing sentences that contain a series of nouns and articles, you can place the article before each noun or before the first noun only. However, it is more common to place the article before each noun.

EXAMPLES:

On her shopping trip, Mrs. Figueroa bought **a** book, **a** dress, and **a** CD.

OR

On her shopping trip, Mrs. Figueroa bought **a** book, dress, and CD.

NOT

~~On her shopping trip, Mrs. Figueroa bought a book, dress, and a CD.~~

Read the following paragraph and correct the five errors in parallel structure with nouns and articles.

Rolleen Laing poured herself a second cup of coffee as she ate her breakfast, which consisted of a fried egg, ~~*an*~~ orange, and a piece of dry toast. She was sixty-two years old and had been successful as a university professor, writer of detective fiction, and an amateur detective. Just then the telephone rang. It was Harry Sadler, a local police detective. Ever since Rolleen had helped Harry crack a murder case several years previously, she had been called in as an unofficial consultant on several cases. She had helped Harry solve cases involving a hit-and-run victim, a murdered television executive, and, most recently, koala stolen from the city zoo.

"Hi, Rolleen. This is Harry. You're needed on another case. It's a robbery this time. Some thieves broke into the art museum and stole a Van Gogh, Picasso, Gauguin, and a Matisse. Meet me at the museum at 10:00, OK?"

In sentences with the passive voice, the auxiliary may be repeated each time or before the first item only. If the parallel items are short, the auxiliary is generally not repeated.

> The prisoner **was arrested**, **tried**, and **found** innocent.

If the parallel items are long, the auxiliary is generally repeated for the sake of clarity.

> The mythical nation of Atlantis **is said** to have existed about twelve thousand years ago, **is thought** to have been located in the Atlantic Ocean west of the Strait of Gibraltar, and **can be regarded** as a thematic source of many present-day legends of lost peoples.

Notice the following nonparallel sentence with two phrases with the passive voice and one with the active.

> The evidence was taken to the crime lab, a team of biochemists analyzed it, and used in a criminal trial.

To put this sentence in parallel structure, change the middle item to the passive voice, eliminating the word *it*.

> The evidence **was taken** to the crime lab, **analyzed by a team of biochemists**, and **used** in a criminal trial.

2 *Each of the following sentences contains an error in parallelism involving active or passive voice. In each case, one item is nonparallel with the others. Correct the nonparallel item.*

1. Yeti is described as a huge creature, ^is^ said to have long, brown hair, and is thought to live in the Himalayan Mountains.

2. According to historical records, the American outlaw Billy the Kid was known as a fearless gunfighter, was hunted by the law, and killed in a gunfight.

3. Anthropologists speculate that the Anasazi might have been attacked by unfriendly tribes, decimated by crop failures, or drought might have driven them away.

4. After Amelia Earhart's airplane was lost, naval investigators searched for debris, interviewed residents of South Pacific islands, but no trace of Earhart and Noonan was found.

5. According to legend, the continent of Atlantis was struck by devastating earthquakes, inundated by floods, and the ocean swallowed it up.

3 *Read the following paragraph about the Judge Crater mystery. Correct the three errors in parallelism with active or passive voice.*

On the evening of August 6, 1930, Judge Force Crater, a wealthy, successful, and good-looking New York lawyer, disappeared without a trace. Earlier in the evening he had been seen with friends at a Manhattan restaurant. At 9:10 P.M. he left the restaurant, hailed a taxi, and ~~was driven~~ *drove* away. No one ever saw or heard from him again. It was ten days before he was even reported missing. On August 16, his wife called his courthouse, the secretary was asked about his whereabouts, and learned that he was probably off on political business. This news reassured Mrs. Crater somewhat, but when he still hadn't turned up by August 26, a group of his fellow judges started an investigation. A grand jury was convened, but its members could not come to any conclusion as to what had happened to Judge Crater. They theorized that the judge might have developed amnesia, run away voluntarily, or been a crime victim. His wife disagreed with the first two possibilities, holding that he had been murdered by someone in the Tammany Hall organization, the political machine that controlled New York City at the time. The mystery remains unsolved to this day. He could have been killed by a Tammany Hall hiree, a girlfriend could have murdered him, or kidnapped by an organized crime group. He might in fact have suffered from amnesia, or he might have planned his own disappearance. Reports of Judge Crater sightings have continued to surface over the last sixty years.

Source: Adapted from E. Randall Floyd, *Great American Mysteries* (Little Rock: August House Publishers, 1990).

4 APPLY IT TO YOUR WRITING

Write a paragraph of six to ten sentences on one of the following topics. Use the passive voice where appropriate.

- An accident or natural disaster that you have witnessed or heard about

- An unsolved mystery that you are aware of

- An unusual or mysterious experience you have had

In your paragraph, include at least one sentence containing verbs in the passive voice in parallel structure. Also include at least one sentence containing a series of nouns in parallel structure. Exchange papers with a partner. Discuss each other's paper and then rewrite your paragraph if necessary. Submit your paragraph to your teacher.

REVIEW OR SELFTEST
ANSWER KEY

I.
1b. was discovered
2. get beaten
3. got hit
4a. we've been getting overcharged
4b. have the company investigated
5a. Aren't they cleaned
5b. didn't get done
6a. are fed
6b. getting fed
6c. They'll be fed

II.
2. He parked his motorcycle in a handicap parking space.
3. When Mason came out of the interview, he discovered that his motorcycle had been removed from the handicap spot.
4. It had been placed upside down in the pool of the adjacent fountain.
5. No one had been noticed in the area.
6. After recovering his motorcycle, Mason said, "I'll never do that again. I deserved what I got."

III.
2. was located
3. were found
4. are assumed
5. is believed
6. should not be considered

IV. Possible Answers
2. Mrs. O'Reilly got stopped by a police officer.
3. Two months ago this old building was being torn down.
4. Now a new stadium is being built here.
5. Mrs. Platt is going to have her toaster repaired.
6. Once a month, Mr. Platt gets his hair cut and his beard trimmed.
7. The yeti is thought to live in the Himalaya Mountains.
8. The lost continent of Atlantis is said to have been located in the Atlantic Ocean west of the Strait of Gibraltar.

V.
2. A
3. B
4. C
5. B
6. A
7. D
8. C
9. D
10. C

VI.
2. was
3. said
4. reported
5. being
6. were
7. started
8. are going to be / will be
9. be launched
10. staffed

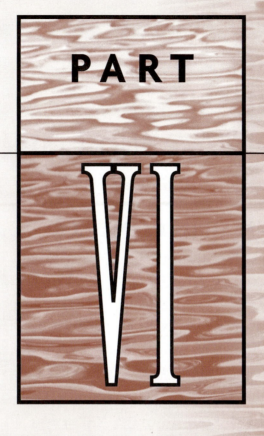

PART VI

AUXILIARIES AND PHRASAL VERBS

AUXILIARIES: CONTRAST AND EMPHASIS

GRAMMAR **IN CONTEXT**

QUESTIONS TO CONSIDER

1. Do you think the order in which children are born determines their character?

2. In your view, can people change their character, or is it basically predetermined?

Read an article about birth order.

DOES IT MATTER WHEN YOU WERE BORN?

DEAR READER,

Let's see if you can answer the following question. No doubt you can. Here goes: There are two men, one named Steve and the other named Jerry. They're pretty similar, when you come right down to it. Steve is a perfectionist. So is Jerry. Jerry, always a high achiever, was president of his high school class. So was Steve. Neither man went to college. Both did become successful businessmen, though. Jerry has been a leader in most of his enterprises. So has Steve. Steve always tries to obey rules. Jerry does, too. Jerry has never liked "liberal" ideas. Neither has Steve. The question is, why are they similar?

"Wait!" you say, "I know what the explanation is: They're identical twins. That's why they're so similar." Well, dear reader, I'm sorry to disappoint you, but that isn't it. They're not twins, or even related to each other. But they are both firstborns. Steve and Jerry are examples of what researchers are calling the birth-order theory. According to this theory, the order in which children are born plays a significant role in the formation of their personalities and in the way they ultimately turn out. Does this sound like some crazy, outlandish new theory? It isn't. It's been around for a while.

The main idea behind the birth-order theory is quite simple: Firstborn children enjoy a special relationship with their parents simply because they were there before any other children were. When other children come along, firstborns know intuitively that these interlopers represent a challenge to their special relationship. For this reason, firstborns tend to be conservative, rule-oriented, and desirous of maintaining the status quo. They want to keep things as they are. Laterborns have a different challenge. They must somehow carve out a niche in their parents' affections. They sense that they have to become different from the oldest child, so they do.

> ... first-, second-, and laterborns often have sharply different characteristics.

One of the leading proponents of the birth-order theory is Frank Sulloway, a researcher who did a twenty-six-year study in which he fed into a computer data about 7,000 famous people in history. The results of the computer analysis led Sulloway to formulate his theory that first-, second-, and laterborns often have sharply different characteristics. According to Sulloway, firstborns are usually self-confident, assertive, conscientious, and conservative. They can also be jealous, moralistic, and inflexible. Winston Churchill, John Wayne, Oprah Winfrey, and Joseph Stalin were all firstborns. Based on this idea, we might expect powerful political figures, such as U.S. presidents, to be firstborns. They usually are, says Sulloway.

Lastborns, Sulloway observes, are usually more social, more agreeable, and more open to new and even revolutionary ideas. This is because, sensing the power of the already-established relationship between the oldest sibling and the parent, they have to turn outward to establish their place in the world. Thus they tend to identify with the underdog in a given situation and to attack the establishment. Famous lastborns, according to Sulloway, are Joan of Arc, Thomas Jefferson, and Leon Trotsky. By the way, perhaps you're wondering whether Sulloway himself might be a lastborn. He is.

What about families in which there are more than two children, or only one? If there are three children in a family, the middle child is usually more flexible than the other two and often has a talent for compromise. And a family in which there is only one child is the least predictable configuration, Sulloway says. Only children aren't as inflexible as firstborns. Like firstborns, they do identify with their parents, however.

Perhaps you're saying to yourself, "But this is all just too much of a generalization, isn't it?" Yes, maybe it is. Sulloway is the first to acknowledge that there are many exceptions to the birth-order theory. A child's inherent temperament has a great deal to do with how he or she turns out. Shy children, for example, may not become movers and shakers even if they are firstborns. And, as Sulloway notes, there have been a lot of famous historical firstborns who became revolutionaries, as well as laterborns who became conservative. Still, the theory of birth order does appear to be valid in its general assumptions.

Assuming that there is some validity to the birth-order theory, what can parents do to achieve the best possible relationships with their

(continued on next page)

children? In Sulloway's view, they should give each child special and unique time and attention. If they do, they probably won't significantly change the influences of birth order, but they will maximize the quality of those relationships.

Source: Based on "Born First or Last: Does it Matter?" by Carol Kramer. Internet. OCP General Research. http://www.eisa.net.au/~santeri/fbol.html

UNDERSTANDING MEANING FROM CONTEXT

Circle the letter of the choice closest in meaning to the italicized word or expression from the reading.

1. When other children come along, firstborns know intuitively that these *interlopers* represent a challenge to their special relationship.

   a. people who interfere
   b. people who are intelligent
   c. people who take control

2. For this reason, firstborns tend to be conservative, rule-oriented, and desirous of maintaining the *status quo*.

   a. situation of special privilege
   b. already-existing situation
   c. newly developing situation

3. They must somehow *carve out a niche in* their parents' affections.

   a. make a special place in
   b. become number one in
   c. not be worried about

4. Thus they tend to identify with the *underdog* in a given situation and to attack the establishment.

   a. person who behaves like an animal
   b. person with the greatest advantage
   c. person with the greatest disadvantage

5. A child's *inherent* temperament has a great deal to do with how he or she turns out.

   a. learned
   b. inborn
   c. created

6. Shy children, for example, may not become *movers and shakers* even if they are firstborns.

   a. athletes
   b. dangerous people
   c. active people

GRAMMAR **PRESENTATION**
BE AND **AUXILIARIES**

REFERENCES TO PRECEDING INFORMATION

Let's see if you can answer the following question. No doubt you **can**.

Does this sound like some crazy, outlandish new theory? It **isn't**.

TAG QUESTIONS AND SHORT ANSWERS

"But this is all just too much of a generalization, **isn't** it?" Yes, maybe it **is**.

SO, TOO, NEITHER, AND *EITHER*

Jerry has been a leader in most of his enterprises. **So has** Steve.

Steve always tries to obey rules. Jerry **does too**.

Jerry has never liked "liberal" ideas. **Neither has** Steve.

Jerry has never liked "liberal" ideas. Steve **hasn't either**.

CONTRAST AND EMPHASIS

They're not twins. But they **are** both firstborns.

Neither man went to college. Both **did become** successful businessmen, though.

Only children aren't as inflexible as firstborns. Like firstborns, they **do identify** with their parents, however.

NOTES	EXAMPLES

1. Auxiliaries are **helping verbs**. They show **tense** and **number** and are used in forming questions and in making sentences negative. They can occur alone in a sentence or along with main verbs. There are four categories of auxiliaries in English:

a. The verb *be*: *am, are, is, was, were*

- Steve and Jerry are examples of what researchers **are** calling the birth-order theory.

b. The verb *do*: *do, does, did*

- **Does** this sound like some crazy, outlandish new theory?

c. The verb *have*: *have, has, had*

- Jerry **has** never liked "liberal" ideas.

d. The modal verbs: *can, could, shall, should, will, would, may, might, must, ought to*

- In Sulloway's view, they **should** give each child special and unique time and attention.
- Let's see if you **can** answer the following question.

2. We often use auxiliaries to refer to **verbs** or **verb phrases** that have already been mentioned. In this way, we do not have to repeat the verb or verb phrase.

- Let's see if you can answer the following question. No doubt you **can**. (*Can* refers to *answer the following question*, which does not have to be repeated.)

We can use the verb *be* to refer to **previously mentioned adjectives** or **noun phrases** without having to repeat those words.

- Does this sound like some crazy, outlandish new theory? It **isn't**. (The verb *isn't* refers to the noun phrase *crazy, outlandish new theory*, which does not have to be repeated.)

3. Auxiliaries are used to form **tag questions** and **short answers**.

- Firstborns tend to identify with their parents, **don't** they?
- Yes, they **do**.

4. Notice how auxiliaries are used with the words *too*, *either*, *so*, and *neither*.

- Steve is a perfectionist. **So is** Jerry. (OR Jerry *is too*.)
- Jerry has never liked "liberal" ideas. **Neither has** Steve. (OR Steve *hasn't either*.)

▶ **BE CAREFUL!** When we make comparative statements with *so* and *neither*, we place these words at the beginning of the sentence and invert the subject and the auxiliary.

- Steve didn't go to college. **Neither did** Jerry.
  NOT Steve didn't go to college. ~~Neither Jerry did~~.

5. When speakers want to place special **emphasis** on a verb (or any other word), they pronounce it with stress. Speakers **stress** words for insistence or for contrast with a preceding statement. Notice the difference between contracted forms and full forms. The contracted forms are the normal ones in conversation. We use the full forms to emphasize something or to contradict a previous statement. Notice that in sentences containing auxiliaries used for contrast and emphasis, there is often a contrast word such as *but*, *though*, *however*, or *still*.

Note: *Be* as a main verb can be used for emphasis and contrast in the same way as auxiliary verbs are used.

In the simple present and simple past tenses, the auxiliaries *do*, *does*, and *did* are used in affirmative sentences to show contrast and emphasis.

- And, as Sulloway notes, there **have** been a lot of famous historical firstborns who became revolutionaries, as well as laterborns who became conservative. (Stressing *have* indicates insistence.)
- They're not twins. But they **are** both firstborns. (Stressing *are* makes a contrast with the first statement.)

- Neither man went to college. Both **did become** successful businessmen, though.

FOCUSED PRACTICE

 DISCOVER THE GRAMMAR

Part A

Look at these sentences from the opening reading. Find and underline the preceding verb, noun, or adjective phrase referred to by the boldface verbs. Draw an arrow between the two.

1. Let's see if you can <u>answer the following question</u>. No doubt you **can**.

2. Steve is a perfectionist. So **is** Jerry.

3. Jerry has been a leader in most of his enterprises. So **has** Steve.

4. Steve always tries to obey rules. Jerry **does** too.

5. Jerry, always a high achiever, was president of his high school class. So **was** Steve.

6. Jerry has never liked "liberal" ideas. Neither **has** Steve.

7. Does this sound like some crazy, outlandish new theory? It **isn't**.

8. They were there before any other children **were**.

9. They sense that they have to become different from the oldest child, so they **do**.

10. Based on this idea, we might expect powerful political figures, such as U.S. presidents, to be firstborns. They usually **are**, says Sulloway.

11. By the way, perhaps you're wondering whether Sulloway himself might be a lastborn. He **is**.

12. "But this is perhaps too much of a generalization, isn't it?" Yes, maybe it **is**.

13. In Sulloway's view, they should give each child special and unique time and attention. If they **do**, they probably won't significantly change the influences of birth order, but they will maximize the quality of those relationships.

Part B

Look again at the opening reading. Find six sentences in which auxiliaries are used to show contrast or emphasis. Write the main parts of those sentences here and underline the auxiliary.

1. Both <u>did</u> become successful businessmen, though.

2. _____

3. _____

4. _____

5. _____

6. _____

② YOU'D BETTER TELL THEM   Grammar Notes 1, 2, 4, 6

Part A

Jeremy Washburn and his sister Sara are having a conversation. Work with a partner. Number the sentences in the correct order to complete the story.

JEREMY: It's not a good time. Dad will be in a bad mood. He just got home from work, didn't he? _____

SARA: You did too break it! Who else could it have been? It must've been you. You shouldn't have been playing there! You know we're only supposed to play ball in the back yard, don't you? _____

JEREMY: I don't think so. It's only cracked, anyway. Besides, they didn't even notice it was broken until you told them. _____

JEREMY: No. I might get in trouble if I tell them. _____

SARA: Tell them what you told me. Tell them you're sorry if you broke it, but you don't think you did because you didn't hear the ball hit the window. Mom and Dad are reasonable people. That should satisfy them. It was an accident, after all. _____

SARA: They did too notice it. They noticed it before I told them. You'd better tell them you did it. You know what Mom always says: "The truth is always the way to go." _____

JEREMY: I know, but we had to stay in the front yard. We knew Jennifer—she's that gorgeous new girl in my class—well, she was going to walk by, and we wanted her to see us playing. _____

SARA: This is the best time to tell them. _____

SARA: You will get in trouble, but you'll get in worse trouble if you don't. How did it get broken, anyhow? _____

JEREMY: I can't do it right now. Maybe after dinner . . . _____

SARA: He got home from work a while ago, and he's in a good mood. He was smiling. I just saw him. _____

JEREMY: I'm scared. What will I say? _____

JEREMY: I honestly don't know. Sam and I were playing ball in the front yard. The ball might've hit the window, but we didn't hear it. Maybe we didn't break it. _____

SARA: Are you going to tell Dad and Mom that you broke that window? ___1___

Part B

Look back at the opening reading, Does It Matter When You Were Born? *Assuming that the birth-order theory is valid, which child, Sara or Jeremy, do you think is older? Talk with a partner. Be ready to support your answer by referring to the article.*

3 LET'S TALK IT OVER

Brent Washburn is having a conversation with his thirteen-year-old son, Jeremy, about Jeremy's recent behavior. Listen to their conversation. Then listen again. Circle the ten auxiliary verbs that show emphasis or make a contrast with a preceding statement.

BRENT: Jeremy, come on into the living room. There are some things we need to talk about.

JEREMY: Dad, if it's about the broken window in the bathroom, I can explain. I guess I did break it, but I didn't mean to. It was an accident, really.

BRENT: It wasn't the window I wanted to talk about. I was wondering how it got broken, though.

JEREMY: It's not the window? What do you want to talk about, then?

BRENT: Well, for one thing, I got a letter in the mail from your teacher, Mrs. Hammond. She says you haven't been studying and you might fail. You do want to pass the seventh grade, don't you?

JEREMY: Of course. And I have been studying, Dad. I just keep forgetting to turn in my homework.

BRENT: She says you don't pay attention in class, either, and you're always staring out the window.

JEREMY: Dad, she's just got it in for me. I do pay attention. Just because I'm not looking at Mrs. Hammond doesn't mean I'm not paying attention to what she's saying. She just doesn't like me. She's boring, too.

BRENT: Jeremy, I've known Mrs. Hammond for a long time. Her classes may not be all fun and games, but she does know how to teach. From now on, I want you to study every evening from 7:00 till 9:00, and I'm going to call Mrs. Hammond every week to see if you're turning in your homework. And I will call every week. Don't think I won't.

JEREMY: Do I still get to watch TV and play video games?

BRENT: Not during the week until your grades improve. You can't have any friends over during the week, either. Of course, you can read a book if you've got your homework done. OK. Now let's talk about the window. What did happen to the window?

4 FAMILY DYNAMICS

Here are excerpts from a dinner table conversation in the Grenough family. Complete the conversations with sentences using verbs to show contrast and emphasis or to refer to a verb or adjective already mentioned.

MRS. GRENOUGH: Kids, come on, now. You should eat your asparagus.

SAMANTHA: Do I have to, Mom? I don't like asparagus.

MOLLY: Neither _____*do I*_____ .

                    1.

MRS. GRENOUGH: Yes, _____ eat it. It's good for you.

                           2.

MOLLY: Mom, if I eat it, it'll make me sick. I know it _____ .

                                                          3.

MRS. GRENOUGH: No, _____ . Don't be silly.

                        4.

MR. GRENOUGH: Steve, what about your homework? You promised me you were going to

do it before dinner.

STEVE: I _____ it, Dad.

               5.

MR. GRENOUGH: You _____ ? When? While you were watching TV?

                         6.

STEVE: From 5:00 to 5:30. It only took me a half hour.

MR. GRENOUGH: What about you, girls? Have you finished your homework? We need to

be leaving for the concert pretty soon.

SAMANTHA: I _____, Dad.
           7.

MOLLY: So _____.
        8.

MRS. GRENOUGH: What was that you said about a concert, John?

MR. GRENOUGH: You know, the big Bonnie Raitt concert—the one we've had tickets to

for a month.

MRS. GRENOUGH: It's not tonight, _____?
               9.

MR. GRENOUGH: Yes. _____. You forgot, _____?
              10.   11.

MRS. GRENOUGH: Oh, no! I'm not ready. Come on, now. Everyone needs to help. Who'll

clear the table?

STEVE: I _____, Mom.
        12.

MR. GRENOUGH: What about the dishwasher?

SAMANTHA: Can't we just leave the dishes in the sink, if we're in such a hurry?

MR. GRENOUGH: No, _____. Now, who'll do it?
              13.

STEVE: Sam _____, Dad.
        14.

SAMANTHA: Thanks a lot, pal!

MR. GRENOUGH: Come on, kids. Let's get going.

5 EDITING

Priscilla Hammond, Jeremy Washburn's seventh-grade teacher, has written a letter to Brent and Anne, Jeremy's parents, to report on Jeremy's progress. The letter was typed from Mrs. Hammond's notes by a secretary. There are eight verb constructions that would be more effective if they were written with auxiliaries that show contrast or emphasis. Find and rewrite these eight constructions, using appropriate auxiliaries.

Madison
Junior High School

February 22

Dear Mr. and Mrs. Washburn,

I'm writing to give you a progress report on Jeremy. In general I'd say he's not out of trouble yet, though ~~he's~~ he is doing better than before. He still has a tendency to daydream a little too much, but he seems to be paying better attention in class. His weakest subject is math, which he's still not passing. He scored high in math on the national achievement tests a month ago, however, so he has a chance of passing math. He's also not passing science, but he's doing very well in English, history, and art. The main problem I'm having is getting Jeremy to turn in his work. He submitted three assignments last week, but he's still missing four others. I appreciate your efforts to monitor his study time in the evenings. I only wish other parents were as concerned as you are. Jeremy could still fail the seventh grade, but he's got a chance to make it, so please keep up the supervised work at home.

Sincerely,

Priscilla Hammond

Priscilla Hammond

COMMUNICATION PRACTICE

6 LISTENING

Listen to a segment of the radio talk show, Do the Right Thing.

Now listen again to the conversation. Work with a partner. Answer these questions.

1. What is the problem of Sally, the first caller?

_____

2. What is she afraid of?

_____

3. What is Mary Mobley's advice to Sally?

_____

4. What is the problem of Jerry, the second caller?

_____

5. What is Jerry's complaint about his children?

_____

6. What is Mary Mobley's advice?

_____

7 INFORMATION GAP: CHILDREARING

Part A

Work with a partner. You are going to read an article about raising children. Each version of the article is missing some information. Take turns asking your partner questions to get information.

Student B, turn to page 274 and follow the instructions there.

Student A, read the following article. Ask questions and fill in the missing information. Then answer Student B's questions.

EXAMPLE:

A: Who have lost their way?

B: American parents have. . . . Where did the American man and his wife take their three children?

A: They took them to the zoo.

ASIAN PARENTS DIFFER ON CHILDREARING

By John Rosemond

A man called the other day from Milwaukee with an interesting story, one that illustrates the extent to which _____ have, in general, lost their way.

He and his wife took their three children, ages _____, to the zoo for what was supposed to be a stress-free afternoon. Instead, pandemonium reigned. The children ran in three directions at once, requiring that two parents run one-half again faster. The children's activity levels were matched, in decibels, by their voices, which were in an incessant state of yell. They demanded _____. Parents saying no resulted in dramatic displays of frustration and anger. So, parents said yes more often than not. The children then began complaining that their hauls were too heavy, so parents wound up carrying armloads of worthless junk.

"Needless to say, John," he went on, "we didn't have a good time. In fact, my wife and I took the kids home early because _____."

To many, this story will have an all-too-familiar ring. Some might even say, "Well, what did they expect, taking three young children to the zoo?" meaning that at least on this occasion, the children were right at home.

But that's not where this father's story ends. In the course of all this mayhem, he and his wife spied an Asian woman with three equally young children. But her children were _____ and followed their mother like ducklings. She spoke to her children in her native tongue, but only rarely. It was apparent that this woman was not giving

(continued on next page)

ASIAN PARENTS DIFFER ON CHILDREARING

her children many instructions. They seemed to know what she expected of them. Neither the mother nor the kids were carrying any junk, yet everyone seemed to be having a good time.

"What's her secret?" asked my man from Milwaukee.

It just so happens I've had several conversations of late with Asian parents, all of whom are recently arrived to these shores. Without exception, they tell me they are appalled at _____ , and fear the bad influence. In the course of these conversations, I've discovered that these parents bring an entirely different set of assumptions to the childrearing process, as 180 degrees removed from those of the average American parent as China is from the United States.

The first of these is that children should pay more attention to parents than parents pay to children. These parents understand that you cannot discipline a child who is not paying attention to you. They also understand that the more attention parents pay to children, the less children will pay to parents.

Second, no attempt is made to persuade children to cooperate. In fact, since cooperation implies a state of equality, these parents don't even seek cooperation. Instead, they expect

_____ .

Third, they don't explain themselves to their children. Therefore, their children's inquiries are directed to what the world is made of and how it works, rather than at the "why?" and "why not?" of their parents' rules and expectations. In fact, these parents are amazed at the amount of time American parents waste dealing with such trivia.

Lastly, these parents do not tolerate misbehavior. Therefore, they do not bribe their children, nor do they threaten them. How enlightening to realize that both bribe and threat are self-fulfilling!

The truly sad aspect of all this, however, is the realization that for the most part America's children used to be as well-behaved as those Asian kids. The good news is, it's not too late to save ourselves.

Source: John Rosemond, "Asian Parents Differ on Childrearing." *Albuquerque Journal*, July 1, 1993.
Family psychologist John Rosemond is the author of 8 best-selling parenting books and is one of America's most popular speakers. For more information, see his website at www.rosemond.com.

Part B: Small Group Discussion

Divide into groups of four and discuss the article. What is John Rosemond's point of view? Do you basically agree or disagree with it? Why? Have one member of the class take notes and report on your discussion to the class.

8 ESSAY

Which kind of childrearing do you think is better—one in which "children pay more attention to parents than parents pay to children" or one in which the opposite is true? Write an essay of three or four paragraphs explaining your viewpoint. Give examples to support your ideas.

9 PICTURE DISCUSSION

Work with a partner. What has happened here? What is the policeman telling Mr. Grenough? What is the situation regarding seatbelts? Invent conversations for the policeman and the Grenoughs, using auxiliaries wherever possible.

INFORMATION GAP FOR STUDENT B

Student B, read the article about raising children. Answer Student A's questions.
Then ask your own questions and fill in the missing information.

EXAMPLE:

A: Who have lost their way?

B: American parents have. . . . Where did the American man and his wife take their three children?

A: They took them to the zoo.

ASIAN PARENTS DIFFER ON CHILDREARING

By John Rosemond

A man called the other day from Milwaukee with an interesting story, one that illustrates the extent to which American parents have, in general, lost their way.

He and his wife took their three children, ages 6, 4, and 3, to _____ for what was supposed to be a stress-free afternoon. Instead, pandemonium reigned. The children ran in three directions at once, requiring that two parents run one-half again faster. The children's activity levels were matched, in decibels, by their voices, which were in an incessant state of yell. They demanded every trinket they set their eyes on. Parents saying no resulted in dramatic displays of frustration and anger. So, parents said yes more often than not. The children then began complaining that their hauls were too heavy, so parents wound up carrying

_____ .

"Needless to say, John," he went on, "we _____ a good time. In fact, my wife and I took the kids home early because we were getting angry at one another."

To many, this story will have an all-too-familiar ring. Some might even say, "Well, what did they expect, taking three young children to the zoo?" meaning that at least on this occasion, the children were right at home.

But that's not where this father's story ends. In the course of all this mayhem, he and his wife spied an Asian woman with _____ equally young children. But her children were well-behaved, calm, quiet and followed their mother like ducklings. She spoke

ASIAN PARENTS DIFFER ON CHILDREARING

to her children in her native tongue, but only rarely. It was apparent that this woman was not giving her children many instructions. They seemed to know what she expected of them. Neither the mother nor the kids were carrying any junk, yet everyone seemed to be having a good time.

"What's her secret?" asked my man from Milwaukee.

It just so happens I've had several conversations of late with Asian parents, all of whom are recently arrived to these shores. Without exception, they tell me they are appalled at the behavior of American children, and fear the bad influence. In the course of these conversations, I've discovered that these parents bring an entirely different set of assumptions to the childrearing process, as 180 degrees removed from those of the average American parent as China is from the United States.

The first of these is that children should pay more attention to parents than parents pay to children. These parents understand that you cannot discipline _____. They also understand that the more attention parents pay to children, the less children will pay to parents.

Second, no attempt is made to persuade children to cooperate. In fact, since cooperation implies a state of equality, these parents don't even seek cooperation. Instead, they expect obedience.

Third, they don't explain themselves to their children. Therefore, their children's inquiries are directed to what the world is made of and how it works, rather than at the "why?" and "why not?" of their parents' rules and expectations. In fact, these parents are amazed at the amount of time American parents waste dealing with such trivia.

Lastly, these parents do not tolerate _____. Therefore, they do not bribe their children, nor do they threaten them. How enlightening to realize that both bribe and threat are self-fulfilling!

The truly sad aspect of all this, however, is the realization that for the most part America's children used to be as well-behaved as those Asian kids. The good news is, _____.

Source: John Rosemond, "Asian Parents Differ on Childrearing." *Albuquerque Journal*, July 1, 1993.
Family psychologist John Rosemond is the author of 8 best-selling parenting books and is one of America's most popular speakers. For more information, see his website at www.rosemond.com.

PHRASAL VERBS

GRAMMAR **IN CONTEXT**

QUESTIONS TO CONSIDER

1. When someone gives you a gift, do you feel you need to give a gift of equal value in return?

2. Have you ever had any surprising experiences with giving gifts cross-culturally? Talk with a partner.

Read an article about gift giving.

Time to Brush Up on Gift Giving

A Chinese woman had lived in Australia for many years. On her birthday, she was invited to the home of an Australian friend to celebrate. When she showed up at the friend's house, she was presented with a beautifully wrapped gift. She thanked her friend and then put the gift away. She was perplexed when her Australian friend seemed to be waiting for something. Finally, the friend asked, "Aren't you going to open it?" Looking forward to unwrapping it in the privacy of her home, she answered, "Oh, no! I don't want to open it now!" Only later, while thinking about her friend's puzzled reaction, did she figure out that she had made a "cultural mistake." Whereas in China it is generally considered courteous not to open a gift in front of the giver, the opposite is true in the Australian culture.

This story illustrates an important point: There's more to getting to know another culture than just being able to speak the language. The Chinese lady spoke excellent English, but she wasn't familiar with the Australian take on gift giving. Of course, if the situation had been reversed and the Australian had been invited to a party in China and been given a present, she would have made a parallel mistake by opening the gift right on the spot instead of setting it aside for later. We all have things to learn about the rules of other cultures, among which gift giving is a key one. Here are some prime examples.

In China, as we have just seen, one is not expected to open a gift immediately upon receiving it. And there are other things to be concerned about. One of the most important considerations is the nature of the gift.

It is important to avoid giving umbrellas, knives, scissors, and clocks. A clock, for example, is not considered a good gift because the receiver may interpret it as a suggestion that he or she is running out of time in life. A gift of knives and scissors is often interpreted as a sign that the giver wants to cut off the friendship. And then there's the umbrella. Since the Chinese word for *umbrella* is the same as the word for *separation,* the receiver may interpret a gift of an umbrella as an indication that the giver wants to break up the relationship.

In Japan, gift-giving practices are somewhat similar. As in China, gift giving is a big deal. Gifts are used to say thank you, offer congratulations, give a welcome, or even to apologize for something. Be sure to take a gift any time you are invited to a Japanese home. Visitors should absolutely not open gifts in front of Japanese people, or expect Japanese people to open gifts in front of them. Avoid giving four of anything. In Japanese (this is also true in Chinese), the word for *four* is *shi,* and another meaning of *shi* in Japanese is *death.* Giving four items may thus be interpreted negatively by your Japanese host. As in China, any gift that is related to cutting (scissors, knives, etc.) should be avoided. Another important consideration is the value of a gift. Give something of approximately the same value of a gift your host has given you. You don't want to show off, so be careful not to overvalue the gift. If you've come up with an idea for a gift for a Japanese friend, think it over carefully. Then run it by another Japanese friend just to see if it's acceptable. Japan also has the custom of giving gifts at set times in the summer (July 1–15) and in the winter (December 1–20).

Another area where it is important to know the rules of gift giving is the Middle East. Consider this situation. A girl named Julie has been going out with Farid, an Iranian, for months. One night Farid invites Julie to dinner at the home of his brother, Reza, and his sister-in-law, Maryam. Julie, an art student, admires Maryam's folk art collection in general and one figurine in particular. Julie is so admiring of the figurine that Maryam insists on giving it to her. Many Middle Easterners feel obligated to give something to someone who admires it. In this case, Julie turns Maryam down on her first offer. Maryam doesn't want to part with the figurine, but she feels constrained to keep offering. Finally Julie gives in to her and accepts the figurine. She is happy, but Maryam isn't. What should Julie have done? She should have kept refusing, for while a Middle Easterner may keep on insisting, you are under no obligation to accept.

Sources: Based on information in *UNESCO Courier*, Feb. 1994, p. 38; Rex Shelley, *Culture Shock! Japan.* (Portland, Oregon: Graphic Arts Center Publishing Company, 1993). Norine Dresser, *Multicultural Manners. New Rules of Etiquette for a Changing Society* (New York: John Wiley & Sons, 1996).

UNDERSTANDING MEANING FROM CONTEXT

We often find synonyms or words with similar meanings either preceding or closely following a difficult or uncommon word. Look at these examples from the reading and then answer these questions about vocabulary.

1. Look at this sentence from paragraph 1: She thanked her friend and then *put the gift away*.

In paragraph 2, find a phrasal verb with a similar meaning to *put the gift away*. Write it here. _____

2. Look at this sentence from paragraph 1: *Whereas* in China it is generally considered courteous not to open a gift in front of the giver, the opposite is true in Australian culture.

What word or words could replace *whereas*? _____

3. Look at this sentence from paragraph 2: She *wasn't familiar with* the Australian take on gift giving.

What phrase in paragraph 2 is closest in meaning to *wasn't familiar with*? _____

4. Look at this sentence from paragraph 3: A gift of knives or scissors is often interpreted as a sign that the giver wants to *cut off* the friendship.

What phrasal verb in paragraph 3 has a similar meaning to *cut off*?

_____

5. Look at this sentence from paragraph 5: Maryam doesn't want to part with the figurine, but she feels *constrained* to keep offering.

What word in paragraph 5 is a synonym of *constrained*?

_____

GRAMMAR **PRESENTATION**
PHRASAL VERBS

PHRASAL VERBS: INSEPARABLE

Maryam doesn't want to **part with** the figurine.

Maryam doesn't want to **part with it**.

PHRASAL VERBS: SEPARABLE

Knives and scissors are often interpreted as a sign that the giver wants to **cut off the friendship**.

Knives and scissors are often interpreted as a sign that the giver wants to **cut the friendship off**.

Knives and scissors are often interpreted as a sign that the giver wants to **cut it off**.

NOTES

1. Phrasal verbs are verbs that are composed of more than one word. A phrasal verb consists of a main verb plus one or more other words following it. The meaning of a phrasal verb is often quite different from the meaning of just the verb alone.

2. There are two types of phrasal verbs: **inseparable** and **separable**. Inseparable phrasal verbs are those that occur in only one order. **Inseparable phrasal verbs** are composed of a verb plus a preposition. The preposition does not move. If a pronoun occurs with an inseparable phrasal verb, it always comes after the preposition.

EXAMPLES

- Knives and scissors are often interpreted as a sign that the giver wants to **cut off** the friendship. (The meaning of *cut off* is quite different from the meaning of *cut*.)

- She was perplexed when her Australian friend seemed to be **waiting for** something.

- Let's assume you've **come up with** an idea for a gift for a Japanese friend.

- Maryam doesn't want to **part with the figurine**.

- Maryam doesn't want to **part with it**. (The pronoun *it* occurs immediately after *with*, not before it.)

3. Separable phrasal verbs are also composed of a verb plus a preposition. However, the preposition can be separated from the main part of the verb (= it can move): If a separable phrasal verb is linked with a noun, the noun can come either before the preposition or after it.

▶ **BE CAREFUL!** In separable phrasal verbs, a pronoun can come *only* between the verb and the preposition.

- She thanked her friend and then **put the gift away**.

  OR

- She thanked her friend and then **put away the gift**.

- She thanked her friend and then **put it away**.
  NOT ~~She thanked her friend and then put away it.~~

4. Like other verbs, phrasal verbs can be used in all tenses and as gerunds, infinitives, and participles.

GERUND
- She would have made a parallel mistake by opening the gift right on the spot and not **setting** it **aside** for later.

INFINITIVE
- But there are other things **to be concerned with**.

PARTICIPLE
- **Looking forward to** unwrapping it in the privacy of her home, she answered, "Oh, no! I don't want to open it now."

5. In pronouncing phrasal verbs, we place the main stress on the preposition.

When we make nouns from phrasal verbs, we move the stress to the beginning of the combination. We usually write the noun with a hyphen or as one word.

- You don't want to **show off**, so don't overvalue the gift. (The main stress is on *off.*)

- You don't want to be **a show-off**, so don't overvalue the gift. (The main stress is on *show.*)

FOCUSED PRACTICE

 DISCOVER THE GRAMMAR

Part A

Look again at the reading on pages 276–277. You will find fourteen inseparable phrasal verbs and nine separable phrasal verbs. Underline the inseparable phrasal verbs. Circle the separable phrasal verbs. If necessary, refer to Appendices 16 and 17 on pages A-8 and A-9 for help in completing this exercise.

Inseparable	**Separable**
brush up on	put away

Part B

Look at these sentences from the reading. Could the first be rewritten as the sentence in parentheses? Why or why not? Could the second be rewritten as the sentence in parentheses? Why or why not?

1. She thanked her friend and then put the gift away. (She thanked her friend and put away the gift.)
2. Maryam doesn't want to part with the figurine. (Maryam doesn't want to part the figurine with.)

Part C

Match the following meanings with phrasal verbs from the reading, writing the phrasal verb as it appears in the text.

1. date _____ going out with _____ (paragraph 5)

2. develop an understanding of _____ (paragraph 2)

3. have no more of something _____ (paragraph 3)

4. reactivate one's knowledge of something already known

   _____ (title)

5. refuse an offer _____ (paragraph 5)

6. give up _____ (paragraph 5)

7. think of _____ (paragraph 4)

8. anticipate favorably _____ (paragraph 1)

9. find a solution by thinking _____ (paragraph 1)

10. did not know something well _____ (paragraph 2)

Part D

Look at these four sentences. Each contains a compound noun made from a phrasal verb. Complete each definition with the appropriate phrasal verb.

1. A show-off is a person who _____ in order to try

to impress other people.

2. The breakup of our friendship happened when we

_____ our relationship after an argument.

3. A set-aside is money that people _____ from

their paychecks or other funds to use at a later time.

4. We had forgotten to pay our electric bill, so the electric company sent us a notice saying

that the cutoff date of our power would occur on January 15. In other words, they said

they were _____ our service unless we paid.

2 MEANINGS   Grammar Notes 1–6

Work with a partner. Student A, ask Student B the first six questions. Student B, ask Student A the last six questions. Both partners answer with a phrasal verb and a pronoun if the sentence has an object.

EXAMPLE:
    A: If you meet friends without planning to meet them, do you run into the friends or run out of the friends?
    B: You run into them.

Student A's Questions

1. If you have no money, have you come into money or run out of money?

2. If you decline someone's offer of a gift, do you turn down the gift or part with the gift?

3. If you know something well, are you concerned about that thing or familiar with that thing?

4. If you make friends with people, are you getting rid of those people or getting to know those people?

5. If you arrive at the answer to a question, do you figure out the solution or think over the solution?

6. If you end a relationship, do you break in the relationship or break up the relationship?

Student B's Questions

7. If you favorably anticipate an event, do you look down on the event or look forward to the event?

8. If you practice and improve skills that you learned in the past, do you brush up on the skills or brush off the skills?

9. If you set a gift aside, do you put the gift off or put the gift away?

10. If you ask a friend's opinion of your idea, do you run the idea over or run the idea by the friend?

11. If a person considered your ideas, did she think over your ideas or set aside your ideas?

12. If your friend Bob gave you his best sweater, did he come up with the sweater or part with the sweater?

 FIGURING OUT THE MEANINGS   Grammar Notes 1, 2, 3, 5, 6

Part A

Study the sentences in which twelve phrasal verbs are used. Make a guess about the meaning of each phrasal verb and write it down.

• The doctor told me to quit smoking, but so far all I've been able to do is **cut down on** cigarettes.

• Near the end of the month, I had spent most of my money, so I had to **do without** entertainment until I got my next paycheck.

• The criminal who robbed $500,000 from the bank has not been caught. So far he's **gotten away with** the crime.

• The boss of the company **put up with** a lot of lateness on the part of his employees until he finally got angry and fired three of them.

• After I cleaned out the garage, I was faced with the task of **getting rid of** all the stuff I wanted to throw away.

• My young brother drives me crazy because he always **puts off** doing his homework until the last minute, and then he asks me to help him do it.

• In a conversation yesterday evening I **found out** that our boss is leaving and that we are going to get a new boss.

• Robert tried for two years before he was finally able to **give up** cigarettes.

• Alice borrowed $500 from her daughter but forgot to **pay** her **back** until her daughter reminded her.

• Every time we're at a party, Jerry always tries to be the center of attention by **showing off**. Last night he told ten jokes in a row.

• Last night for my Russian homework I had to **look up** fifty words I didn't know in my Russian–English dictionary.

• Mrs. Giuliani **tried on** twelve pairs of shoes before she finally found a pair that fit.

Part B

Work with a partner. Look at the pictures. On a separate piece of paper, write a phrasal verb from the list in Part A for each picture. Then discuss the meaning of each phrasal verb with your partner and write a short definition for each one.

4 EDITING

Read the letter from Catherine, a Singaporean exchange student in Australia, to her friend Yukiko in Singapore. Find and correct the ten errors in phrasal verbs.

Sydney, July 20

Dear Yukiko,

Sorry it's taken me so long to write. I've just been so busy. I'm really looking forward ^to the holidays and seeing all of you guys again.

School is going well. It's tough but really interesting. I've gotten to know a lot of new people, including several Australians. I have this one really good friend, a girl named Jane. She invited me to her house last week for a party. Actually, it was my birthday, but I didn't know she knew that. I thought it was a party like any other. I thought I'd better take some kind of gift, but I couldn't figure it out what to take. Finally I came up the idea of a bouquet of flowers. As soon as I got to the party, I gave them to Jane, and she was really happy to get them. But then the funniest thing happened: This was a surprise party—for me. As soon as I took on my coat, a lot of people jumped up from behind sofas and other places where they'd been hiding and shouted, "Surprise! Happy birthday!" I was embarrassed and didn't know what to think. But everybody was really friendly, and pretty soon I forgot my embarrassment about. Then they gave me presents. I was about to put away them, but Jane said, "Aren't you going to open them?" I didn't know what to do, but everyone wanted me to open up them right on the spot, so I did. The nicest gift was a new blouse from Jane. She wanted me to go and try on it immediately. So I did. It's beautiful. Anyway, what a party! I thought I knew all about Australian culture, but I guess I'm not as familiar it with as I thought. The custom of opening presents in front of the gift giver is a strange one to me!

The weather is kind of chilly. How is it back in Singapore? Nice and warm?

Well, Yukiko, I'm running space out of, so I'd better sign off. Write soon.

Best,
Catherine

COMMUNICATION PRACTICE

5 LISTENING

Read the following questions. Then listen to the telephone conversation.

Now listen again. Answer the questions, using a phrasal verb in each item.

1. Who has shown up for the party? _____

2. Who are they waiting for? _____

3. Has Mom figured out what's going on? _____

4. What is Mom looking forward to? _____

5. What is the problem Dad and Ray are having? _____

6. Does Bev think they can get away with not giving Mom a gift today?

_____

7. What did Mom get rid of last week? _____

8. According to Bev, what does her mother have to do in order to buy a dress?

_____

9. What are Dad and Ray running out of? _____

10. What does Bev suggest that Dad and Ray look for?

_____

6 INFORMATION GAP: GIFT GIVING PRACTICES

Work with a partner. You are going to read a description of a gift giving experience. Each version is missing some information. Take turns asking your partner questions to get information.

Student A, read the description on page 287. Ask questions and fill in the missing information. Then answer Student B's questions.

Student B, read the description on page 289 and follow the instructions there.

> **EXAMPLE:**
> **A:** What is Tina specializing in?
> **B:** She is specializing in Asian design and graphics. What does she make for the birthday of her close friend Inga?
> **A:** She makes a pair of elephant bookends.

ELEPHANT TRUNKS—UP OR DOWN?

Tina, an artist specializing in _____, makes a pair of elephant bookends for the birthday of her close friend Inga. She decorates the elephants with traditional _____. At first, Inga is thrilled. However, when Inga's boyfriend Roberto sees the elephants, he insists that Inga return them to Tina at once.

Tina made the elephants showing their trunks facing downward. For Roberto, a Mexican, this symbolized that _____. He was so adamant about this that he convinced Inga to return the bookends to Tina.

Tina felt crushed to have the elephants returned, and she was incredulous at the reason. As an expert in Indian art, she was skeptical. She had never heard of this belief before. A folklorist later convinced her that this belief was real and prevalent all over _____, where there are additional beliefs about replicas of elephants: They should face the front door so that their upward trunks can hold all the good fortune as it enters the home. One should not have one but _____ elephants—one that was purchased, one that was received as a gift, and one that was found.

It is ironic that these strong beliefs flourish in Latin America where no elephants have lived naturally, whereas in _____, where elephants abound, the belief is nonexistent. In the United States, it makes no difference how an elephant's trunk is depicted.

Source: Norine Dresser, "Elephant Trunks—Up or Down?" *Multicultural Manners. New Rules of Etiquette for a Changing Society* (New York: John Wiley & Sons, Inc., 1996).

7 CHARADES

Divide into two teams. As a team, select ten phrasal verbs from the unit for the other team to act out or illustrate in some way. Write each phrasal verb on a slip of paper and place it in a hat. A member of the other team draws a slip and has one minute to act out the phrasal verb. He or she may not use any words in acting out the verb. The other team members try to guess the phrasal verb.

8 ESSAY

What is the most satisfying or interesting experience you have ever had with giving or receiving a gift? Write an essay of three or four paragraphs about it. It could be a situation in which you received a very special gift, did not receive the gift you expected or wanted, or gave a gift and the result was good or bad. Give as many supporting details as possible.

9 PICTURE DISCUSSION

Talk with a partner. Look at the two pictures. What do you think they show about potential problems with gift giving? How many gifts are enough? If someone gives you a gift, are you obligated to give one in return? To whom do you give gifts?

Student B, read the description of a gift giving experience. Answer Student A's questions. Then ask your own questions and fill in the missing information.

EXAMPLE:
A: What is Tina specializing in?
B: She is specializing in Asian design and graphics. What does she make for the birthday of her close friend Inga?
A: She makes a pair of elephant bookends.

ELEPHANT TRUNKS—UP OR DOWN?

Tina, an artist specializing in Asian design and graphics, makes a pair of elephant

_____ for the birthday of her close friend Inga. She

decorates the elephants with traditional Indian motifs. At first, Inga is thrilled. However,

when Inga's boyfriend Roberto sees the elephants, he insists that

_____.

Tina made the elephants showing their trunks facing downward. For Roberto, a

Mexican, this symbolized that all luck entering the house would slip away. He was so

adamant about this that he convinced Inga to _____.

Tina felt crushed to have the elephants returned, and she was incredulous at the

reason. As an expert in Indian art, she was _____. She

had never heard of this belief before. A folklorist later convinced her that this belief was

real and prevalent all over Latin America, where there are additional beliefs about replicas

of elephants: They should face the front door so that

_____. One should not have one but three

elephants—one that was purchased, one that was received as a gift, and one that

was found.

It is ironic that these strong beliefs flourish in Latin America where no elephants have

lived naturally, whereas in India, where elephants abound, the belief is nonexistent. In the

United States, it makes no difference how an elephant's trunk is depicted.

Source: Norine Dresser, "Elephant Trunks—Up or Down?" *Multicultural Manners. New Rules of Etiquette for a Changing Society* (New York: John Wiley & Sons, Inc., 1996).

I. *Complete the following conversations between a job interviewer and various applicants. Use contracted verbs for nonemphatic statements and full forms for emphatic (contrasting) statements.*

1. **A:** What languages do you know, Ms. Suzuki? Do you speak Mandarin?

   B: No, I _____don't speak_____ Mandarin. I _____do speak_____
   ‎   a. (not / speak)   b. (speak)
   Japanese and Spanish, though.

   A: Are you fluent in those languages?

   B: I _____ fluent in Japanese. I _____
   ‎   c. (be)   d. (not / be)
   fluent in Spanish, but I _____ conversant in it.
   ‎   e. (be)

2. **A:** Mr. Quinn, your resume says that you attended college. Did you earn

   a bachelor's degree?

   B: No, I _____ my B.A. I _____ an
   ‎   a. (not / earn)   b. (earn)
   associate degree, though.

3. **A:** Ms. Liu, this job requires overseas experience. Have you lived abroad?

   B: I _____ abroad, but I _____ extensively
   ‎   a. (not / live)   b. (travel)
   in Europe and the Far East.

4. **A:** Mr. Travolta, this _____ a full-time position.
   ‎   a. (not / be)
   It _____ a three-quarter-time job, though, and it
   ‎   b. (be)
   _____ an excellent benefits package. Are you interested?
   ‎   c. (have)

   B: The job sounds interesting. I _____ some time to think
   ‎   d. (would like)
   it over, however. Could I let you know by next Monday?

II. *Complete the conversations with* **so**, **neither**, **too**, *or* **either** *plus the appropriate auxiliary.*

1. **A:** Avocados have a disgusting texture, I think. I can't stand them.

   B: _____Neither can_____ I. They're at the bottom of my list.

2. A: What did you think of *The Phantom Menace*? I thought it was pretty neat, all in all.

B: _____ I. I really liked Liam Neeson and Ewan McGregor.

3. A: Janice has never been to Mexico City.

B: Joe _____. He wants to go this summer, though.

4. A: Helena won't be able to come to the party Wednesday afternoon.

B: _____ Josh. He has a doctor's appointment.

5. A: How do you feel about hunting whales? I'm against it.

B: I _____. I can understand both sides of the issue, but it still seems

cruel to the whales.

6. A: Did you hear that Bill spent $2,000 on a new bicycle? I wouldn't spend that much.

B: _____ I. There are better things to do with your money.

7. A: Can you believe it? Priscilla had never heard of George Lucas.

B: Well, I _____ before his new movie came out. You just can't keep

up with everything.

8. A: I can't believe it! My mother says she believes in ghosts.

B: Really? _____ my mother. She says she saw one once.

III. *Examine the following statements about famous world figures. Fill in the blanks
in the statements with regular or emphatic forms of the verbs provided, placing
emphatic forms in the parts of sentences that make a contrast.*

On August 9, 1974, Richard M. Nixon _____resigned_____ the presidency of the
1. (resign)
United States, disgraced by his involvement in the Watergate scandal. Many

_____ he would always be hated, but he persevered and
2. (predict)
_____ to rehabilitate himself politically by the time of his death in 1994.
3. (manage)
On September 8, 1974, President Gerald R. Ford _____ Richard M.
4. (pardon)
Nixon for any federal crimes he might have committed while he was president. This action

probably _____ Ford the 1976 presidential election, but it
5. (cost)
_____ the United States to recover from Watergate.
6. (help)

On March 26, 1979, Egyptian president Anwar el-Sadat _____ the Camp
7. (sign)

David Accords with Prime Minister Menachem Begin of Israel. This action probably

_____ Sadat's assassination in 1981, but it _____ peace
8. (cause)   9. (promote)

between Egypt and Israel.

On February 11, 1990, South African president F. W. de Klerk _____
10. (free)

black nationalist leader Nelson Mandela from imprisonment, initiating the process of

dismantling apartheid and creating a multiracial society. Although South Africa's road

ahead may be fraught with peril, the country _____ a good chance to
11. (have)

become a racially harmonious society.

In the late 1800s, Elizabeth Cady Stanton and Susan B. Anthony _____
12. (found)

the National Woman Suffrage Association. Their actions _____ to the
13. (lead)

eventual granting of the vote to women in the United States and _____ the
14. (influence)

achievement of women's rights elsewhere in the world. While women today may not yet

enjoy complete equality with men, they _____ increased political power.
15. (have)

IV. *Look at the pictures. Write two statements about each picture, one with a noun
and one in which you change the noun to a pronoun. Use a phrasal verb in
each case.*

1.

2.

They're waiting for their guests.

_____

They're waiting for them.

_____

3.

4.

5.

6.

V. *Circle the letter of the choice that correctly completes each sentence.*

1. I don't really like any of these pairs of shoes, but I'll try
_____ if that will make you happy.

A B Ⓒ D

   (A) it on   (C) them on

   (B) on it   (D) on them

2. My daughter doesn't like many cooked vegetables. She
_____ most raw vegetables, though.

A B C D

   (A) does like   (C) likes

   (B) did like   (D) liked

3. My son asked me to help him with his math homework, but I couldn't   A B C D
_____ .

   (A) figure out it   (C) figured it out

   (B) figure them out   (D) figure it out

4. Frank is against capital punishment, and _____ .   A B C D

   (A) I'm too   (C) so do I

   (B) so am I   (D) neither I am

5. There used to be a factory on this corner, _____ ?   A B C D

   (A) didn't it   (C) didn't there

   (B) wasn't it   (D) wasn't there

6. Betsy didn't think I'd really done the work, but I _____ .   A B C D

   (A) had   (C) did

   (B) would   (D) have

7. I know where Chichicastenango is. _____ to   A B C D
Guatemala, you know.

   (A) I'd been   (C) I have been

   (B) I was   (D) I'll go

8. Sam asked me for the money he'd lent me, but I'd already   A B C D
_____ . He just forgot.

   (A) paid them back   (C) paid back them

   (B) paid it back   (D) paid back it

9. Neither of my uncles went to college. Both _____   A B C D
successful businessmen, however.

   (A) became   (C) becoming

   (B) become   (D) did become

10. It's late. We'd better leave, _____ ?   A B C D

   (A) hadn't we   (C) didn't we

   (B) wouldn't we   (D) won't we

▶ *To check your answers, go to the Answer Key on page 298.*

FROM GRAMMAR TO WRITING
UNITY, SUPPORT, AND COHERENCE

Three important aspects of writing in English are unity, support, and coherence. A well-written paragraph, composition, or longer essay will demonstrate each of these characteristics.

UNITY

If a piece of writing has unity, every sentence in it is on target. In other words, every sentence is related to the main idea and supports that main idea. The following paragraph is not unified because one sentence is not related to the main idea.

EXAMPLE:

For me, a dog is a better pet than a cat. When I come home from work, for example, my dog comes to meet me at the door. He is always glad to see me. My cat, on the other hand, couldn't care less whether I'm at home or not, as long as I keep filling his food dish. Another good thing about a dog is that you can teach him tricks. Cats, however, can't be bothered to learn anything new. My neighbor has a beautiful Siamese cat that sits all day long on the windowsill looking out at what is happening. The best thing about a dog, though, is that he's a great companion. I can take my dog on hikes and walks. He goes everywhere with me. As we all know, you can't take a cat for a walk.

The sentence *My neighbor has a beautiful Siamese cat that sits all day long on the windowsill looking out at what is happening* is off target. It has nothing to do with the writer's main idea: that a dog is a better pet than a cat. That sentence should be removed from the paragraph.

 Read the following paragraph. Find the three sentences that are not related to the main idea of the paragraph. Write them on the lines provided.

Our family vacation last summer was the best we've ever had. We spent two weeks in Mexico and traveled around by train and bus. We started our trip in the city of Chihuahua, where we caught the train that travels across northern Mexico through the "Copper Canyon" and ends up in the city of Los Mochis on the Pacific. I've

(continued on next page)

always loved train trips. When we got to Los Mochis, we stayed in a pension where we met some interesting travelers from many different places. We even got a chance to practice our Spanish. Spanish was always my best subject in school. After Los Mochis we traveled on down the Pacific Coast and stopped in Mazatlán, where we spent a few relaxing days on the beach. From there we took a bus to Mexico City. I was astonished to discover how gigantic the city is, but we were able to get around it on the metro. In my opinion, every city should have a metro system. The highlight of the trip, however, was seeing the Pyramids north of Mexico City. They were incredibly beautiful, and you can even climb them. All in all, we had such a wonderful time that we're planning another trip to Mexico next summer.

1. _____

2. _____

3. _____

SUPPORT

In a piece of writing, ideas must be supported with specific examples. These examples are called supporting details. There are three specific supporting details in the following paragraph:

> **EXAMPLE:**
> One reason why I'm going to stop driving my car to work is that I can't afford to pay for traffic tickets. The other day, for example, I was driving on the Evergreen Expressway, and a police officer stopped me for speeding. I had to pay a $90 fine even though I was only driving seven miles over the speed limit.

The three specific details are the name of the highway (the Evergreen Expressway), the amount of the fine ($90), and the speed at which the writer was driving (seven miles over the speed limit).

2 *The following paragraph contains four statements relating to the main idea. Two of them contain supporting details, and two do not. Which two statements need specific supporting details? Write those two sentences on a separate piece of paper.*

> There are several reasons why I'm really happy in my new job. For one thing, the hours are flexible: I can work from 9:00 to 5:00 on some days and 12:00 noon to 8:00 on other days. Second, the job pays well—$20 an hour as a minimum. Third, my boss is supportive of me and of the other employees. Best of all, I love the work because I've always been fascinated by solving problems. I think I'll be working at this job for a long time.

Now write examples of supporting details for these two sentences.

COHERENCE

A paragraph or larger piece of writing is coherent when its parts are in an effective order. When we are arranging points we are making in writing, the recommended order is usually from least important to most important. That is, you should place your least important detail or reason first and your most important detail or reason last. Look at this paragraph:

> **EXAMPLE:**
>
> There are four main reasons why I am in favor of the death penalty for capital crimes such as murder. First, it saves the taxpayers money because they don't have to pay for supporting prisoners for twenty or more years. Second, it reduces the number of prisoners, and prisons are already overcrowded. Third, it provides justice and a degree of satisfaction to the families of murder victims. Most importantly, despite what many have said, it prevents some potential murderers from committing capital crimes because they fear they will eventually be executed themselves.

This writer believes that the least important reason is that capital punishment saves taxpayers money and that the most important reason is that it prevents some people from committing murder.

3 *Rewrite the following paragraph in what you believe to be the most effective order.*

> There are four main reasons why I am against the death penalty. First, I don't believe that any human has the right to make a life-or-death decision about the life of another human. Second, it deprives the criminal of a chance to reform and become a better person. Third, it is cruel and unusual punishment. Most importantly, it is not enforced uniformly but tends to target minorities.

1. First, _____

2. Second, _____

3. Third, _____

4. Most importantly, _____

4 APPLY IT TO YOUR WRITING

Write a paragraph of five or six sentences about something you are for or against. Begin with a topic sentence and provide supporting details in the form of reasons. Then rewrite your paragraph, adding one sentence that is off target—that doesn't support your point of view. Also, put your sentences in a different and less effective order. Then work with a partner. Read each other's paper. Find the sentence that is off target. Suggest a more effective order for the sentences. Modify your paper if necessary and submit it to your instructor.

PART

VI

REVIEW OR SELFTEST
ANSWER KEY

I.
1. **c.** 'm
   d. 'm not
   e. am
2. **a.** didn't earn
   b. did earn
3. **a.** haven't lived
   b. have traveled
4. **a.** isn't
   b. is
   c. does have
   d. would like

II.
2. So did
3. hasn't either
4. Neither will
5. am too
6. Neither would
7. hadn't either
8. So does

III.
2. predicted
3. did manage
4. pardoned
5. cost
6. did help
7. signed
8. caused
9. did promote
10. freed
11. does have
12. founded
13. led
14. influenced
15. do have

IV. Possible Answers
2. The people who live here need to get rid of the garbage. They need to get rid of it.

   OR

   The people who live here need to throw away the garbage. They need to throw it away.
3. He can't do without coffee. He can't do without it.
4. They ran into their friends at the movies. They ran into them at the movies.
5. They've run out of money. They've run out of it.
6. He's putting off the job. / He's putting the job off. He's putting it off.

V.
2. A	5. C	8. B
3. D	6. A	9. D
4. B	7. C	10. A

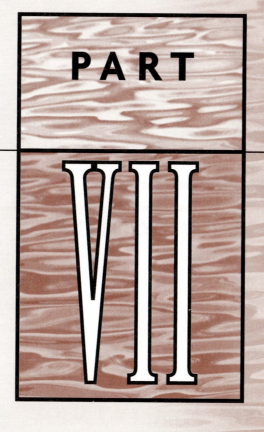

PART

VII

GERUNDS AND INFINITIVES

GERUNDS

GRAMMAR **IN CONTEXT**

QUESTIONS TO CONSIDER

1. What are your favorite hobbies and pastimes?
2. Do you have enough time to pursue the pastimes you really enjoy?
3. Do you think that TV watching is passive, or not?

Read the article.

DO YOU REALLY ENJOY BEING A COUCH POTATO?

Are you having an exciting time surfing, dear?

A husband and wife come home from work, exhausted and stressed out. They don't feel like preparing a real dinner, so they pop something in the microwave. Then they sit down on the couch for an evening of being mesmerized by the TV set. Hours later, after having fallen asleep, they wake up and stumble off to bed. Each day they continue to do the same thing: Get up, go to work, come home, grab a bite, then sit down and vegetate in front of the TV set. Does this sound like you? If so, are you satisfied with your existence? Isn't there more to life than being a couch potato?

Some people apparently don't think so. In their recent book *Time for Life,* researchers John Robinson and Geoffrey Godbey state that the average amount of time that people in the United States have to devote to leisure activities is actually increasing. While this may sound unlikely, Robinson and Godbey claim that Americans now spend almost forty hours a week doing leisure-time activities, and something similar may be true all over the industrialized world. Here's what Robinson and Godbey say are the top five leisure activities among Americans: Watching television, at 15.0 hours a week, is by far the most popular. Number two on the list is socializing—6.7 hours a week. Number three, at 4.4 hours weekly, is home communication. Reading, at 2.8 hours a week, ranks number four. And number five on the list, engaging in hobbies, comes in at 2.7 hours a week. Judging from these statistics, we might conclude that many Americans seem to enjoy being couch potatoes. Now, if you want to spend your leisure time channel surfing, that's your choice. There are, however, many rewarding pursuits out there. With all the extra leisure time that we supposedly have, it behooves us to know how to spend it interestingly. Here are three of the more unusual and interesting popular hobbies.

Roller coasting has become so popular that there's even an organization called ACE (American Coaster Enthusiasts) that is dedi-

cated to preserving, appreciating, and enjoying roller coasters. The precursors of roller coasters originated in Russia as ice slides built high into the air, and the first actual mechanical roller coasters were also constructed in Russia. From there the idea migrated to Paris, where a kind of roller coaster with wheels was built in 1804. Eventually the roller coaster made its way to the United States, with more and more coasters being built until Depression times. Then they began to fall out of fashion, and many were torn down. It was not until the 1950s, with Walt Disney's opening of the first Disneyland, that roller coasters began to make a comeback. Now they're being built at breakneck speed. Marie Miller, a member of ACE now in her eighties, is a major enthusiast. She figures she's ridden on most of the roller coasters in the United States, saying, "There was a time when I rode every wooden coaster in the United States, Canada, and Mexico, but I can't keep up with them. One thing's certain: I'll never stop riding until I'm in my grave."

Another fascinating pastime is orienteering, a combination of map reading and cross-country skiing or running. Orienteers are given a map that shows where a set of "control points" are located. They try to follow the map by interpreting it carefully and using a compass to plot their course. Each time they succeed in finding a control point, they stamp a card that validates their having completed that part of the game. The sport is competitive: Participants get a starting time and have a prescribed time period for locating all of the control points. Orienteering has become extremely popular. Why? There are several reasons. It's interesting and healthy. You get the chance to enjoy the outdoors. Best of all, it taxes both your physical strength and your mental acumen.

Then there's letterboxing, a hobby that is like a combination of orienteering and treasure hunting. It began in England in 1854, when an English gentleman put his calling card (a little like today's business card) into a bottle and left it on the bank of a pond. Someone else found it and contacted him, and from this the hobby sprang up. What happens is this: People put a notebook and a rubber stamp in a bottle (the letterbox) and they provide special clues for finding the bottle. Participants have to follow the clues by hiking in certain sections of the English countryside until they finally locate the letterbox and stamp their notebook. For some aficionados, letterboxing is so enjoyable that it's become a way of life.

(continued on next page)

These are just three examples of captivating pastimes. Why are they all so popular? One principal reason is that they're basically active, not passive. Aficionados of these hobbies get out and act rather than passively sitting in front of the TV screen. Suppose that at some future time we start engraving, on our tombstones, not only the names and the dates of people's births and deaths but also their hobbies and accomplishments. Which would look better on a gravestone: JOHN L. DOE, COUCH POTATO, or JOHN L. DOE, ORIENTEER?

JOHN L. DOE

COUCH POTATO R.I.P.

Sources: Includes information from Michael Raphael, "Survey Says You've Got It Easier," Copyright The Associated Press, *Newsday*, June 5, 1997, p. A49; Ellen Sweets, "Runaway Favorites: Coaster to Coaster, Americans Love Life on the Fast Tracks," *Dallas Morning News*, July 4, 1996, p. 1C; Harley Jebens, "Getting One's Bearings: Orienteering Combines Map-Reading and Compass Work with Cross-Country Running," *Dallas Morning News*, December 27, 1998, p. 21B; and Chris Granstrom, "They Live and Breathe Letterboxing," *Smithsonian* Magazine, April 1998.

UNDERSTANDING MEANING FROM CONTEXT

Circle the letter of the choice closest in meaning to the italicized word or phrase from the reading.

1. With all the extra leisure time that we supposedly have, it *behooves* us to know how to spend it interestingly.

    a. benefits   **b.** interests   **c.** frightens

2. The *precursors of roller coasters* originated in Russia as ice slides built high into the air.

    a. first roller coasters   **b.** devices that later developed into roller coasters   **c.** inventors of roller coasters

3. Best of all, it taxes both your physical strength and your mental *acumen*.

    a. enjoyment   **b.** appreciation   **c.** skill

4. These are just three examples of *captivating* pastimes.

    a. attractive   **b.** inexpensive   **c.** demanding

5. For some *aficionados*, letterboxing is so enjoyable that it's become a way of life.

    a. fans   **b.** participants   **c.** spectators

GRAMMAR **PRESENTATION**
GERUNDS

GRAMMATICAL FUNCTIONS

GERUND AS SUBJECT

Watching television, at 15.0 hours a week, is by far the most popular.

GERUND AS OBJECT

We might conclude that many Americans seem to enjoy **being** couch potatoes.

They don't feel like **preparing** a real dinner, so they pop something in the microwave.

It was not until the 1950s, with Walt Disney's **opening** of the first Disneyland, that roller coasters began to make a comeback.

GERUND AS SUBJECT COMPLEMENT

Number two on the list is **socializing**—6.7 hours a week.

GERUND AS APPOSITIVE

And number five on the list, **engaging** in hobbies, comes in at 2.7 hours a week.

FORMS

VERB + GERUND		
VERB	**GERUND**	
I'll never **stop**	**riding**	until I'm in my grave.

PERFECT FORM

Hours later, after **having fallen** asleep, they wake up and stumble off to bed.

PASSIVE FORM

Then they sit down on the couch for an evening of **being mesmerized** by the TV set.

NOTES	**EXAMPLES**
1. A **gerund** is a noun made from a verb. To form a gerund, add *-ing* to the base form of a verb and make any necessary spelling changes. Gerunds perform the same functions as nouns.	• **Reading**, at 2.8 hours a week, ranks number four. (The gerund *reading* is made by adding *-ing* to the verb *read*.)
Gerunds act as **subjects**.	• **Watching** television, at 15.0 hours a week, is by far the most popular. (*Watching* is the subject of the verb *is*.)
Gerunds act as **direct objects**.	• Do you really enjoy **being** a couch potato? (*Being* is the direct object of the verb *enjoy*.)
Gerunds act as **objects of prepositions**.	• Participants have to follow the clues by **hiking** in certain sections of the English countryside. (*Hiking* is the object of the preposition *by*.)
Gerunds act as **subject complements** (phrases that further describe the subject of the sentence).	• Number two on the list is **socializing**. (*Socializing* explains the subject, *number two on the list*.)
Gerunds act as **appositives** (phrases, placed next to a noun, that explain the noun and are equivalent to it).	• And number five on the list, **engaging** in hobbies, comes in at 2.7 hours a week. (The appositive *engaging in hobbies* explains and is equivalent to the phrase *number five on the list*.)
2. Gerunds can be used in perfect form (*having* + **past participle**). This form suggests the past in relation to some other time.	• Hours later, after **having fallen** asleep, they wake up and stumble off to bed. (*They fell asleep. Hours later, they woke up and stumbled off to bed.*)
3. Gerunds can occur in passive form with *being* or *getting* + **past participle** or *having been* or *gotten* + **past participle**.	• Then they sit down on the couch for an evening of **being mesmerized** by the TV set.

4. Use a possessive noun or pronoun before a gerund.

- It was not until the 1950s, with **Walt Disney's opening** of the first Disneyland, that roller coasters began to make a comeback.

USAGE NOTE: Native speakers often informally use a regular noun or an object pronoun (instead of a possessive) before a gerund or gerund phrase.

- They stamp a card that validates **their having completed** that part of the game. (more formal)

- They stamp a card that validates **them having completed** that part of the game. (more informal)

5. BE CAREFUL! Remember that some verbs can be followed by gerunds or infinitives. See Appendices 9, 10, 11, and 12 on pages A-6, and A-7 for listings of all these categories.

a. Some verbs and verb phrases are followed only by gerunds. Examples of these are *avoid, consider, enjoy, feel like, have trouble, keep, mind, miss,* and *spend time*.

- Do you really **enjoy being** a couch potato?

b. Some verbs are followed only by infinitives. These include *decide, expect, manage, learn, need, seem, want,* and *would like*.

- Now, if you **want to spend** your leisure time channel surfing, that's your choice.

c. Some verbs are followed by gerunds or infinitives with no significant meaning change. These include *begin, can't stand, continue, hate, like, love, prefer,* and *start*.

- In fact, each day they **continue to do** the same thing.

  OR

- In fact, each day they **continue doing** the same thing.

(continued on next page)

d. Some verbs are followed by gerunds or infinitives with a significant meaning change. These include *forget, go on, quit, regret, remember, stop,* and *try*.

- Marie Miller says she'll never **stop riding** until she's in her grave. *(stop the activity of riding)*

- Marie Miller would **stop** doing any other thing **to ride** a roller coaster. (stop doing something else *in order to* ride a roller coaster)

- They **try to follow** the map by interpreting it carefully and using a compass to plot their course. (*Try* means "attempt." They do not know if they will succeed or not.)

- If you want an interesting hobby, **try letterboxing**. (*Try* means "sample an activity.")

6. BE CAREFUL! Do not confuse gerunds with verbs in the progressive form, adverbial phrases, or present participles. See Unit 21 for a discussion of adverbial phrases.

- The average amount of time that people in the United States have to devote to leisure time is actually **increasing**. (*Increasing* is a verb in the progressive form.)

- **Judging** from these statistics, we might conclude that many Americans seem to enjoy being couch potatoes. (*Judging from these statistics* is an adverbial phrase.)

- Another **fascinating** pastime is orienteering. (*Fascinating* is a present participle used as an adjective.)

FOCUSED PRACTICE

 DISCOVER THE GRAMMAR

Part A

Look back at the reading on pages 300–302. Find and underline the thirty-five gerunds or gerund phrases.

1. <u>feel like preparing</u>

Part B

Could the following sentences from the reading be rewritten using the phrases in parentheses without a meaning change? Why or why not?

1. In fact, each day they continue to do the same thing. (continue doing the same thing)

2. We might conclude that many Americans enjoy being couch potatoes. (enjoy to be couch potatoes)

3. I'll never stop riding until I'm in my grave. (stop to ride)

4. Suppose that at some future time we start engraving on our tombstones, not only the names and the dates of people's births and deaths, but also their hobbies and accomplishments. (start to engrave)

Part C

*Are the **-ing** words in each of the following sentences gerunds? Answer **yes** or **no**.*

1. Isn't there more to life than being a couch potato? _____

2. If you want to spend your leisure time channel surfing, that's your choice. _____

3. Now they're being built at breakneck speed. _____

4. Participants get a starting time . . . _____

5. These are just three examples of captivating pastimes. _____

6. Aficionados of these hobbies get out and act rather than passively sitting in front of the TV screen. _____

2 ALL WORK AND NO PLAY Grammar Notes 4, 5

Brian Hansen is constantly tired and not satisfied with his life. He has gone to a doctor to see if there is anything physically wrong with him. Fill in the blanks in their conversation with gerunds or infinitives. If both a gerund and an infinitive can be used without a change in meaning, provide both answers.

DOCTOR: Well, Brian, what seems to be the problem?

BRIAN: Well, it's the rat race, I guess. I feel like I'm on a treadmill. Some nights when I come home from work I'm so exhausted I don't feel like _____<u>doing</u>_____
1. do
anything but _____ on the sofa. I just want
2. collapse
_____ in front of the TV. Is there anything physically wrong
3. vegetate
with me?

DOCTOR: No, I've looked at the test results, and you're healthy. How long have you been feeling like this?

BRIAN: Oh, two or three months, I guess. Long enough so that I've started
_____ about _____ any energy. Basically I'm
4. worry **5. never have**
not doing anything besides _____ a time clock.
6. punch

DOCTOR: How much are you working?

BRIAN: Well, I'm putting in a lot of overtime—all in all, at least sixty hours a week, I'd say.

DOCTOR: Why are you doing this? Are you trying to kill yourself?

BRIAN: Well, _____ overtime is what pays the bills. The other thing is
7. work
that I only recently moved here, and I hardly know anyone, so I've decided
_____ on _____ money for a while. I like
8. concentrate **9. make**
_____, but I don't know quite how to go about
10. socialize
_____ new people.
11. meet

DOCTOR: You're not married, then?

BRIAN: No, I'm not.

DOCTOR: Well, paying off bills is one thing, but killing yourself is another. I think you need
to stop _____ so much and start _____ a
12. work **13. play**
little—to put things in balance. I'd say you need _____ a hobby.
14. find

BRIAN: Seriously? You mean some boring thing like stamp _____?
15. collect

DOCTOR: No! I mean, that's an OK hobby if you like it, but there are a lot more interesting ones.

BRIAN: Like what?

DOCTOR: Like _____ a karaoke club. Do you like _____?
16. join **17. sing**

BRIAN: It sounds like fun, but I'm not much of a singer.

DOCTOR: Well, how about _____?
                          18. orienteer

BRIAN: What's that?

DOCTOR: People use a map and a compass and try _____ the first person
                                                        19. be

to find locations of hidden clues.

BRIAN: Now that I'd like _____. Where can I find out more about it?
                                   20. do

DOCTOR: I've got a friend who belongs to an orienteering club. I'll give you her number.

BRIAN: Super. Thanks.

---

③ TOGETHERNESS Grammar Note 4

_Read the two conversations that follow. In the first conversation, Lois Walker is
talking with family counselor Brenda Matthews and is using more formal language.
In the second conversation, Lois is talking with a close friend, and her language is
more informal. Complete the first conversation with **possessive** + **gerund** forms
and the second conversation with **object pronoun** or **noun** + **gerund** forms._

Conversation 1

MATTHEWS: What can I do for you, Mrs. Walker?

WALKER: Well, it's about our family. I thought you might have some suggestions for . . .

     _____our improving_____ our lifestyle, for lack of a better way of putting it.
              1. improve

MATTHEWS: What seems to be the problem?

WALKER: Well, my husband and I are both really busy with our jobs, and the kids are

teenagers now. It just seems like we've all become strangers. We don't spend

any time together. Would you recommend _____ an athletic
                                         2. join

club? Or doing some sort of family hobby? Or maybe we should just take a

vacation together. It's been years since we've done that.

MATTHEWS: Well, those could all be good ideas. But it might be better to start with

something a little more basic. Let me just ask this: Do you have any meals

together now?

WALKER: No, we don't. _____ such different schedules makes that
              3. Everybody / have

really difficult.

MATTHEWS: Well, I understand the difficulty, but I'd say that _____ at

4. a family / get together

least once each day is crucial for their relationship. Isn't there one meal when

you could do that?

WALKER: Well, I suppose dinner might be a possibility. The kids have school activities in

the evening starting at seven. My husband Joe and I don't get home until six.

That doesn't leave much time. And the kids don't like _____

5. we / try

to "control their lives," as they put it.

MATTHEWS: Well, Mrs. Walker, I think you'll have to make a decision, but I don't think

_____ _____ one meal together each day is

6. you / insist on   7. the family / have

unreasonable. Why don't you and your husband just say that this is the way

things are going to be? I'd recommend _____ a different

8. you / assign

person to be responsible for dinner each night—you and your husband

included, of course. It's worth a try, I think. Later on, you can think about

joining an athletic club and taking a family vacation.

WALKER: You know, I think you're right. I think I'll give it a try.

Conversation 2

MARTHA: Hi, Lois. What's on your mind? You said you wanted to talk.

LOIS: Hi, Martha. I wanted to tell you about the session I had with the family

counselor. I asked her about how we could get some family togetherness. She's in

favor of _____ at least one meal together every day. I

9. families / eat

remember _____ you and Hank and your kids always have

10. you / say

breakfast and dinner together. How do you manage it?

MARTHA: How do we manage it? I don't know. We just do it. That's just been a rule in our

house for as long as I can remember. Don't you have any family meals now?

LOIS: No, we don't. _____ different schedules makes it really tough.

11. Everybody / have

MARTHA: Well, I understand your problem, but I'd say that _____

12. a family / eat

together at least once a day is pretty necessary if they're really going to be a

family. Isn't there one time when you could all be there?

LOIS: Well, maybe dinner. The kids have school stuff every night starting at seven. Joe

and I don't get home until six. That doesn't leave much time. Plus, the kids don't

like _____ to "run their lives." That's the way they put it.

    13. we / try

MARTHA: There's nothing wrong with _____ _____

        14. you and Joe / insist on   15. everybody / be

there at dinner. Give it a try.

LOIS: Yeah, I think you're right. OK, I will.

❹ A LIFESTYLE SURVEY   Grammar Notes 1, 3

Part A

Work with three partners. Find out about each other's lifestyle, likes, and differences. Using the pictures and the prompts, ask each other a question for each item. Use gerunds in each question and answer. Share your results with the other groups.

> **EXAMPLE:**
> **A:** Do you like **being woken up** by an alarm clock or **waking up** by yourself?
> **B:** I like **waking up** by myself. I hate **being woken up** by an alarm clock.

Part B

Now continue by making up three questions of your own.

_____

_____

_____

5 EDITING

There are fifteen missing gerunds in this letter from a visitor to a dude ranch in New Mexico. Find and correct them.

July 28

Dear Adam,

I've been here for three days and am having a great time, but I can't help

~~wish~~ *wishing* you were here too. Tell your boss I'm really angry at him. His not let you

take any vacation time qualifies him for the Jerk-of-the-Year Award. (Just kidding.

Don't say that!) Believe it or not, the first night I missed hear all the city noises,

but I haven't really had any trouble get used to the peace and quiet since then.

Everything's all so relaxed here—there's no rush around or write things down in your

Daily Planner. Get out of New York City was definitely what I needed, even if it's

only for two weeks. The ranch has lots of activities—horseback ride, river raft on the

Rio Grande, hike in the wilderness—you name it. The ranch employees do everything

for you—getting taken care of is nice, for a change, and I love be chauffeured around

Santa Fe in the ranch limousine. Tonight a bunch of us are going out to a country and

western dancing place called Rodeo Nites in Santa Fe, so my having taken those

two-step lessons last summer will come in handy. It's just too bad you couldn't come

along so we could both kick up our heels. Tomorrow we're all going to Taos Pueblo to

watch some weave being done and to see some Native American dance, which is

great because I'm really interested in learn more about Native American culture. And

I'm looking forward to see *The Magic Flute* at the Santa Fe Opera on Saturday.

I'll write again in a day or two. Miss you lots.

Love,
Louise

COMMUNICATION PRACTICE

6 LISTENING

Brian Hansen and Jane Travanti are having a telephone conversation. Brian is asking Jane about the orienteering group she belongs to. Listen to the conversation. Then listen again and mark the following statements **True**, **False**, *or* **I don't know** *based on what you heard about the group.*

	True	False	I don't know
1. Brian has been in an orienteering group before.	❏	❏	❏
2. Dr. Stevens wants Brian to stop working.	❏	❏	❏
3. Brian has a lot of free time.	❏	❏	❏
4. Being experienced in orienteering is necessary to join Jane Travanti's group.	❏	❏	❏
5. Jane is married.	❏	❏	❏
6. It is summer now.	❏	❏	❏
7. Jane's club tries to go orienteering at least twice a month.	❏	❏	❏
8. Brian has done cross-country skiing before.	❏	❏	❏
9. People in the club are interesting people.	❏	❏	❏
10. Membership in Jane's club is free.	❏	❏	❏
11. Being married is necessary for membership in Jane's club.	❏	❏	❏
12. On their next orienteering activity, the group will stop at a restaurant to eat lunch.	❏	❏	❏

7 INFORMATION GAP: LETTERBOXING

Part A

Work with a partner. You are going to read an article about letterboxing. Each version of the article is missing some information. Take turns asking your partner questions to get information.

Student A, read the article. Ask questions and fill in the missing information. Then answer Student B's questions.

Student B, turn to page 316 and follow the instructions there.

EXAMPLE:

A: What does a screw-top bottle contain?

B: It contains a small notebook and a unique rubber stamp. What are hidden throughout the wild country of Dartmoor National Park?

A: Thousands of letterboxes are hidden throughout the wild country of Dartmoor National Park.

THEY LIVE AND BREATHE
LETTERBOXING

A letterbox is a plastic, screw-top bottle that contains _____.

Thousands of letterboxes are hidden throughout the wild country of Dartmoor National Park in

southwestern England. Letterboxing is a sort of combination of _____

that consists of using maps, clues, and compasses to find the hidden containers. Once a box is

located, the finder inks the stamp from the box and presses it into his notebook, then inks his

personal stamp and presses that into the notebook kept in the box. The stamp copy he takes home

is _____. Many letterboxers have collected hundreds of stamp

copies, which they enjoy reviewing at their leisure.

Letterboxing gives enthusiasts an excellent excuse for spending long days

_____. The great challenge is to interpret the complicated clues

to the whereabouts of each box. The clues are given on _____,

available from letterboxers (all of the boxes hidden in Dartmoor have been put out over the years

by letterboxers themselves) and an organization that publishes a clue catalogue.

Letterboxers trace their hobby back to 1854, when _____

put his calling card in a bottle and stuck the bottle into a bank at Cranmere Pool, in a remote part

of Dartmoor. Who could have foreseen that from such a modest beginning would emerge an

elaborate pastime that has become almost a way of life for many of its aficionados?

Source: Chris Granstrom, "They Live and Breathe Letterboxing." Originally appeared in *Smithsonian* Magazine, April 1998. Reprinted by permission of the author.

Part B

In small groups, discuss these questions. Share your views with the rest of the class.

1. Does the activity of letterboxing appeal to you? Why or why not? Would you participate in an activity like this if you had the opportunity?

2. If you wanted to take the basic idea of letterboxing and adapt it to your situation, how would you change it?

3. Do you know of any activities similar to letterboxing? If so, describe them.

8 ESSAY

What is the most interesting hobby or pastime you or someone that you know pursues? Write an essay of three or more paragraphs about it. Say what it is and why you consider it interesting, exciting, or fulfilling. Try to use gerunds and gerund phrases in your essay, including a passive gerund and a gerund phrase with **having** + **past participle**.

9 PICTURE DISCUSSION: A DAY IN THE LIFE OF TED

Work with a partner. Talk about one day in the life of Ted. Using as many gerunds and gerund phrases as possible, talk about Ted's likes and dislikes.

Student B, read the article. Answer Student A's questions. Then ask your own questions and fill in the missing information.

EXAMPLE:

A: What does a screw-top bottle contain?

B: It contains a small notebook and a unique rubber stamp. What are hidden throughout the wild country of Dartmoor National Park?

A: Thousands of letterboxes are hidden throughout the wild country of Dartmoor National Park.

THEY LIVE AND BREATHE
LETTERBOXING

A letterbox is a plastic, screw-top bottle that contains a small notebook and a unique rubber stamp. _____ are hidden throughout the wild country of Dartmoor National Park in southwestern England. Letterboxing is a sort of combination of orienteering and treasure hunting that consists of _____. Once a box is located, the finder inks the stamp from the box and presses it into his notebook, then inks his personal stamp and presses that into the notebook kept in the box. The stamp copy he takes home is his reward for the effort. Many letterboxers have collected hundreds of stamp copies, which they enjoy reviewing _____.

Letterboxing gives enthusiasts an excellent excuse for spending long days tramping over the moors. The great challenge is _____. The clues are given on detailed clue sheets, available from letterboxers (all of the boxes hidden in Dartmoor have been put out over the years by _____) and an organization that publishes a clue catalogue.

Letterboxers trace their hobby back to 1854, when a Victorian gentleman put his calling card in a bottle and stuck the bottle into a bank at Cranmere Pool, in a remote part of Dartmoor. Who could have foreseen that from such a modest beginning would emerge an elaborate pastime that has become _____?

Source: Chris Granstrom, "They Live and Breathe Letterboxing." Originally appeared in *Smithsonian* Magazine, April 1998. Reprinted by permission of the author.

INFINITIVES

GRAMMAR **IN CONTEXT**

QUESTIONS TO CONSIDER

1. What are the dangers of procrastination?

2. Do you ever put things off until it is too late or almost too late to do anything about it?

Read the story and think about the questions.

I Meant to Call . . .

The clock radio boomed on at 8:30 and jarred Steve Reynolds awake.

It was a Saturday morning, and as Steve rolled over he caught a glimpse through the window of heavy, dark clouds in the sky. He heard the sound of rain pouring down. It looked like it was going to be another one of those rainy, sleepy days. Even though it was Saturday, he needed to go to work, and he'd asked one of the security people to open the office so that he could use the computer to work on the annual report. It was supposed to have been completed and left on his boss's desk three days ago. It had to be done today! Steve sighed and pulled the covers up over his head. He didn't want to go to work, but he knew he had to. But to sleep for just a few more minutes wouldn't hurt, would it?

When Steve woke up the second time, the clock read 10:35. He'd better get rolling if he was going to get anything done today. He went into the kitchen and put a cup of coffee into the microwave to heat it up. He glanced at two pieces of mail that had been lying on the counter for more than a week now. One was a postcard from his veterinarian reminding him that Omar, his pet cat, was supposed to have gotten his distemper and feline leukemia shot a month ago. The other piece of mail was a letter from his mother, who lived in a nursing home in a town thirty miles away. The letter was actually two weeks old. Steve hadn't spoken to his mother recently, and he was sure she expected him to have written or called by now, though of course she hadn't said anything about it. He really should give her a call—maybe when he came back from work tonight. He sat down at the dining room table and glanced at the newspaper while he drank his coffee and ate a doughnut. Omar, who loved to be held, jumped up into his lap, but Steve pushed him off, annoyed. "Not now, Omar—I don't feel like holding you right now. Later!" *(continued on next page)*

317

Steve's plan was to spend just a couple of hours finishing the report, but it took him all day. When he got home at 6:30 in the evening, he was drained and irritable. The message light on his answering machine was blinking, but Steve thought he'd wait until later to listen to the messages. Feeling too tired to cook a regular meal, he called and ordered some Chinese food to be delivered. He'd planned to fix a leaky faucet, but it was so late that he decided it wasn't worth starting, so he settled down in front of the TV set.

The next day was Sunday. It had stopped raining, and the sun was shining brilliantly. Steve got up at 8:00 feeling refreshed and spent a leisurely hour reading the Sunday paper. He'd arranged to meet his friend Anne at 1:00 for lunch at a new restaurant that was rumored to have excellent omelets. The lunch was delicious, and Steve enjoyed Anne's company. Driving by a shopping mall on his way home, Steve stopped to get his mother a birthday present. Her seventy-fifth birthday had actually occurred a month previously, but they had agreed it wasn't important to celebrate the exact day. The important thing was the thought, no matter when the gift came. Steve had said, "Mom, I want to get you the right thing, something really nice. I don't want to be rushed into it." His mother had agreed, saying, "Of course, son. I'm long past the age when I expect to be fussed over for a silly birthday or be given a birthday party."

When Steve walked into his apartment, he noticed that the red phone message light was still blinking, and he realized he had forgotten to listen to his messages the evening before. He pressed the play button and heard the first message:

Hi, Steve, this is Mom. I wanted to tell you that I'm going into the hospital for a couple of days. I just haven't been feeling well these last two weeks or so, and the doctor thinks I need to have some tests. Maybe you could give me a call later if you have time. My number at the hospital is 688–9294.

The machine beeped, and then the second message came on:

Steve, this is Doctor O'Brien at Parkland General Hospital. Please give me a call right away at 688–9299.

Steve's heart was racing now, and he quickly dialed the number. The phone was answered by an aide, and it took several minutes for Dr. O'Brien to be tracked down. Finally, Steve heard the doctor's voice on the other end:

"This is Mark O'Brien."

"Hello, Dr. O'Brien, this is Steve Reynolds. I got a message on my machine this morning from my mother. She said she was going into the hospital. Then I got your message. Is everything OK? She's all right, isn't she?"

"Steve, your mother had a heart attack yesterday afternoon. She's in intensive care. Her condition is stable, but she's in pretty serious condition. You'd better get down here right away."

UNDERSTANDING MEANING FROM CONTEXT

Circle the letter of the choice closest in meaning to the italicized word or phrase from the reading.

1. As Steve rolled over he caught a *glimpse* through the window of heavy, dark clouds in the sky.

   a. flash of light   **b.** brief look   **c.** long look

2. He'd better *get rolling* if he was going to get anything done today.

   a. start the day's activities   **b.** start breakfast   **c.** start the car

3. When he got home at 6:30, he was *drained* and irritable.

   a. wet   **b.** sick   **c.** exhausted

4. He'd arranged to meet his friend Anne at 1:00 at a new restaurant that *was rumored to have* excellent omelets.

   a. people said had   **b.** advertisers said had   **c.** his friend Anne said had

5. I'm long past the age when I expect to be *fussed over for* a silly birthday or be given a birthday party.

   a. given a lot of criticism regarding   **b.** paid a lot of attention regarding   **c.** asked a lot of questions regarding

6. It took several minutes for Dr. O'Brien to be *tracked down*.

   a. telephoned   **b.** talked to   **c.** located

COMPREHENSION

1. Do you think Steve cared about his mother?

2. Why did he wait so long to get in touch with her? Is this a good example of procrastination?

GRAMMAR **PRESENTATION**
INFINITIVES

GRAMMATICAL FUNCTIONS

INFINITIVE AS SUBJECT

To sleep a few minutes longer wouldn't hurt, would it?

INFINITIVE AS OBJECT

Mom, I want **to get** you the right thing, something really nice.

INFINITIVE AS SUBJECT OR ADJECTIVE COMPLEMENT

Steve's plan was **to spend** just a couple of hours finishing the report.

They had agreed it wasn't important **to celebrate** the exact day.

FORMS

VERB + INFINITIVE

	VERB	**INFINITIVE**	
He	**needed**	**to go**	to work later.

VERB + OBJECT + INFINITIVE

	VERB	**OBJECT**	**INFINITIVE**	
He'd	**asked**	**one of the security people**	**to open**	the office.

PERFECT FORM

He was sure his mother expected him **to have written or called** by now.

PASSIVE FORM

I'm long past the age when I expect **to be given** a birthday party.

INFINITIVE OF PURPOSE

He put a cup of coffee into the microwave **to heat it up**.

ELLIPSIS OF FULL INFINITIVE

Steve had meant to call his mother, but so far he hadn't had a chance **to**.

NOTES	**EXAMPLES**
1. An **infinitive** is *"to"* plus the base form of a verb. Infinitives often take the place of nouns, performing the same functions as regular nouns.	
Infinitives act as **subjects**.	subject • **To sleep a few minutes longer** wouldn't hurt, would it?
Infinitives act as **direct objects**.	direct object • He'd arranged **to meet his friend Anne for lunch**.
Infinitives act as **subject complements** (words or phrases that describe or explain the subject). To form an infinitive subject complement, add an infinitive after the subject noun.	subject complement • Steve's plan was **to spend just a couple of hours finishing the report**. (*To spend just a couple of hours finishing the report* shows what the plan was.)
Infinitives act as **adjective complements** (words or phrases that describe or explain adjectives in the sentence). To form an infinitive adjective complement, add an infinitive that refers to an adjective.	adjective complement • Feeling too tired **to cook a regular meal**, Steve ordered some Chinese food. (*To cook a regular meal* describes the adjective *tired*.)
2. Infinitives can be used in **perfect form** (*to* + *have* + **past participle**). This form suggests the past in relation to some other time.	• His mother expected him **to have called or written by now**. (*She had expected him to call or write before now*.)

(continued on next page)

3. Infinitives can occur in **passive form** (*to* + *be* or *get* + **past participle**).

- The report was supposed **to have been completed and left** on his boss's desk three days ago.

4. An **infinitive of purpose** explains the purpose of an action. It often answers the question "why?"

- Steve stopped at a nearby shopping mall **to get** his mother a birthday present. *(explains why Steve stopped at the mall)*

An infinitive of purpose can be stated in the longer form *in order to*.

- Steve stopped at a nearby shopping mall **in order to get** his mother a birthday present.

▶ **BE CAREFUL!** Don't use *for* directly before an infinitive of purpose.

- He could use the computer **to work** on the annual report.
  NOT ~~He could use the computer for to work on the annual report~~.

5. When **verb** + **infinitive** constructions refer to a verb mentioned earlier, it is not necessary to repeat the base form of the preceding verb. The *to* alone is enough and is understood to stand for the earlier verb. This process is called **ellipsis**.

- Steve had meant to call his mother, but so far he hadn't had a chance **to**. *(hadn't had a chance to call his mother)*

Ellipsis also occurs with the *to* of the modal-like expressions *have to, have got to, had to, ought to, be supposed to, be about to*, and *be able to*.

- Steve didn't want to go to work, but he knew he had **to**. *(had to go to work)*

6. **BE CAREFUL!** Remember that some verbs can be followed by infinitives or gerunds. See Appendices 9–12 on pages A-6 and A-7 for listings of these categories.

a. Some verbs and verb phrases are followed only by infinitives. These include *appear, begin, decide, hope, manage, need, pretend, seem, want,* and *would like*.

- Steve didn't **want to go** to work.

b. Some verbs and verbs phrases are followed only by gerunds. Examples of these are *avoid, be worth, can't help, consider, enjoy, feel like, have trouble, keep, mind, miss,* and *spend* (time).

- Steve **spent** all day **finishing** the report.
- He'd planned to fix a leaky faucet, but it was so late that he decided it **wasn't worth starting**.

c. Some verbs are followed by infinitives or gerunds with no significant meaning change. These include *begin, can't stand, continue, hate, like, love, prefer,* and *start*.

- Steve didn't **like to work** on Saturdays.
  OR
- Steve didn't **like working** on Saturdays.

d. Some verbs are followed by infinitives or gerunds with a significant meaning change. These include *forget, go on, quit, regret, remember, stop,* and *try*.

- Driving by a shopping mall on his way home, Steve **stopped to get** his mother a birthday present. *(stopped in order to get the present)*

- It had **stopped raining**. *(stopped the activity of raining)*

- Steve had **forgotten to listen** to his messages. *(hadn't remembered to listen)*

- Steve had **forgotten listening** to his messages. *(forgotten that he had listened to them)*

FOCUSED PRACTICE

1 DISCOVER THE GRAMMAR

Part A

1. *Go back to the unit opener. Underline all the infinitives and infinitive phrases, including the word* **to** *if it is an ellipsis.*

2. *Draw a second line under the perfect forms.*

3. *Circle the passive forms.*

Part B

Look at these sentences from I Meant to Call . . . *Then circle* **True (T)** *or* **False (F)**, *according to the meaning of each sentence.*

1. It was supposed to have been completed and left on his boss's desk three days ago.

    T   F   Steve had only three more days to complete the project.

2. Omar, his pet cat, was supposed to have gotten his distemper and feline leukemia shot a month ago.

    T   F   Omar should have had the shot by now, but he hadn't.

3. He was sure she expected him to have written or called by now.

    T   F   Steve was already later than his mother would have expected.

4. Feeling too tired to cook a regular meal, he called and ordered some Chinese food to be delivered.

    T   F   Steve didn't have the time to cook a regular meal.

5. Driving by a shopping mall on his way home, Steve stopped to get his mother a birthday present.

    T   F   He stopped looking for his mother's present.

6. I don't want to be rushed into it.

    T   F   I want to take my time.

Part C

Could the following sentences from the reading be rewritten using the phrases in the parentheses without a significant change in meaning? Why or why not?

1. Even though it was Saturday, he needed to go to work. (needed going to work)

_____

2. Omar, who loved to be held, jumped up into his lap. (who loved being held)

_____

3. Not now, Omar—I don't feel like holding you right now. (feel like to hold you)

_____

4. Driving by a shopping mall on his way home, Steve stopped to get his mother a

birthday present. (stopped getting his mother a birthday present)

_____

5. He realized he had forgotten to listen to his messages the evening before. (had

forgotten listening)

_____

2 **WHAT WOULD YOU EXPECT?** Grammar Notes 1–4, 6

Work with a partner. Read the description of each situation and look at the
appropriate picture. Ask your partner a question for each item. Each question and
answer must contain at least one infinitive structure.

1. On your second day of a new job, you are two
hours late to work. (get / fire)

   Would you expect to get fired?

_____

2. You have a flat tire on a busy freeway.
(someone / stop / help you)

_____

3. Your son or daughter borrowed the car and was supposed to be home by 11:00 P.M. It is now 2:00 A.M. (him / her / call / by now)

_____

_____

4. You have borrowed your parents' car and it has stalled. It is 2:00 A.M. and no one has come by to help you. (your parents / worried)

_____

_____

5. You have put off paying your phone bill for more than a month. (phone service / be / disconnect)

_____

_____

③ SEIZE THE DAY   Grammar Notes 1, 3, 4, 6

Writer Jessica Taylor has again interviewed psychiatrist Robert Stevens for an article in Pocket Digest *magazine. Read the excerpt on pages 327–328 about the basis of procrastination. Complete the sentences in the conversation by supplying active or passive infinitive structures of the verbs in the following box. You will use some of the verbs more than once.*

put off	tell	turn out	be	procrastinate	stick
resist	change	not put off	do	fail	take
avoid	make	invite	turn down	ask	reject

TAYLOR: Dr. Stevens, the last time we talked, you spoke about the expectation syndrome. This time I wanted ____to ask____ you if there's such a thing
1.
as a procrastination syndrome.

STEVENS: Well, I don't know if we could go so far as to call it a syndrome, but for many people procrastination is a very serious problem.

TAYLOR: Yes, that certainly seems _____ the case for a lot of
2.
individuals. What causes them _____, anyway? Laziness?
3.

STEVENS: That's a popular notion, but I'd have to say that laziness is a relatively minor cause. No, I think that fear is really the most important force that motivates people _____ doing something until later.
4.

TAYLOR: Fear? Not laziness? You'll have to explain that to me a little bit.

STEVENS: Well, it's actually somewhat related to the expectation syndrome. A lot of people feel they have to live up to other people's expectations. They're afraid _____. Many times they fear they won't be able to do
5.
something perfectly or well. They're afraid _____ mistakes, or
6.
maybe they don't want _____ or _____ no. They let
7.   8.
fear take control of them, and they put off any action.

TAYLOR: What would be an example of that?

STEVENS: Well, suppose someone wants _____ people to a party—let's
9.
say it's a young woman named Blanche. She's always been afraid of these kinds of things, and she expects, either consciously or subconsciously,

_____, so she delays calling people until the very last moment.
10.
Her invitation is at such short notice that not many people are going to be able to accept. And that's what happens. Hardly anyone can come. In an ironic way, Blanche's fear has caused things _____ like this.
11.

TAYLOR: Uh-huh. Well, what if someone is a procrastinator and wants

_____? What would you advise that person _____?
12.   13.

(continued on next page)

STEVENS: Well, there are three principles I try _____ to. The first is never

_____ until tomorrow what needs _____ today. The
     15.   **16.**

second comes from Eastern philosophy, and that's not _____
                                                     17.

the needle—in other words, don't try _____ painful things. The
                                                     18.

third comes from Western philosophy and is summed up in the Latin

phrase _carpe diem_. Seize the day. Consider everything that comes before

you as an opportunity. If it seems like a good and proper thing

_____ , do it, regardless of whether it's going to provide pain or
     19.

pleasure. Don't even think about whether it makes you afraid or not. I'm

not advising people _____ unnecessary or foolish risks, but I
                               20.

am urging them _____ living. They may not get another chance.
                 21.

TAYLOR: Well, Doctor Stevens, thanks for another stimulating discussion.

---

4 EDITING

Read this tongue-in-cheek Procrastinator's Creed and correct the twelve errors in infinitives and gerunds. Some sentences have more than one error.

Procrastinator's Creed

1. I believe that if anything is worth ~~to do~~ _doing_, it would have been done already.

2. I shall never move quickly, except to avoiding more work or find excuses.

3. I shall never rush do a job without a lifetime of consideration.

4. I shall meet all of my deadlines directly in proportion to the amount of bodily injury I could expect receiving from missing them.

5. I firmly believe that tomorrow holds the chance to creating new technologies, making astounding discoveries, and getting a reprieve from my obligations.

6. I truly believe all deadlines are impossible to meet regardless of the amount of time given.

7. I shall always decide not to decide, unless of course I decide to have changed my mind.

8. I know that the cycle of work is not to planning / starting / finishing, but to waiting / planning / planning.

9. I will never put off until tomorrow what I can forget do forever.

Source: Adapted from Nigel Mendez, "Procrastinator's Creed," nhmen@CONNCOLL.EDU. Internet Website: Stefani Banerian.

5 HELPING PROCRASTINATORS GET TO IT

Part A

Read the following excerpts from an article about procrastination. Complete the sentences with the infinitive or gerund forms of the appropriate verbs from the box below.

avoid	clean	do	finish	procrastinate
be	complete	deal	start	make

HELPING PROCRASTINATORS GET TO IT

When you ignored your mother's advice to never put off until tomorrow what you can do today, the worst you probably suffered was a lecture about ____*cleaning*____
                                                                                                    1.
your room. But if you're still putting things off as an adult, the consequences are more serious: you are probably missing deadlines and breaking promises.

There are remedies, says psychologist Linda Sapadin, author of the new book *It's About Time.* And the key to change is in the past.

Not all procrastinators are cut from the same cloth. There are six **procrastination styles**, Sapadin says, based on harmful patterns learned in childhood, such as a tendency to perfectionism or worrying. Rather than face new challenges, procrastinators learned as children _____ them.
                                                              2.

Procrastinators are neither disorganized nor lazy, she says. Time management tips won't help them: understanding the emotional patterns that still hobble them will.

Most who chronically put things off are a blend of several types, but they have one predominant style. You can identify your own procrastination patterns from the following list and deal with them, she says.

PERFECTIONISTS

They are reluctant _____ because they might fall short of their
                          3.
unrealistically high standards. They get buried in details, hoping _____
                                                                        4.
mistakes.

▶

DREAMERS

They tend to be vague, unrealistic, romantic. Grandiose ideas are not turned into solid goals and plans. They're unable _____ with details.
5.

WORRIERS

These procrastinators have a small "comfort zone" and easily become overwhelmed. They avoid risk or change and lack confidence in their ability _____ decisions. The mantra of the worrier: "What if . . . ?"
6.

CRISIS MAKERS

They are proud of saying they can't get motivated until the last minute. They live for the adrenaline rush, life on the edge, and will create a crisis by _____
7.
and then ride in like a superhero to solve it. They have very low boredom thresholds and avoid _____ and _____ routine projects.
8.   9.

DEFIERS

There are two types: the aggressive, argumentative, sulky one and the passive–aggressive who promises _____ something and doesn't. The
10.
second is a big problem in marriages.

OVERDOERS

They're always working, so they may not seem like procrastinators. But overdoers make extra work and don't focus on what really needs _____ done.
11.
They have difficulty saying no and delegating; they're candidates for early burnout.

Part B

Does your perfectionism cause you problems? Psychologist Linda Sapadin identifies six types of procrastinators. This quiz is adapted from It's About Time *and is designed to test specifically for a perfectionist procrastinator: Circle* **F** *if this behavior is* **Frequent**; **S** *if* **Sometimes**; **R** *if* **Rare**. *The scoring key follows.*

• Do I get preoccupied with details that others don't seem to care about?	F	S	R
• Do I have difficulty starting / finishing a task because my own standards haven't been met?	F	S	R
• Am I reluctant to delegate tasks or work with others unless they work my way?	F	S	R
• Do others say I am rigid, stubborn, finicky?	F	S	R
• Am I critical of my accomplishments or how long they took?	F	S	R
• Does my work have to be as good as it possibly can be in order to satisfy me?	F	S	R
• Do I look at my failures as embarrassments I would not want revealed?	F	S	R
• Do I have trouble maintaining a sense of humor while learning something new?	F	S	R
• Am I upset if I don't perform as well as a peer?	F	S	R
• Do I think about situations in terms of black and white, in extremes?	F	S	R

Scoring: Give yourself two points for each **F** *answer and one for each* **S**. *If your total score is 10 or above, you are a major perfectionist procrastinator.*

Source: Adapted from Karen S. Paterson, "Helping Procrastinators Get to It," *USA Today*, July 22, 1997, p. 7D. Copyright 1997, USA TODAY. Reprinted with permission.

Part C

Now discuss your answers as a class.

COMMUNICATION PRACTICE

6 LISTENING

Kenny Anaya is a junior in high school and has difficulty getting his work done. Listen to the conversation between Kenny and his mother.

Now listen again. Circle the letter of the choice that gives correct information about what is happening.

1. **a.** Kenny hopes Mom will be able to write his paper for him.

   b. Kenny hopes Mom will be able to type his paper for him.

2. **a.** Mom won't have time to type the paper.

   b. Mom won't have time to go to the party.

3. **a.** Kenny says Mom must turn in the paper.

   b. Kenny says Mom must type the paper.

4. **a.** Kenny is afraid of getting kicked out of school.

   b. Kenny isn't afraid of getting kicked out of school.

5. **a.** Mom thinks Kenny will get kicked out of school.

   b. Mom doesn't think Kenny will get kicked out of school.

6. **a.** Kenny thinks he might have to repeat the year in school.

   b. Kenny thinks he will have to repeat the year in school.

7. **a.** Kenny says he didn't finish his paper because of a problem with his dog.

   b. Kenny says he didn't finish his paper because of a problem with his cat.

8. **a.** Kenny promises to get his work done on time in the future.

   b. Kenny promises to type the paper himself.

9. **a.** Mom is not going to bail Kenny out of his difficulties.

   b. Mom is not going to attend the party.

10. **a.** Kenny may need to get a snack.

    b. Kenny may need to stay up all night.

7 INFORMATION GAP: ON THE LOOSE

Work with a partner. You are going to read the transcript of a police bulletin about a dangerous fugitive who has escaped from prison. Each version is missing some information. Take turns asking your partner questions to get information.

Student A, read the following transcript. Ask questions and fill in the missing information. Then answer Student B's questions.

Student B, turn to the Information Gap on page 335 and follow the instructions there.

EXAMPLE:

A: Who are reported to have escaped from the maximum security facility?

B: The infamous prisoner Charles Gallagher and two other inmates are reported to have escaped from the maximum security facility. Where is the maximum security facility they are reported to have escaped from?

A: The facility is in Grandview.

Official Transcript

Here is a bulletin from the Mason County Sheriff's Office. _____ are reported to have escaped from the maximum security facility in Grandview. The three prisoners are thought to _____ out of the prison in a laundry truck. Prison authorities are noncommittal as to how the break could have taken place, but according to usually reliable sources, the three men are believed to have been aided in their escape by a confidant within the prison. Ironically, _____ was supposed to have been installed two months ago, but because of unexplained delays and apparent bureaucratic problems, it is not yet operative. Listeners should be aware that the three prisoners are thought _____ and are believed to be heading in the direction of Aberdeen. Listeners are also warned not to _____ but are asked to contact the Mason County Sheriff's Office or call the toll-free number, 1-800-555-9999, if they have any information.

8 ESSAY

All of us have procrastinated at one time or another. Write an essay of three to five paragraphs about a time when you put off doing something that needed to be done. Tell about the results. Speculate about the reasons for your procrastination and discuss the consequences.

9 PICTURE DISCUSSION

Work with a partner. Describe what is happening, using present tenses. Complete the mother and daughter's conversations. Then tell the story a second time, using past tenses. Use as many infinitives and infinitive phrases as possible.

INFORMATION GAP FOR STUDENT B

Student B, read the transcript. Answer Student A's questions. Then ask your own questions and fill in the missing information.

EXAMPLE:

A: Who are reported to have escaped from the maximum security facility?

B: The infamous prisoner Charles Gallagher and two other inmates are reported to have escaped from the maximum security facility. Where is the maximum security facility they are reported to have escaped from?

A: The facility is in Grandview.

Official Transcript

Here is a bulletin from the Mason County Sheriff's Office. The infamous prisoner Charles Gallagher and two other inmates are reported to have escaped from the maximum security facility in _____. The three prisoners are thought to have been smuggled out of the prison _____. Prison authorities are noncommittal as to how the break could have taken place, but according to usually reliable sources, the three men are believed to have been aided in their escape by a confidant within the prison. Ironically, a new state-of-the-art security system was supposed to have been installed _____, but because of unexplained delays and apparent bureaucratic problems, it is not yet operative. Listeners should be aware that the three prisoners are thought to be armed and are believed to be heading _____. Listeners are also warned not to approach the fugitives but are asked to contact _____ or call the toll-free number, 1-800-555-9999, if they have any information.

REVIEW OR SELFTEST

I. *Complete the conversations with a gerund or infinitive form of the indicated verb. Include both forms if either a gerund or infinitive can be used.*

1. **A:** What do you want _____to do_____ tonight?

a. (do)

   B: I feel like _____ to a movie.

b. (go)

2. **A:** It's not so bad _____ a white lie, is it?

a. (tell)

   B: I don't think _____ is ever right.

b. (lie)

3. **A:** It isn't wrong _____ yourself, is it?

a. (defend)

   B: I think _____ yourself is the right thing to do if you have

b. (defend)

   a good reason.

4. **A:** Why did you end up _____ in forestry?

a. (major)

   B: I've always loved _____ outdoors. And I've always had

b. (be)

   trouble _____ desk jobs.

c. (do)

II. *Read the following magazine article about historical situations of fortunate and unfortunate events. Fill in the blanks with gerund phrases containing a possessive + past participle. Include **having** if necessary.*

 ## Timing Is Everything

Is there such a thing as good or bad timing—a moment in time when events and currents combine fortuitously or unfortuitously to cause major changes? Apparently there are such moments, though of course the labels good and bad depend heavily on one's viewpoint.

On August 3, 1492, for example, Christopher Columbus set sail for what would later become known as the New World.

_____His having persuaded_____ the Spanish monarchs, King Ferdinand and
　　　　1. (He / persuade)

Queen Isabella, to sponsor his voyage at a moment when they were disposed to

help him is a classic example of historical good timing—from the European

viewpoint, that is.

Another example of good timing occurred on March 30, 1867, when the United

States purchased Alaska from Russian for $7.2 million as a result of the efforts of

U.S. Secretary of State William H. Seward. _____ the
　　　　　　　　　　　　　　　2. (Seward / perceive)

potential worth of Alaska later disproved the criticisms of his detractors, who called

the territory "Seward's Icebox" and the purchase "Seward's Folly."

A momentous example of good timing occurred on December 5, 1955, in

Montgomery, Alabama, when Rosa Parks, a black woman, refused to give up her

seat and move to the back of a city bus out of deference to white people. The U.S.

Supreme _____ school segregation a year and a half
　　　　　3. (Court / outlaw)

previously had set the stage for the event. _____ not to
　　　　　　　　　　　　　　　4. (Parks / decide)

give up her seat and _____ to back down set in motion
　　　　　5. (she / refuse)

the Montgomery Bus Boycott, a movement that brought to prominence the pastor

of Parks's church, Martin Luther King, Jr., and immeasurably affected the U. S. Civil

Rights movement.

_____ to make a political trip to Dallas, Texas, on
　　6. (John F. Kennedy / agree)

November 22, 1963, the day of his assassination, is a tragic example of bad timing,

especially in light of _____ by several advisors not to go
　　　　　　　7. (he / be / warn)

to Dallas at that time.

Another example of bad timing occurred in 1968 in Prague, when the brief

experiment with the democratization of the Communist regime in Czechoslovakia

ended with Warsaw Pact forces invading the country and quashing the hopes of the

reformers. _____ the resolve of the Soviets apparently
　　　8. (They / misjudge)

(continued on next page)

paved the way for the invasion. In November 1989, however, amidst the tide of

revolt that was sweeping Eastern Europe,

_____ new elections led to the

    9. (protesters / seize the moment / and / demand)

resignation of the Communist leadership and to the end of communism in

Czechoslovakia. Their timing was certainly right the second time around.

III. *Complete the traffic report with gerund or infinitive forms of the indicated verbs.*
Place the verbs in the appropriate tense. Some verb forms need to be passive.

You'll have trouble _____commuting_____ this afternoon, folks. Interstate 5 is blocked for
                1. (commute)

two miles north and south of 80th Street, so I suggest _____ an alternate
                                              2. (use)

route if possible. Construction on the Factoria interchange has caused

_____ on I-405, so use caution there. Repairs on the Evergreen Point Bridge
    3. (slow)

_____ by 6:00 A.M. today, but the bridge is still closed. The Highway
    4. (expect / complete)

Department issued a statement apologizing for _____ further
                                      5. (cause)

inconvenience to motorists, but the repairs are taking longer than planned. The repairs are

expected _____ by 5:00 A.M. Tuesday. Meanwhile, an accident involving an
              6. (finish)

overturned van in the left lane on the 509 freeway isn't expected _____ for
                                                                  7. (clear)

at least half an hour, so avoid the 509 northbound. You can improve your commute by

_____ Highway 99, where traffic is smooth and relatively light. This is Hank
    8. (take)

Simmons for KXYZ Traffic Watch.

IV. *Complete the conversations, using ellipsis. Make the verbs negative if necessary.*

1. A: Why didn't Alex and Anna come to the party?

    B: They _____were going to_____, but they got called to the hospital.
                (be going)

2. A: Wasn't Gabe going to bring hot dogs to the picnic?

    B: He _____, but I don't see any. I don't think he did.
        (be supposed)

3. A: Are you going to attend the university?

B: I'm _____, but I have to earn some money first.
(plan)

4. A: Doesn't Amanda know how to cook?

B: She _____. She's worked in a restaurant for more than a year.
(ought)

5. A: Why didn't you type my paper? It's due tomorrow!

B: I _____. I had my own work to do.
(have time)

6. A: Aren't you going to buy that house?

B: No, I _____, after all. It doesn't have a view.
(want)

V. *Describe a day in the life of Alice Matthews, using the indicated verb and a gerund or infinitive. Include both forms if either a gerund or infinitive can be used.*

1. Alice Matthews _____ enjoys taking the _____

_____ bus to work _____. (enjoy)

2. She _____

_____ because

of the trafffic. (avoid)

3. She _____

_____ at 9:00 A.M.

(start)

4. She _____

_____ in meetings.

(have trouble)

5. She _____

_____ at 5:00 P.M.

(finish)

6. She usually _____

_____.

(spend / evenings)

VI. *Circle the letter of the choice that correctly completes each sentence.*

1. We are in favor of _____ the bridge.　　　　　A (B) C D
   (A) build　　　　　　　　　　(C) to build
   (B) building　　　　　　　　(D) having built

2. I asked Juanita _____ the proposal.　　　　　A B C D
   (A) review　　　　　　　　　(C) to review
   (B) reviewing　　　　　　　(D) having reviewed

3. "Bobby, can you type my paper?"
   "I don't have time _____ right now.　　　　　A B C D
   Maybe later."
   (A) to　　　　　　　　　　　(C) to doing
   (B) to do　　　　　　　　　(D) to have done

4. _____ my lifestyle is the best thing I ever did.　　A B C D
   (A) My having changed　　　(C) Me having changed
   (B) Having changing　　　　(D) My change

5. You're expected _____ well prepared for a job interview.　A B C D
   (A) be　　　　　　　　　　　(C) being
   (B) to be　　　　　　　　　(D) having been

6. "The report was supposed _____ completed by March 1.　A B C D
   What happened?"
   (A) being　　　　　　　　　(C) have been
   (B) be　　　　　　　　　　　(D) to have been

7. The sign warned pedestrians _____ on the grass.　　A B C D
   (A) not walking　　　　　　(C) not walk
   (B) not to walk　　　　　　(D) not to have walked

8. Ms. Francis was said _____ the article.　　　　A B C D
   (A) to write　　　　　　　　(C) to have written
   (B) writing　　　　　　　　(D) write

9. When the teacher asked the students _____, they　　A B C D
   kept making noise.
   (A) stop talking　　　　　　(C) stopped to talk
   (B) to stop to talk　　　　(D) to stop talking

10. Harriet tried _____ the sport of snowboarding but　　A B C D
    was never able to get the hang of it.
    (A) to master　　　　　　　(C) to have mastered
    (B) mastering　　　　　　　(D) having mastered

▶ *To check your answers, go to the Answer Key on page 345.*

FROM GRAMMAR TO WRITING PARALLELISM OF GERUNDS AND INFINITIVES

Remember that in parallel structure all items in a series are in the same grammatical form: singulars with singulars, plurals with plurals, actives with actives, passives with passives, and so forth. Parallelism makes our speaking and writing more communicative. Mixing gerunds and infinitives in the same series is a common parallelism error.

EXAMPLES:

gerund   gerund   gerund

My summer hobbies are **hiking**, **boating**, and **mountain biking**.

NOT

gerund   gerund   infinitive

~~My summer hobbies are hiking, boating, and to go mountain biking~~.

infinitive

As my friend Pam started college, her goals were **to make** new

infinitive

friends and **to become** well educated.

NOT

infinitive

~~As my friend Pam started college, her goals were to make new~~

gerund

~~friends and becoming well educated~~.

A series of infinitive phrases may be presented with the word *to* before each item or before the first item only.

Helen loves **to read**, **to write**, and **to attend** the opera.

OR

Helen loves **to read**, **write**, and **attend** the opera.

NOT

~~Helen loves to read, write, and to attend the opera~~.

Remember that in any series, a common element can either be used before each item or before the first item only, though often one form will sound better than the other. See *From Grammar to Writing* after Part V, on page 252, for a discussion of this feature of parallel structure.

If a sentence is long, it is often best to include the word **to** before each infinitive phrase.

> In his sensitivity training at work, Bob learned **to listen** carefully to other people, **to consider** their feelings, and **to imagine** himself in their situations.

Gerunds or gerund phrases containing a possessive and / or *having* + past participle should also be presented in parallel structure.

> I want to thank everyone for making this party a success. I especially appreciate **Sarah's having invited** the guests, **Jack's having cooked** the food, and **Jennifer's having organized** the whole thing.

Similarly, long infinitive phrases should be presented in parallel structure.

> Applicants to the university are expected **to have completed** a college preparatory program, **to have graduated** in the upper third of their high school class, and **to have participated** in extracurricular activities.

---

❶ *Each of the following sentences contains an error involving parallelism with gerunds or gerund phrases. Correct the nonparallel items.*

1. Kenneth loves camping, ~~to~~ collect ^ing^ stamps, and surfing the Internet.

2. Lately I've been trying to stop speeding in traffic, to schedule too many activities, and rushing through each day like a crazy person.

3. To have a happier family life, we should all focus on eating meals together, on airing our problems and concerns, and on take time to talk to one another.

4. Mr. Mason's planning the agenda, Ms. Bono renting the hall, and Mrs. Tanaka's arranging for the guest speakers made the conference a success.

5. Ken's life is vastly changed because of his having stopped working all the time, joined a singles group, and having met some interesting new friends.

---

❷ *Each of the following sentences contains an error in parallelism with infinitives or infinitive phrases. Correct the nonparallel items.*

1. On our vacation this year we want to see the Butchart Gardens in Victoria, British Columbia, camp near Great Slave Lake, and ~~to~~ drive up the Alaska Highway.

2. I'm advising you not to sell your property, take out a loan, and not to buy a new house right now.

3. Most presidents want to be reelected to a second term, taken seriously by other world leaders, and to be remembered fondly after they leave office.

4. To be hired in this firm, you are expected to have earned a bachelor's degree and having worked in a bank for at least two years.

3 *Read the following paragraph about speech anxiety. Correct the ten errors in parallelism with gerunds and infinitives.*

What are you most afraid of? Are you worried about being cheated, ~~to lose~~ *losing* your job, or contracting a deadly disease? Well, if you're like the vast majority of Americans, you fear standing up, to face an audience, and to deliver a speech more than anything else. Surveys have found that anxiety about public speaking terrifies Americans more than dying does. Somehow, people expect to be laughed at, ridiculed, or to be scorned by an audience. Many college students fear public speaking so much that they put off taking a speech class or even to think about it until their last term before graduation. Speech instructors and others familiar with the principles of public speaking stress that the technique of desensitization works best for overcoming speech anxiety. This idea holds that people can get over their fear of speaking in public by enrolling in a course, to attend the class faithfully, and to force themselves to perform the speech activities. Once they have discovered that it is rare for people to die, making fools of themselves, or to be laughed at while making a speech, they're on their way to success. Consequently, their anxiety becomes a little less each time they get up and talk in public. It may take a while, but eventually they find themselves able to stand up willingly, speaking comfortably, and expressing themselves clearly.

4 **APPLY IT TO YOUR WRITING**

Write a paragraph of six or seven sentences on one of these topics:

- ways you enjoy spending your leisure time
- things you like to do
- things you have difficulty doing

In your paragraph, include examples of parallelism of gerunds, of infinitives, or of both. Then work with a partner. Edit each other's paragraph. Pay particular attention to correctness of parallel structures.

REVIEW OR SELFTEST
ANSWER KEY

I.
1. **b.** going
2. **a.** to tell
   b. lying
3. **a.** to defend
   b. defending
4. **a.** majoring
   b. being, to be
   c. doing

II.
2. Seward's having perceived
3. Court's having outlawed
4. Parks's deciding
5. her refusing
6. John F. Kennedy's having agreed
7. his having been warned
8. Their having misjudged
9. protestors' having seized the moment and demanded *or* having demanded

III.
2. using
3. slowing
4. were expected to have been completed
5. having caused / causing
6. to be finished
7. to be cleared
8. taking

IV.
2. was supposed to
3. planning to
4. ought to
5. didn't have time to
6. don't want to

V. Possible Answers
2. avoids driving
3. starts working / starts to work
4. has trouble staying awake in meetings
5. finishes working
6. spends her evenings reading

VI.
2. C	5. B	8. C
3. A	6. D	9. D
4. A	7. B	10. A

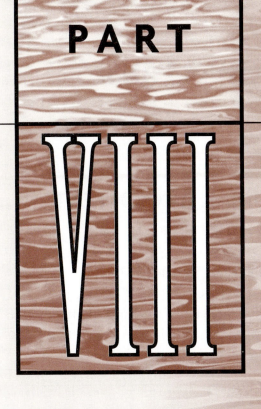

PART

VIII

ADVERBS

ADVERB CLAUSES

GRAMMAR **IN CONTEXT**

QUESTIONS TO CONSIDER

1. What is your view of sports? Is it basically positive, basically negative, or somewhere in between?

2. In recent years, "extreme" sports, such as bungee jumping and skiing off cliffs, have become increasingly popular. What is your view of these kinds of activities? Are they really sports?

Read the article.

GOING TO EXTREMES?

A pickup truck rolls to the center of a deserted bridge. Several people get out. Two of them, a thirty-something young man and a twenty-something young woman, are both wearing a strange-looking harness on their backs. The others with them check their harnesses to make sure all is well. As soon as they complete these preparations, they attach a long cord to each harness and securely fasten the cords to the bridge. When that is finished, the young man and woman climb up onto the bridge rail, wave to the crowd below, and jump. No, this is not a suicide attempt. The elastic cords attached to their backs are so strong and flexible that the young people will be able to drop close to the canyon floor below without hitting it. This is bungee jumping, one of a new set of sports that are being described as "extreme."

Most people, if they're really honest with themselves, will admit they like sports at least a little bit. When the first Olympic Games began in Greece in 776 B.C., something within the

bungee jumping

human spirit was tapped. Most of us like to be challenged, and many of us are at least moderately competitive. Sports provide benefits: they amuse and excite us, provide jobs for many people, and allow individuals who might not have other opportunities to achieve success. Although sports have long been popular, something significant has changed in the last ten to twenty years. A whole new set of sports has been created. They are called "extreme" because participants are pushing themselves to extreme (and even dangerous) levels.

ski jumping

windsurfing

Why do people participate in extreme sports? Mark Musgrave, an "extreme" sportsman who windsurfs all year around, says people do it because it's a question of attitude, not the activity per se. "These sports are so hard," says Musgrave, "they don't attract the masses; I think that's one of the appealing things about it. You can excel in it if you put your mind to it. There's not a thousand people out there crowding you or doing what you're doing." He adds, "There is no right. There is no wrong. There are no rules. You can do what you want and no one cares."

So what are some of these new extreme sports? Musgrave's own sport of windsurfing is one, though windsurfing on a quiet summer day at a speed of 2 miles an hour hardly qualifies. If you want to become extreme, you'll have to travel much faster, above the water, with a much more powerful wind blowing while you're trying to do a forward flip.

mountain biking

Then there's mountain biking, although riding your mountain bike down a gentle slope at a leisurely speed doesn't make you an extreme biker. What does is piloting that bike down a steep, rocky mountain path at a speed of at least 35 miles per hour. You can also call yourself an extreme sports enthusiast if you ski off cliffs, jump out of a plane and sky surf, or go in-line skating.

in-line skating

(continued on next page)

By now, someone somewhere is probably mounting a campaign to make extreme sports safer to save extreme sports enthusiasts from themselves. Are these sports too dangerous? Perhaps. Even if they are, isn't a personal choice involved here? It occurs to this writer that the development of extreme sports is understandable, even quite predictable. We live in such a globalized, homogenized world today that a counterrevolution seems to have started. Wherever we go, we see sameness: a McDonald's in Moscow is only marginally different from one in Paris or in Pensacola, Florida. There seem to be far fewer singular, individualized experiences today than there were in the past. Maybe extreme-sport people are merely striking a blow for truly individualized and unique experiences.

sky surfing

Source: Based on information in Nara Schoenberg, "Carrying Things to the Extreme, Pushing It to the Limit Seems to Be, ahh, Absolutely Everywhere." *St. Louis Post-Dispatch*, September 4, 1996, p. 3E.

UNDERSTANDING MEANING FROM CONTEXT

Look at the italicized word or expression in each of the following sentences. Make a guess as to its meaning and write your guess in the blank provided. Then rewrite each word or phrase in another way.

1. When the first Olympic Games began in Greece in 776 B.C., something within the human spirit was *tapped*.

   _____   _____

2. Mark Musgrave, an "extreme" sportsman who windsurfs all year around, says people do it because it's a question of attitude, not the activity *per se*.

   _____   _____

3. We live in such a globalized, *homogenized* world today that a counterrevolution seems to have started.

   _____   _____

4. A McDonald's in Moscow is only *marginally* different from one in Paris or in Pensacola, Florida.

   _____   _____

5. Maybe extreme-sport people are *merely* striking a blow for truly individualized and unique experiences.

   _____   _____

GRAMMAR **PRESENTATION**
ADVERB CLAUSES

CLAUSE OF REASON

They are called "extreme" **because participants are pushing themselves to extreme (and even dangerous) levels**.

CLAUSE OF CONTRAST

Although sports have long been popular, something significant has changed in the last ten to twenty years.

CLAUSE OF CONDITION

Most people, **if they're really honest with themselves**, will admit they like sports at least a little bit.

CLAUSE OF TIME

When that is finished, the young man and woman climb up onto the bridge rail.

CLAUSE OF PLACE

Wherever we go, we see sameness.

CLAUSE OF COMPARISON

There seem to be far fewer singular, individualized experiences today **than there were in the past**.

CLAUSE OF RESULT

The elastic cords attached to their backs are so strong and flexible **that they allow the young people to drop close to the canyon floor below without hitting it**.

NOTES	EXAMPLES

1. A **clause** is a group of words that contains at least **a subject** and **its verb**. Clauses can be either independent or dependent. **Independent clauses** (also called main clauses) can stand alone as complete sentences. They do not need another clause to be fully understood.

Dependent clauses (also called subordinate clauses) do need another clause to be fully understood.

INDEPENDENT CLAUSE

- They attach a long cord to each harness and securely fasten the cords to the bridge. (does not need another clause to be fully understood)

DEPENDENT CLAUSE

- as soon as they complete these preparations (needs another clause to be fully understood)

- **because it's a question of attitude**, **not the activity per se** (dependent clause—not completely understandable)

- People do it **because it's a question of attitude, not the activity per se**. (Now it is part of an independent clause, so it is fully understandable.)

Sentences made up of an independent clause and a dependent clause are called **complex sentences**. In a complex sentence, the main idea is in the independent clause.

- **When that is finished**, the young man and woman climb up onto the bridge rail, wave to the crowd below, and jump. (*When that is finished* is the dependent clause; the main idea is in the independent clause.)

2. Adverb clauses are dependent clauses that answer the questions *how, when, where,* or *why* in the same way that single adverbs do. They are introduced by subordinating conjunctions, which can be either single words or phrases. See Appendix 19 on page A-9 for a list of subordinating conjunctions.

- They are called "extreme" **because those who participate in them are pushing themselves to extreme (and even dangerous) levels**. (answers the question of why they are called extreme)

▶ **BE CAREFUL!** Remember that in future time sentences, *will* and *be going to* are used in the independent clause but not in the dependent clause.

- If you want to become extreme, you'll have to travel much faster . . .
  NOT ~~If you'll want to become extreme, you'll have to travel much faster . . .~~

3. Speakers and writers use adverb clauses to combine thoughts and show connections between ideas. They also use them to vary their writing style. Compare these two ways to convey an idea.

- You can excel in it. You put your mind to it.
- You can excel in it **if you put your mind to it**. (shows the connection between the two ideas)

4. Here are seven important types of adverbial clauses and certain subordinating conjunctions that can introduce each type of clause. See Appendix 19 on page A-9 for a more complete list of subordinating conjunctions.

a. Adverb clauses of reason: introduced by *because, since, on account of the fact that*. These clauses answer the question *why*.

- People do it **because it's a question of attitude, not the activity per se**.

b. Adverb clauses of contrast: introduced by *although, though, even though, even if, in spite of the fact that*. These clauses contrast the idea expressed in the independent clause.

- Musgrave's own sport of windsurfing is one, **though windsurfing on a quiet summer day at a speed of two miles an hour hardly qualifies**.
- **Even if they are**, isn't a personal choice involved here?

c. Adverb clauses of condition: introduced by *if, unless, in case, provided (that)*. These clauses answer the question *under what conditions*.

- You can also call yourself an extreme sports enthusiast **if you ski off cliffs** . . .

d. Adverb clauses of time: introduced by *when, whenever, before, after, as, as soon as, once, while, until*. These clauses answer the question *when*.

- **As soon as they complete these preparations**, they attach a long cord to each harness and securely fasten the cords to the bridge.

e. Adverb clauses of place: introduced by *where, wherever*. These clauses answer the question *where*.

- **Wherever we go**, we see sameness.

f. Adverb clauses of comparison: introduced by *than, as much as, as many as*. These clauses make comparisons of quantity.

- There seem to be far fewer singular, individualized experiences today **than there were in the past**.

g. Adverb clauses of result: introduced by *so (that)* or containing the expressions *so + **adjective** + that* or *such + **noun phrase** + that*. These clauses present the result of a situation stated in the independent clause. The word *that* is sometimes omitted, especially in conversation.

- The elastic cords attached to their backs are so strong and flexible **(that) they allow the young people to drop close to the canyon floor below without hitting it**.

5. Except for clauses of comparison and result, adverb clauses can come either before or after the independent clause. When the adverb clause comes first, we place a comma after it. When the adverb clause comes second, we generally do not place a comma before it.

We place a comma before a dependent clause, however, if the dependent clause sets up a contrast.

- **Wherever we go**, we see sameness.

OR

- We see sameness **wherever we go**.

- Then there's mountain biking, **although riding your mountain bike down a gentle slope at a leisurely speed doesn't make you an extreme biker**.

6. Unlike the other adverb clauses, adverb clauses of comparison and result cannot normally be moved. This is because their meaning is linked to or dependent on a particular element in the independent clause.

- There seem to be far fewer singular, individualized experiences today **than there were in the past**. (The clause *than there were in the past* cannot be moved because it is dependent on the meaning of *fewer* in the independent clause.)

▶ **BE CAREFUL!** Note the difference between *so* and *such*. *So* occurs before an adjective or adverb with no following noun. *Such* occurs before a noun or noun phrase.

- The elastic cords attached to their backs are **so strong and flexible** that they allow the young people to drop close to the canyon floor below without hitting it.

OR

- There is **such strength and flexibility** in the cords attached to their backs that the young people are able to drop close to the canyon floor below without hitting it.

FOCUSED PRACTICE

 DISCOVER THE GRAMMAR

Part A

Look at paragraph 2 of the opening reading. Underline the four adverb clauses in that paragraph.

Look at paragraph 3. Underline the three adverb clauses in that paragraph.

Part B

In each of the following sentences, underline the dependent clause once and the independent clause twice. Then determine the role each dependent clause plays in the sentence. Write **where**, **when**, **why**, *or* **under what conditions** *above the clauses that answer those questions. Write* **result**, **comparison**, *or* **contrast** *above the clauses that present results, comparisons, or contrasts.*

<dl>

1. *when*
As soon as they complete these preparations, they attach a long cord to each harness and securely fasten the cords to the bridge.

2. "These sports are so hard," says Musgrave, "they don't attract the masses."

3. Musgrave's own sport of windsurfing is one, though windsurfing on a quiet summer day at a speed of 2 miles an hour hardly qualifies.

4. If you want to be extreme, you've got to be traveling much faster, above the water, with a much more powerful wind blowing.

5. You'll have to travel much faster . . . while you're trying to do a forward flip.

6. We live in such a globalized, homogenized world today that a counterrevolution seems to have started.

7. There seem to be far fewer singular, individualized experiences today than there were in the past.

8. Wherever we go, we see sameness.

9. Mark Musgrave, an "extreme" sportsman who windsurfs all year around, says people do it because it's a question of attitude, not the activity per se.

</dl>

Part C

Look at Part B. In which items could the dependent clause be moved? In which items could they not be moved?

② KEY MOMENTS IN SPORTS

Look at the pictures. Complete the sentence describing each picture with an adverb clause. Use a different subordinating conjunction in each clause.

1. The Sharks will win the game _____

_____

_____ .

OR

2. The other team can't win _____

_____ .

_____ .

3. _____

_____ ,

their fans still love them.

4. There are more people in the game _____

_____

_____ .

OR

5. There aren't as many people in the audience

_____

_____ .

6. The slope was _____ icy

_____

_____ .

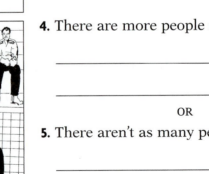

③ WHEN SPORTS BECOME TOO EXTREME Grammar Note 4

Part A

Read the following excerpt from an article about extreme sports. Then answer the questions.

WHEN SPORTS BECOME TOO EXTREME

BY ALEX SALKEVER

As some of the best professional big-wave surfers in the world looked out over 40-foot waves crashing onto the shore of Oahu's Waimea Bay, the decision seemed disappointingly clear. The Quiksilver Invitational surfing competition had to be cancelled. The waves were just too big.

But on that same late-January day, relatively unknown big-wave rider Greg Russ had to be physically restrained by lifeguards from launching out into the biggest surf in more than a decade. The guards were interfering with his "constitutional right" to make money, he said.

The incentive: $50,000 from the surf-equipment manufacturer K2 to anyone who can ride the biggest wave of the year and get it on film.

From ice climbing to mountain biking to big-wave surfing, more people are becoming extreme athletes, putting their lives in danger for the ultimate rush. But the K2 contest, and the growing popularity of extreme sports worldwide, has raised questions about the financial and human consequences for athletes and the rescuers who watch over them. For many, the incident at Waimea perfectly illustrates the dangers unleashed when big money, big egos, and big challenges are mixed.

Although exact figures on how many extreme athletes exist are hard to come by, isolated statistical evidence and virtually all anecdotal evidence point to a rapid increase. For example, the number of climbers attempting the summit of Alaska's 20,300-foot Mt. McKinley—the tallest peak in North America—has increased from 695 in 1984 to 1,110 in 1997.

"It's a numbers deal, and clearly there are more people getting hurt in the back country than there were when I started doing rescues 20 years ago," says Dan Burnett, a mission coordinator with the all-volunteer Summit County Search and Rescue Group in Colorado. "We're responding into areas now that even four years ago I would have thought we didn't need to check because nobody goes there."

Some strides have been made toward creating a safer extreme-sports world. Three years ago, Denali National Park in Alaska, for instance, instituted a mandatory $150 fee for climbers seeking to ascend Mt. McKinley. The fee pays for an educational program that park rangers credit with dramatically reducing the number of search-and-rescue missions and fatalities. And the system has arrested skyrocketing rescue costs.

Source: Alex Salkever, Special to *The Christian Science Monitor*, "When Sports Become Too Extreme." *The Christian Science Monitor*, March 24, 1988, p. 1. Reprinted by permission of the author.

1. Find the adverb clause in paragraph 1. What subordinating conjunction could replace the subordinating conjunction that begins the clause while keeping the basic meaning?

_____

2. Combine the last two sentences in paragraph 1 into one sentence containing an adverb clause. _____

_____

3. Read paragraph 2. Complete this sentence in your own words: Big-wave rider Greg Russ had to be physically restrained by lifeguards because _____

_____ .

4. Read paragraph 3. Complete this sentence in your own words: You'll get $50,000 from the surf-equipment manufacturer if _____

_____ .

5. Read paragraph 4. Complete this sentence: More people are becoming extreme athletes and putting their lives in danger because _____

_____ .

6. Read paragraph 5. Find the adverb clause. What two subordinating conjunctions could replace the subordinating conjunction that begins this clause? _____

_____

7. Read paragraph 6. Find the first adverb clause and write it here.

_____

8. Find the second adverb clause in paragraph 6. If you replaced **when** with **whenever**, would the sentence still make sense? _____

9. Find the third adverb clause in paragraph 6. What subordinating conjunction could replace the subordinating conjunction that begins this clause?

_____

10. Read paragraph 7. Complete this sentence: Because _____

_____ , the number of

search-and-rescue missions and fatalities has been reduced.

Part B

In groups, discuss these questions:

1. Should there be any limits on extreme athletes?

2. Who should pay for the costs of rescuing extreme athletes who get into trouble?

3. If you or someone close to you got into trouble and needed to be rescued, would you expect the government to pay for the cost of the rescue?

4 EDITING

Read the student essay. Find and correct the ten errors in adverb clauses, including subordinating conjunctions that need to be changed.

Why Sports?

by Jamal Jefferson

A lot of people are criticizing school sports these days. Some say there's too much emphasis on football and basketball and not enough on education. Others say the idea of the scholar-athlete is a joke. Still others say sports are a way of encouraging violence. I think they're all wrong. If anything, school sports help prevent violence, not encourage it. Fortunately, most of the heads of high schools and colleges haven't accepted this concept. Why do I think sports are a positive force?

For one thing, sports are positive ~~even though~~ *because* they give students opportunities to be involved in something. Every day on TV we hear that violence is increasing. I think a lot of people get involved in crime on account of they don't have enough to do to keep themselves busy. After you'll play two or three hours of basketball, baseball, or any other kind of sport, you're such tired that it's hard to commit a violent act.

Second, sports teach people a lot of worthwhile things, especially at the high school level. By playing on a team, students learn to get along and work with others. Wherever their team wins, they learn how to be good winners; when their team will lose, they find out they have to struggle to improve. They discover that winning a few and losing a few are part of the normal ups and downs of life. Also, there's no doubt that students improve their physical condition by participating in sports.

Finally, sports are positive although they give students who do not have enough money to go to college an opportunity to get a sports scholarship and improve their chances for a successful life. Unless a young basketball player from a small village in Nigeria can get a scholarship to play for, say, UCLA, he will have a chance to get an education and probably make his life better. Unless a young woman with little money is accepted on the University of Toronto swim team and gets a scholarship, she'll have the chance to earn a college degree and go on to a high-paying job. In spite of school sporting programs have some deficiencies that need to be ironed out, their benefits outweigh their disadvantages. I should know because I'm one of those students. School sports must stay.

COMMUNICATION PRACTICE

5 LISTENING

Look at these questions. Then listen to the interview with a sports star.

1. Why did Lillian Swanson become successful?

_____

2. Where and when did Lillian learn to swim?

_____

3. Why did Lillian and her family spend a lot of time at the beach?

_____

4. Where was it more difficult to swim than in a pool?

_____

5. Under what conditions did Lillian's parents agree to pay for lessons?

_____

6. What didn't Lillian have as much time to do as her friends did?

_____

7. Why can't Lillian imagine herself doing anything else?

_____

Now listen again to the interview and answer the questions.

6 THE NAME OF THE GAME

Divide into two teams. Each team rearranges the words in its group to make six sentences, each containing an adverb clause. The other team guesses which sport is being referred to. Score points.

EXAMPLE:
when / innings / been / The / game / leading / ends / one / played / is /
and / nine / have / team
A: The game ends **when nine innings have been played and one team is leading**.
B: Baseball.

Team A's prompts

1. ticket / can / to / Before / lift / buy / , / a / you / you / have / start

2. you've / ten / knock / scored / you / If / strike / a / ball / with / , / down / one / pins

3. better / parachute / along / case / You'd / extra / one / an / open / take / the / doesn't / first / in

4. player's / love / zero / If / score / , / the / one / forty / is / is / score

5. puck / unless / can't / You / ice / have / game / you / skates / a / and / this / play

6. kilometers / You've / you've / 41.3 / course / finished / run / the / when

Team B's prompts

7. whenever / ball / net / of / scores / ground / a / point / Your / you / side / opponents' / the / the / on / team / the

8. bat / until / Your / team / team / can't / outs / three / makes / the / other

9. head / hands / Though / may / you / you / can't / use / your / your / use / ,

10. scores / touchdown / try / point / Your / after / may / it / for / extra / an / a / team

11. free / line / throw / You / after / you've / go / the / to / fouled / been

12. mouth / protector / Since / hit / will / opponent / , / your / you / the / in / a / tooth / need / you

⑦ ESSAY

Choose one of the following topics and write an essay of three to five paragraphs on it. Support your ideas with examples from your personal experience, if possible.

- Sports are valuable to society because they provide entertainment.

- Sports have become too violent.

- Sports provide opportunities to people who have no other opportunities.

- Sports stars earn ridiculously large salaries.

8 PICTURE DISCUSSION

Talk with a partner. In your view, how does this picture reflect sports in the world today? What is happening here? Have sports everywhere become too violent, or is this sort of behavior just "part of the game"? A common saying holds that "It's not whether you win or lose that's important; it's how you play the game." Is this idea followed in sports today, or is it important to win at all costs?

ADVERBS: VIEWPOINT, FOCUS, NEGATIVE, SEQUENCE

GRAMMAR **IN CONTEXT**

QUESTIONS TO CONSIDER

1. Are you in favor of or against cloning?
2. What are some possible benefits of genetic engineering? What are some disadvantages?

Read the transcript of a radio call-in show.

TIME TO SOUND OFF

Show #126

STEWART: Good evening, all you talkers out there, and welcome to *Sound Off*, the international program that allows you to express your no-holds-barred opinions on the controversial issues of the day. I'm Russell Stewart. Tonight's topics are cloning and genetic engineering. Where do you stand on these closely related issues? These are clearly controversies that have gotten people stirred up, so let's see if we can shed some light on them. Give me a call and we'll talk. I ask only one thing: that you keep your language clean. . . . All right, here we go with our first caller, Jeff Franke, from Nassau in the Bahamas. Go ahead, Jeff. Where do you stand?

FRANKE: Hi, Russell. Thanks for taking my call. So here's where I stand: I say, let's get on with it. Genetic engineering, I mean.

STEWART: I take that to mean you feel genetic engineering would be a good thing. Is that right?

(continued on next page)

FRANKE: I do, absolutely. And not only do I think it would be a good thing, but I also think it's essential if the world is going to get out of its present difficulties.

STEWART: Why? What difficulties are you referring to?

FRANKE: Everything. Poisoned food. Not enough food. More and more debilitating diseases. Violence.

STEWART: Violence? What's the relationship between genetic engineering and violence?

FRANKE: Well . . . hopefully, scientists will find the gene responsible for violence in certain individuals. They'll isolate and eliminate that gene in future generations.

STEWART: Hmm. I'll tell you, Jeff—I'm a pretty accepting guy, but even I find that suggestion off the wall. . . . So what do you think about cloning?

FRANKE: That's slightly more controversial, but I'm in favor of cloning, too, basically.

STEWART: Just cloning of plants and animals, or humans, too?

FRANKE: Plants and animals, certainly, but I'm even in favor of cloning humans.

STEWART: Really? A lot of people think that's playing God. What would you say to them?

FRANKE: Give me a break! The fact that the technology exists to clone living organisms obviously means that we were meant to use that technology. Take some dread disease, for example, like polio. Once upon a time people who got polio were doomed to die or be crippled. Then along came the technology to develop the vaccine. It wasn't playing God to make the vaccine available to everyone then. Neither is cloning people now.

STEWART: Whew! OK, Jeff, very interesting. I expect we'll hear some pretty spirited responses to what you've said. Our next caller is Janice

Stone from Brighton, England. Janice has been waiting a good long time, so here she is. Janice, go ahead. What do you think about Jeff's comments? Fuzzy thinking?

STONE: Thanks, Russell. I couldn't disagree more with what your first caller said. No, it's not fuzzy thinking. He made his point clearly. I just don't agree with it.

STEWART: OK. Why do you disagree?

STONE: I especially take exception to what he said about our being meant to do something just because technology makes it possible. I don't think that's true at all. Plus, the violence comment is outrageous. I almost think this guy's gone around the bend.

STEWART: Give me an example to support your viewpoint.

STONE: All right. Nuclear weapons. They've been available for use for at least sixty years. Fortunately, we haven't used them—except during World War II. Hopefully we won't. If we start thinking like Mr. Franke, there goes our morality down the tube.

STEWART: All right, Janice. But maybe Jeff has a point about the potential benefits of genetic engineering. What if it would allow us to eliminate certain dread diseases? Shouldn't it be used?

STONE: Obviously there might be some superficial benefits. But it would open up a Pandora's box. We don't know what it might lead to. It could upset the balance of nature. And not only could it do that, but it might also lead to a decline in species diversity. You know that sheep—Dolly—that the Scottish scientists cloned? Well, she's already getting old. Who knows what will happen if we keep up this kind of thing? It's not worth the risk.

STEWART: OK, Janice. Thanks for your comments. Let's see where we go with this. Our next caller is from Hong Kong, China. Here's Mu Han. Mu, what's your view?

UNDERSTANDING MEANING FROM CONTEXT

Match the words and expressions in Column A with their synonyms in Column B.

Column A

_____ **1.** no-holds-barred

_____ **2.** down the tube

_____ **3.** around the bend

_____ **4.** a Pandora's box

_____ **5.** off the wall

_____ **6.** shed some light on them

Column B

a. crazy

b. unbelievable, outrageous

c. help people understand better

d. unrestricted

e. in a lost or unrecoverable location

f. an event or situation which opens up dangers and difficulties

GRAMMAR **PRESENTATION**
ADVERBS: VIEWPOINT, FOCUS, NEGATIVE, LOCATION, SEQUENCE

VIEWPOINT ADVERBS

These are **clearly** controversies that have gotten people stirred up . . .

Hopefully, scientists will find the gene responsible for violence in certain individuals.

That's slightly more controversial, but I'm in favor of cloning, too, **basically**.

But **maybe** Jeff has a point about the potential benefits of genetic engineering.

FOCUS ADVERBS

I ask **only** one thing: that you keep your language clean.

Plants and animals, certainly, but I'm **even** in favor of cloning humans.

I especially take exception to what he said about our being meant to do something **just** because technology makes it possible.

NEGATIVE ADVERBS

And **not only** do I think it would be a good thing, but I also think it's essential if the world is going to get out of its present difficulties.

It wasn't playing God to make the vaccine available to everyone then. **Neither** is cloning people now.

I don't think that's true **at all**.

LOCATION AND SEQUENCE ADVERBS

Then **along came the technology** to develop the vaccine.

Here is Janice Stone.

Here she is.

NOTES	**EXAMPLES**

1. Viewpoint adverbs* (sometimes also called **sentence adverbs**) give the speaker's or writer's viewpoint or comment about the statement made, modifying entire sentences rather than elements within them. They include words such as *fortunately, unfortunately, clearly, obviously, certainly, luckily, surely, evidently, frankly, really, apparently, actually, perhaps,* and *maybe*. Note the difference in meaning in the example sentences. The adverb *clearly* in the first sentence modifies *made*, showing the manner in which he made his point. The word *clearly* in the second sentence is a viewpoint adverb that shows the speaker's or writer's comment about the situation.

- He made his point **clearly**.
  (not a viewpoint adverb—modifies *made*, showing how he made his point)
- These are **clearly** controversies that have gotten people stirred up.
  (viewpoint adverb—modifies the entire idea; *it is clear that these are controversies that have gotten people stirred up*)

Viewpoint adverbs can appear at the beginning of a sentence, in its middle, or at the end. When they appear at the beginning of a sentence, they often have a comma separating them from the rest of the sentence. When they appear at the end of a sentence, they are always preceded by a comma. If they appear in the middle, they are always close to the verb and are usually enclosed in commas when they precede the verb. In general, writers use the comma when they want to separate the viewpoint adverb from the rest of the sentence.

- I'm in favor of cloning, **basically**.
- **Basically**, I'm in favor of cloning.
- I'm in favor, **basically**, of cloning.

*The author wishes to acknowledge L. G. Alexander regarding the terms **viewpoint adverb** and **focus adverb** (*Longman Advanced Grammar, Reference and Practice*, New York: Longman Publishing, 1993.)

2. Focus adverbs* include words such as *only, just, even,* and *almost*. Like viewpoint adverbs, they are flexible words that can appear in different places in a sentence. In writing and formal speaking, we place focus adverbs just before or after words or phrases that we want to focus on specifically. The meaning of a sentence often changes if the focus adverb is moved.

- I **just** don't agree with it.
  (The basic point is that I don't agree with it.)
- I don't **just** agree with it.
  (I not only agree with it, but I support the idea strongly.)
- I **almost** think this guy's gone around the bend.
  (modifies the verb think—I am close to thinking this.)
- I think this guy's **almost** gone around the bend.
  (He is almost crazy.)

In informal speech and writing, the adverb *only* usually occurs before the verb, and the meaning is made clear through stress and intonation.

- I **only ask** one thing: that you keep your language clean.
  (informal, conversational usage)
- I **ask only** one thing.
  (more formal usage)

3. The **focus adverb** *even* is used to show that something is unexpected or unusual. Notice how the meaning of *even* changes in different places in the sentence.

- Plants and animals, certainly, but I'm **even** in favor of cloning humans.
  (Even modifies in favor of cloning humans—it is rather unusual for a person to be in favor of this.)
- I'm a pretty accepting guy, but **even** I find that suggestion off the wall.
  (Even modifies I find—with his reputation, the talk show host might be expected to accept almost any idea, but he doesn't accept this one.)

▶ **BE CAREFUL!** Don't confuse *even* with *even if*.

- He **even** believes in cloning.
- **Even if** some kinds of cloning become legal, its overall use should be restricted.

4. Negative adverbs include words and expressions like *never, rarely, seldom, scarcely, not only,* only then, neither, hardly, little, on no account*. Because negative adverbs are already negative, the verb in the sentence doesn't need the word *not*. Negative adverbs are sometimes placed at the beginning of a sentence for emphasis in writing or more formal speech. When they come at the beginning, they force the subject and auxiliary to invert.

In sentences in the simple present or simple past, a negative adverb at the beginning of the sentence forces the appearance of the auxiliary *do / does / did*.

Placing most negative adverbs at the beginning of the sentence sounds somewhat formal to most native speakers and is less common in conversation than in writing. However, it is common to place *neither* at the beginning of the sentence in both formal and informal English.

- And **not only do** I think it would be a good thing, but I also think it's essential if the world is going to get out of its present difficulties.

- It wasn't playing God to make the vaccine available to everyone then. **Neither is** cloning people now.

- The second caller on the radio show doesn't support cloning. **Neither does** the third caller.

5. Like the negative adverbs, certain **location** and **sequence adverbs** sometimes occur at the beginning of a sentence, particularly in descriptive writing. When they do, the subject and verb are inverted if the subject is a noun. In both formal and informal English, this type of inversion is common if the sentence begins with *here* or *there*.

▶ **BE CAREFUL!** Inversion with location or sequence adverbs occurs only when the subject is a noun. If the subject is a pronoun, the word order is normal.

- Then **along came the technology** to develop the vaccine. (The sequence adverb *along* forces the subject and verb to invert.)
- **There goes our morality** down the tube.
- **There it goes**.
- **Here is Janice Stone** from Brighton, England. (noun— inversion)
- **Here she is**. (pronoun—no inversion)

6. The adverbial phrase *at all* occurs only in negative and interrogative sentences. It is usually used with the indefinite pronouns. It also never begins a sentence.

- I don't think that's true **at all**.

---

* *Not only* often occurs with *but also*. When it does, it functions as both a negative adverb and a conjunction.

FOCUSED PRACTICE

1 **DISCOVER THE GRAMMAR** **Grammar Notes 1–6**

Part A

Look again at the opener, Time to Sound Off. *You will find ten different viewpoint adverbs. Circle them in the reading. Count uses only one time.*

1. clearly

Part B

You will find three sentences containing negative adverbs that force inversion of the subject and the verb. Write the parts of those sentences showing the inversion here.

1. _____

2. _____

3. _____

Part C

Look at the following sentences from the reading. Could they be correctly rewritten as shown in parentheses? Why or why not?

1. Fortunately, we haven't used them. (We haven't used them, fortunately.)

_____

2. Our next caller is from Hong Kong, China. Here's Mu Han. (Here's he.)

_____

3. I don't think that's true at all. (At all I don't think that's true.)

_____

4. Then along came the technology to develop the vaccine. (Then along the technology came . . .)

_____

Part D

Look at this sentence from the reading. How would the meaning of the sentence change if the word **even** *were moved as shown?*

Plants and animals, certainly, but I'm even in favor of cloning humans.
Plants and animals, certainly, but even I'm in favor of cloning humans.

1. _____

② SCIENCE AND TECHNOLOGY

Read these pairs of sentences about scientific and technological developments in the twentieth century. On a separate sheet of paper, combine the ideas in each pair by using a viewpoint adverb. Note that a viewpoint adverb can appear in at least three places in a sentence. Write three sentences for each numbered item.

1. The world has become very dependent on computers. This is obvious.

> *Obviously, the world has become very dependent on computers.*

> *The world has obviously become very dependent on computers.*

> *The world has become very dependent on computers, obviously.*

2. Some people think computers are intelligent machines that can do anything. This is apparent.

3. Computers can do only what they are programmed to do. This is the actual situation.

4. Scientists have been able to genetically engineer tomatoes that will stay fresh for a long time. This is fortunate.

5. These tomatoes often don't have much taste. This is unfortunate.

6. Some progress has been made in fighting AIDS. This is certain.

7. A cure will be found. This is what people hope.

③ THE POWER OF TECHNOLOGY

Read the following statements about the role of technology in today's world. Then rewrite them, beginning each sentence or clause with the negative adverb provided.

1. We think about how dependent we are on technology to make things work. (Seldom)

> *Seldom do we think about how dependent we are on technology to make things work.*

2. If one of our technological conveniences breaks down, the average person knows how to fix it. (Rarely)

3. It might be good if we had to do without our modern conveniences for a while. We would appreciate how much technology provides for us. (Only then)

4. We know how much of our lives is directed and controlled by computers. (Little)

(continued on next page)

5. Most women don't know how a computer works. Most men don't. (Neither)

_____

6. We could easily give up our modern conveniences. (In no way)

_____

4 **PICTURE TIME**   Grammar Notes 2, 3

Look at the pictures. Write a statement about each picture, using the adverb provided.

1.

(only)

Only one student has

a home computer.

2.

(even)

_____

_____

3.

(even)

_____

_____

4. Marriage Counseling 1900 A.D.

(just)

_____

_____

5. Marriage Counseling 2000 A.D.

(just)

_____

_____

5 EDITING

Find and correct the ten errors in adverbs in the following letter.

April 15

Dear Mom,

I'm sitting in the train station, waiting for the 5:25 to come along, so ~~just I~~ ^{I just} thought I'd

drop you a quick note. I've been attending the conference on genetic engineering and cloning at

the university. Very interesting. Actually, I almost didn't get to go to the conference because

almost we didn't get our taxes done on time, but Jonathan and I stayed up until midnight

last night, and I mailed the forms this morning.

I hate income taxes! Only once in the last ten years we have gotten a refund, and this time

the tax return was so complicated that Jonathan got even upset, and you know how calm he

is. Maybe we should clone ourselves so we'd make more money! Just kidding.

Besides that, we've been having a few problems with Allison. It's probably nothing more

serious than teenage rebellion, but whenever we try to lay down the law, she gets defensive.

Rarely if ever she takes criticism well. The other night she and her boyfriend stayed out until

2 A.M.—this was the second time in two weeks—and when we asked her what they'd been

doing she said, "Just we were talking and listening to dance music at the Teen Club. Why

can't you leave me alone?" Then she stomped out of the room. Fortunately, Karen and Kenny

have been behaving like angels—but they're not teenagers! Speaking of cloning, I don't think

I'd want to have another Allison around right now.

Meanwhile, Allison's school has started a new open-campus policy. Students can leave the

campus whenever they don't have a class. Even they don't have to tell the school office where

they're going and when they'll be back. Jonathan and I approve of that policy at all. School

time is for studying and learning, not for socializing. Little those school officials realize how

much trouble teenagers can get into whenever they're roaming around unsupervised.

Well, here the train comes. I'll sign off now. Write soon.

Love,
Sue

COMMUNICATION PRACTICE

 *Read these questions. Then listen to the caller on Russell Stewart's radio call-in show.*

1. How often does the third caller get a chance to listen to the program?

   _____

2. Is the third caller basically closer to the viewpoint of the man or the woman?

   _____

3. On what point does this caller agree with the woman?

   _____

4. On what point does this caller agree with the man?

   _____

5. How does this caller feel about cloning?

   _____

6. What disease does the caller use as an example to support his statement about genetic engineering?

   _____

 *Now listen again and answer the questions.*

7 **ESSAY**

Choose one of the following topics and write an essay of three or four paragraphs on it. Try to use at least two viewpoint adverbs, two focus adverbs, and two negative adverbs in your essay. Support your viewpoint with specific examples.

- Cloning should be allowed in all situations.
- Cloning should be prohibited in all situations.
- Cloning should be allowed in some situations and prohibited in others.

8 **PICTURE DISCUSSION**

Assume that the moment is sometime in the future. Cloning of humans and animals has become legal. You are a member of a government board that approves or disapproves applications for cloning. Look at the pictures. Work with a partner. Discuss which applications you would approve and which you would disapprove. Explain your reasons.

DISCOURSE CONNECTORS

GRAMMAR **IN CONTEXT**

QUESTIONS TO CONSIDER

1. What is your earliest memory?
2. What are methods that help you to remember things?

Read an article about memory.

Try to Remember

Have you ever had this experience? You're sitting at the breakfast table, and you notice that the little saucer you usually put your vitamins on is empty. Did you take them, or didn't you? You can't remember taking them, nor can you even remember whether you put the vitamins on the saucer. Or what about this experience? You're in a drugstore with a friend, and suddenly up walks somebody you've known for a long time. You want to introduce this new person to your friend. However, just as you say, "Nancy, I'd like you to meet _____," your mind goes blank, and you can't remember the person's name to save your life. It's embarrassing and maybe a little worrisome. I wouldn't be too concerned, though, for it's also very common. As we get older, we tend to become more forgetful, especially of things we've experienced recently.

How does memory work, and what can we do to improve it? Let me tell you, I was worried about what I perceived to be memory loss on my part. I felt it was incumbent on me, therefore, to do some research into the problem. Here's what I learned. ⇩

First, let's distinguish between two types of memory, long-term and short-term. Long-term memory refers to things that we experienced a long time ago and that form the core of our knowledge of ourselves. Short-term memory can be called "working" memory—the type we use in every-day activity. It is involved in processing such things as phone numbers, names of new people we meet, statistics, e-mail addresses and phone numbers, and the like. As we grow older, our long-term memory holds up remarkably well. Thus we are able to intimately remember and recount the vacation we took at the age of ten to Everglades National Park and the alligators we saw there. Meanwhile, things have been happening to our short-term memory. It, in contrast, doesn't hold up as well as our long-term memory does. Because of this, we may have difficulty remembering people's names right after we meet them, or remembering someone's phone number we heard only twice. Memory problems are generally short-term memory problems.

Second, let's look a little at the physicality of the memory process. The frontal lobes of the brain are the area where short-term memory operations occur. As we age, these lobes tend to lose mass, as much as 5 to 10 percent per decade, though this of course varies with the individual. There is also a structure in the brain called the hippocampus, a key player in memory processing. This structure tends to atrophy the older a person gets. In addition, there is a brain chemical called acetylcholine, which transmits signals between nerve cells. As time goes on, the brain tends to produce less of it. So the problem is really that our brains, as we grow older, do not take things in as well as they once did—and this is the root of short-term memory problems. However, not all is gloomy on this score. There are things we can do to slow memory decline. Maintaining a steady supply of glucose can mitigate the problem of shrinking lobes. Consequently, elderly people would do well to eat several smaller meals each day rather than two or three big ones. There is also evidence that staying mentally active can help prevent memory deterioration.

Another aspect of memory that is interesting to consider involves the many materials on the market designed to help us remember things better. Some of them are relatively cheap; some are expensive. The key question is this: Do they work? Well, yes and no. All memory courses, books, audiotapes, or whatever, depend on the creation of a peg, or mental picture on which to hang something we want to recollect. Suppose, for example, that you have trouble remembering your car license plate number. I had this problem until I created a peg. My license number is 409 FGO. It occurred to me that FGO reminded me of *Fargo,* one of my favorite movies. The 409 reminded me of the liquid cleaner of that name, the product that is supposed to clean anything. Since my car always looks dirty, there was certainly an association here. It may sound silly, but it worked for me. Or suppose you have difficulty, as most of us do, remembering names. ⮕

> **There are things we can do to slow memory decline.**

Try to Remember (continued)

Let's say, for instance, that you're at a cocktail party and are introduced to a man named Terry Baer. You look at him. He has long, thick, black hair, rather like that of a black bear. Baer = bear. Furthermore, the first syllable of "Terry" rhymes with "bear." Ter and Baer. It might work. The point is that you need to create a mental picture that you can relate to the person, place, or thing you want to recall. If the picture is outrageous, so much the better. The more vivid the association, the greater the chance that you'll remember it.

There is one particularly salient point in all this, and that is that memory improvement takes work. If we think carefully about our own involvement in remembering things, we may realize that the real problem is usually not in remembering something that we learned earlier but in the fact that we weren't paying enough attention when we learned it. Think about the last time you were introduced to someone whose name you immediately forgot. Were you really paying attention to the person's name? Or were you, instead, focusing on yourself and the impression you might be making? Memory books and courses can work, of course, but they depend on techniques that we can create and perform for ourselves. The real trick lies in our willingness to tap what's within us and to expend effort in tapping it.

Source: Based on information in Emily Yoffe, "How Quickly We Forget," *U.S. News & World Report,* October 13, 1997, p. 52.

UNDERSTANDING MEANING FROM CONTEXT

Match the ten words and expressions in Column A with their synonyms in Column B.

Column A	Column B
1. to save your life	**a.** relieve
2. incumbent on	**b.** decrease in size or power, weaken
3. intimately	**c.** worsening, decay
4. recount	**d.** supporting structure
5. atrophy	**e.** very prominent, conspicuous, or important
6. mitigate	**f.** obligatory for
7. deterioration	**g.** use
8. peg	**h.** tell about
9. salient	**i.** no matter how hard you try
10. tap	**j.** very closely or well

Two of these words, though they are different parts of speech, are close in meaning to each other. Which two are they?

11. _____

GRAMMAR **PRESENTATION**
DISCOURSE CONNECTORS

COORDINATING CONJUNCTIONS

You're sitting at the breakfast table, **and** you notice that the little saucer you usually put your vitamins on is empty.

It may sound silly, **but** it worked for me.

Did you take them, **or** didn't you?

I wouldn't be too concerned, though, **for** it's also very common.

As time goes on, the brain tends to produce less of it. **So** the problem is really that our brains, as we grow older, do not take things in as well as they once did . . .

You can't remember taking them, **nor** can you even remember whether you put the vitamins on the saucer.

TRANSITIONS

You want to introduce this new person to your friend. **However**, just as you say, "Nancy, I'd like you to meet _____," your mind goes blank.

I felt it was incumbent on me, **therefore**, to do some research into the problem.

In addition, there is a brain chemical called acetylcholine, which transmits signals between nerve cells.

Meanwhile, things have been happening to our short-term memory.

NOTES

1. Discourse connectors are words and expressions that tie together the ideas in a piece of writing or in speech. They join ideas both within sentences and between sentences or larger stretches of text.

Two important types of discourse connectors are **coordinating conjunctions** and **transitions**.

EXAMPLES

• You're sitting at the breakfast table, **and** you notice that the little saucer you usually put your vitamins on is empty. (coordinating conjunction)

• I felt it was incumbent on me, **therefore**, to do some research into the problem. (transition)

2. The coordinating conjunctions, *and, but, or, nor, for, so,* and *yet,* normally connect ideas within sentences, joining two independent clauses. Sentences made up of two or more independent clauses joined by a coordinating conjunction are called **compound sentences**.

Note that the coordinating conjunction *nor* connects negative statements. Like other negative words at the beginning of a clause, *nor* forces the subject and the verb or auxiliary to invert.

- Memory books and courses can work, of course, **but** they depend on techniques that we can create and perform for ourselves.
  (two independent clauses joined by the coordinating conjunction *but*)

- You can't remember taking them, **nor can you** even remember whether you put the vitamins on the saucer.

3. Some people object to beginning a written sentence with a coordinating conjunction, particularly in academic writing. However, many writers use coordinating conjunctions to connect ideas from sentence to sentence.

- You can't even remember whether you put the vitamins on the saucer. **Or** what about this experience?
  (The coordinating conjunction *or* connects two ideas in the text.)

- As time goes on, the brain tends to produce less of it. **So** the problem is really that our brains, as we grow older, do not take things in as well as they once did.
  (The coordinating conjunction *so* connects these two ideas.)

4. When we use coordinating conjunctions to join two independent clauses in a compound sentence, we generally place a comma before the conjunction.

- There is one particularly salient point in all this, **and** that is that memory improvement takes work.

5. Be careful! Do not confuse *so* as a coordinating conjunction with *so that* (= *in order that*) or *so . . . that* as a subordinating conjunction that introduces a clause of result.

- **So** the problem is really that our brains do not take things in as well as they once did.
  (coordinating conjunction)
- I write things down **so that** I can remember them.
  (*in order that*)
- I've got **so** much on my mind **that** I can hardly even remember my own name, let alone someone else's.
  (subordinating conjunction introducing a clause of result)

6. Transitions are words and phrases such as *however, therefore, in addition, consequently, in fact, first, second,* and *finally.* We use them to connect ideas between sentences or larger sections of text.

- Maintaining a steady supply of glucose can mitigate the problem of shrinking lobes. **Consequently**, elderly people would do well to eat several smaller meals each day rather than two or three big ones.
  (*Consequently* shows the connection between these two ideas in the text.)

7. Transitions can come at the beginning of a sentence, within it, or at the end, depending on what the writer or speaker wants to emphasize. They are usually separated from the rest of the sentence by a comma or commas.

- **However**, not all is gloomy on this score.

  OR

  Not all, **however**, is gloomy on this score.

  OR

  Not all is gloomy on this score, **however**.

8. There are four principal types of transitions. See Appendix 20 on page A-10 for a more complete list. Note that some transitions can function in more than one category. See Note 11.

Some transitions show an "and" relation, adding information. These include *also, in addition (to), additionally, for one thing, moreover, furthermore, plus, besides (that), for example, for instance, likewise, in fact, as a matter of fact, indeed*.

- Embarrassing, isn't it? Yes, but it's **also** very common.
  (*Also* shows an additional point to be made about forgetfulness.)

Some transitions show a "but" relation, offering contrasting information to an idea presented earlier. These include *however, still, nevertheless, nonetheless, in contrast, in fact, instead, in spite of (this / that), despite (this / that), on the contrary, on the other hand*.

- You want to introduce this new person to your friend. **However**, just as you say, "Nancy, I'd like you to meet _____," your mind goes blank, and you can't remember the person's name to save your life.
  (*However* makes a contrast with the first statement.)

Some transitions show a cause-and-effect relationship, presenting a cause for or showing a result of an action or situation discussed earlier. These include *therefore, thus, because of this / that, on account of this / that, consequently, accordingly, otherwise, as a result*.

- Maintaining a steady supply of glucose can mitigate the problem of shrinking lobes. **Consequently**, elderly people would do well to eat several smaller meals each day rather than two or three big ones.
  (*Consequently* shows the logical result of the first fact; since it's important to take in glucose, a good way to do this is to eat several smaller meals each day.)

Some transitions show relationships of actions, events, or ideas in time. These include *next, then, afterwards, meanwhile, after this / that, first, second, third, finally, in conclusion*.

- **Second**, let's look a little at the physicality of the memory process.
  (*Second* indicates that the writer will discuss the next point to be made.)

9. **BE CAREFUL!** Be sure to place a period or a semicolon—not a comma—before a transition when it is the first word in a sentence or clause. A comma in this location is incorrect and creates an error called a **comma splice**. See *From Grammar to Writing* after Part X, page 489, for further discussion of comma splices.

You want to introduce this new person to your friend. **However**, just as you say . . .
(The two clauses are connected by a period.)

You want to introduce this new person to your friend; **however**, just as you say . . .
(The two clauses are connected by a semicolon.)

NOT ~~You want to introduce this new person to your friend, however, just as you say~~ . . .
(comma splice)

---

10. Transitions often parallel coordinating conjunctions in meaning. However, note the differences in punctuation between sentences containing coordinating conjunctions and those containing transitions.

- It may sound silly, **but** it worked for me.
- It may sound silly. **Nonetheless**, it worked for me.
- Write it down, **or** you're likely to forget it.
- Write it down; **otherwise**, you're likely to forget it.
- I don't remember the situation, **nor** do I want to remember it.
- I don't remember the situation. **Besides that**, I don't want to remember it.

---

11. The word *though* can be a subordinating conjunction or a transition. It is normally a transition when it comes at the end of a sentence or clause.

- **Though** it may sound silly, it worked for me.
(subordinating conjunction)
- I wouldn't worry too much, **though**.
(transition; *though* = *however*)

The expression *in fact* can both add and contrast.

- We are not doomed to forget everything when we are old. **In fact**, we can even improve our memories.
(adds information)
- Some people think they'll be able to remember everything. **In fact**, they'll forget a great deal.
(contrasts)

FOCUSED PRACTICE

1 DISCOVER THE GRAMMAR

Part A

Look again at Try to Remember. *You will find fifteen coordinating conjunctions that connect clauses. Circle them in the reading. Circle them only if they connect independent clauses.*

Part B

Find the eight transitions in the reading that show an "and" relation. Write the phrases in which they occur here.

1. for it's also very common

2. _____

3. _____

4. _____

5. _____

6. _____

7. _____

8. _____

Part C

Find the five transitions that show a "but" relation. Write the phrases in which they occur here.

1. However, just as you

2. _____

3. _____

4. _____

5. _____

Part D

Find the four transitions that show a "cause-and-effect" relation. Write the phrases in which they occur here.

1. therefore, to do some research

2. _____

3. _____

4. _____

Part E

Find the three transitions that show a time relation. Write the phrases in which they occur here.

1. First, let's distinguish

2. _____

3. _____

Part F

Look at this sentence. Is the word though *a transition or a subordinating conjunction?*

As we age, these lobes tend to lose mass, as much as 5 to 10 percent per decade, though this of course varies with the individual.

2 A MEMORY TEST
Grammar Notes 1, 2, 6–10

Part A

🔲 *Close your book and listen to the following segment of a radio newscast. It was recorded during a thunderstorm, and static makes it impossible to hear some parts of it. Write down as many details as you can remember. Then compare your list of details with a partner's. Which details were you able to remember, and why?*

Part B

🔲 *Now listen again to the broadcast. Note the details you got correct and those you missed. Then complete the text with discourse connectors from the box.*

meanwhile	otherwise	first	in fact	however
therefore	and	second	also	~~next~~

_____Next_____ we focus on the aftermath of the recent California
1.

earthquake. Investigators have determined that it will cost approximately 6 billion dollars

to rebuild damaged highways. According to the governor, two actions have to be taken:

_____, the federal government will have to approve disaster funds to
2.

pay for reconstruction; _____, insurance investigators will need to
3.

determine how much their companies will have to pay in the rebuilding effort. With luck,

the governor says, some key highways could be rebuilt within six months. He cautioned,

_____, that the six-month figure is only an estimate. The process
4.

depends on timely allocation of funds, and certain insurance companies have in the past

been slow to approve such funds. The rebuilding effort could, _____,
5.

drag on for at least a year. _____, bad weather could hamper the
6.

speedy completion of the project. _____, it is taking some people as
7.

long as four hours to commute to work, and others haven't been able to get to work at all.

Interviewed by our news team, one commuter who works in an office downtown said,

"This has been ridiculous. It took me six hours to drive to work last Friday. I knew I'd have

to find some other way of getting there; _____, I'd never make it. Well,
8.

yesterday I took the train and got there in 50 minutes. _____ you
9.

know, the trip was really pleasant. I had the chance to read the morning paper.

_____, I'm going to switch permanently to the train."
10.

3 A STRING AROUND HIS FINGER?

Look at the pictures. On a separate piece of paper, write two sentences describing what is happening in each picture. Use the suggested prompts.

1.

(and / also)

2.

(but / however)

3.

(so / consequently)

4.

(nor / besides that)

5.

(while this was happening / meanwhile)

6.

(or / otherwise)

4 **EDITING**

Correct the thirteen mistakes, providing a correct connector in each case. You may add or eliminate words, but do not change word order or punctuation.

MY CAR IS MOVING TO THE SUBURBS
by James Griffith

The other day I drove my car to the downtown campus of the college. I usually have a certain amount of trouble finding a parking place, ~~however~~ but this time really took the cake. There were simply no parking places anywhere in the vicinity of the campus, therefore I had to park in the downtown mall, which is about a mile from the campus. When I finished class, I walked back to the mall. In addition, I couldn't remember where I'd parked my car! Believe it or not, it took me forty-five minutes to find it, and I was about ready to panic when I finally did. That was the last straw. I've decided that I'm going to send my car to a new home in the suburbs.

I used to think that a car was the most wonderful thing in the world. I loved the freedom of being able to come and go to my part-time job or to the college whenever I wanted. A year ago I was in a carpool with four other people, however I hated having to wait around on account of my carpool members weren't ready to leave, so I started driving alone.

Although, I've changed my mind since then. Now it's clear to me that there are just too many disadvantages to having a car in town. For one thing, sitting stalled in your car in a traffic jam is stressful, besides it's a phenomenal waste of time. In addition, it would cost me $200 a month to park my car in the city (which is why I don't do that), also there's always the chance it will be vandalized.

Nonetheless, I've decided to leave it at my cousin Brent's house in the suburbs. Or, I'll end up going broke paying for parking or memory improvement. My car will have a good home, also I'll use it just for longer trips. When I'm in the city, although, I'll take the bus or the trolley, otherwise I'll walk. Who knows? They say that you can meet some interesting people on the bus. Maybe I'll find the love of my life. My only problem will be remembering which bus to take.

COMMUNICATION PRACTICE

5 LISTENING

Read these questions. Then listen to the following excerpt from a memory training workshop.

1. What is the first point the workshop leader makes?

_____

2. According to her, why is it important to remember clients' names?

_____

3. What's the second point the leader makes?

_____

4. What does the visitor tell the people in the workshop to do?

_____

5. and 6. What are the two reasons one of the women knows the visit was staged?

_____

_____

7. Why were they all able to remember the last word the visitor said?

_____

8. According to the workshop leader, what is the most important thing the participants in the workshop have to learn to do?

_____

Now listen again. Complete the answers to the questions.

6 THE MEMORY GAME

The class divides into two teams. Students on each team prepare one statement each. Statements should test the other team's memory and may be either factual or personal. Each statement must contain a discourse connector of some sort. Teams take turns making their statements one at a time while the other team listens. When all the statements have been made, teams attempt to reproduce the other team's statements. Score points: one point for the correct connector and one point for correct content.

EXAMPLE:
Team A: Washington is the capital of the United States. However, it's not the largest city.

Team B: I have been to France three times, and I've been to Britain twice.

7 ESSAY

Write an essay of three or four paragraphs about a significant memory you have. Explain clearly why this memory is important to you. Use specific details to support your ideas.

8 PICTURE DISCUSSION

When your instructor signals you to begin, look at this picture for one minute. Then close your book. Work with a partner. Write down as many details as you can remember. Then open the book and look at the picture again. How accurate was your memory? Which kinds of things were you able to remember best? Speculate as to why you were able to remember some things better than others.

ADVERB PHRASES

GRAMMAR **IN CONTEXT**

QUESTIONS TO CONSIDER

1. What is your definition of compassion?

2. How important a value is compassion in society?

Read the article.

Compassion

It was the evening of September 29, 1994. Having spent a wonderful day exploring the ruins at Paestum in southern Italy, Reg and Maggie Green were driving south in the area of Italy known as the boot, their children Nicholas and Eleanor sleeping peacefully in the back seat. Suddenly an old and decrepit car pulled up alongside them, and an Italian with a bandana over his face screamed at them, signaling them to stop. Not knowing what to do, Reg weighed the gravity of the situation. If they stopped, they risked a potentially deadly confrontation with criminals; if they sped away, they might escape. Guessing that their newer-model car could probably get away from the old car the criminals were

driving, Reg floored the gas pedal. Shots rang out, shattering both windows on the driver's side of the

(continued on next page)

Compassion *(continued)*

car. The Greens' car took off, easily outdistancing the bandits' car. Checking the children, Reg and Maggie found them still sleeping peacefully in the back seat. A bit farther down the road, Reg saw a police car parked on the shoulder and pulled over to alert the authorities. Upon opening the door, he saw blood oozing from the back of Nicholas's head. Rushed to a hospital, Nicholas lay in a coma for two days. Then doctors declared him brain-dead.

This was not the end of the story, however. As Nicholas lay on his deathbed, Reg and Maggie decided that something good ought to come out of the situation. Realizing that it would be far better to return good for evil than to seek revenge, they offered Nicholas's organs for transplant. "Someone should have the future he lost," Reg said. Profoundly moved by the gesture, Italians poured out their emotions. Maurizio Costanzo, the host of a talk show, summed up the common feeling by saying, "You have given us a lesson in civility . . . shown us how to react in the face of pain and sorrow."

The great irony of this tragedy was that it was a mistake. Investigators later determined that Nicholas was killed by two small-time Calabrian thugs who thought the Greens were jewelers carrying precious stones. Having been turned over to the police, apparently by the Calabrian Mafia, they were placed on trial.

People all over Europe and North America reacted in sorrow. Headlines in Italian newspapers spoke of LA NOSTRA VERGOGNA ("Our shame"). Wherever the Greens went, they met Italians who begged their forgiveness. The Greens were given a medal, Italy's highest honor, by the Prime Minister.

Some good has indeed come out of Nicholas's death. Seven Italians received Nicholas's heart, liver, kidneys, islet cells, and corneas. Perhaps more importantly, a blow was struck for organ donation. Having heard Reg and Maggie speak on French television, 40,000 French people pledged to donate their organs when they died. After returning to the United States, the Greens began to receive requests to tell their son's story and speak about organ donation. "It gradually dawned on us," says Reg, "that we'd been given a life's work."

Nicholas Green is gone, but others live on because of his parents' compassionate act. How many of us would do the same thing if given the chance? ༄

Source: Based on information in Brad Darrach, "Journey: A Brave Family Changes Horror into Healing after a Child Dies," *Life,* October 1, 1995, pp. 42+.

UNDERSTANDING MEANING FROM CONTEXT

Find two synonyms for **criminals** *in the reading.*

1. a. _____ **b.** _____

Find a synonym for **get away from**.

2. _____

Find an approximate synonym for **sped away**.

3. _____

Look at these sentences from the reading. Write a synonym or approximate definition for each italicized word or expression.

4. a. Suddenly an old and *decrepit* car pulled up alongside them.

_____

  b. Not knowing what to do, Reg *weighed the gravity* of the situation.

_____

  c. Guessing that their newer-model car could probably get away from the old car the criminals were driving, Reg *floored* the gas pedal.

_____

  d. Upon opening the door, he saw blood *oozing from* the back of Nicholas's head.

_____

  e. The great *irony* of this tragedy was that it was a mistake.

_____

  f. "*It gradually dawned on us,*" says Reg, "that we'd been given a life's work."

_____

GROUP DISCUSSION

Talk with a partner. What would you have done if you had been in the position of Reg and Maggie Green? What would you do if you were in a similar position now?

GRAMMAR **PRESENTATION**
ADVERB PHRASES

WITH A PRESENT PARTICIPLE

Guessing that their newer-model car could probably get away from the old car the criminals were driving, Reg floored the gas pedal.

WITH *BY* PLUS A PRESENT PARTICIPLE

Maurizio Costanzo, the host of a talk show, summed up the common feeling **by saying, "You have given us a lesson in civility . . . shown us how to react in the face of pain and sorrow."**

WITH A PAST PARTICIPLE

Rushed to a hospital, Nicholas lay in a coma for two days.

WITH *HAVING* PLUS A PAST PARTICIPLE

Having spent a wonderful day exploring the ruins at Paestum in southern Italy, Reg and Maggie Green were driving south in the area of Italy known as the boot.

WITH A SUBORDINATING WORD

After returning to the United States, the Greens began to receive requests to tell their son's story and speak about organ donation.

How many of us would do the same thing **if given the chance**?

WITH THE INFINITIVE OF PURPOSE

A bit farther down the road, Reg saw a police car parked on the shoulder and pulled over **to alert the authorities**.

NOTES

1. When sentences contain an adverb clause and a main clause, the adverb clause modifies the main clause. Remember that a clause contains a subject and a verb. A phrase may or may not contain a subject and a verb. You can convert an adverb clause into an **adverb phrase** by changing the verb into a present or past participle (a form that does not show time). Often it is necessary to eliminate the subject as well.

2. You can combine two sentences into one sentence with an independent clause and an adverb phrase if the subjects of the two sentences refer to the same person, place, or thing. In this type of sentence, the adverb phrase can come either before or after the independent clause. Note that we simply place *not* before the participle to make the statement negative.

3. There are five main types of adverb phrases.

  a. With a present participle: Use this form when you are talking about two actions or events that occur or occurred in the same general time frame. Place the idea that you consider more important in the independent clause. Make sure that the verb in the adverbial phrase is in the *-ing* form.

EXAMPLES

- Reg and Maggie Green were driving south in the area of Italy known as the boot while their children Nicholas and Eleanor were sleeping peacefully in the back seat.
  (independent clause modified by adverb clause)

- Reg and Maggie Green were driving south in the area of Italy known as the boot, **their children Nicholas and Eleanor sleeping peacefully in the back seat**.
  (adverb phrase; *were* and the subordinating adverb *while* have been deleted)

- Reg didn't know what to do. He weighed the gravity of the situation.

- **Not knowing what to do**, Reg weighed the gravity of the situation.
  (same subject in both sentences—*Reg* and *he*)

  OR

- Reg weighed the gravity of the situation, **not knowing what to do**.

- Shots rang out, **shattering both windows on the driver's side of the car**.
  (same time frame)

b. With *by* plus a present participle:
Use this form when there is a clear sense of intention or purpose—i.e., that one action causes a certain result. Make sure that *by* is followed by a present participle.

- Maurizio Costanzo, the host of a talk show, summed up the common feeling **by saying**, "You have given us a lesson in civility . . . shown us how to react in the face of pain and sorrow."
(Costanzo made his point by making this statement.)

c. With a past participle: Use this form when you want to communicate a passive meaning. Replace the subject and the auxiliary with a past participle.

- **Rushed to a hospital**, Nicholas lay in a coma for two days.
(passive meaning; past participle *rushed*)

d. With *having* plus a past participle:
Use this form when you are talking about actions or events that occurred at different times. Replace the subject and verb with *having* + past participle.

- **Having spent a wonderful day exploring the ruins at Paestum in southern Italy**, Reg and Maggie Green were driving south in the area of Italy known as the boot.
(Actions at two different times: *First they spent a day exploring the ruins. Later they drove south.*)

e. With a subordinating conjunction:
An adverb phrase is sometimes a reduced form of an adverb clause in which the subordinating conjunction is maintained but the subject and any auxiliary verbs are deleted. The main verb is changed to an *-ing* form or left as a past participle. Common subordinating conjunctions in this kind of phrase are *after, although, before, even though, if, though, unless, until, upon, when, whenever, while.* To reduce a clause in this way, delete the subject and any auxiliary verbs from the adverb clause, change the verb to an *-ing* form, and keep the subordinating conjunction.

- **After they returned to the United States**, the Greens began to receive requests to tell their son's story.
(adverb clause and independent clause)

- **After returning to the United States**, the Greens began to receive requests to tell their son's story and speak about organ donation.
(adverb phrase and main clause)

- How many of us would do the same thing **if we were given the chance**?
(adverb clause)

- How many of us would do the same thing **if given the chance**?
(adverb phrase with a past participle)

4. The infinitive of purpose is often used as an adverb phrase. Use this form when there is an infinitive phrase and a sense of purpose involved in the action.

The sentence with the adverb phrase can also be written with *in order to*.

- A bit farther down the road, Reg saw a police car parked on the shoulder and pulled over **to alert the authorities**.

- A bit farther down the road, Reg saw a police car parked on the shoulder and pulled over **in order to alert the authorities**.
  (shows why he pulled over)

---

5. BE CAREFUL! If we combine two sentences with different subjects into one sentence with an independent clause and an adverb phrase, we create an incorrect, illogical sentence. This error is called a **dangling modifier** because the phrase "dangles," having nothing in the sentence to modify.

- As **Nicholas** lay on his deathbed, **Reg and Maggie** decided that something good ought to come out of the situation.
  (two different subjects:— *Nicholas* and *Reg* and *Maggie*; illogical to combine the two into one sentence)
  NOT ~~Lying on his deathbed, Reg and Maggie decided that something good ought to come out of the situation.~~
  (dangling modifier)

To avoid this error, make sure that two sentences have the same subjects. One way to do this is to draw a rectangle around the subject in each sentence and connect the rectangles with an arrow. If the two subjects refer to the same person, place, or thing, they can be combined logically and correctly.

- **Italians** were profoundly moved by the gesture. **They** poured out their emotions.
  (Two subjects, *Italians* and *they*, referring to the same entity; the sentences can logically be combined.)

- **Profoundly moved by the gesture**, Italians poured out their emotions.

To correct a dangling modifier, add a subject in one of the clauses and any other words necessary to make the sentence logical.

- **With Nicholas lying on his deathbed**, Reg and Maggie decided that something good ought to come out of the situation.
  (correct sentence)

▶ **BE CAREFUL!** Dangling modifiers often occur when one of the parts of the sentences is in the passive voice. To correct a dangling modifier, it is sometimes necessary to change the passive to the active and add a subject.

WRONG ~~Not knowing what to do, the gravity of the situation was weighed (by Reg).~~
(incorrect—dangling modifier)

- Not knowing what to do, **Reg weighed** the gravity of the situation.
  (correct—same subject in both parts)

FOCUSED PRACTICE

 DISCOVER THE GRAMMAR

Part A

Look again at Compassion. *You will find eight adverb phrases with a present participle. Underline them in the reading.*

> **EXAMPLE:**
> their children Nicholas and Eleanor <u>sleeping peacefully</u> in the back seat

Part B

Find the two adverb phrases with a past participle and write them here.

1. _____

2. _____

Part C

Find the three adverb phrases with **having** *+ past participle and underline them in the reading.*

Part D

Find the adverb phrase which contains an infinitive of purpose and write it here.

1. _____

Part E

Find the three adverb phrases that contain a subordinating conjunction and write them here.

1. _____

2. _____

3. _____

2 **SENTENCE COMBINING**

Look at these sentences taken or adapted from Compassion. *Identify the subject of each sentence or clause by drawing a rectangle around it. Connect the rectangles. If the subjects refer to the same thing, combine them into a sentence with the form independent clause + adverb phrase. If the subjects are different, write "cannot be combined."*

1. Suddenly an old and decrepit car pulled up alongside them. An Italian with a bandanna over his face screamed at them.

   different subjects – cannot be combined _____

2. Reg weighed the gravity of the situation. He considered whether to stop or speed away.

_____

3. If they stopped, they risked a potentially deadly confrontation with criminals.

_____

4. Reg saw a police car parked on the shoulder. He pulled over to alert the authorities.

_____

5. As Nicholas lay on his deathbed, Reg and Maggie decided that something good ought to come out of the situation.

_____

6. Two Calabrian thugs killed Nicholas. They thought the Greens were jewelers carrying precious stones.

_____

3 **ENTERPRISE**   **Grammar Notes 3, 4**

Look at the pictures. On a separate piece of paper, write a sentence with an adverb phrase and a main clause to describe the situation. Use the suggested grammatical prompt.

1.

(present participle)

Coming out of the train station, the

tourists saw a boy selling things.

2.

(*by* + present participle)

(continued on next page)

3.

(*not* + present participle)

4.

(past participle)

5.

(infinitive of purpose)

6.

(*having* + past participle)

7.

(*after* + present participle)

8.

(*having* + present participle)

4 EDITING

Correct a writer's article about his overseas trip. It contains eleven sentences with adverbial phrases. Underline the six sentences that are incorrect because of dangling modifiers. Then, on your own paper, correct each sentence by adding a subject in one part of the sentence and changing word order.

A Helping Hand

BY JIM LAMOREUX

If you are at all like me, you tire of requests to help others. Barraged by seemingly constant appeals for money to support public television, the Policemen's Benevolent Association, or the Special Olympics, worthy organizations all, I tend to tune out, my brain numbed. It's not that I'm selfish, I don't think. It's just that there are so many of these requests. Subjected to many stimuli, *I only remember the crucial ones.* only the crucial ones are remembered. By arguing to myself that I don't have enough money to help others, the request is able to be ignored. At least that was the way I saw the situation until the magazine I write for sent me to a small village in South America to do a human interest story on homeless children. Having seen and heard many television requests asking viewers to sponsor a child overseas, I had always said to myself, "I'll bet the money gets pocketed by some local politician." My opinion changed when I saw the reality of the life of a poor child. Having landed in Santa Simona, a taxi took me to my hotel in the center of town, and that's where I met Elena. Sitting on a dirty blanket on the sidewalk in front of the hotel, my eye was caught by her. She didn't beg. Instead, she was trying to scratch out a living by selling mangoes. Smiling up at me, she asked, "Mangos, señor?—Mangoes, sir?" I bought some mangoes and some other fruit, and we got to talking. Her parents were both dead, and she lived with an elderly great-aunt who had no job and sold firewood for money.

I learned from her aunt that Elena had suffered from polio at the age of five and now walked with a distinct limp. While talking later with a nun at a nearby convent that administers gift money from other countries, a lot of worthwhile information was given to me. She proved to my satisfaction that money from sponsors does indeed get to those who need it. Learning that I could sponsor Elena for less than a dollar a day, I began to feel ashamed. After all, I spend more than that on my dogs. But what remains most vivid in my mind is my vision of Elena. She didn't beg, and she didn't feel sorry for herself. Selling her mangoes, a semblance of a living was earned, and her spirit shone through in the process. So I say to you reading this: The next time you hear an ad about sponsoring a child, pay attention.

COMMUNICATION PRACTICE

5 LISTENING

Read these questions. Then listen to the news broadcast.

1. What has happened to the cease fire in Franconia?

_____

2. What answer did dissident leader Amalde give when asked whether he would attend the peace conference?

_____

3. According to Amalde, on what does the success of the conference depend?

_____

4. According to Amalde, how can Mr. Tintor demonstrate good faith?

_____

5. On what basis was President Tintor's aide interviewed?

_____

6. What is one of the key issues to be discussed?

_____

7. What have members of the Global Health Foundation acknowledged?

_____

8. What has WASA done with Magna Maria, the existing telescope?

_____

9. How much will the new telescope cost?

_____

10. According to the new president of Illyria, what will the new nation need in order to be a viable state?

_____

Now listen again. Answer the questions.

6 INFORMATION GAP: A CARING ELEPHANT

Part A

Working with a partner, complete the text. Each of you will read a version of the same article. Each version is missing some information. Take turns asking your partner questions to get the missing information.

Student A, read the article about a caring elephant. Ask questions and fill in the missing information. Then answer Student B's questions.

Student B, turn to page 406 and follow the instructions there.

EXAMPLE:

Student A: In what condition did Damini refuse to move, to eat, to drink?

Student B: Distressed by a companion's death, Damini refused to move, to eat, to drink. For what reason did zoo keepers and veterinarians try everything they could think of?

Student A: They did this to save an elephant who seemed determined to die.

A Caring Elephant That Died of Grief
She refused to move or eat after companion's death

BY SUTAPA MUKERJEE, *The Associated Press*

LUCKNOW, India.—_____, Damini refused to move, to eat, to drink. For 24 days, zoo keepers and veterinarians tried everything they could think of to save an elephant who seemed determined to die.

Caretakers cooled her with a water spray and fans as she lay under a makeshift tent they erected of fragrant medicinal grass in a zoo in this northern Indian town. They tempted her with tons of sugarcane, bananas and grass—her favorites. They even fed her intravenously.

Despite all their efforts, Damini died yesterday in her enclosure—_____ protruding bones, bed sores covering much of her body.

"In the face of Damini's intense grief, all our treatment failed," said Dr. Itkarsh Shukla, veterinarian at the Prince of Wales Zoo in Lucknow, about 350 miles southeast of New Delhi.

Zoo officials said Damini was 72. She came to the zoo last year, after _____. She was alone for five months until the arrival in September of a pregnant younger elephant named Champakali.

Champakali came from Dudhwa National Park, 310 miles southeast of New Delhi, where she had worked carrying around tourists. _____, apparently by a wild bull elephant, park officials decided to send her to the zoo in Lucknow for a kind of maternity leave.

Zoo officials were worried about caring for Champakali, but, Shukla said, "Damini took up the job instantaneously."

(continued on next page)

A Caring Elephant That Died of Grief *(continued)*

The two elephants "became inseparable in no time," said zoo keeper Kamaal, who goes by one name. Damini made herself available at all hours for Champakali, who lapped up the attention.

According to elephant experts, such attachments commonly develop among elephants, with older elephants serving as caretakers for younger ones, especially in pregnancy.

"Elephants are very social animals. They can form very close bonds with others in their social group," said Pat Thomas, curator of mammals at the Bronx Zoo in New York City. "It's been pretty well documented that they do exhibit emotions that we would consider grieving" _____.

However, he said, an age-related medical problem should not be discounted as well in the case of an elephant as old as Damini.

When Champakali died on April 11 giving birth to a stillborn calf, Damini seemed to shed tears, then showed little interest in food or anything else, according to zoo officials.

For days, Damini stood still in her enclosure, _____ the 2 tons of sugarcane, bananas and grass heaped in front of her.

Her legs soon swelled up and eventually gave way. After that, Damini lay still on her side, head and ears drooping, trunk curled. Tears rolled down her eyes and the 4-ton elephant rapidly lost weight.

She simply lay "_____, moist with tears," Kamaal said.

A week ago, Damini completely stopped eating or drinking her usual daily quota of 40 gallons of water, despite the 116 degree heat.

Alarmed, veterinarians pumped more than 25 gallons of glucose, saline and vitamins through a vein in her ear.

Yesterday, Damini died.

For the second time in a month, Kamaal dug a big pit to bury an elephant.

"It will take me some time to get over the death of my two loved ones," he said.

Source: Sutapa Mukerjee, "A Caring Elephant That Died of Grief," *The Seattle Post-Intelligencer*, May 6, 1999. Copyright: The Associated Press.

Part B

In groups of four or five, discuss these questions. Share your answers with the class.

1. Compare animals and humans in regard to showing emotion. Are animals capable of compassion or any kind of emotion?

2. Give a personal example of a compassionate animal.

7 ESSAY

Write an essay about an act you have witnessed that you believe qualifies as compassionate. Describe the situation fully. What made the act compassionate? Did the compassionate person have anything to gain from showing compassion?

8 PICTURE DISCUSSION

In small groups, discuss Sir Edwin Landseer's painting The Old Shepherd's Chief Mourner. *What is happening in the picture? What is the dog doing? Are animals able to show compassion? In your discussion, consider the title of the painting, along with the article* "A Caring Elephant That Died of Grief."

Part A

Student B, read the article about a caring elephant. Answer Student A's questions.
Then ask your own questions and fill in the missing information.

EXAMPLE:

Student A: In what condition did Damini refuse to move, to eat, to drink?

Student B: Distressed by a companion's death, Damini refused to move, to eat, to drink. For what reason did zoo keepers and veterinarians try everything they could think of?

Student A: They did this to save an elephant who seemed determined to die.

A Caring Elephant That Died of Grief

She refused to move or eat after companion's death

BY SUTAPA MUKERJEE, *The Associated Press*

LUCKNOW, India.—Distressed by a companion's death, Damini refused to move, to eat, to drink. For 24 days, zoo keepers and veterinarians tried everything they could think of _____.

Caretakers cooled her with a water spray and fans as she lay under a makeshift tent they erected of fragrant medicinal grass in a zoo in this northern Indian town. They tempted her with tons of sugarcane, bananas and grass—her favorites. They even fed her intravenously.

Despite all their efforts, Damini died yesterday in her enclosure—loose gray skin hanging over her protruding bones, _____ her body.

"In the face of Damini's intense grief, all our treatment failed," said Dr. Itkarsh Shukla, veterinarian at the Prince of Wales Zoo in Lucknow, about 350 miles southeast of New Delhi.

Zoo officials said Damini was 72. She came to the zoo last year, after she was confiscated from owners who were illegally transporting her. She was alone for five months until the arrival in September of a pregnant younger elephant named Champakali.

Champakali came from Dudhwa National Park, 310 miles southeast of New Delhi, where she had worked _____. When she became pregnant,

A Caring Elephant That Died of Grief

apparently by a wild bull elephant, park officials decided to send her to the zoo in Lucknow for a kind of maternity leave.

Zoo officials were worried about caring for Champakali, but, Shukla said, "Damini took up the job instantaneously."

The two elephants "became inseparable in no time," said zoo keeper Kamaal, who goes by one name. Damini made herself available at all hours for Champakali, who lapped up the attention.

According to elephant experts, such attachments commonly develop among elephants, _____ for younger ones, especially in pregnancy.

"Elephants are very social animals. They can form very close bonds with others in their social group," said Pat Thomas, curator of mammals at the Bronx Zoo in New York City. "It's been pretty well documented that they do exhibit emotions that we would consider grieving" when a calf or other elephant dies.

However, he said, an age-related medical problem should not be discounted as well in the case of an elephant as old as Damini.

When Champakali died on April 11 _____, Damini seemed to shed tears, then showed little interest in food or anything else, according to zoo officials.

For days, Damini stood still in her enclosure, barely nibbling at the the 2 tons of sugarcane, bananas and grass heaped in front of her.

Her legs soon swelled up and eventually gave way. After that, Damini lay still on her side, _____. Tears rolled down her eyes and the 4-ton elephant rapidly lost weight.

She simply lay "staring at the staff with her eyes, moist with tears," Kamaal said.

A week ago, Damini completely stopped eating or drinking her usual daily quota of 40 gallons of water, despite the 116 degree heat.

Alarmed, veterinarians pumped more than 25 gallons of glucose, saline and vitamins through a vein in her ear.

Yesterday, Damini died.

For the second time in a month, Kamaal dug a big pit _____.

"It will take me some time to get over the death of my two loved ones," he said.

Source: Sutapa Mukerjee, "A Caring Elephant That Died of Grief," *The Seattle Post-Intelligencer*, May 6, 1999. Copyright: The Associated Press.

REVIEW OR SELFTEST

I. *Read the conversations. Underline all of the adverb clauses.*

1. A: Honey, we're going to be late for the play <u>if we don't leave right now.</u>

 B: OK. We can leave as soon as you back the car out of the garage.

2. A: Harry is a lot more responsible than he used to be.

 B: Yeah, I know. He never used to do his chores unless I threatened him. Now he does things without being told.

3. A: I'll call you when the plane gets in.

 B: OK, but you'd better take down Harriet's number in case I'm not home.

4. A: Wasn't that a great dinner? I ate so much that I can hardly move.

 B: Yeah. Dad is such a fabulous cook that I end up gaining a few pounds whenever I come home to visit.

5. A: You know, there aren't as many high-quality TV shows as there used to be.

 B: Oh, I don't know. You have access to some pretty impressive programming—provided that you have cable.

6. A: Joe, since you didn't turn in your term paper, you didn't pass the course—even though you did well on the tests.

 B: Yes, I know. I didn't do the term paper because I couldn't think of anything to write about.

7. A: When is your new house going to be finished?

 B: It'll be at least two months. Once they've laid the foundation, they can start building.

II. *Choose transitions from the box to complete the news item. Use each transition only once.*

otherwise	moreover	however	in fact	thus	~~next~~

> We focus _____*next*_____ on the mission of the Ares, the manned
> 1.
> space mission of WASA, the World
> Aeronautics and Space Association.
>
> The Ares was launched seven months ago from Woomera Spaceport in
> Australia. _____,
> 2.
> contact had been lost with the Ares for

the past three weeks, and WASA officials had feared the worst. WASA officials were _____ **3.** elated when they received a radio message today confirming that the Ares has made a successful landing on Mars. Harald Svendorf, chief of WASA, had this to say in today's news conference: "We needed a victory; _____, we might **4.** have lost our United Nations funding.

This successful landing should silence our critics, who have been calling the Ares Project a boondoggle. The project will _____ be one of **5.** the most cost-effective missions in the history of space exploration. _____, it will pave **6.** the way toward realization of other manned missions to the Jovian moons and to Venus."

III. *Combine the two sentences into one sentence with a dependent clause and an independent clause. Use the indicated subordinating conjunction.*

1. Mel and Sarah Figueroa were in a difficult situation. They both had jobs and didn't have daycare for their two children. (because)

> Mel and Sarah Figueroa were in a difficult situation because they both had jobs
>
> and didn't have daycare for their two children.

2. They had been leaving the children with Sarah's mother. This wasn't a satisfactory situation. (though)

_____

_____

_____

3. One of them was going to have to quit working. They could find a solution to the problem. (unless)

_____

_____

_____

4. One of their neighbors proposed the creation of a daycare co-op involving seven families. Their problem was solved. (when)

_____

_____

_____

5. Each day, one of the parents in the co-op cares for all of the children. The other parents are working. (while)

_____

_____

_____

IV. *Correct the eight mistakes in negative and focus adverbs in the letter.*

A note from Barb…

Dear Samantha,

   I wanted to thank you again for your hospitality while we were in Vancouver. Not only ~~you~~ did you and Michael showed us a wonderful time, but we got to re-establish the close ties we used to have. The even kids enjoyed the trip, and you know how kids can be on vacations. Only I hope that Dan and I can reciprocate sometime.

   The drive back to Edmonton was something else; almost we didn't make it back in one piece. About 4:30 on the day we left, there was an ice storm near Calgary which turned the highway into a sheet of ice. Little we knew that it would take us four hours to get through the city! Never I have been in such a colossal traffic jam. By the time we got off the freeway, it was 11:30 at night, and the kids were crying. We stopped at a motel to try to get a room; they were full up, but when we asked the proprietors if just we could spend the night in their lobby, they took pity on us and made us up a bed in their living room. People can be so kind sometimes. Never again I will think twice about helping people when they need it. By the next morning, the roads had been cleared, and we made it safely back to Edmonton.

   So, that's all for now. Thanks again.

               Love,
               Barb

V. *Punctuate the following sentences, which form a narration, with commas or semicolons. Do not add periods or capital letters.*

1. Tim and Zeya Donovan felt that their children were watching too much television but they didn't know what to do about the problem.

2. They tried combinations of threats, punishments, and rewards however, nothing seemed to work.

3. Tim and Zeya both got home about 5:30 P.M. and they needed to occupy the children's attention while they were fixing dinner.

4. Though they felt so much TV watching wasn't good they allowed it because they had no alternative.

5. Their children weren't getting enough exercise also, they weren't interacting with the neighborhood children.

6. Since a lot of their neighbors were having the same problem with their children someone came up with the idea of starting a neighborhood activities club.

7. The club met every afternoon from 5:00 until 6:30 and two parents from different families supervised activities.

8. The club has been a big success none of the children have watched very much television lately.

VI. *Circle the letter of the one underlined word or phrase that is not correct.*

1. <u>By</u> <u>pool</u> the world's food supply, we might <u>conceivably</u> avert   A Ⓑ C D
     A   B   C
   starvation—<u>provided that</u> the food were disbursed evenly.
                  D

2. <u>To feel</u> that pleas to sponsor orphans in Third World nations were <u>only</u>   A B C D
     A   B
   rip-off schemes, I refused <u>until</u> recently <u>even</u> to consider giving money.
                  C   D

3. Drivers should be <u>extremely</u> careful <u>when</u> <u>giving</u> a ride to   A B C D
                  A   B   C
   hitchhikers, <u>even</u> they look completely respectable.
           D

4. <u>Though</u> his prose is dense, columnist James Makela, <u>having written</u>   A B C D
     A
   in the *Carson City Courier*, <u>forcefully</u> makes the point that only rarely
                           C
   <u>is capital punishment</u> carried out in an evenhanded manner.
           D

5. Automobiles <u>certainly</u> cause many problems, <u>however</u> they   A B C D
                 A   B
   <u>fortunately</u> provide us with benefits <u>also</u>.
       C   D

6. <u>Feeling</u> that the subject was beneath me, I <u>unfortunately</u> learned
  A   B

  <u>something</u> at all <u>when</u> I took calculus last quarter.
   C   D

                      A B C D

7. <u>Happily</u>, the leaders of <u>almost</u> all world nations seem to have realized
  A   B

  that something must <u>quickly</u> be done <u>controlling</u> the problem of toxic
          C   D

  waste.

                      A B C D

8. <u>My having landed</u> at Orly Airport, <u>a taxi took me</u> <u>speedily</u> to the hotel
   A   B   C

  <u>where</u> the conference was to be held.
   D

                      A B C D

9. Bruce does not accept constructive criticism <u>well</u>, <u>nor</u> <u>he does</u> <u>even</u>
               A B C D

  appear to listen to it.

                      A B C D

10. I <u>actually</u> thought Ben wasn't going to be able to come to the party
   A

  <u>at all</u>, <u>but</u> here <u>comes he</u> now.
   B C   D

VII. *Go back to your answers for Part VI. Write the correct form for each item that you believe to be incorrect. You may change single words or expressions, but do not change punctuation.*

1. __pooling__

6. _____

2. _____

7. _____

3. _____

8. _____

4. _____

9. _____

5. _____

10. _____

▶ *To check your answers, go to the Answer Key on page 417.*

FROM GRAMMAR TO WRITING SENTENCES AND FRAGMENTS

As you have learned, a sentence must have at least one independent, or main, clause. (See From Grammar to Writing after Part I, page 52, for a discussion of the sentence.) If a group of words does not have an independent clause, it is a **fragment**, not a sentence.

EXAMPLES:

We need to do something about violence. (sentence—independent clause)

Because it's tearing apart the fabric of societies everywhere. (fragment—dependent clause)

For correctness in writing, we normally avoid sentence fragments. To correct a fragment, we often attach it to an independent clause. We can do this with the fragment above.

We need to do something about violence **because it's tearing apart the fabric of societies everywhere**.

If there is no independent clause nearby, we can correct a fragment by adding a subject and its verb.

Interviewed by our news team. (fragment—no independent clause)

One commuter was interviewed by our news team. (sentence)

1 *In the following sentences, underline dependent clauses once and independent clauses twice. Do not underline phrases. In the blank to the left of each item, write **S** for **Sentence** or **F** for **Fragment**.*

_S_ **1.** Though there are benefits to genetic engineering, there are also dangers.

_____ **2.** As soon as I've saved enough money.

_____ **3.** Although China is overpopulated, it is trying to correct the problem.

_____ **4.** We won't solve the problem of illiteracy until we provide enough teachers.

_____ **5.** If a young basketball player from Nigeria can get a scholarship.

_____ **6.** Because I was one of those students.

(continued on next page)

_____ **7.** The economy is perhaps too dependent on high-tech industries.

_____ **8.** Carried out right, this procedure would cause the economy to expand.

_____ **9.** By the time the train finally arrived in Santa Cruz.

_____ **10.** We need to make some personal sacrifices if we want to help.

2 *Read the following paragraph. Correct the eight fragments by joining them to the independent clauses to which they are logically connected. Where necessary, add commas and change capitalization, but do not add words.*

The life of Dorothy and Patrick Tien has improved immeasurably, Since they both got new jobs. Dorothy got a position as a proofreader and editor at a publishing company. That is pioneering new workplace methods. Patrick was hired as a full-time consultant for an engineering firm. The difference between their new jobs and their old ones can be summed up in one word: flextime. Until they secured these new positions. Dorothy and Patrick had a very difficult time raising their two small children. Their life was extremely stressful. Because they were at the mercy of a nine-to-five schedule and had to pay a lot for day care. In order to get to work on time. They had to have the children at the day care center by 7:30 every morning. Both of their new companies, however, offer a flextime schedule. As long as Dorothy and Patrick put in their forty hours a week. They are free to work. When it is convenient for them. Now they can take turns staying home with the children, and day care is just a memory. Best of all, the children are much happier. Because they are getting the attention they need.

If a sentence has only one clause, it is called a **simple** sentence.

> **EXAMPLE:**
> I bought a new car last month. (simple sentence—one independent clause)

If two independent clauses are connected by a coordinating conjunction (*and, but, or, nor, for, so, yet*), the larger sentence is called a **compound** sentence. We place a comma before the coordinating conjunction.

> **EXAMPLE:**
> The tea was virtually flavorless. The sandwich tasted like cardboard.
> The tea was virtually flavorless, **and** the sandwich tasted like cardboard.

We don't normally place a comma before a coordinating conjunction if it does not connect two independent clauses.* That is, there must be a subject and its verb in both clauses.

> **EXAMPLE:**
> We can go out to a movie or stay home and watch television.
> (There is no subject in the second half of the sentence.)

Note, though, that if we join two very short independent clauses with a coordinating conjunction, we can eliminate the comma before the coordinating conjunction.

*Remember, however, that you can use a comma before a coordinating conjunction when it is being used before the last item in a series. (I don't like pie, cake, or ice cream.)

EXAMPLE:

I love movies but I hate television.

If a sentence contains an independent clause and one or more dependent clauses, it is called a **complex** sentence. If the dependent clause comes first, we normally put a comma after it. If it comes second, we normally don't put a comma before it unless the dependent clause establishes a contrast.

EXAMPLES:

Because they provide activity, school sports are worthwhile.

School sports are worthwhile **because they provide activity**.

Though they aren't everything, jobs are important.

Jobs are important, **though they aren't everything**.

(The subordinating conjunction *though* establishes a contrast, so there is a comma before it.)

---

3 *Place commas wherever possible in the following sentences. In the blank to the left of each item, write **S** for a **Simple Sentence**, **CPD** for a **Compound Sentence**, or **CX** for a **Complex Sentence**.*

CPD **1.** Violence exists nearly everywhere in the world, and it is spreading.

_____ **2.** Since we usually watch TV at home in our living room a TV show doesn't seem like a special event.

_____ **3.** The population will continue to increase but natural resources won't.

_____ **4.** We must make trains viable again if we expect people to use them.

_____ **5.** I listened politely for a while and then excused myself.

_____ **6.** The governor isn't in favor of higher taxes nor does she encourage the development of mass transit.

_____ **7.** We don't have to buy a lot of groceries at once for we can always stop at the supermarket on the way home from work.

_____ **8.** Tim passed his driving exam with flying colors though he could use some practice in parallel parking.

_____ **9.** As I was entering the dining car a violent lurch of the train threw me to the left.

Coordinating conjunctions, subordinating conjunctions, and transitions often have similarities in meaning but are used with different sentence patterns and punctuation. Notice the use of *but, although,* and *however* in the following sentences.

EXAMPLES:

Dams provide many benefits, **but** they also do considerable harm to wildlife.

Although dams provide many benefits, they also do considerable harm to wildlife.

Dams provide many benefits. **However**, they also do considerable harm to wildlife.

The meanings of these three examples are similar, but the emphasis is different. It is also correct to use a semicolon and a lowercase letter in the third example.

4 *For each of the following sentences, write two other sentences that express a similar meaning, using the connectors given.*

Drake tried to think of a justification for his actions. However, he was unable to come up with a single thing.

1. (but)

_____

_____

2. (although)

_____

_____

Dams provide a great many economic benefits, so I don't think they should be removed.

3. (because)

_____

_____

4. (therefore)

_____

_____

In addition to being an excellent athlete, Bruce is a top student.

5. (and)

_____

_____

6. (also)

_____

_____

5 **APPLY IT TO YOUR WRITING**

Write a paragraph of six to ten sentences on one of these topics or a similar topic that interests you:

- One reason why sports are so popular today
- One danger of cloning
- My earliest memory
- A kind act I experienced

*In your paragraph, include at least one transition (**however**, **therefore**, etc.), one coordinating conjunction (**and**, **but**, etc.), and one subordinating conjunction (**because**, **as soon as**, etc.) Leave your paragraph unpunctuated. Then exchange papers with a partner. Read and punctuate each other's paper, paying particular attention to avoiding fragments and to correct use of commas and semicolons. Discuss your papers together. Then rewrite your paragraph and submit it to your teacher.*

REVIEW OR SELFTEST
ANSWER KEY

PART VIII

I.
1. **B:** as soon as you back the car out of the garage
2. **A:** than he used to be
   B: unless I threatened him
3. **A:** when the plane gets in
   B: in case I'm not home
4. **A:** that I can hardly move
   B: that I end up gaining a few pounds / whenever I come home to visit
5. **A:** as there used to be
   B: provided that you have cable
6. **A:** since you didn't turn in your term paper / even though you did well on the tests
   B: because I couldn't think of anything to write about
7. **B:** Once they've laid the foundation

II.
2. However
3. thus
4. otherwise
5. in fact
6. Moreover

III.
2. Though they had been leaving the children with Sarah's mother, this wasn't a satisfactory situation.
3. One of them was going to have to quit working unless they could find a solution to the problem.
4. When one of their neighbors proposed the creation of a daycare co-op involving seven families, their problem was solved.
5. Each day, one of the parents in the co-op cares for all of the children while the other parents are working.

IV.

The even kids	→ Even the kids
Only I hope	→ I only hope
almost we didn't	→ we almost didn't
Little we knew	→ Little did we know
Never I have been	→ Never have I been
just we could spend	→ we could just spend
Never again I will	→ Never again will I

V.
2. . . . rewards; however, . . .
3. . . . 5:30 P.M., and . . .
4. . . . good, they . . .
5. . . . exercise; also, . . .
6. . . . children, someone . . .
7. . . . until 6:30, and . . .
8. . . . success; none . . .

VI.
2. A
3. D
4. B
5. B
6. C
7. D
8. A
9. C
10. D

VII.
2. Feeling
3. even if
4. writing
5. but
6. nothing
7. to control
8. After I landed
9. does he
10. he comes

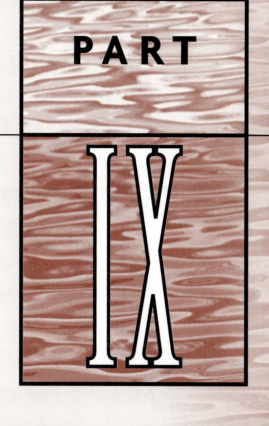

PART

IX

NOUN CLAUSES

NOUN CLAUSES: SUBJECTS AND OBJECTS

GRAMMAR **IN CONTEXT**

QUESTIONS TO CONSIDER

1. What kinds of things make you laugh?

2. What benefits do humor and laughter provide us?

 Read the story.

HAVE YOU HEARD THIS ONE?

A disconsolate young man was walking along a beach in southern California. What was making him sad was the fact that his ladylove wasn't with him. She was in Hawaii, and he was in California. Suddenly, on the sand in front of him, he spied what looked like a magic lamp. "I wonder if this is one of those magic lamps, like Aladdin's?" he mused. "I guess that there's only one way to find out." Picking up the lamp, he began to rub it. Immediately, a genie popped out. Let me tell you, though—this wasn't your usual type of genie. This was a genie with an attitude.

"Thanks for letting me out, man. It was getting a little stuffy in there. . . . Anyway, you know the drill. You let me out; I grant you one wish. So what's your wish?"

"Wait a minute," said the young man. "I thought you always got three wishes when you let a genie out of a lamp or a bottle."

Have You Heard This One?

"Yeah, well, times have changed," retorted the genie. "Inflation, you know. My contract says that whoever lets me out gets one wish. Take it or leave it. What's your fondest wish?"

The young man pondered the question. He took so long that the genie finally said, exasperated, "Hey, man, come on. I haven't got all day. What do you want?"

"You'll grant me whatever I wish?"

"Whatever."

"I'm having a real problem figuring out what I want. The fact that you're restricting me to one wish really isn't kosher, you know. . . . But . . . if you insist . . . here it is. What I want is for you to build me a bridge to Hawaii."

"Say what?" the genie replied. "I thought you said you wanted a bridge to Hawaii. I'm going to have to get my hearing checked."

"I did say that. I want a bridge to Hawaii. You see, I'm afraid of flying. I flew one time, and I almost had a nervous breakdown, what with the possibility of plane crashes, and the airline food, and all."

"So take a boat."

"I get seasick on boats. Deathly ill. I can't travel on boats. But if you build me a bridge to Hawaii, I can drive there. And I really need to go to Hawaii."

Chagrined, the genie asked, "Do you understand what you're asking me to do? I can't do that. Do you realize how far it is to Hawaii? It's 2,000 miles. I'd have to sink pilings into the ocean floor . . . Do you know how much cement that would take? And I'd probably have to attach all kinds of pontoons, and it would take months just to do a geologic survey and prepare an environmental impact statement. I'm tired after all those centuries inside that lamp. I don't think I have the energy. . . . No, this request is simply out of the question. Ask me something else. I'll give you another chance. Is there someone special you want to see? I can transport whomever you'd like right here in the twinkling of an eye. The queen of England. Madonna. Whomever. I can bring however many people you want—a whole army. Or maybe there's some possession you desire. A Rolls-Royce, perhaps? Money is no object."

Again the young man cogitated for a considerable time. Finally, he said, "Yes, I do have one more wish."

"All right," responded the genie. "Now we're getting somewhere. Make it; make it."

"Well," said the young man, "I've always been fascinated by the mysteriousness and the unpredictability of women. Have you ever been able to figure them out? I haven't. So that's my wish."

"What?" said the genie.

"To understand them. I've always wanted to know what makes women tick. I'll be satisfied if you can answer that question for me. That'll be my wish."

. . . "So did you want two lanes or four on the bridge?" the genie said.

Source: Several versions of this joke exist. One is from S. Comey@aol.com. See netsong.com/Jokes/oj211.htm.

UNDERSTANDING MEANING FROM CONTEXT

1. *Find three synonyms for* **thought** *in the reading and write them here.*

a. _____ b. _____ c. _____

2. *Write synonyms or definitions for each of the following italicized words and expressions.*

a. A *disconsolate* young man was walking along a beach in southern

California. _____

b. Anyway, *you know the drill.* _____

c. The fact that you're restricting me to one wish really isn't *kosher*,

you know. _____

d. I can transport whomever you'd like right here *in the twinkling of*

an eye. _____

e. I've always wanted to know *what makes women tick.*

_____

3. *Look at this sentence from the reading:*

He took so long that the genie finally said, exasperated, . . .

In the first blank, write a definition of **exasperated**. *In the second,
write the word in the story closest in meaning to* **exasperated**.

a. _____

b. _____

4. *Look at this sentence from the reading:*

"Wait a minute," said the young man.

In addition to **said**, *three other reporting verbs are used in the reading.
Write them here.*

a. _____ b. _____ c. _____

COMPREHENSION

*Talk with a partner. Do you think this story is funny? Why or
why not? Whether or not the joke makes you laugh, explain what
the intended humor is.*

GRAMMAR PRESENTATION
NOUN CLAUSES: SUBJECTS AND OBJECTS

SUBJECT
What was making him sad was the fact that his ladylove wasn't with him.
The fact that you're restricting me to one wish really isn't kosher, you know.
My contract says that **whoever lets me out** gets one wish.

OBJECT
"I guess **that there's only one way to find out**."
"I thought you said **(that) you wanted a bridge to Hawaii**."
He spied **what looked like a magic lamp**.
"You'll grant me **whatever I wish**?"
"I wonder **if this is one of those magic lamps, like Aladdin's**?"
"Do you realize **how far it is to Hawaii**?"
"I'm having a real problem figuring out **what I want**."
"I can transport **whomever you'd like** right here in the twinkling of an eye."

NOTES

1. Noun clauses are dependent clauses that perform the same functions that regular nouns do: They can be subjects, direct objects, indirect objects, or objects of prepositions. See Unit 23 for a discussion of noun clauses as complements.

EXAMPLES

- Suddenly, on the sand in front of him, he spied **what looked like a magic lamp**.
  (*What looked like a magic lamp* is a noun clause functioning as a direct object.)

- **What was making him sad** was the fact that his ladylove wasn't with him.
  (*What was making him sad* is a noun clause functioning as a subject.)

- "I'm having a real problem figuring out **what I want**."
  (*What I want* is a noun clause functioning as the object of a preposition.)

(continued on next page)

2. Noun clauses are often introduced by *what, that, who, whom, where, whatever, whichever (one), wherever, whomever,* and *however.*

- "My contract says **that whoever lets me out gets one wish**."
- "You'll grant me **whatever I wish**?"
- "**What I want** is for you to build me a bridge to Hawaii."

▶ **BE CAREFUL!** Don't confuse *however* as a clause introducer with *however* as a transition.

- "I can bring **however many people you want—a whole army**."
  (*However* is a clause introducer.)
- "**However**, I can't build you a bridge."
  (*However* is a transition similar in meaning to *but*.)

3. Remember the distinction between *who* and *whom, whoever* and *whomever. Who* and *whoever* are used as subjects, while *whom* and *whomever* are used as objects in formal English. Many native speakers don't use *whom* and *whomever.*

- "My contract says **that whoever lets me out gets one wish**."
  (*Whoever* is the subject of the clause verb *lets*.)
- "I can transport **whomever you'd like** right here in the twinkling of an eye."
  (*Whomever* is the object of the clause verb *like*.)

▶ **BE CAREFUL!** If you are unsure whether to use *whoever* or *whomever,* remember that noun clauses (like all clauses) must have both a subject and a verb.

Look at this sentence. It would seem to require the object form *whomever.* However, the verb in the noun clause must have a subject, so *whoever* is the correct choice.

- The genie had to grant one wish to **whoever let him out of the lamp**.
  (*Whoever* is the subject of the clause verb *let*.)

USAGE NOTE: Although native speakers often replace *whom* and *whomever* in conversation or informal writing, in careful speech and formal writing the use of *whom* and *whomever* is recommended.

- "I can transport **whomever you'd like** right here in the twinkling of an eye." (formal, precise, correct)
- I can transport **whoever you'd like** right here in the twinkling of an eye. (informal and conversational but not strictly correct)

4. When a noun clause beginning with *that* or *whom* functions as a direct object, the words *that* and *whom* may be omitted.

- "I guess **that there's only one way to find out**."

    OR

- "I guess **there's only one way to find out**."
  (The clause functions as a direct object, so *that* may be omitted.)

5. Noun clauses are sometimes **embedded questions** with *if* and *whether (or not)*. *If* and *whether (or not)* are similar in meaning and can be used interchangeably.

- "I wonder **if / whether this is one of those magic lamps, like Aladdin's**."

6. Embedded questions beginning with *wh-* words *(who, whom, which, when, where, how, how many, how much)* are also noun clauses.

▶ **BE CAREFUL!** When we embed a question in a noun clause, we use normal word order, not question word order.

- "How far is it to Hawaii?"
- "Do you realize **how far it is to Hawaii**?"
  NOT ~~Do you realize how far is it to Hawaii?~~

7. **Indirect (reported) speech** is expressed in noun clauses. Remember to follow the sequence of tenses in changing direct speech to indirect (reported) speech.

- "You always get three wishes when you let a genie out of a lamp or bottle."
- "I thought **you always got three wishes when you let a genie out of a lamp or a bottle**."
  (The verbs change to the past to match *thought*.)

8. Note that a noun clause sometimes includes the phrase ***the fact that***. See Unit 23 for more work on clauses with *the fact that*.

- **The fact that you're restricting me to one wish** really isn't kosher, you know.

FOCUSED PRACTICE

1 DISCOVER THE GRAMMAR

Part A

Look again at Have You Heard This One? *Underline the noun clauses and classify them as* **Subjects (S)**, **Direct Objects (DO)**, *or* **Objects of Prepositions (OP)**.

Part B

There are four noun clauses that are embedded questions. Write each direct question before it was embedded.

1. _____

2. _____

3. _____

4. _____

Part C

You will find one sentence in which a noun clause functioning as a subject lies within a noun clause functioning as an object. Write both clauses here.

1. _____

2. _____

2 PARTS OF NOUN CLAUSES   Grammar Notes 1, 2

Look at these four sentences with noun clauses. Underline the noun clause. Label a **Subject (S)**, *a* **Verb (V)**, *and a* **Direct Object (O)** *in the noun clause.*

1. I'm having a real problem figuring out what I want.

2. Do you understand what you're asking me to do?

3. You'll grant me whatever I wish?

4. I can transport whomever you'd like right here in the twinkling of an eye.

3 A THUMBNAIL SKETCH OF HUMOR　Grammar Note 6

Part A

Work with a partner. Student A asks four direct questions. Student B answers with an embedded question inside a phrase such as **I don't know, I'm not entirely sure, I really don't know, I have no idea, I don't have a clue,** *and so on. Then Student B asks Student A four questions and Student A answers similarly.*

EXAMPLE:

what / happen / to our diaphragm / when we laugh

Student A: What happens to our diaphragm when we laugh?

Student B: I don't know what happens to our diaphragm when we laugh.

1. what / a pun

   _____

   _____

2. what / *hyperbole* / mean

   _____

   _____

3. what / the humor of the unexpected happening

   _____

   _____

4. how / repetition / work in humor

   _____

   _____

5. what / the humor of the incongruous situation

   _____

   _____

6. how / sarcasm / differ from other humor

   _____

   _____

7. why / it / impossible to tickle yourself

_____

_____

8. what / endorphins

_____

_____

Part B

Read A Thumbnail Sketch of Humor. *Then answer the questions in Part A.*

A Thumbnail Sketch of Humor

Pun A pun is a kind of humor that depends on similarities in sound or meaning between two words. Someone says one word but means another. EXAMPLE: A woman saw a bear a week before her baby was born. Frightened, she asked the doctor, "Will seeing that *bear* affect my baby?" After the baby was born, the doctor said, "Yes, your baby has two *bare* feet."

Hyperbole Hyperbole, much used in humor, is exaggeration. EXAMPLE: Bill: "Mary, why are you so tired?" Mary: "I've been working about a million hours a week; that's why."

Humor of the unexpected happening A great deal of humor depends on what is called the humor of the unexpected happening. EXAMPLE: In a movie, a woman in a restaurant opens her purse, and a bird flies out of it.

Repetition Many humorous stories are structured on the basis of repetition of an element, most often three times. EXAMPLE: A man can't find his car and tries to hitchhike. It is pouring rain. The first driver who comes along honks his horn and doesn't stop. The second car that comes by splashes water from a mud puddle all over him. Then another man comes out and unlocks the door of his parked car, next to the first man. Furious, the first man goes up to him,

shakes him, and says, "I wouldn't accept a ride from you if you paid me."

Incongruous situation The humor of the incongruous situation depends on normal things happening in unusual places. No one thinks twice about seeing a dog in someone's yard, but if a dog enters an elevator in a downtown building, people will laugh.

Sarcasm Sarcasm is a kind of irony. It can be mild and gentle, but it is more often biting and hurtful. EXAMPLE: **A:** "What do you think of Jones as a political candidate? I think he's pretty sharp." **B:** "Oh, he's sharp, all right. He's got a mind as good as any in the twelfth century."

Tickling Tickling is a not-completely-understood phenomenon. It is thought, however, that in order to experience tickling as a pleasant or laughter-producing experience, we must perceive it as a pretended, not real, attack. Therefore, it must be reasonably gentle. This explains why it is impossible for us to tickle ourselves. Our brain is aware of itself.

Physiological aspects of laughter When we laugh, our diaphragm moves quickly up and down. Endorphins, hormones that are created in the brain when we laugh or exercise, are instrumental in lessening pain and contributing to a sense of well being.

HUMOR

Includes material adapted from "Humor," *The World Book Encyclopedia*, Volume H, Chicago: World Book, 1998, pp. 435–436; and "Humour and Wit," *Encyclopedia Britannica*, Macropaedia, Chicago: Encyclopedia, 1998, p. 686.

4 BUMPER STICKERS

Work with a partner. Examine each of the following bumper stickers, all of which have been found on the rear bumpers or on the backs of cars. With your partner, discuss the meaning of each bumper sticker. Then, on a separate piece of paper, write one or two sentences explaining the meaning of each, making sure to use a noun clause. Use phrases such as those in the box in your noun clauses:

what's funny about this	what this means	what the humor depends on
the fact that	what this is referring to	what this is about

EXAMPLE:

Is there life before coffee?

What this is referring to *is the fact that many people cannot start the day without coffee. They act like they're dead.*

OR

What's funny about this *is the fact that many people cannot start the day without coffee. They act like they're dead.*

1. **Go ahead and hit me.** I need the money.

2. **HONK** If you're illiterate.

3. If You Don't Like the Way I Drive, **Stay OFF the Sidewalk.**

4. Sometimes I wish life had subtitles.

5. MISSING: HUSBAND AND DOG. ATTENTION: <u>$100 REWARD</u> FOR DOG.

6. CHANGE IS INEVITABLE— EXCEPT FOR VENDING MACHINES

7. I IS A COLLEGE STUDENT.

8. *Welcome to Oregon.* NOW GO HOME.

9. **Eschew obfuscation.**

Source: www.rider.edu/users/grushow/humor/bumper.html

5 EDITING

Read the following statements about the proper way to tell a joke. Find and correct the ten errors in noun clauses.

Ten Pieces of Advice about Telling a Joke

1. Make sure ~~that~~ the joke you're telling ^is^ funny.

2. The best jokes are broad enough so that everyone can enjoy them. Be certain that no one will be embarrassed by that you tell.

3. Also make certain that however you're saying won't embarrass anyone.

4. Ask yourself is the joke you want to tell vulgar. If it is, don't tell it.

5. Before you begin, be certain you remember what are the key details. Run through them in your mind before you start speaking.

6. Make sure what you have everybody's attention when you're ready to start.

7. Be certain that you remember what is the punch line of the joke. Nothing is worse than listening to a joke when the teller can't remember the punch line.

8. The fact can you remember a joke doesn't guarantee success. You have to make the experience a performance. Be animated and dramatic.

9. Don't panic if you get interrupted. Let whomever is talking finish what he or she is saying. Then say something like, "OK, folks, listen up. I want to finish the joke I was telling you."

10. Many comedians are criticized because they laugh at their own jokes. Don't laugh at that you're saying. Let others do the laughing.

COMMUNICATION PRACTICE

6 LISTENING

🔲 *Look at these questions. Then listen to the conversation.*

1. What bothers Greg about jokes?

_____

2. According to Greg, what is the expectation when someone tells a joke?

_____

3. According to Greg, what does everyone think if you don't laugh?

_____

4. What is Greg's other problem with jokes?

_____

5. What does he feel like in this situation?

_____

6. What was the problem that some girls at a middle school were causing?

_____

7. What did the principal of the school decide?

_____

8. What did the principal have the custodian clean the mirror with?

_____

🔲 *Now listen again. Write answers to the questions. Use noun clauses where possible.*

7 GROUP DISCUSSION: WHAT'S FUNNY ABOUT THAT?

Read the article on page 432. Then work with a partner. Tell your partner which jokes you find funny and which ones you don't find funny. If you do find a joke funny, explain what makes you laugh about it. Explain to your partner what makes each joke a joke.

They Do Have a Sense of Humor

By David Field *USA Today*

Airline crews may seem like a dour group as they walk through the airport terminal with that look of determination and dedication on their faces. But behind the serious demeanor, they are a funny lot. Here are some classic airline jokes culled from the collective memory of aviation writers.

Flight Attendant Quips

Before the no-smoking announcement: "This is a nonsmoking flight. If you must smoke, please ring your attendant-call bell and one of us will escort you out to the wing."

After the no-smoking announcement: "Any passenger caught smoking in the lavatories will be asked to leave the plane immediately."

First-Time Fliers

Then there was the woman who, when asked if she wanted a window seat, responded, "No, not by the window. I've just had my hair done."

One passenger wanted to know how a plane could get from Chicago to Detroit, cities separated by a time zone, in just 15 minutes.

Although the flight time was 75 minutes, the time zone made the airline's scheduled departure seem like the flight took only 15 minutes. He was finally satisfied with the explanation that it was a *very* fast airplane.

Pilot Humor

When controllers are uncertain what a pilot plans or wants to do, they usually say, "Please state your intentions."

Few pilots are daring enough to respond literally. But one was once overheard: "I intend to retire to a small farm in Georgia and raise peaches."

Faux Paws

Two airline cargo handlers were removing a pet carrier from a plane's cargo hold and discovered the dog inside was dead.

Fearful of the bereaved owner's anger, the two went to the nearest dog pound and found an animal of the same breed, size and color, and proudly delivered it to its destination.

As the animal leaped out of the cage, the owner gasped in shock, turned to the cargo handlers, and exclaimed, "This is not my dog! My dog was dead when I shipped him! He was stuffed!"

Airport Humor

Years ago, a bank had an office in a North Carolina Airport. Right next to the Eastern Airlines counter, the local bank had put up a sign asking, "Have you written your will yet?"

Plane Humor

Pilots and maintenance crews usually communicate in writing. A pilot typically writes up an item to be repaired such as a cockpit gauge or switch.

An overnight maintenance crew responds in writing that the work was done or wasn't needed or couldn't be done.

A pilot once left a note complaining "Dead bugs are on the cockpit windshield." When the pilot came back in the morning, maintenance had replied: "Sorry, live bugs not available." ◆

Source: David Field, "They Do Have a Sense of Humor," *USA Today*, August 22, 1998.

8 ESSAY

Write an essay of three to five paragraphs about a situation that you witnessed or participated in that you found humorous. Describe the situation fully, using plenty of supporting details. Explain why the situation was funny to you.

OR

If you know an extended joke (like the opening story in this unit), write it.

9 PICTURE DISCUSSION

Look at this cartoon for a few minutes. Talk with a partner. What are the dogs trying to do? Do you find the cartoon funny? Why or why not? What main point do you think the artist wanted to make in drawing this cartoon?

THE FAR SIDE By GARY LARSON

Knowing how it could change the lives of canines everywhere, the dog scientists struggled diligently to understand the Doorknob Principle.

UNIT

23 NOUN CLAUSES AND PHRASES: COMPLEMENTS

GRAMMAR IN CONTEXT

QUESTIONS TO CONSIDER

1. Do you think the majority of people are happy in life?

2. What kinds of things make you happy?

Read an article about happiness.

Happiness Is . . . ?

Singers sing about it: Dorothy, for example, sang about what she hoped to find "Over the Rainbow" in *The Wizard of Oz*. Bobby McFerrin's advice to us in song was "Don't worry, be happy." Filmmakers often make movies with happy endings. Fairy tales typically end with "And they all lived happily ever after." People go to psychiatrists and psychologists to find out if they've got it or to get it if they haven't. There's a common belief that it's essential for us to be happy in life. The American Declaration of Independence says people are entitled to "life, liberty, and the pursuit of happiness." It's clear that happiness is central to human existence. But what is it? How can we get it, and how can we keep it?

And they all lived happily ever after.

Happiness Is . . . ?

It was difficult for me to come up with answers to these questions, so I went to *The American Heritage Dictionary* and looked up "happy." Here's the main definition I found: "Enjoying, showing, or marked by pleasure, satisfaction, or joy." OK. That seems like a reasonable definition. But the concept of happiness is nonetheless elusive. We tend to say things like, "If only I could find someone I could really love, I'd be happy forever," or "I'd be so happy if I just had enough money to buy the things I want and need." That things and even people are not the key to happiness is quite clear, however. How many times have we gone all out to get something we really wanted, only to discover that it wasn't so great once we had it? I decided to do some additional research about happiness. I found out some interesting things.

hap•py Enjoying, showing, or marked by pleasure, satisfaction, or joy

The first thing I learned about happiness is that there's a big difference between what we think will make us happy and what actually does. According to psychologist Daniel Gilbert of Harvard University, we human beings are very good at describing our feelings and emotions at the moment of a significant experience. What we're not so good at is predicting what our feelings will be like in the future and how long we'll have those feelings. This is because feelings are produced by certain brain chemicals right after we've had an experience. The feelings are recorded in our memory, but the specific chemicals associated with the experience fade rather soon. When we look back on emotional experiences, we still feel the emotions we once felt but not as strongly as before. It's evident that some force in our brain seeks to keep our emotions on an even keel. When we have a humiliating or irritating experience, for example, our brain takes steps to lessen the impact of this experience in order to maintain mental equilibrium. Gilbert likens this process to the way an oyster produces a layer of pearl around an invading grain of sand. It appears that the brain reduces the emotional impact of very positive experiences as well. A few weeks after a positive experience, we've gotten over the "high," and our feelings have returned to "normal."

Psychological experiments bear out this notion that humans are not good at predicting their future happiness. In one case, a number of lottery winners who had won large jackpots were interviewed after they had won. They expected to feel happy for a long time afterwards. They did, in fact, feel euphoria for a short time, but this feeling faded, and their level of happiness was soon back to its usual state. In another experiment, students were interviewed about where they thought they would feel happier attending school, in a warm climate like that in California or in a colder climate. Most predicted that they would be happier in warm California, but later interviews

(continued on next page)

Happiness Is . . . ?

showed that students felt equally happy in warm and cold climates. In a third case, people who had been tested for Huntington's disease or AIDS expected that they would be devastated if they got bad news. Most of them, however, were not. It was those who decided not to be tested who suffered the greatest anxiety.

The second thing I learned about happiness is that it apparently centers around our ability to adapt to a situation and live through it, especially under adverse circumstances. For example, a professor recounted an experience he'd had with his wife regarding which curtains they should buy for their bedroom. The professor's wife wanted some brown curtains with vertical stripes. The professor hated them and was sure he would always hate them. His wife was adamant, however, and the professor felt it was important that he not get into an argument with her. They went ahead and bought the brown curtains. In time, he got used to them. In fact, not only did he adapt to them, but he also came to like them. It may be the same with most of our experiences. It's not things or people or relationships in themselves that make us happy; it's the process of experiencing and adapting to them that brings us joy and satisfaction.

So it appears that the secret to happiness lies not in thinking about what makes us happy but in just "doing it." Perhaps Bobby McFerrin had it right when he said, "Don't worry, be happy."

Sources: (1) *The American Heritage Dictionary* (New York: Houghton Mifflin Company 1993), p. 618; (2) Based on information in Philip J. Hilts, "In Forecasting Their Emotions, Most People Flunk Out," *The New York Times*, February 16, 1999, p. F-2.

UNDERSTANDING MEANING FROM CONTEXT

Look carefully at paragraphs 3, 4, and 5 of the reading. Match the meanings of the words and phrases from the reading in column A to their equivalent meanings in column B.

Column A

1. on an even keel (par. 3)
2. likens (par. 3)
3. bear out (par. 4)
4. jackpots (par. 4)
5. euphoria (par. 4)
6. devastated (par. 4)
7. adamant (par. 5)

Column B

a. insistent
b. intense joy
c. reasonably steady
d. support
e. compares
f. destroyed mentally
g. rewards

GRAMMAR **PRESENTATION**

COMPLEMENTS

ADJECTIVE COMPLEMENTS

It	LINKING VERB	ADJECTIVE	NOUN CLAUSE
It	's	clear	**that happiness is central to human existence.**

It	LINKING VERB	ADJECTIVE OF URGENCY	NOUN CLAUSE
It	was	important	**that he not get into an argument with her.**

It	LINKING VERB	ADJECTIVE	NOUN PHRASE
It	's	essential	**for us to be happy in life.**

NOUN COMPLEMENTS

The first thing I learned about happiness is **that there's a big difference between what we think will make us happy and what actually does.**

NOTES

1. Complements are words, phrases, or clauses that add information about or further explain an adjective or noun. One common type of complement is a **noun clause.**

EXAMPLES

- It's evident **that some force in our brain seeks to keep our emotions on an even keel.**
  (The noun clause *that some force in our brain seeks to keep our emotions on an even keel* adds information about *evident.*)

- There's a common belief **that it's essential for us to be happy in life.**
  (The noun clause *that it's essential for us to be happy in life* adds information about *belief.*)

2. One type of noun clause functions as an adjective complement. It follows the pattern *It* + linking verb + adjective. (Common linking verbs are *be, appear, seem, feel, smell, look, taste,* etc.) The clause further identifies or explains the adjective. The clause introducer *that* may be omitted.

We can restate this kind of sentence so that the noun clause becomes the subject of the sentence. When we do this, *that* cannot be omitted.

A sentence rearranged in this way is more common in writing than in conversation.

- It's clear **(that) the concept of happiness is central to human existence**.
  (The noun clause *[that] the concept of happiness is central to human existence* explains the adjective *clear. That* can be omitted.)

- **That the concept of happiness is central to human existence** is clear.
  (The noun clause is now the subject. *That* cannot be omitted.)

3. When noun clauses functioning as adjective complements follow **adjectives of urgency**, **necessity**, or **advice**, the noun clause must contain the base (= subjunctive) form of the verb, since it is not known whether the action in the noun clause will ever take place. Expressions showing these meanings include *it is essential, it is necessary, it is important, it is advisable, it is desirable, it is crucial.*

See Unit 25 for more practice on this structure.

See Appendix 21 on page A-10 for a list of verbs and adjectives of urgency, necessity, and advice that require the subjunctive.

Sentences of this type can be restated, with the noun clause becoming the subject and occurring at the beginning of the sentence. Note that *it* is not needed in this restated sentence.

A sentence arranged in this way is rarely heard in conversation.

- There's a common belief **that it's essential (that) we be happy in life**.
  (The base form *be* is used instead of *are.*)
  NOT ~~There's a common belief that it's essential we are happy in life.~~

- The professor felt it was **important that he not get into an argument with her**.
  (*Important* is an adjective of urgency. It is followed by the base [= subjunctive] form, *get.*)
  NOT ~~It was important that he didn't get into an argument with her.~~

- **That it's essential we be happy in life** is a common belief.
- **That he not get into an argument with his wife** was important.

4. Another type of noun clause functions as a **noun complement**.

In formal and academic writing this type of sentence often includes the words *the fact that* or *the belief that*.

- The first thing I learned about happiness is **that there's a big difference between what we think will make us happy and what actually does**.
  (The clause talks about the noun *thing*.)
- There's a common **belief that it's essential for us to be happy in life**.
- The problem in defining happiness is **(the fact) that expectations don't coincide with reality**.

5. Noun phrases can also function as complements. They follow the pattern *It* + adjective + *for* + object pronoun + infinitive. This pattern is common both in writing and in conversation.

Sentences containing noun clauses following adjectives of urgency, necessity, or advice can be restated as noun phrases.

- **It** was **difficult for me to come up** with answers to these questions.

- It was **important that the professor not get into an argument with her**.

  OR

- It was **important for the professor not to get into an argument with her**.

FOCUSED PRACTICE

1 DISCOVER THE GRAMMAR

Part A

Look again at the opening reading. Find and underline all the noun clauses.
Classify them as **noun complements (NC)** *or* **adjective complements (AC)**.

1. There's a common belief that it's essential for us to be happy in life. (NC)

Part B

Find and circle the two noun phrases functioning as adjective complements.

2 A FAMILY

This is a picture of the Brands' living room. Study the picture and then write eight
sentences about it, each containing a noun clause functioning as a complement.
Use the indicated prompts.

1. It's obvious that the Brands enjoy being with each other.
(It's obvious that . . .)

2. _____
(It appears that . . .)

3. _____
(It appears that . . .)

4. _____
(It's clear that . . .)

5. _____
(It's apparent that . . .)

6. _____
(It's possible that . . .)

7. _____
(It's evident that . . .)

8. _____
(It's likely that . . .)

3 **WHAT MAKES YOU HAPPY?**   Grammar Notes 3, 4

Part A

Write four sentences about things that make you happy. In each sentence, use a noun phrase that contains an adjective of urgency, necessity, or advice (**important**, **necessary**, **essential**, **crucial**, *and the like).*

> **EXAMPLE:**
> It's important **for me to have an interesting job**.

Part B

Now write four sentences about things that make someone you know happy— your spouse, a parent, a friend, a sibling, and the like. In each sentence, use a noun clause that contains an adjective of urgency, necessity, or advice.

> **EXAMPLE:**
> It's essential **that my brother have a lot of friends**.

Part C

Share your answers with the class. Do a class tabulation about the things that seem to be necessary to make class members happy.

4 EDITING

For an English class assignment, a student wrote a composition comparing two high school classes. Find and correct the ten errors involving noun clauses and phrases.

Night and Day

I'm in college now, and the other day I got into a discussion about whether ~~was I~~ ^{I was} satisfied with my high school education and whether high school had been a happy time for me. I thought about it for a while and then remembered two classes I took in my senior year that typify my feelings about high school. The two classes were ancient history and Spanish. My motivations for signing up for these two were quite different. I enrolled in history because it was reputed to be a "Mickey Mouse" course that anyone could breeze through. I took Spanish only because it was a requirement. The two classes were as different as night and day.

The history class was taught by Mr. Bolt, the soccer coach. From the start of the semester, it was obvious what the class was going to be a total waste of time. Mr. Bolt made it clear right away that the soccer players going to be his special pets. Just about all we ever did was watch him diagram soccer plays on the chalkboard and listen to him tell stupid jokes. To pass the course, there were only two things that were necessary for you do. One was that you were there every day to laugh at his jokes. The other was that you turn in a take-home midterm and final exam that you mostly copied out of the textbook. At first I was happy in ancient history because I wanted to slide through the class without doing much work. I wasn't learning anything eventually got to me, however.

Mrs. Arellano's Spanish class was 180 degrees away from Mr. Bolt's class. Starting on the first day, Mrs. Arellano made it clear that we be there to learn Spanish. I can still remember what she told us: "If students are going to learn Spanish, or any language, it's absolutely essential for they to speak it. We're going to be doing a lot of speaking in this class." Well, we did speak. We also read, wrote, listened to Spanish music, learned the geography of the Spanish-speaking countries, and even taught our own mini-lessons. The class was hard, and at first some of the students didn't like Mrs. Arellano kept us active for the whole fifty minutes every day. But by the end of the year, most of us could carry on a decent conversation in Spanish.

I didn't think I'd like Spanish very much, but I did. I'm happy that I took Mrs. Arellano's class, and I'm not really very happy to take Mr. Bolt's. It's obvious for schools to need more teachers like Mrs. Arellano.

COMMUNICATION PRACTICE

5 LISTENING

Look at these statements. Then listen to the conversation.

1. It's obvious that this conversation

_____ .

2. It's evident that Mike is going to

_____ .

3. Mike is sure

_____ .

4. It's clear that Mike

_____ .

5. It appears that Carol didn't

_____ .

6. It's clear that Carol doesn't

_____ .

7. It's likely that Mike and Carol

_____ .

Now listen again. Complete each statement.

6 MOODS

Part A

Answer the following questions **True (T)** *or* **False (F)** *according to your opinion.*
Then read the article.

_____ **1.** In general, women's lives are more stressful than men's.

_____ **2.** In general, women are more emotional than men.

_____ **3.** In general, women stay in a bad mood longer than men do.

(continued on next page)

In a Bad Mood—for a Good Reason

By Nancy Stedman

According to a researcher at Harvard University, in any 24-hour period, married women are 50 percent more likely to complain of being in a bad mood than their Y-chromosomed counterparts. The reason, he theorizes, is that married women typically juggle more roles than men do, so they encounter more opportunities for things to go wrong in their lives.

Dr. Ronald C. Kessler, a sociologist in the department of health care policy at Harvard Medical School, and a colleague studied 166 couples who kept diaries of their emotions for six weeks.

Women, Dr. Kessler said, "tend to the home, the plumber, their husband's career, their jobs, and, oh yes, the kids." By contrast, he said, men operate with a narrower focus. "For men, it's, 'How are things at work? The end,'" said Dr. Kessler.

The study was reported in a recent issue of the *Journal of Personality and Social Psychology.*

Dr. Kessler said women also pay more attention to the problems of friends, coworkers, and distant relatives, while men tend to limit their "range of caring" to their spouses and children. "Men's emotional antennae are not spread as wide," he said, adding, "Men get to participate in the good stuff like parties, while their wives pay the price for maintaining social networks."

But the research challenges the idea that women are unhappy more often because they "hold on to bad feelings more," Dr. Kessler said. Women appear to be no more likely than men to remain in foul moods. Wives have more bad days than husbands, said the report, simply "because they experience more frequent daily stressors."

Source: Nancy Stedman, "In a Bad Mood—for a Good Reason," *The New York Times*, December 1, 1998, p. F-7. Reprinted by permission of the author.

Part B

Talk with a partner. Do you agree or disagree with some of the points made in the article? Or are you somewhere in between? Do you think women have more stress in their lives, in general, than men do? Are they unhappy more often than men are? Discuss your answers to the quiz.

7 ESSAY

Write an essay of three to five paragraphs on one of the following topics. Provide supporting details from your own experience to support your ideas.

- Describe your life. Is it basically happy, unhappy, or somewhere in between?
- What does it take to produce a happy life?
- Describe the life of someone you consider happy. What makes it that way?

8 PICTURE DISCUSSION

This picture is an advertisement for life insurance. What does it say or imply about happiness? Why do you think the life insurance company used this picture in its advertisement? Talk with a partner about the picture and speculate about the advertiser's intent.

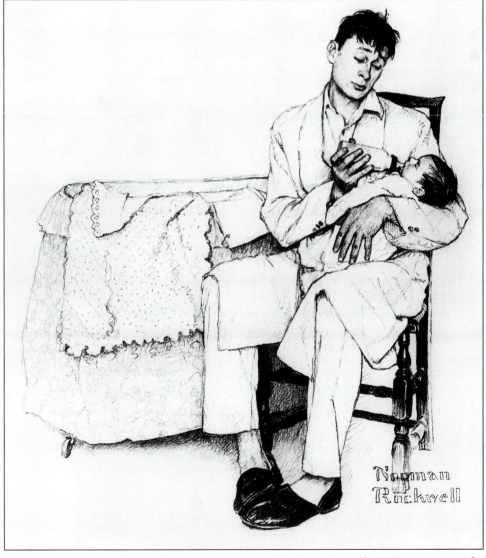

Source: Norman Rockwell: (detail) Massachusetts Mutual "Father Feeding Infant." Photo courtesy of the Normal Rockwell Museum at Stockbridge.

REVIEW OR SELFTEST

I. *Read the conversations and underline each noun clause.*

1. A: I don't know <u>what we should do tonight</u>.

    B: Whatever you want to do is fine with me.

2. A: We haven't decided where we want to go on vacation.

    B: Don't you think Hawaii would be nice?

3. A: How do we decide who wins the prize?

    B: Give the prize to whoever gets the most points.

4. A: Do you think she's guilty?

    B: Well, the fact that she waited so long to contact the police doesn't help

    her case.

5. A: I can't believe what I'm seeing. The Bengals might even win this game.

    B: Yeah, I know. I'm amazed that they've been able to do this well.

6. A: Mr. Brown, I'm sorry to report that I need more time to complete

    the assignment.

    B: That's all right. Take however long you need to do the job well.

7. A: In your view, what is the answer to the problem of violence in schools?

    B: I think that we need to ban weapons of all kinds.

8. A: What is Samantha's problem?

    B: Well, it's clear that she's very unhappy.

II. *Read the letter and correct the eight errors in pronouns that introduce noun clauses.*

November 28

Dear Manny,

    Well, my first month as a literacy volunteer is over, and I feel exhilarated!
~~*That*~~ What *I like best is the chance to work with real people. In the mornings I report to it's called "Open Classroom." I'm assigned to tutor whomever comes in and asks for help. Most of the students are wonderful; sometimes I'm amazed what they're so motivated to learn. In the afternoons I tutor my regular students. I usually work with a lady from Vietnam named Mrs. Tranh. When I started working with her she could hardly read at all, but I'm really impressed by that she's learned. At first I chose the assignments, but now we work on however Mrs. Tranh chooses. If she wants to practice oral reading, that's which we do. If she wants to work on comprehension, we do that for whenever long she wants to do it. Sometimes we spend all afternoon on one thing, but it's very rewarding.*

    Well, that's all for now. Write soon, and I'll do the same.

                            Best,
                            Diane

III. *Complete the conversations with noun clauses, using the prompts given. Begin each noun clause with a word selected from the box.*

that	whoever	where	however	the fact that	whatever

1. A: How long do you want to spend in Buenos Aires?

  B: <u>However long you want to spend</u>   is fine with me.
              a. (long / you / want / spend)

(continued on next page)

2. A: Where's Hattie?

B: I don't know _____. Maybe she's out in the backyard.
    b. (she / be)

3. A: Do you think _____?
    c. (Bill / be / an asset to our firm)

B: Well, _____ says something, I think.
    d. (he / ill a great deal)

4. A: What do you think we need to do about Bill's excessive absences?

B: I think _____ _____.
    e. (we / need / do)   f. (be / necessary)

5. A: Who do you think is behind this rumor?

B: I don't know, but _____ needs a talking to. It's
    g. (it / be)

obvious _____ Ron. He has too much to lose.
    h. (it / not be)

IV. *Look at the pictures. Using the main verbs and clause introducers indicated, write a sentence containing a noun clause to explain each picture.*

(clear / need)

It was clear that the Martins needed
a bigger house.

But can we afford that house? It's kind of expensive.

RESIDENTIAL REALTY

(wonder / if)

_____

_____

3.

(Mrs. Martin's father / ask / where)

_____

_____

4.

(important / that)

_____

_____

5.

(tell / that)

_____

_____

6.

(thrilled / that)

_____

_____

V. *Read the following sentences, all of which deal with education. Circle the letter of the choice that correctly completes each sentence.*

1. ___The fact that___ student test scores have not improved in the last decade suggests that the American educational system is in need of a major overhaul.
   A **Ⓑ** C D

   (A) The fact which   (C) Which

   (B) The fact that   (D) What

(continued on next page)

2. Many educators seem convinced _____ students would
respond favorably to a change in the system.   A B C D

(A) what   (C) that
(B) the fact   (D) whatever

3. _____ America needs now is a two-track program in   A B C D
high schools.

(A) Whatever   (C) That
(B) What   (D) Whichever

4. In the majority of high schools at present, many students are allowed   A B C D
to take _____ courses they want.

(A) whoever   (C) whichever
(B) however   (D) whenever

5. In a two-track system, students would choose after the eighth grade   A B C D
_____ educational track they wanted to study—
academic or vocational.

(A) which   (C) whom
(B) who   (D) when

6. _____ was interested in a college education would   A B C D
study in the academic track.

(A) Whatever   (C) Whomever
(B) Whoever   (D) Whichever

7. _____ wanted to go right into the workplace after   A B C D
graduation would choose the vocational track.

(A) Whoever   (C) Whatever
(B) However   (D) Whomever

8. _____ America is one of only two industrialized   A B C D
nations without a two-track choice is a telling statistic.

(A) The fact which   (C) What
(B) Which   (D) The fact that

9. It is obvious _____ the country needs this educational   A B C D
reform.

(A) what   (C) which
(B) who   (D) that

10. It's important _____ that what they're learning is   A B C D
worthwhile.

(A) the fact that students believe   (C) whatever students believe
(B) for students to believe   (D) however students believe

▶ *To check your answers, go to the Answer Key on page 455.*

FROM GRAMMAR TO WRITING WRITING DIRECT AND INDIRECT SPEECH

Direct speech (or quoted speech) quotes the exact words or thoughts of a speaker. Indirect speech (or reported speech) reports the words or thoughts of a speaker and contains most but not all of that speaker's exact words or thoughts.

Both direct and indirect speech usually occur in noun clauses, normally as direct objects.

> **EXAMPLES:**
>
> direct speech
> Chuck asked Marie, **"Do you think Taylor should go to a private school?"** (The quotation is the direct object of the sentence, answering the question, "What did Chuck ask?")
>
> indirect speech
> Chuck asked Marie **if she thought Taylor should go to a private school**. (The noun clause *if she thought Taylor should go to a private school* is the direct object, answering the question, "What did Chuck ask?")

In direct speech, quotation marks surround the quotation. The reporting verb, such as *said, told,* or *responded*, is followed by a comma if it introduces the quotation. Quotation marks come <u>after</u> a final period, question mark, or exclamation point.

> **EXAMPLES:**
>
> Taylor said**,** "Mom, I want to keep going to public school**."** (statement)
>
> Marie asked Chuck**,** "Can we afford to send Taylor to a private school**?"** (question)
>
> Taylor said to Chuck and Marie**,** "I won't go**!"** (exclamation)

If the reporting statement comes after the quotation, a comma follows the last word of the quotation, and the second set of quotation marks comes after the comma. A period ends the sentence.

> **EXAMPLE:**
>
> "I don't want to go to a private school**,"** Taylor said**.**

If the quotation is a question or an exclamation, that question or exclamation ends with a question mark or exclamation point.

EXAMPLES:

"Taylor, do you like school**?"** asked Aunt Emily.

"I won't go to a private school**!"** Taylor yelled.

If the reporting statement comes within the quotation, each part of the quotation is enclosed in quotation marks. The part of the quotation after the reporting statement does not begin with a capital letter if the remainder of the quotation is not part of a new sentence. Look at the quotation marks, the commas, and the capitalization in this example:

"Ms. Baldwin," **the reporter asked**, "why are you all participating in this demonstration?"

In indirect speech there are no quotation marks. The first word of the indirect speech is not capitalized, and the reporting statement is not followed by a comma. An indirect question does not have a question mark at the end of the sentence. Note that indirect speech is presented as a noun clause and can be introduced by the word *that*. *That* is sometimes omitted in conversation and informal writing.

EXAMPLES:

Taylor said **(that) he wanted to keep going to public school**.

Taylor told his mother **(that) he wanted to keep going to public school**.

Marie asked Chuck **if they could afford to send Taylor to a private school**.

Taylor told Chuck and Marie **(that) he wouldn't go**.

 Punctuate the following sentences in direct speech. Add capital letters if necessary.

1. "Dad, I want to quit school and go to work," Jim murmured.

2. Sally, how would you evaluate your education the reporter queried

3. I absolutely love going to school Sally responded (exclamation)

4. Jim, Frank said, you're crazy if you think it's going to be easy to get a job

5. Frank said Jim, don't be a fool (exclamation)

6. The union spokesperson asked the management team when are you going to start taking our concerns seriously

2 *Correct the capitalization and punctuation of the following examples of indirect speech.*

1. Union spokesperson Frances Baldwin said/ that the management had even refused to talk to them.

2. Company President Bates responded that "There was simply no money for salary raises."

3. TV reporter Joan Matthews asked Fumiko if, she agreed with Janice that cloning should be banned.

4. Frank asked Jim, What he would do if he couldn't find a job after he quit school?

5. Professor Martin asked Zeya if she intended to go to graduate school after earning her bachelor's degree

---

In conversation and informal writing, the most common reporting verbs in both direct and indirect speech are *say, tell,* and *ask.* In more formal writing, the following reporting verbs are often used: *report, respond, query, wonder, confess, claim, maintain, add,* and *comment.*

> Chairman Bates **maintained** that the school district had no money to raise teachers' salaries. (*argued*)

> The union representative **claimed** that the company C.E.O. hadn't considered the union's demands. (*expressed the opinion*)

3 *In the following paragraph, change each instance of **said** to another reporting verb from the box.*

~~responded~~   claimed   added   commented   maintained

Reporter Jennifer Goodenough asked Heidi Dennison what the single most enjoyable experience in her Peace Corps Service had been. Heidi ~~said~~ *responded* that it had **1.** been the vacation she had taken to Kenya, Tanzania, and Uganda at the end of her first year. Jennifer <u>said</u> that she was surprised at Heidi's answer because she had **2.** expected her to mention one of her accomplishments in Nigeria. Many people <u>said</u> **3.** the purpose of the Peace Corps was to give Americans the chance to take vacations in exotic places. But Heidi <u>said</u> that the chance to learn about other countries was a **4.** valuable learning experience. She <u>said</u> that she thought it would contribute to **5.** international understanding in the long run.

4 *Rewrite the following paragraph, changing all indirect speech to direct speech.*

At dinner one night, Marie ~~told~~ Chuck_{said,} ~~that she thought~~ it _{I think} ~~had been~~ _{was} a mistake to put Taylor in a private school. Chuck asked Marie what had made her come to that conclusion. Marie responded that Taylor didn't have any real friends in the school. She added that his teacher had said he'd seemed miserable for quite a long time. Chuck said that he thought Marie was probably right. He asked her if they should switch him to the public school.

1. At dinner one night, Marie said, "Chuck, I think it was a mistake to put Taylor in a private school."

2. _____

_____

3. _____

_____

4. _____

_____

5. _____

_____

6. _____

_____

5 **APPLY IT TO YOUR WRITING**

*Interview a friend, classmate, or a relative about a short, humorous incident that happened to the person. Write down the person's answers. Then write a one-paragraph record of the conversation in direct speech, paying particular attention to correctness in the use of commas and quotation marks. Use the verbs **asked, said, told**, and any others that seem appropriate. Then rewrite the paragraph in indirect speech. Exchange papers with a partner. Proofread each other's paper and discuss the results. Then submit both of your paragraphs to the teacher.*

REVIEW OR SELFTEST
ANSWER KEY

I.
1. **B:** Whatever you want to do
2. **A:** where we want to go on vacation

   B: Hawaii would be nice
3. **A:** who wins the prize

   B: whoever gets the most points
4. **A:** she's guilty

   B: the fact that she waited so long to contact the police
5. **A:** what I'm seeing

   B: that they've been able to do this well
6. **A:** that I need more time to complete the assignment

   B: however long you need to do the job well
7. **B:** that we need to ban weapons of all kinds
8. **B:** that she's very unhappy

II.

. . . I report to it's called . . .	→	. . . I report to what's called . . .
. . . to tutor whomever comes in . . .	→	. . . to tutor whoever comes in . . .
. . . I'm amazed what they're so motivated . . .	→	. . . I'm amazed that they're so motivated . . .
. . . impressed by that she's learned . . .	→	. . . impressed by what she's learned . . .
. . . work on however Mrs. Tranh chooses . . .	→	. . . work on whatever Mrs. Tranh chooses . . .
. . . that's which we do . . .	→	. . . that's what we do . . .
. . . for whenever long . . .	→	. . . for however long . . .

III.
b. where she is
c. that Bill is an asset to our firm
d. the fact that he's ill a great deal
e. that we need to do
f. whatever is necessary
g. whoever it is
h. that it isn't / is not Ron

IV. Possible Answers
2. They wondered if they could afford this house.
3. Mrs. Martin's father asked where the house was located.
4. Mrs. Martin's mother said it was important that they have the house they needed.
5. Mrs. Martin's father told them that they would help with the down payment.
6. They're thrilled that they were able to get the house they wanted.

V.

2. C	5. A	8. D
3. B	6. B	9. D
4. C	7. A	10. B

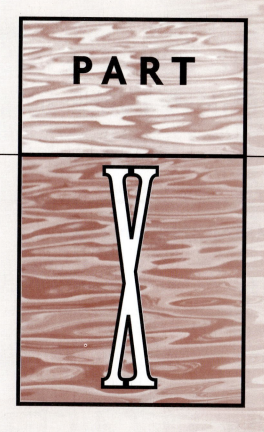

PART

X

UNREAL CONDITIONS

24 UNREAL CONDITIONALS AND OTHER WAYS TO EXPRESS UNREALITY

GRAMMAR **IN CONTEXT**

QUESTIONS TO CONSIDER

1. What do you understand by "intuition"? Do you believe in intuition?

2. Have you had any experiences in which your or someone else's intuition proved correct?

Read the story and think about the questions.

Intuition

It was a sweltering day. Thain and Aurora were driving down Maple Street, looking for a yard sale, when they spotted the old man. Waving at them with a halfhearted gesture, he looked as though he hadn't eaten for days.

"Nine-thirty in the morning, and it's already beastly hot. I wish I had an iced tea right now. Open your window, will you, Thain?"

"Wow! Look at that old man, Aurora. Boy, I'd sure get out of this heat if I were him. . . . Pull over, will you? Let's give him a ride. He's going to faint if he doesn't get out of the sun."

"Thain, I wish you would stop taking pity on every weirdo you see. He's probably an ax murderer. I bet he'll kill us and steal the car if we pick him up."

"I don't think so. He looks harmless to me—just a poor old guy. He's acting as if he's sick."

"But Sweetie, we've got to get to that yard sale. There won't be anything worth buying if we don't get there soon. If only no one buys that chest of drawers they

advertised."

"My male intuition is telling me we'd better stop."

"If I had a nickel for all the times we've done things because of your male intuition, I'd be a rich woman. Aren't females supposed to have the intuition, anyway? OK. I just hope we don't end up in the newspaper headlines. I can see it all now: YOUNG MARRIED COUPLE MUTILATED BY SERIAL KILLER!"

They pulled up to the curb in front of the old man. "Need some help, sir?" Thain asked.

The old man smiled. "Yes, thank you. Could you take me to a pharmacy? I'm diabetic and I've run out of medicine. I'm on a trip around the country, but I keep forgetting to buy enough insulin. If I don't take my

YARD SALE
SAT. 10-5
18 Lily Pond
Lane

Intuition

medicine regularly, I go into shock. . . . If only I weren't so forgetful."

They found a pharmacy and got the insulin. Back in the car, the old man said, "Now, if you can just take me to the bus station, I'll be on my way." Aurora frowned. Thain said, "Sure. We can do that." At the bus station, they helped the old man out of the car. "Can you tell me your names and your address? When I get back home, I'll send you a token of my appreciation." They gave him their names and address, said good-bye, and proceeded to the yard sale.

As Aurora had predicted, all of the good merchandise had been sold. "I wish we'd been able to get here in time to buy that chest of drawers," she said, "but I'm glad we stopped for the old guy. He did need our help. I'll be surprised if we ever hear from him, though. You don't really believe all that about his taking a trip around the country, do you, Thain?"

In a few days they had forgotten about the incident. Three months later they returned from a short vacation, and Aurora was going through the pile of mail that had accumulated in their absence. She opened a long envelope with no return address.

"What in the world? Thain, come here and look at this!" There was a letter inside, neatly typed, which said,

Dear Thain and Aurora,

I finished my trip around the country and had a marvelous time. I'm now back at home and won't be traveling anymore, I don't think. I met some wonderful people in my travels, the two of you among them.

Thank you for your kindness to a forgetful old man. If you hadn't come along when you did and taken me to the pharmacy, I might have died. At the very least, I would have become quite ill. I wish there had been time for us to get to know one another. If I had been fortunate to have any children of my own, I couldn't have had any nicer ones than you two. At any rate, I am enclosing a token of my gratitude. My warmest regards,

Quentin Wilkerson

Something fluttered out of a second sheet of folded paper. It was a check for fifty thousand dollars.

UNDERSTANDING MEANING FROM CONTEXT

Look at the following sentences from the reading. Write each italicized word or phrase in another way.

1. It was a *sweltering* day.

   _____

2. Thain, I wish you would stop taking pity on every *weirdo* you see.

   _____

3. YOUNG MARRIED COUPLE *MUTILATED* BY SERIAL KILLER!

   _____

4. When I get back home, I'll send you a *token* of my appreciation.

   _____

5. Something *fluttered* out of a second sheet of folded paper.

   _____

GRAMMAR **PRESENTATION**
UNREAL CONDITIONALS AND OTHER WAYS TO EXPRESS UNREALITY

UNREAL CONDITIONALS
If I **had** a nickel for all the times we've done things because of your male intuition, I**'d be** a rich woman.
If you **hadn't come** along when you did and **taken** me to the pharmacy, I **might have died**.
At the very least, I **would have become** quite ill.

OTHER WAYS TO EXPRESS UNREALITY
I **wish** (that) you **would stop** taking pity on every weirdo you see.
I **wish** (that) there **had been** time for us to get to know one another.
If only I **weren't** so forgetful.
. . . he looked **as though** he **hadn't eaten** for days.

NOTES

EXAMPLES

1. Conditional sentences consist of two clauses, a dependent *if*-clause and an independent result clause.

Real conditionals are sentences that describe situations that are true or likely in the present or future. In present-time situations, simple present tense verbs are used to describe habitual or regularly occurring actions.

In future-time situations, the simple present tense is used in the *if*-clause and the future with *will* or *be going to* in the result clause.

Unreal conditionals are sentences that describe situations that are untrue—contrary to fact. In present-time situations, use the simple past tense form of the verb in the *if*-clause and *would*, *could*, or *might* plus the base form of the verb in the result clause.

Note that when you use the simple past tense verb form in a conditional sentence, it does not have past meaning.

- If I **don't take** my medicine regulary, I **go** into shock (a regularly occurring action).

- There **won't be** anything worth buying if we **don't get** there soon.

- If I **had** a nickel for all the times we've done things because of your male intuition, **I'd be** a rich woman. (Contrary to fact: *Aurora doesn't have a nickel for every time this has happened, and she's not a rich woman.*)

- Boy, **I'd** sure **get** out of this heat if I **were** him.

▶ **BE CAREFUL!** Remember to use *were* for all persons with the verb *be*.

To express contrary-to-fact ideas in past time, use *had* plus a past participle in the *if*-clause, and use *would, could,* or *might* + *have* + past participle in the result clause.

- If you **hadn't come** along when you did and **taken** me to the pharmacy, I **might have died**. (Contrary to fact: *You did come along.*)
  NOT ~~If you wouldn't have come along when you did and taken me to the pharmacy, I might have died.~~

USAGE NOTE: You will hear some native speakers use *would have* in the *if*-clause. However, this usage is not acceptable in formal speaking or writing. Use *would have* only in the result clause.

2. Notice the difference between ***hope*** and ***wish***. *Hope* is used to express a desire or an expectation about something considered real, possible, or probable. *Wish* is used to express a desire or a regret about something that is not the case (contrary to fact). The speaker wants a different situation but does not know if the situation will change or not. *Hope* and *wish* are followed by noun clauses. In conversation, the word *that* is often omitted.

- I **hope** (that) the sun **comes** out later.
- I **wish** (that) it **weren't raining** right now.

Use *hope* + the simple present to describe a present or future desire or expectation.

- Mr. Wilkerson is back home now. I **hope** he's happy. (present)
- I just **hope** we **don't end up** in the newspaper headlines. (future)

Use *wish* + a simple past or past progressive verb to express a desire for a different present state.

- I **wish** I **had** an iced tea right now.
  (Contrary to fact: *Aurora doesn't have an iced tea right now.*)

Use *wish* + *would* + the base form to express a desire for a change in a habitual action in the present or future.

- Thain, I **wish** you **would stop** taking pity on every weirdo you see.
  (*This is what Aurora wants, but she doesn't know if Thain will change his behavior or not.*)

(continued on next page)

Use *wish* + *would* or *could* + the base form to express a desire for a different situation in the future.	• I wish we **could visit** Mr. Wilkerson next summer. • I wish Mr. Wilkerson **would come back and visit** us.
Use *wish* + *had* + past participle to express a desire about a past action or state.	• I **wish** there **had been** time for us to get to know one another. (Contrary to fact: *There wasn't time.*)

3. The phrase *if only* has meanings similar to those of *wish* and *hope*.

Use the simple past tense form after *if only* to express a wish about something that is contrary to fact at present.	• **If only** I **weren't** so forgetful. (Contrary to fact: *The man is forgetful.*)
Use *had* + a past participle after *if only* to express a wish that something had happened differently in the past.	• **If only** I **had remembered** to buy enough insulin. (Contrary to fact: *The man didn't remember to buy enough insulin.*)
Use a simple present tense after *if only* to express a hope that something will be true in the present or future.	• **If only** no one **buys** that chest of drawers they advertised. (*Aurora thinks this is possible.*)

4. *As if* and *as though* are often followed by past verb forms to express situations that appear contrary to fact.

• Waving at them with a halfhearted gesture, he looked **as though** he **hadn't eaten** for days. (Probably contrary to fact—*no doubt he had eaten recently.*)

When *as if* and *as though* are followed by simple present tense forms or *will* + base form, they express situations that appear to be true.

• He's acting **as if** he**'s** sick. (*He probably is sick.*)

FOCUSED PRACTICE

 DISCOVER THE GRAMMAR

Look again at the opening reading. Answer the following questions.

Part A

Find the one real conditional sentence that does not show future meaning. Write it here.

1. _____

Find the four real conditional sentences that show future meaning. Write them here.

2. He's going to faint if he doesn't get out of the sun._____

3. _____

4. _____

5. _____

*Find the two sentences with **if only**. Rewrite them using **wish** in one sentence and **hope** in the other.*

6. _____

7. _____

Find two present unreal conditional sentences. Write them here.

8. _____

9. _____

Find the three past unreal conditional sentences. Write them here.

10. _____

11. _____

12. _____

*Rewrite this sentence, replacing **'d been able** with another structure with the same basic meaning.*

I wish we*'d been able* to get here in time to buy that chest of drawers.

13. _____

What would this sentence mean if **as if he's sick** *were changed to* **as if he were sick**?

He's acting as if he's sick.

14. _____

Part B

How do you think the story ended? Would it have been ethical for Thain and Aurora to cash the check Mr. Wilkerson sent them? Why or why not? Write an ending to the story. Read your ending to the class.

② HOPES AND WISHES

Grammar Note 2

Look at the pictures. Write a sentence for each, using **wish** *or* **hope**, *as indicated.*

1.

(hope)

They hope it doesn't rain. (or)

They hope it won't rain.

2.

(wish)

_____

_____

3.

(hope)

_____

_____

4.

(wish)

_____

_____

5.

(wish)

_____

_____

6.

(hope)

_____

_____

 TRAGEDY   Grammar Notes 1–2

Part A

*Read and think about the poem. Then write past conditional sentences based on the
verbs given. Use* **would** *unless another auxiliary, such as* **might** *or* **could***, is given.*

> ## "Out, Out—"
>
> ### ROBERT FROST
>
> The buzz-saw snarled and rattled in the yard
> And made dust and dropped stove-length sticks of wood,
> Sweet-scented stuff when the breeze drew across it.
> And from there those that lifted eyes could count
> Five mountain ranges one behind the other
> Under the sunset far into Vermont.
> And the saw snarled and rattled, snarled and rattled,
> As it ran light, or had to bear a load.
> And nothing happened: day was all but done.
> Call it a day, I wish they might have said
> To please the boy by giving him the half hour
> That a boy counts so much when saved from work.
> His sister stood beside them in her apron
> To tell them "Supper." At the word, the saw,
> As if to prove saws knew what supper meant,
> Leaped out at the boy's hand, or seemed to leap—
> He must have given the hand. However it was,
> Neither refused the meeting. But the hand!
> The boy's first outcry was a rueful laugh,

(continued on next page)

As he swung toward them holding up the hand,
Half in appeal, but half as if to keep
The life from spilling. Then the boy saw all—
Since he was old enough to know, big boy
Doing a man's work, though a child at heart—
He saw all spoiled. "Don't let him cut my hand off—
The doctor when he comes. Don't let him, sister!"
So. But the hand was gone already.
The doctor put him in the dark of ether.
He lay and puffed his lips out with his breath.
And then—the watcher at his pulse took fright.
No one believed. They listened at his heart.
Little—less—nothing!—and that ended it.
No more to build on there. And they, since they
Were not the one dead, turned to their affairs. ❀

1. If the boy had been in school, he wouldn't have died.
    (the boy / be / in school / he / not / die)

2. _____
    (the doctor / arrive / sooner / he / might / be able / save / the boy)

3. _____
    (the boy / not / doing / a man's job / he / probably / not / be killed)

4. _____
    (the saw / cut / the boy's finger instead of his hand / the boy / could probably / survive)

5. _____
    (the boy / might / not / be / cut by the saw / the sister / not / say "Supper" / at a crucial moment)

6. _____
    (the work boss / say / "Call it a day" / the boy / escape / his fate)

Part B

Now assume that the time is the present and that the accident has just happened. Write sentences about what certain people probably **wish** *or* **hope***.*

7. The sister probably wishes (that) everyone had decided to quit work early.
    (the sister / probably / wish / everyone / decide / quit work early)

8. _____
    (the doctor / probably wish / he / arrive sooner)

9. _____
    (the boy's parents / probably wish / they / not allow / the boy / work at a man's job)

10. _____
    (other parents / probably hope / this kind of accident / not happen / to their children)

④ WHAT WOULD HAVE HAPPENED IF . . . ? Grammar Note 1

Read the story. Then write six past unreal conditional sentences about what would or might have happened if events had occurred differently.

Stella and Hideyuki were at the new racetrack one afternoon and were standing near a betting window. They hadn't even planned on going to the track except that their friends had invited them to meet there and then go out for dinner. The friends hadn't shown up, though, and now Stella and Hideyuki were about to leave the racetrack and go home. Neither of them had ever bet on a horse before and had no intention of doing so this time. There's a first time for everything, however, and it suddenly occurred to Stella that this was that first time. "As long as we're here, we might as well bet on a horse," she said. Hideyuki didn't want to bet, but Stella twisted his arm. Finally he agreed. "But what horse shall we bet on? I don't have any idea," he said. Stella looked at the racing form, trying to figure out which one to choose. She scanned the list of races previously won by the horses. Hideyuki said, "Let's bet on the one that's won the most." Stella thought for a minute and then said, "No, let's not. Let's bet on Static. He's the one that's won the fewest races. We're only betting twenty dollars." Hideyuki said, "Why? That one is the least likely to win." "I don't know," said Stella. "I just have an inkling." "Oh, all right," Hideyuki grumbled, and went to the betting window to place the bet. Then they proceeded to the stands to watch the race. At first it looked like Hideyuki's original idea had been correct, for Magic Dancer, the favored horse, was running in the lead. In the last minute, though, Static moved up suddenly and finally passed Magic Dancer at the finish line. Stella and Hideyuki couldn't believe their eyes. They'd won ten thousand dollars.

1. _____

2. _____

3. _____

4. _____

5. _____

6. _____

5 EDITING

Read the following diary entry. Correct the ten errors in conditionals.

June 4

Dear Diary,

                                                  had

This has been one of those days when I wish I ~~would have~~ stayed in
bed. It started at 7:30 this morning when Trudy called me up and
asked me for "a little favor." She's always asking me to do things for
her and never wants to take any responsibility for herself. She acts as
if the world owe her a living. I wish she won't do that. Today she
wanted me to take her to the mall because she had to get her mother a
birthday present. I told her I had to be downtown at ten A.M. for a job
interview, and she said it wouldn't take long to drive to the mall and
I'd have plenty of time to get downtown. I gave in and agreed to take
her, but something told me I shouldn't. If I would have listened to
my inner voice, I might had a job today. When we were on the freeway,
there was a major accident, and traffic was tied up for over an hour.
By the time we got to the mall, it was ten-thirty, so I missed my job
interview. I think I probably would get the job if I would have managed
to make it to the interview, because my qualifications are good. If only
I wouldn't have listened to Trudy! I just hope she never asked me to do
something like this again, and if she does, I hope I didn't agree.

COMMUNICATION PRACTICE

6 LISTENING

Listen to the conversation between two women who are members of Warm Hearts, *a matchmaking service. Then listen again. For each item given, circle the letter of the sentence that explains the meaning of certain sentences you heard.*

1. **a.** Rosa has met some interesting people.
   b. Rosa hasn't met any interesting people.

2. **a.** Phyllis followed her gut feeling.
   b. Phyllis didn't follow gut feeling.

3. **a.** Phyllis went out with Les.
   b. Phyllis went out with Wayne.

4. **a.** Phyllis didn't pay attention to her intuition.
   b. Phyllis did pay attention to her intuition.

5. **a.** Phyllis is in a good relationship now.
   b. Phyllis isn't in a good relationship now.

6. **a.** Wayne seemed to think he was Phyllis's boss.
   b. Wayne didn't seem to think he was Phyllis's boss.

7 **a.** Phyllis thinks it's possible or likely that Wayne is gone for good.
   b. Phyllis thinks it's unlikely or improbable that Wayne is gone for good.

8. **a.** Phyllis doesn't regard herself as a coward.
   b. Phyllis regards herself as a coward.

9. **a.** Rosa thinks Phyllis puts herself down too much.
   b. Rosa doesn't think Phyllis puts herself down too much.

10. **a.** Phyllis thinks it's possible that Les hasn't found someone else.
    b. Phyllis is sure that Les has found someone else.

7 THE CONDITIONAL GAME

Divide into two teams. Each team uses the prompts to construct eight conditional questions, four in the present and four in the past. Then each team creates two questions of its own, for a total of ten questions. The other team guesses the person or thing referred to. Score points.

> **EXAMPLE:** What / doing / if / you / spelunking
> **A:** What would you be doing if you were spelunking?
> **B:** We'd be exploring a cave.

(continued on next page)

Team A's Prompts

1. Where / be / if / you / in the capital of Honduras

2. Who / be / if / you / the Secretary-General of the United Nations

3. Where / be traveling / if / the monetary unit / the won

4. Where / be / if / visiting Angkor Wat

5. Who / been / if / the emperor of France in 1802

6. Who / been / if / the first prime minister of India

7. What country / been from / if / Marco Polo

8. What mountain / climbed / if / with Edmund Hillary and Tenzing Norgay

Team B's Prompts

1. Who / be / if / the president of Mexico

2. Where / be traveling / if / in Machu Picchu

3. What / be / if / the largest mammal

4. What country / be in / if / standing and looking at Angel Falls

5. Who / been / if / the inventor of the telephone

6. What kind of creature / been / if / a brontosaurus

7. What / been your occupation / if / Genghis Khan

8. Who / been / if / Siddartha Gautama

8 ESSAY

Write an essay of at least three paragraphs about a time when you ignored your intuition and inner "gut" feelings and opted instead for a rational decision that turned out unsuccessfully. Describe your original intuitive feelings, explain why you ignored them, and speculate on what would or might have happened if you had acted intuitively. Use conditional sentences and clauses with **wish** *and* **hope** *where appropriate.*

9 PICTURE DISCUSSION

Work with a partner. Discuss the situation. In the first picture, what does the wife probably wish? What does she hope? In the second picture, what has happened? What do the children probably hope? What does the husband probably wish? What would have happened if they'd bought the more expensive tent?

THE SUBJUNCTIVE; INVERTED AND IMPLIED CONDITIONALS

GRAMMAR IN CONTEXT

QUESTIONS TO CONSIDER

1. In your opinion, what is the difference between being assertive and being aggressive?

2. Do you agree with the saying "Don't say yes when you mean no"?

Read the letter to the advice columnist and the columnist's response.

*Ask*Pamela . . .

Dear Pamela,

I've always been considered a "nice person," but I guess you could also call me "a soft touch." A year ago my husband's sister, Sarah, was in a desperate situation and needed a thousand dollars immediately to pay off a loan she had defaulted on. She asked us to lend her the money. At first I suggested that she go through the usual channels and get a bank loan. She said she'd tried that and had been turned down. She pressured my husband for a loan, and he pressured me. Sarah assured us that if we lent her the money, she would pay it back with interest. I gave in and advanced her a thousand dollars from my own account, but I shouldn't have. In fact, had I known what was going to happen, I never would have said yes. We didn't put anything in writing, and Sarah hasn't paid us a red cent. I am extremely angry about this, but whenever I mention it to Carl, my husband, he says that Sarah suffers from low self-esteem and is going through a rough time right now. And, he says, it's important that we keep peace in the family. Were I to confront Sarah, he says, it would be the straw that broke the camel's back. Pamela, what should I do? What if I confront her and it ends up being a blow to her self-esteem or it causes trouble in the family?

Furious in Frankfort

Dear Furious,

Sweetie, it's one thing to be a nice person, but it's another to be a doormat. It sounds like you let people take advantage of you. If so, I'd say it's time you got some assertiveness training. Without it, you'll just keep letting people tell you what to do. In my view, you should have insisted that Sarah sign a notarized agreement spelling out the terms of repayment. It's too late for that now, though, so I recommend that you arrange a meeting between yourself and Sarah. And, if I were you, I wouldn't worry too much about Sarah's self-esteem. Leave Carl out of it. Call Sarah and ask her to meet you for lunch at a restaurant. At the lunch meeting, tell her calmly but in no uncertain terms that you're angry and that this thing has gone far enough. Insist that she start making immediate repayments. Should she balk at what you're saying or mention Carl, simply tell her that this is between you and her, that you don't want family squabbles, and that there won't be any as long as she makes the payments. Make it clear that she must make the payments; if not, you'll take her to small claims court. It's essential that Sarah understand you're serious; otherwise, she'll simply go on taking advantage of you. Tell Carl what you've done after you've met with Sarah. You don't need to get angry. Just say that it was your money that was lent, that this is the way things are going to be from now on, and that you'd rather the two of you didn't get into a fight about it. Then look around for a course in assertiveness. With a little work, you can learn not to be a wimp. Good luck, and be calm but courageous!

Pamela

UNDERSTANDING MEANING FROM CONTEXT

Find words or phrases from the reading equivalent in meaning to each of the following:

1. a person easily taken advantage of (letter 1)

   _____

2. not even a tiny amount of money (letter 1)

   _____

3. the situation that finally caused a disaster (letter 1)

   _____

4. a person who lets others control him or her (Find two expressions for this.) (letter 2)

   a. _____

   b. _____

5. small fights or quarrels (letter 2)

   _____

GRAMMAR **PRESENTATION**
THE SUBJUNCTIVE; INVERTED AND IMPLIED CONDITIONALS

SUBJUNCTIVE FOLLOWING CERTAIN VERBS AND ADJECTIVES

At first I **suggested** that she **go** through the usual channels and get a bank loan.

It**'s essential** that Sarah **understand** you're serious.

You**'d rather** the two of you **didn't get** into a fight about it.

I'd say it**'s time** you **got** some assertiveness training.

INVERSION

In fact, **had I** known what was going to happen, I never would have said yes.

Were I to confront Sarah, he says, it would be the straw that broke the camel's back.

Should she balk at what you're saying or mention Carl, simply tell her that this is between you and her.

IMPLIED CONDITIONALS

It sounds like you let people take advantage of you. **If so**, I'd say it's time you got some assertiveness training.

Without it, you'll just keep letting people tell you what to do.

What if I confront her and it ends up being a blow to her self-esteem?

NOTES

1. The **subjunctive form** (= the base form) of the verb is used in noun clauses following verbs or adjectives of urgency, necessity, and advice. It is impossible to know whether the action in the noun clause will ever occur.

EXAMPLES

- At first I **suggested** that she **go** through the usual channels and get a bank loan.
  NOT I suggested that she went . . .

- It's **essential** that Sarah **understand** you're serious . . .
  NOT It's essential that Sarah understands . . .

▶ **BE CAREFUL!** Note that the base form is used regardless of whether the main verb is in the present or past.

Common **verbs of urgency**, **necessity**, and **advice** that take the subjunctive are *demand, suggest, insist*, and *recommend*. See Appendix 21 on page A-10.

Note that some verbs often take the subjunctive but can also occur in the pattern verb + object + infinitive. These verbs include *ask, order, require*, and *urge*.

Common **adjectives of urgency**, **necessity**, and **advice** that take the subjunctive are *essential, necessary, advisable*, and *important*. See Appendix 21 on page A-10.

- She **asked** that **we lend** her the money.

  OR

- She **asked us to lend** her the money.

---

2. You can express an unreal condition by deleting *if* and inverting the auxiliaries *had, were*, or *should* and the subject in an *if*-clause.

- In fact, **had I known** what was going to happen, I never would have said yes. *(If I had known . . .)*
- **Were I to confront** Sarah, he says, it would be the straw that broke the camel's back. *(If I were to confront . . .)*

---

3. Unreal and real conditionals are sometimes implied rather than stated directly with an *if*-clause and a result clause. **Implied conditionals** often use the following phrases and words: *if so, if not, otherwise, with, without*, and *what if*.

- It sounds like you let people take advantage of you. **If so**, I'd say it's time you got some assertiveness training. *(If you let people take advantage of you . . .)*
- **Without it**, you'll just keep letting people tell you what to do. *(If you don't get some assertiveness training . . .)*

---

4. Two commonly used expressions, ***it's time*** and ***would rather***, are often followed by the subjunctive. After these two expressions, the verb form is usually the simple past rather than the base form.

- I'd say **it's time** you **got** some assertiveness training.
- You**'d rather** the two of you **didn't get** into a fight about it.

FOCUSED PRACTICE

 DISCOVER THE GRAMMAR Grammar Notes 1–4

Part A

Look again at the opening reading. Find six sentences containing subjunctive verb forms in which a main verb is followed by the base form of another verb. Find two sentences in which the main verb is followed by the past form of another verb. On a separate piece of paper, write the eight sentences containing subjunctive usage.

1. I suggested that she go through . . .

Part B

Find the three inverted conditionals in the opening reading. Write them here, and then rewrite them using normal word order.

1. Had I known . . . / If I had known . . .

2. _____

3. _____

Part C

There are six implied conditionals in the opening reading. On a separate piece of paper, write the parts of the sentences in which they occur and the longer conditionals which they imply.

1. What if I confront her . . . / What would happen if I confronted her . . .

Part D

Could each of the following sentences be correctly restated as the sentence in parentheses? Why or why not?

1. You should have insisted that Sarah sign a notarized agreement. (You should have insisted Sarah to sign a notarized agreement.)

   No. "Insist" is followed only by the base form.

2. I recommend that you arrange a meeting between yourself and Sarah. (I recommend you to arrange a meeting between yourself and Sarah.)

   _____

3. Call Sarah and ask her to meet you for lunch at a restaurant. (Call Sarah and ask that she meet you for lunch at a restaurant.)

   _____

4. Tell Carl you'd rather the two of you didn't get into a fight about it. (Tell Carl you'd rather the two of you aren't getting into a fight about it.)

   _____

2 GROWING UP

Complete the sentences with past forms of the indicated verbs after **what if**, **would rather**, *as if*, *and* **it's time**.

DAD: Liz, the swim meet starts in an hour. It's time we _____left_____.
1. (leave)

LIZ: Dad, can't I just go by myself? I'd rather you and Mom _____ me drive.
2. (let)

I do have my license, you know.

DAD: Liz, it's a dangerous world out there. What if you _____ into
3. (get)

an accident?

LIZ: Dad, I'm sixteen years old. It's time you and Mom _____ treating me
4. (start)

like an adult.

DAD: You're not an adult yet, Liz.

LIZ: OK, maybe not, but you treat me as if I _____ a baby. It's embarrassing,
5. (be)

always getting dropped off.

DAD: Hmm. All right. Do you really think you can handle it?

LIZ: Of course, Dad.

3 JOB HUNTING

Fill in the blanks in the story with items from the box.

if so	if not	with
otherwise	~~had she known~~	were she to have stayed

Helen Hilliard had recently moved to Atlanta from Ponders, the small town where she

had grown up. ___Had she known___ how difficult it would be to find employment, she might
1.

have stayed in her hometown. She loved the big city, though, and she felt that,

_____ in Ponders, she would have fallen into a rut that she would never
2.

escape from. The only problem was that Helen needed to find a job soon;

_____, she wouldn't be able to pay next month's rent, and she'd have to go
3.

back to Ponders.

(continued on next page)

The trouble was, she was shy about asking for work. One day Helen was wandering around downtown, feeling that _____ a bit of luck she might find something.
4.
She saw a pleasant-looking florist's shop. Maybe they were hiring. _____, she
5.
might get a job. _____, she wouldn't lose anything by going in and asking.
6.
Without even thinking further, she walked in.

"I'm Helen Hilliard, and I was wondering whether you were doing any hiring. I have a lot of experience with flowers and gardening."

The manager said, "Actually, we do need someone to work part-time. I was just going to put up a sign in the window. Tell me more about your experience."

Helen got the job.

Now rewrite the phrase in each blank above with an **if**-clause that restates the meaning.

7. _Had she known / If she had known_ _____
(she / know)

8. _____
(she / stay)

9. _____
(she / not / find / work)

10. _____
(she / have)

11. _____
(they / be / hiring)

12. _____
(they / not / be / hiring)

④ AGGRESSIVE OR ASSERTIVE?   Grammar Notes 1, 4

Look at the pictures on page 479. Using the suggested verb or expression in each case, write a sentence containing a subjunctive to describe each situation.

1.

(demanded)

The boss demanded (that)

somebody turn off the fan.

2.

(suggested)

3.

(insisting)

4.

(recommends)

5.

(it's time)

6.

(she'd rather)

5 EDITING

Read the letter and correct the eight verb errors.

December 10

Dear April,

I wanted to write and fill you in on what's been happening since I left Ponders.
                                                                        go
I finally got a job! Remember when you suggested I just ~~went~~ walking around,

getting a sense of what Atlanta was like? A few weeks ago I was really getting

worried, and I had spent almost all the money I had saved up to tide me over until

I found work. I had gotten to the point where it was absolutely essential that I found

something or just came home. So I decided to follow your advice. Had I know how

easy this would be, I would have tried it in the first week I was here. I started

walking around in the downtown area, and before I knew it, I saw a beautiful little

florist's shop. I walked right in as if I have courage and experience and asked

whether they needed anyone. Can you believe that they did?

I was really happy in my job until my boss hired a new assistant manager who

has been making my life miserable. He treats me as if I be his personal slave. I took

this job to work with plants, not to serve him coffee. I think it's time I'm telling him

where I stand.

I have a few days off for the holidays. What if I had come home as a surprise to

Mom and Dad? Could we plan some kind of party? Write and let me know, OK?

Love, Helen

COMMUNICATION PRACTICE

6 LISTENING 1

Part A

Read these questions. Then listen to the radio commercial on assertiveness training and answer the questions.

1. How many times has your friend asked you to baby-sit? _____

2. What time was it the last time this happened? _____

3. Under what conditions would you not have answered the phone?

_____

4. Why couldn't Mary use a day care service? _____

5. What did you swear you wouldn't do? _____

6. According to the ad, how are you feeling now? _____

7. What is the name of the company offering this service? _____

8. What if you're not satisfied with their service? _____

Part B

Listen to the commercial again. Write equivalent ways of saying the following.

1. asked you to baby-sit her children _____

2. if you had known . . . _____

3. insist on her coming and picking up her kids _____

4. suggested Mary's looking into day care _____

5. treats you like her slave _____

6. if this sounds like you _____

7. if you get a little bit of practice _____

7 LISTENING 2

Read these statements. Then listen to a segment of the radio talk show Wimp No More.

_____ **1.** Callers are supposed to turn down their radios when they're on the air.

_____ **2.** Mildred's mother-in-law takes Buddy shopping every day.

(continued on next page)

_____ **3.** Mildred's mother-in-law owns the house Mildred and Buddy live in.

_____ **4.** Buddy's mother treats Mildred like an intruder.

_____ **5.** Buddy doesn't want his mother to set foot in the house.

_____ **6.** Buddy doesn't want Mildred to excite his mother.

_____ **7.** Forrest thinks Mildred needs to do something about the situation soon.

_____ **8.** Forrest will sit down with Buddy and tell him the situation can't continue.

_____ **9.** Forrest thinks Buddy should find his mother a new place to live.

_____ **10.** Buddy got mad and chose his mother over Mildred.

_____ **11.** Forrest suggests that Buddy take a chance and get married.

Now listen again and mark the statements **True (T)** *or* **False (F)** *based on what you hear.*

⑧ DISCUSSION

Part A

Read these statements. Then mark **Agree (A)**, **Disagree (D)**, *or* **In Between (IB)** *according to your personal beliefs.*

A Quiz

_____ **1.** Adults have a harder time saying no to people's requests than children do.

_____ **2.** Your friend wants to spend the night at your house. The room isn't tidy, and the bed isn't made. You should tidy it up and make the bed yourself.

_____ **3.** Your boss has asked you to complete a task and then suddenly asks you to do another within the same time frame. You have time to do only one. It's reasonable to tell your boss that you can only complete one of the tasks by the deadline.

_____ **4.** Parents should come to their children's aid whenever their children ask them.

_____ **5.** It's good to do volunteer work.

_____ **6.** Women have a harder time saying no than men do.

_____ **7.** It's reasonable to do things because you're pressured to do them.

_____ **8.** You should do things for others not because you're required or compelled to do so but as a gift to them.

_____ **9.** People should make their own needs a priority.

_____ **10.** It is better to say "I choose to do this" than "I should do this."

Part B

In groups of four or five, discuss your answers to the quiz above. Share your group's opinions with the rest of the class.

⑨ ESSAY

Choose one of the following topics and write a narrative essay of three or four paragraphs. Support your statements with specific details.

- A time when being assertive was a mistake for you. What should you have done instead? What might have happened had you behaved differently?

- A time when you weren't assertive and should have been. What was the situation? What did you do? What could you have done?

- A time when you were successfully assertive. What was the situation? What action did you take? Why was it successful?

⑩ PICTURE DISCUSSION

In groups of four or five, discuss the three types of classrooms in the pictures. What is happening in each classroom? What is each teacher like? What kind of learning is taking place? Use subjunctive verb expressions in your descriptions. Also use as much new vocabulary as you can.

REVIEW OR SELFTEST

I. *Read the paragraph about Brandon's car problem. Then complete the sentences with conditional forms.*

> Recently I had an experience that taught me a lesson. I'd been meaning to get the oil in my car changed, but I kept putting it off. Last Tuesday on the Appleton Expressway, I was on my way to a job interview when the car just quit. The engine seized because it was out of oil. Before I could make it to the side of the road, another car rear-ended me. That did about a thousand dollars worth of damage to the car, and I had to have the car's engine completely replaced. I had to pay a towing bill of $150, and I didn't make it to the job interview, either. Hopefully, I've learned my lesson.

1. <u>Brandon wished he had not put off changing the oil in his car.</u>
(Brandon / wish / not put off / change / the oil in his car)

2. _____
(If / he / change / the oil / the engine / not seize)

3. _____
(If / the engine / not seize / the other car / not rear-end him)

4. _____
(He / not / have to / pay a towing bill)

5. _____
(He / not / have to / replace the engine)

6. _____
(He / could / make it to the job interview / if / all this / not happen)

7. _____
(If / he / make it to the job interview / he / might / get the job)

8. _____
(Brandon / hope / that / he / learn his lesson)

II. *Complete the conversations with **as if / as though** and the correct form of the verb.*

1. A: Harriet is really arrogant, don't you think?

B: Yes. She's always acting _____<u>as if she were</u>_____ the boss.
(as if / she / be)

2. A: How's the weather there?

B: Well, an hour ago it looked _____ pour. The sun
(as though / it / going to)

is shining now, though.

3. A: Chief, Mr. Bransford is acting _____ guilty.
(as if / he / be)

 B: Just remember, officer, that he's innocent until proven guilty.

4. A: Where did you get this dog? He's really cute.

 B: We found him on the street. He looked _____ in some sort of
(as though / he / be)

 accident. He's OK now, though.

5. A: What do you think of our new boss?

 B: She needs to be more decisive. She's acting _____ one of the
(as if / she / be)

 employees.

6. A: What are you so mad about?

 B: You're behaving _____ this whole thing was my fault. I didn't
(as though / you / think)

 have anything to do with it, remember?

III. *Read the answer from an advice columnist. Then complete five subjunctive
sentences that restate the columnist's suggestions.*

> ### To Mary in Montreal:
>
> No one should have to put up with a dog that barks all night. First, it's essential
> for you to talk with your next-door neighbor. At the same time, though, it's
> important not to lose your temper while you're explaining your side of the
> issue. Ask your neighbor to bring the dog in at night. Stay calm. If she refuses,
> insist on her getting rid of the animal. If she doesn't do something about the
> problem, I'd recommend calling the animal control bureau.
>
> *Pamela*

1. It is essential that Mary

 talk with her next-door neighbor _____.

2. It is important that Mary

 _____ while she is

 explaining her side of the issue.

3. Mary should ask that her neighbor

 _____.

(continued on next page)

4. If she refuses, Mary should insist that she

_____ .

5. The columnist recommends that Mary

_____ if her

neighbor doesn't do something about the problem.

IV. *Complete the conversation by completing the verb phrases with* **wish**, **hope**, *and* **if only**.

AURORA: I can't believe Mr. Wilkerson sent us a check for fifty thousand dollars. I wish

_____*we'd been able to*_____ get better acquainted with him the day he was here.
　　　　　1. (we / be able to)

THAIN: Yeah. If only _____ what was happening.
　　　　　　　　　　2. (we / realize)

AURORA: I just hope _____ taking his insulin, and I hope
　　　　　　　　　3. (he / keep)

_____ someone around to remind him in case he forgets.
4. (there / be)

THAIN: You know, I really wish _____ him in some way. The
　　　　　　　　　　　　5. (we / can contact)

trouble is, there's no return address on the envelope. Hey! What about the

postmark? Where is that envelope, anyway?

AURORA: Here it is. Oh, no. Look at this! If only the postmark _____
　　　　　　　　　　　　　　　　　　　　　6. (not / be)

so blurred. You can't see the city name.

THAIN: I wish _____ a magnifying glass . . . Hey, wait; I can make
　　　　　7. (we / have)

out the zip code. It's . . . 93302. Honey, get the almanac, will you?

AURORA: Here it is. Zip codes that start with nine are on the West Coast, aren't they? I

hope _____ like finding a needle in a haystack. Try
　　　8. (this / not be)
California.

THAIN: OK . . . Here it is! 93302—that's Bakersfield. I wish _____
　　　　　　　　　　　　　　　　　　　　　9. (we / know)

someone in Bakersfield.

AURORA: I know! Let's just get on the Internet and call up the Bakersfield telephone

directory. Maybe his name will be listed. Let's hope _____ ,
　　　　　　　　　　　　　　　　　　　　　10. (it / be)
anyway.

V. *Look at the pictures. Using the indicated prompts, write a conditional or subjunctive sentence to describe each situation.*

1.

(suggested)

Sam suggested that they

stay just fifteen minutes.

2.

(insisted)

_____

_____

3.

(not stay up late)

_____

_____

4.

(get some gas)

_____

_____

5.

(take a taxi)

_____

_____

6.

(listen to Karen's advice)

_____

_____

VI. *Circle the letter of the choice that correctly completes each sentence.*

1. You need to get some job retraining. <u>Without</u> it, you risk being laid off. A B C (D)
   (A) If so   (C) With
   (B) If not   (D) Without

2. I recommend that Miriam _____ a boarding school. She'd be A B C D
   much more challenged academically.
   (A) attends   (C) is attending
   (B) attend   (D) were attending

3. Ambrose had to take a job at a fast-food restaurant; _____, he A B C D
   wouldn't have been able to make his car payment.
   (A) otherwise   (C) had he done so
   (B) if so   (D) were that the case

4. I hope you _____ make it to the family reunion on the fifteenth. A B C D
   Everyone will be there.
   (A) could   (C) can
   (B) were   (D) would

5. I hope Anna passed her exams. _____, she'll have to repeat her A B C D
   senior year.
   (A) If not   (C) With
   (B) Without   (D) If so

6. At this point, Shannon wishes she _____ mechanical drawing. She A B C D
   hates the course.
   (A) didn't take   (C) hadn't taken
   (B) wouldn't take   (D) were to take

7. You were right when you suggested I _____ my intuition in this A B C D
   business deal. I did, and it worked.
   (A) follow   (C) were to follow
   (B) followed   (D) had followed

8. I wish we _____ to get to know one another better in the time we had. A B C D
   (A) will be able   (C) would have been able
   (B) were able   (D) had been able

9. My wife will be home by seven P.M. on the eighteenth. _____ A B C D
   before her, please water the lawn.
   (A) Should arrive   (C) You should arrive
   (B) Should you arrive   (D) Should you have arrived

10. It sounds like something is wrong with the car's engine. _____, A B C D
    we'd better take it to the garage immediately.
    (A) Otherwise   (C) If not
    (B) Without it   (D) If so

▶ *To check your answers, go to the Answer Key on page 494.*

From Grammar to Writing
Avoiding Run-on Sentences and Comma Splices

A sentence is made up of at least one independent clause. A sentence containing more than one independent clause must be punctuated properly to avoid two kinds of errors: the run-on sentence and the comma splice.

A run-on sentence is a group of words containing at least two independent clauses without any punctuation separating them; the sentences are "run together."

independent clause — independent

Thain and Aurora were on their way to a yard sale an old man

clause

waved feebly to them.

The following are four ways to correct a run-on sentence.

a. Separate the two independent clauses with a period. Capitalize the first word of the second clause.

Thain and Aurora were on their way to a yard sale. **A**n old man waved feebly to them.

b. Separate the two independent clauses with a semicolon. Do not capitalize the first word of the second clause.

Thain and Aurora were on their way to a yard sale**;** **a**n old man waved feebly to them.

c. Join the two independent clauses with a comma and a coordinating conjunction.

Thain and Aurora were on their way to a yard sale**, and** an old man waved feebly to them.

d. Make one of the independent clauses dependent by adding a subordinating conjunction, and separate the two clauses with a comma if the dependent clause comes first.

When Thain and Aurora were on their way to a yard sale**,** an old man waved feebly to them.

Correct the following run-on sentences by using the method suggested.

1. The old man had forgotten to buy medicine. He went into diabetic shock. (period)

2. Thain asked Aurora to pull over his intuition told him the old man needed their help. (semicolon)

3. Kate knew she had to change her relationship with her boss she didn't know how to do it. (coordinating conjunction and comma)

4. Aurora wished they had gotten to the yard sale on time she was glad they had stopped to help the old man. (subordinating conjunction at beginning of sentence and comma)

A **comma splice** is the joining of two independent clauses with only a comma. A comma, however, does not provide adequate punctuation.

    ⎯⎯⎯⎯ **independent clause** ⎯⎯⎯⎯⎯ ⎯ **independent clause** ⎯

Marsha read *The Assertive Individual's Handbook,* she learned a lot about

expressing herself in the process.

A comma splice can be corrected by the same four methods used to correct a run-on sentence.

a. Use a period.

Marsha read *The Assertive Individual's Handbook.* **She** learned a lot about expressing herself in the process.

b. Use a semicolon.

Marsha read *The Assertive Individual's Handbook;* **she** learned a lot about expressing herself in the process.

c. Use a comma and a coordinating conjunction.

Marsha read *The Assertive Individual's Handbook,* **and** she learned a lot about expressing herself in the process.

d. Make one of the clauses dependent by adding a subordinating conjunction.

When Marsha read *The Assertive Individual's Handbook,* **she** learned a lot about expressing herself in the process.

A fifth way of correcting a comma splice is to convert one of the clauses into an adverb phrase if the subjects of the two clauses are the same.

> Marsha read *The Assertive Individual's Handbook*, **learning** a lot about expressing herself in the process.

The period and semicolon are similar punctuation marks in that they are both used between independent clauses. The period can be thought of as separating two clauses, and the semicolon can be thought of as joining two clauses.

Do not capitalize the first word after a semicolon (unless it is "I" or a proper noun).

> The teachers considered the Board of Education's offer**; then** they went on strike.

Use a semicolon instead of a period to join independent clauses if you feel that the two clauses have a close connection in meaning.

> Kate's job situation deteriorated a great deal**; she** had to speak to her boss.

> ▶ **BE CAREFUL!** Do not use a semicolon to connect an independent clause and a dependent clause.

> While I was learning to be assertive**, I** learned many things about myself.
>
> NOT
>
> ~~While I was learning to be assertive; I learned many things about myself.~~

 Correct each of the following comma splices by using the suggested method in each case.

1. The old man looked ill⨟he needed to get out of the sun quickly. (semicolon)

2. Thain and Aurora drove to a pharmacy, they got the old man his insulin. (period)

3. Aurora wanted to get to the yard sale, there was a chest of drawers for sale.

(semicolon)

4. Aurora didn't want to stop for the old man, Thain persuaded her it was necessary.

(comma and coordinating conjunction)

(continued on next page)

5. Harold says he will seek professional help to overcome his anger, there is no assurance that he will carry out his promise. (subordinating conjunction at beginning of sentence / dependent clause and comma)

6. Nancy felt dominated by her mother-in-law, she needed to take assertive action. (Convert the first clause to an adverb phrase and place the noun subject in the second clause.)

Notice the specific types of punctuation in sentences containing transitions.

> You are three months behind in paying your electric bill; therefore, we are terminating your service.

> You need to take some positive action. Also, you need to respect yourself.

If a transition begins a clause, place a period or semicolon before it. Use a semicolon if you feel that the clauses connected are closely related in meaning; otherwise, use a period.

3 *Correct the following run-on sentences, using the suggested punctuation mark in each case. Capitalize where necessary.*

1. A tiny voice inside Jeremy told him he would hate the job; therefore, he turned it down. (semicolon)

2. Nancy says she wants to do something worthwhile if so, she should do volunteer work. (period)

3. I need to get a bank loan otherwise, I'll have to file for bankruptcy. (semicolon)

4. Ben and Carolyn would like to send Jim to a private school however, the school is expensive, and Jim doesn't want to go. (period)

5. Fred and Claudia love their new neighborhood in fact, they're going to buy a house there. (semicolon)

4 *Carefully read and study the following passage, which contains thirteen independent clauses. Correct the eleven errors in run-on sentences and comma splices by adding periods or semicolons and capitalizing correctly.*

Call it either intuition or good vibrations whatever you want to call it, it works last summer, I was one of four members of a committee to hire a new head nurse at the nursing home where I work we interviewed two candidates as finalists, a man named Bob and a woman named Sarah on paper, Bob was better qualified he had a master's degree while Sarah had only a bachelor's degree however, Sarah was the one who really impressed us she answered all of the questions straightforwardly and simply Bob, on the other hand, evaded some of our questions while simultaneously trying to make us think he knew everything and could do everything all of us on the committee just liked Sarah better in fact, she got the job because she was the person we all felt we wanted to work with. Our intuition wasn't wrong she's turned out to be a wonderful nurse.

5 **APPLY IT TO YOUR WRITING**

Write a paragraph (six to ten sentences) on one of the following topics or a similar topic that interests you.

- A Problem I Overcame
- A Problem I Need to Overcome
- A Time When My Intuition Proved Correct

Begin your first sentence with a capital letter, and end the last sentence with a period. However, do not include any other punctuation or capital letters at the beginnings of sentences. Exchange papers with a partner. Read your partner's paper and add punctuation and capitalization, paying particular attention to avoiding run-on sentences and comma splices. Discuss your papers. Then rewrite your paragraph and submit it to your teacher.

REVIEW OR SELFTEST
ANSWER KEY

I.

2. If he had changed the oil, the engine wouldn't have seized.
3. If the engine hadn't seized, the other car wouldn't have rear-ended him.
4. He wouldn't have had to pay a towing bill.
5. He wouldn't have had to replace the engine.
6. He could have made it to the job interview if all this hadn't happened.
7. If he had made it to the job interview, he might have gotten the job.
8. Brandon hopes that he has learned his lesson.

II.

2. as though it were going to
3. as if he were
4. as though he had been
5. as if she were
6. as though you thought

III.

2. not lose her temper
3. bring the dog in at night.
4. get rid of the animal.
5. call the animal control bureau

IV.

2. we'd realized
3. he keeps (or he'll keep)
4. there's (or there will be)
5. we could contact
6. weren't
7. we had
8. this won't be (or this isn't)
9. we knew
10. it is (or it will be)

V. Possible Answers

2. At 12:00, Karen insisted that they leave.
3. If Sam hadn't stayed up so late, he wouldn't have overslept.
4. If Sam had gotten some gas, he would have been able to drive to the interview.
5. If Sam had taken a taxi, he might not have gotten stuck in traffic.
6. Sam might have made it to the interview on time if he'd listened to Karen's advice.

VI.

2. B	5. A	8. D
3. A	6. C	9. B
4. C	7. A	10. D

APPENDICES

1 Irregular Verbs

Base Form	Simple Past	Past Participle
arise	arose	arisen
awake	awoke / awaked	awaked / awoken
be	was, were	been
bear	bore	borne
beat	beat	beaten / beat
become	became	become
begin	began	begun
bend	bent	bent
bet	bet	bet
bite	bit	bitten
bleed	bled	bled
blow	blew	blown
break	broke	broken
bring	brought	brought
broadcast	broadcast / broadcasted	broadcast / broadcasted
build	built	built
burn	burned / burnt	burned / burnt
burst	burst	burst
buy	bought	bought
cast	cast	cast
catch	caught	caught
choose	chose	chosen
cling	clung	clung
come	came	come
cost	cost	cost
creep	crept	crept
cut	cut	cut
deal	dealt	dealt
dig	dug	dug
dive	dived / dove	dived
do	did	done
draw	drew	drawn
dream	dreamed / dreamt	dreamed / dreamt
drink	drank	drunk
drive	drove	driven
eat	ate	eaten
fall	fell	fallen
feed	fed	fed
feel	felt	felt
fight	fought	fought
find	found	found
fit	fitted / fit	fitted / fit
flee	fled	fled
fling	flung	flung
fly	flew	flown
forbid	forbade / forbad	forbidden / forbid
forget	forgot	forgotten
forgive	forgave	forgiven
forgo	forwent	forgone
freeze	froze	frozen

Base Form	Simple Past	Past Participle
get	got	gotten / got
give	gave	given
go	went	gone
grind	ground	ground
grow	grew	grown
hang	hung / hanged*	hung / hanged*
have	had	had
hear	heard	heard
hide	hid	hidden / hid
hit	hit	hit
hold	held	held
hurt	hurt	hurt
keep	kept	kept
kneel	knelt / kneeled	knelt / kneeled
knit	knit / knitted	knit / knitted
know	knew	known
lay	laid	laid
lead	led	led
leap	leaped / leapt	leaped / leapt
leave	left	left
lend	lent	lent
let	let	let
lie (down)	lay	lain
light	lighted / lit	lighted / lit
lose	lost	lost
make	made	made
mean	meant	meant
pay	paid	paid
prove	proved	proved / proven
put	put	put
quit	quit / quitted	quit / quitted
read / riᵞd /	read / rɛd /	read / rɛd /
rid	rid / ridded	rid / ridded
ride	rode	ridden
ring	rang	rung
rise	rose	risen
run	ran	run
saw	sawed	sawed / sawn
say	said	said
see	saw	seen
seek	sought	sought
sell	sold	sold
send	sent	sent
set	set	set
sew	sewed	sewn / sewed
shake	shook	shaken
shave	shaved	shaved / shaven
shear	sheared	sheared / shorn

*hung = hung an object
 hanged = executed by hanging

(continued on next page)

Base Form	Simple Past	Past Participle	Base Form	Simple Past	Past Participle
shine	shone / shined**	shone / shined **	strike	struck	struck / stricken
shoot	shot	shot	swear	swore	sworn
show	showed	shown / showed	sweep	swept	swept
shrink	shrank / shrunk	shrunk / shrunken	swell	swelled	swelled / swollen
shut	shut	shut	swim	swam	swum
sing	sang	sung	swing	swung	swung
sink	sank / sunk	sunk	take	took	taken
sit	sat	sat	teach	taught	taught
slay	slew	slain	tear	tore	torn
sleep	slept	slept	tell	told	told
slide	slid	slid	think	thought	thought
sneak	sneaked / snuck	sneaked / snuck	throw	threw	thrown
speak	spoke	spoken	undergo	underwent	undergone
speed	sped / speeded	sped / speeded	understand	understood	understood
spend	spent	spent	upset	upset	upset
spill	spilled / spilt	spilled / spilt	wake	woke / waked	waked / woken
spin	spun	spun	wear	wore	worn
spit	spat / spit	spat / spit	weave	wove / weaved	woven / weaved
split	split	split	weep	wept	wept
spread	spread	spread	wet	wet / wetted	wet / wetted
spring	sprang / sprung	sprung	win	won	won
stand	stood	stood	wind	wound	wound
steal	stole	stolen	withdraw	withdrew	withdrawn
stick	stuck	stuck	wring	wrung	wrung
sting	stung	stung	write	wrote	written
stink	stank / stunk	stunk			
strew	strewed	strewn			

**shone = intransitive: The sun shone brightly.
  shined = transitive: He shined his shoes.

② Common Verbs Usually Used Statively

Example:
She **seems** happy in her new job.

APPEARANCE	EMOTIONS	MENTAL STATES		PERCEPTION AND THE SENSES	POSSESSION	WANTS AND PREFERENCES
appear	abhor	agree	hesitate	ache	belong	desire
be	admire	amaze	hope	feel	contain	need
concern	adore	amuse	imagine	hear	have	prefer
indicate	appreciate	annoy	imply	hurt	own	want
look	care	assume	impress	notice	pertain	wish
mean (= signify)	desire	astonish	infer	observe	possess	
parallel	detest	believe	know	perceive		**OTHER**
represent	dislike	bore	mean	see		cost
resemble	doubt	care	mind	sense		include
seem	empathize	consider	presume	smart		lack
signify (= mean)	envy	deem	realize	smell		matter
	fear	deny	recognize	taste		owe
	hate	disagree	recollect			refuse
	hope	disbelieve	remember			suffice
	like	entertain (= amuse)	revere			
	love	estimate	see (= understand)			
	regret	expect	suit			
	respect	fancy	suppose			
	sympathize	favor	suspect			
	trust	feel (= believe)	think (= believe)			
		figure (= assume)	tire			
		find	understand			
		guess	wonder			

③ Common Uses of Modals and Modal-like Expressions

1. ABILITY

can	I can speak French.
could	She could talk when she was a year old.
was / were able to	Henry was able to get a scholarship.
will be able to	Sarah will be able to buy a new house.

2. ADVICE

should	You should study harder.
ought to	You ought to sing in the choir.
should have	You should have acted sooner.
ought to have	We ought not to have said that.
had better	You'd better do something fast.
shall	Shall I continue? *

3. CERTAINTY: PRESENT AND PAST

must	He's not here. He must be on his way.
must have	I must have forgotten to pay the bill.

4. CERTAINTY: FUTURE

should	They should be here by nine.
ought to	That ought to help the situation.

5. EXPECTATION: PRESENT AND PAST

be to	You are to report to the traffic court on April 1. He was to be here by nine.
be supposed to	A person accused of a crime is supposed to have a speedy trial. The boys were supposed to feed the pets.

6. FUTURITY

will	He will do it.
shall	I shall never travel again. **
be going to	They are going to visit us.
be about to	The bell is about to ring.

7. HABITUAL ACTION: PAST

used to	I used to procrastinate, but I don't anymore.
would	When I was a child, we would spend every summer at our beach cabin.

8. HABITUAL ACTION: PRESENT AND FUTURE

will	Many people will gossip if given the chance.

9. IMPOSSIBILITY: PRESENT AND PAST

can't	This can't be happening.
couldn't	She couldn't be here. I heard she was ill.
can't have	They can't have arrived yet. It's a two-hour trip.
couldn't have	They couldn't have bought a car. They didn't have any money.

10. LACK OF NECESSITY: PRESENT AND PAST

don't have to	We don't have to leave for work yet.
didn't have to	Frank didn't have to work yesterday.
needn't	You needn't rewrite your essay.
needn't have	She needn't have bothered to call. Mary wasn't home.

11. NECESSITY: PRESENT AND PAST

must	Everyone must pay taxes.
have to	She has to have surgery.
have got to	We've got to do something about the situation.
had to	John had to fly to New York for a meeting.

12. NECESSITY NOT TO

mustn't	You mustn't neglect to pay your car insurance.

13. OPPORTUNITY

could	We could go to the park this afternoon.
could have	You could have done better in this course.

14. POSSIBILITY: PRESENT AND PAST

may	He may be sick.
may have	Zelda may have saved enough money.
might	I might go to the play; I'm not sure.
might have	The money might have been stolen.
could	Frank could be on his way.
could have	They could have taken the wrong road.

15. PREFERENCE

would rather	Martha would rather stay home tonight than go to the play.

16. WILLINGNESS (VOLITION)

will	I'll help you with your homework.

*The use of *shall* in a question to ask another's opinion or direction is the only common use of *shall* in American English.

**Shall* used to express futurity is rare in American English.

4 Irregular Noun Plurals

SINGULAR FORM	PLURAL FORM	SINGULAR FORM	PLURAL FORM	SINGULAR FORM	PLURAL FORM
alumna	alumnae	fish	fish, fishes**	people	people ****
alumnus	alumni	foot	feet	phenomenon	phenomena
amoeba	amoebas, amoebae	genus	genera	(no singular form)	police*****
analysis	analyses	goose	geese	policeman	policemen
antenna	antennae, antennas	half	halves	policewoman	policewomen
appendix	appendices, appendixes	index	indexes, indices	postman	postmen ***
		knife	knives	protozoan	protozoa, protozoans
axis	axes	leaf	leaves		
basis	bases	life	lives	radius	radii
businessman	businessmen	loaf	loaves	series	series
businesswoman	businesswomen	louse	lice	sheaf	sheaves
calf	calves	mailman	mailmen ***	sheep	sheep
(no singular form)	cattle	man	men	shelf	shelves
child	children	millennium	millennia, millenniums	species	species
crisis	crises			thesis	theses
criterion	criteria	money	moneys, monies	tooth	teeth
datum	data	moose	moose	vertebra	vertebrae, vertebras
deer	deer	mouse	mice		
dwarf	dwarfs, dwarves	octopus	octopuses, octopi	wife	wives
elf	elves	ox	oxen	woman	women
fireman	firemen*	paramecium	paramecia		

* Also: firefighter, firefighters
** fishes = different species of fish
*** Also: letter carrier, letter carriers, postal worker, postal workers
**** Also: person, persons; a people = an ethnic group
***** Also: police officer, police officers

5 Common Non-Count Nouns

ABSTRACTIONS		ACTIVITIES		AILMENTS	SOLID ELEMENTS	GASES
advice	inertia	badminton	golf	AIDS	calcium	carbon dioxide
anarchy	integrity	baseball	hiking	appendicitis	carbon	helium
behavior	love	basketball	reading	cancer	copper	hydrogen
chance	luck	biking	sailing	chicken pox	gold	neon
choice	momentum	billiards	singing	cholera	iron	nitrogen
decay	oppression	bowling	skating	diabetes	lead	oxygen
democracy	peace	boxing	soccer	flu (influenza)	magnesium	
energy	pollution	canoeing	surfing	heart disease	platinum	
entertainment	responsibility	cards	talk	malaria	plutonium	
entropy	slavery	conversation	tennis	measles	radium	
evil	socialism	cycling	volleyball	mumps	silver	
freedom	spontaneity	dancing	wrestling	polio	tin	
fun	stupidity	football		smallpox	titanium	
good	time			strep throat	uranium	
happiness	totalitarianism			tuberculosis (TB)		
hate	truth					
hatred	violence					
honesty						

FOODS	LIQUIDS	NATURAL PHENOMENA	OCCUPATIONS	PARTICLES	SUBJECTS	MISCELLANEOUS
barley	coffee	air	banking	dust	accounting	clothing
beef	gasoline	aurora australis	computer	gravel	art	equipment
bread	juice	aurora borealis	technology	pepper	astronomy	furniture
broccoli	milk	cold	construction	salt	biology	news
cake	oil	electricity	dentistry	sand	business	
candy	soda	fog	engineering	spice	chemistry	
chicken	tea	hail	farming	sugar	civics	
fish	water	heat	fishing		computer	
meat		ice	law		science	
oats		lightning	manufacturing		economics	
pie		mist	medicine		geography	
rice		rain	nursing		history	
wheat		sleet	retail		Latin	
		smog	sales		linguistics	
		smoke	teaching		literature	
		snow	writing		mathematics	
		steam	work		music	
		thunder			physics	
		warmth			psychology	
					science	
					sociology	
					speech	
					writing	

 Some Common Ways of Making Non-Count Nouns Countable

ABSTRACTIONS
a piece of advice
a matter of choice
a unit of energy
a type *or* form of entertainment
a piece *or* bit of luck

ACTIVITIES
a game of badminton, baseball, basketball,
    cards, football, golf, soccer, tennis, etc.
a badminton game, a baseball game, etc.

FOODS
a grain of barley
a cut *or* piece of beef
a loaf of bread
a piece of cake
a piece *or* wedge of pie
a grain of rice
a portion *or* serving of—

LIQUIDS
a cup of coffee, tea
a gallon *or* liter of gasoline
a can of oil
a can *or* glass of soda
a glass of milk, water, juice

NATURAL PHENOMENA
a drop of rain
a bolt *or* current of electricity
a bolt of lightning
a clap *or* bolt of thunder

PARTICLES
a speck of dust
a grain of pepper, salt, sand, sugar

SUBJECTS
a branch of accounting, art, astronomy,
    biology, business, chemistry, civics,
    economics, geography, literature,
    linguistics, mathematics, music, physics,
    psychology, science, sociology, etc.

MISCELLANEOUS
an article of clothing
a piece of equipment
a piece *or* article of furniture
a piece of news *or* a news item *or* an item
    of news
a period of time

⑦ Countries Whose Names Contain the Definite Article

The Bahamas
The Cayman Islands
The Central African Republic
The Channel Islands
The Comoros
The Czech Republic

The Dominican Republic
The Falkland Islands
The Gambia
The Isle of Man
The Leeward Islands
The Maldives (the Maldive Islands)

The Marshall Islands
The Netherlands
The Netherlands Antilles
The Philippines
The Solomon Islands
The Turks and Caicos Islands

The United Arab Emirates
The United Kingdom (of Great
    Britain and Northern Ireland)
The United States (of America)
The Virgin Islands
The Wallis and Futuna Islands

8 Selected Geographical Features Whose Names Contain the Definite Article

GULFS, OCEANS, SEAS, AND STRAITS

The Adriatic Sea
The Aegean Sea
The Arabian Sea
The Arctic (Ocean)
The Antarctic (Ocean)
The Atlantic (Ocean)
The Baltic Sea
The Black Sea
The Caribbean (Sea)
The Caspian Sea
The Coral Sea
The Gulf of Aden
The Gulf of Mexico

The Gulf of Oman
The Indian (Ocean)
The Mediterranean (Sea)
The North Sea
The Pacific (Ocean)
The Persian Gulf
The Philippine Sea
The Red Sea
The Sea of Japan
The South China Sea
The Strait of Gibraltar
The Strait of Magellan
The Yellow Sea

MOUNTAIN RANGES

The Alps
The Andes
The Appalachians
The Atlas Mountains
The Caucasus

The Himalayas
The Pyrenees
The Rockies
   (The Rocky Mountains)
The Urals

RIVERS

The Amazon
The Colorado
The Columbia
The Danube
The Euphrates
The Ganges
The Hudson
The Indus
The Jordan
The Mackenzie
The Mekong
The Mississippi
The Missouri
The Niger
The Nile

The Ob
The Ohio
The Orinoco
The Po
The Rhine
The Rhone
The Rio Grande
The St. Lawrence
The Seine
The Tagus
The Thames
The Tiber
The Tigris
The Volga
The Yangtze

OTHER FEATURES

The Equator
The Far East
The Gobi (Desert)
The Middle East (Near East)
The North Pole
The Occident
The Orient
The Panama Canal
The Sahara (Desert)
The South Pole
The Suez Canal
The Tropic of Cancer
The Tropic of Capricorn

9 Common Verbs Followed by the Gerund (Base Form of Verb + -ing)

Example:
Jane **enjoys playing** tennis and **gardening**.

abhor
acknowledge
admit
advise
allow
anticipate
appreciate
avoid
be worth
can't help
celebrate

confess
consider
defend
delay
deny
detest
discontinue
discuss
dislike
dispute
dread

endure
enjoy
escape
evade
explain
fancy
feel like
feign
finish
forgive
give up (= stop)

imagine
keep (= continue)
keep on
mention
mind (= object to)
miss
necessitate
omit
permit
picture

postpone
practice
prevent
put off
recall
recollect
recommend
report
resent
resist

resume
risk
shirk
shun
suggest
support
tolerate
understand
urge
warrant

10 Common Verbs Followed by the Infinitive (*To* + Base Form of Verb)

Example:
The Minnicks **decided to sell** their house.

agree
appear
arrange
ask
attempt
beg
can / can't afford
can / can't wait
care
chance
choose

claim
come
consent
dare
decide
demand
deserve
determine
elect
endeavor
expect

fail
get
grow (up)
guarantee
hesitate
hope
hurry
incline
learn
manage

mean (= intend)
need
offer
pay
prepare
pretend
profess
promise
prove
refuse

remain
request
resolve
say
seek
seem
shudder
strive
struggle
swear

tend
threaten
turn out
venture
volunteer
wait
want
wish
would like
yearn

11 Verbs Followed by the Gerund or Infinitive without a Change in Meaning

attempt	can't bear	continue	like	prefer	regret
begin	can't stand	hate	love	propose	start

12 Verbs Followed by the Gerund or the Infinitive with a Change in Meaning

forget	go on	quit	remember	stop	try

forget
I've almost **forgotten meeting** him. (= At present, I can hardly remember.)
I almost **forgot to meet** him. (= I almost didn't remember to meet him.)

go on
Jack **went on writing** novels. (= Jack continued to write novels.)
Jack **went on to write** novels. (= Jack ended some other activity and began to write novels.)

quit
Ella **quit working** at Sloan's. (= She isn't working there anymore.)
Ella **quit to work** at Sloan's. (= She quit another job in order to work at Sloan's.)

remember
Velma **remembered writing** to Bill. (= Velma remembered the activity of writing to Bill.)
Velma **remembered to write** to Bill. (= Velma wrote to Bill. She didn't forget to do it.)

stop
Hank **stopped eating**. (= He stopped the activity of eating.)
Hank **stopped to eat**. (= He stopped doing something else in order to eat.)

try
Martin **tried skiing**. (= Martin sampled the activity of skiing.)
Martin **tried to ski**. (= Martin tried to ski but didn't succeed.)

13 Verbs Followed by Object + Infinitive

Example:
I **asked Sally to lend** me her car.

advise	choose*	expect*	hire	order	persuade	teach	want*
allow	convince	forbid	invite	pay*	remind	tell	warn
ask*	encourage	force	need*	permit	require	urge	would like*
cause							

*These verbs can also be followed by the infinitive without an object.
Example:
I **want to go**.   *or*   I **want Andy to go**.

14 Common Adjectives Followed by the Infinitive

Example:
I was **glad to hear** about that.

afraid	curious	disturbed	fascinated	hesitant	pleased	reluctant	surprised
alarmed	delighted	eager	fortunate	impossible	possible	right	touched
amazed	depressed	easy	frightened	interested	prepared	sad	unlikely
angry	determined	ecstatic	furious	intrigued	proud	scared	unnecessary
anxious	difficult	embarrassed	glad	likely	ready	shocked	willing
astonished	disappointed	encouraged	happy	lucky	relieved	sorry	wrong
careful	distressed	excited	hard	necessary			

These expressions are followed by nouns, pronouns, or gerunds.

Example:
I'm not **familiar with** that writer.

accustomed to	careful of	furious with	nervous about	sick of
afraid of	concerned with / about	glad about	obsessed with / about	slow at
amazed at / by	content with	good at	opposed to	sorry for / about
angry at / with	curious about	guilty of	pleased about	suited to
ashamed of	different from	happy about	poor at	surprised at / about / by
astonished at / by	excellent at	incapable of	ready for	terrible at
aware of	excited about	intent on	responsible for	tired from
awful at	famous for	interested in	sad about	tired of
bad at	fascinated with / by	intrigued by / at	safe from	used to
bored with / by	fed up with	mad at (= angry at,	satisfied with	weary of
capable of	fond of	angry with)	shocked at / by	worried about

Example:
We **got rid of** our old furniture.
We **got rid** of it.

advise against	come out	get behind	let up	run across
apologize for	come over	get by (on)	listen in on	run into
approve of	come through	get even (with)	listen to	run out of
back out (of)	come to	get in	live up to	run through
bear up	come up	get into	look after	stand up to
be familiar with	come upon	get off	look at	stick to
believe in	come up with	get on	look back on	stoop to
brush up (on)	complain about	get out of	look down on	succeed in
carry on (with)	count on	get over	look for	take after
catch up (on)	cut down on	get rid of	look forward to	take care of
catch up (with)	deal with	get through	look like	talk about
choose between / among	do without	get through to	look out for	think about
come about	dream about / of	get through with	look up to	try out for
come across	feel like	get to know	make up (= become	turn into
come along	fill in for	get up (= rise)	friendly again)	turn out for
come apart	follow up on	give up on	make up for	turn up (=appear
come around	get about	go back on	miss out (on)	suddenly)
come between	get after	go in for	object to	wait for
come by	get ahead	go through	part with	walk out on
come down with	get along (with)	hurry up to	plan on	watch out for
come in	get around	insist on	put up with	wonder about
come into	get away (with)	keep up with	rely on	work up to
come off	get back	laugh at	resort to	write about

Common Separable Phrasal Verbs

Example:
I **figured out** the answer.
I **figured** the answer **out.**
I **figured** it **out.**

bring about	drop off	make up (= invent)	stir up
bring along	figure out	make up one's mind	take away
bring around	fill out	(= decide)	take back
bring in	fill up	mix up	take off (= remove)
bring on	find out	pay back	take on
bring over	get across	pick up	take over
bring through	give away	put across	take up
bring up	give back	put away	think over
call off	give up	put off	try on
call up	hand out	put on	try out
clear up	have on	put out	turn down
cut off	hold up	run by / past	turn off
cut up	look over	set aside	turn on
do over	look up	show off	turn up (=increase the volume)

 Coordinating Conjunctions

Example:
We went to the party, **but** we really didn't have a good time there.

and	but	for	nor	or	so	yet

19 **Common Subordinating Conjunctions: Single Words and Phrases**

after	before	in spite of the fact that	such . . . that
although	despite the fact that	no matter if	though
as	due to the fact that	no matter whether	till
as if	even if	on account of the fact that	unless
as long as	even though	once	until
as many as	even when	plus the fact that	when
as much as	however (= the way in which)	provided (that)	whenever
as soon as	if	providing (that)	whereas
as though	if only	since	whether (or not)
because	inasmuch as	so that	while
because of the fact that	in case	so . . . that	

Transitions: Single Words and Phrases

A. To show an "and" relation

additionally
again
along with this / that
also
alternatively
as a matter of fact
besides
by the way
finally
first
for example
for instance
furthermore
in addition
incidentally
indeed
in fact
in other words
in the same way
likewise
that is

B. To show a "but" relation

actually
anyhow
anyway
as a matter of fact
at any rate
despite this / that
even so
however
in any case
in either case
in spite of this / that
instead (of this / that)
nevertheless
nonetheless
on the contrary
on the other hand
rather
still

C. To show a "why / because" relation

accordingly
arising out of this / that
as a result
because of this / that
consequently
for this / that reason
hence
in consequence
in such an event
in this / that case
on account of this / that
otherwise
then
therefore
this / that being so
thus
to this end

D. To show a time / sequence relation

after this / that
afterwards
an hour later (several hours later, etc.)
at last
at the same time
at this moment
before this / that
briefly
first(ly)
from now on
henceforth
hitherto
in conclusion
in short
in sum
in summary
in the end

in the meantime
just then
meanwhile
next
on another occasion
previously
second(ly)
then
third(ly) (fourth, fourthly, etc.)
to resume
to return to the point
to summarize
under the circumstances
until then
up to now

---

21 Verbs and Expressions Followed by the Subjunctive (Base Form)

Examples:
We **demand that** he **do** it.
It is **essential that** he **do** it.
The professor **suggested that** we **read** his book.

ask*	it is desirable that	it is required that	propose
demand	it is essential that	move (= formally propose in a	recommend
insist	it is important that	meeting)	request*
it is advisable that	it is mandatory that	order*	suggest
it is crucial that	it is necessary that	prefer*	urge*

* These verbs also take the form verb + object pronoun + infinitive:
  We ask that she be present.   *or*   We ask her to be present.

---

22 Expressions That Can Be Followed by Unreal Conditional Forms

as if   as though   if only   it is time   what if   would rather (that)

Examples:
She acts **as if (as though)** she were president.
If only I **had** more time.
It's time we left.
What if we **had** a million dollars?
I'd rather (that) we **didn't** stay.

INDEX

This Index is for the full and split editions. All entries are in the full book.
Entries for Volume A of the split edition are in black. Entries for Volume B are in color.